Modeling, Optimization and Control of Robotic Systems

Modeling, Optimization and Control of Robotic Systems

Editors

Ahmad Taher Azar
Amjad J. Humaidi
Ammar K. Al Mhdawi

Basel • Beijing • Wuhan • Barcelona • Belgrade • Novi Sad • Cluj • Manchester

Editors

Ahmad Taher Azar
College of Computer and
Information Sciences (CCIS),
Prince Sultan University
Riyadh
Saudi Arabia

Amjad J. Humaidi
University of Technology
Baghdad
Iraq

Ammar K. Al Mhdawi
Edge Hill University
Ormskirk
UK

Editorial Office
MDPI
St. Alban-Anlage 66
4052 Basel, Switzerland

This is a reprint of articles from the Special Issue published online in the open access journal *Actuators* (ISSN 2076-0825) (available at: https://www.mdpi.com/journal/actuators/special_issues/1CX3LAWYR6).

For citation purposes, cite each article independently as indicated on the article page online and as indicated below:

Lastname, A.A.; Lastname, B.B. Article Title. *Journal Name* **Year**, *Volume Number*, Page Range.

ISBN 978-3-7258-1235-6 (Hbk)
ISBN 978-3-7258-1236-3 (PDF)
doi.org/10.3390/books978-3-7258-1236-3

© 2024 by the authors. Articles in this book are Open Access and distributed under the Creative Commons Attribution (CC BY) license. The book as a whole is distributed by MDPI under the terms and conditions of the Creative Commons Attribution-NonCommercial-NoDerivs (CC BY-NC-ND) license.

Contents

Preface vii

Jianguo Duan, Hongzhi Zhang, Qinglei Zhang and Jiyun Qin
Research on Neural Network Terminal Sliding Mode Control of Robotic Arms Based on Novel Reaching Law and Improved Salp Swarm Algorithm
Reprinted from: *Actuators* **2023**, *12*, 464, doi:10.3390/act12120464 1

Siyong Xu, Zhong Wu and Tao Shen
High-Precision Control of Industrial Robot Manipulator Based on Extended Flexible Joint Model
Reprinted from: *Actuators* **2023**, *12*, 357, doi:10.3390/act12090357 18

Hongwei Yan, Pengyang Zhao, Canjun Xiao, Dengxiao Zhang, Shaoni Jiao, Haibing Pan and Xi Wu
Design and Kinematic Characteristic Analysis of a Spiral Robot for Oil and Gas Pipeline Inspections
Reprinted from: *Actuators* **2023**, *12*, 240, doi:10.3390/act12060240 35

Tero Kaarlela, Tomi Pitkäaho, Sakari Pieskä, Paulo Padrão, Leonardo Bobadilla, Matti Tikanmäki, et al.
Towards Metaverse: Utilizing Extended Reality and Digital Twins to Control Robotic Systems
Reprinted from: *Actuators* **2023**, *12*, 219, doi:10.3390/act12060219 51

Changlong Ye, Yang Su, Suyang Yu and Yinchao Wang
Development of a Deformable Water-Mobile Robot
Reprinted from: *Actuators* **2023**, *12*, 202, doi:10.3390/act12050202 71

Honggang Wu, Xinming Zhang, Linsen Song, Yufei Zhang, Chen Wang, Xiaonan Zhao and Lidong Gu
Parallel Network-Based Sliding Mode Tracking Control for Robotic Manipulators with Uncertain Dynamics
Reprinted from: *Actuators* **2023**, *12*, 187, doi:10.3390/act12050187 89

Pengjie Xu, Xinyi Chen and Qirong Tang
Design and Coverage Path Planning of a Disinfection Robot
Reprinted from: *Actuators* **2023**, *12*, 182, doi:10.3390/act12050182 106

Yufei Liu, Dong Tang and Jinyong Ju
Electromechanical Coupling Dynamic and Vibration Control of Robotic Grinding System for Thin-Walled Workpiece
Reprinted from: *Actuators* **2023**, *12*, 37, doi:10.3390/act12010037 121

Namhyun Kim, Daejin Oh, Jun-Young Oh and Wonkyun Lee
Disturbance-Observer-Based Dual-Position Feedback Controller for Precision Control of an Industrial Robot Arm
Reprinted from: *Actuators* **2022**, *11*, 375, doi:10.3390/act11120375 138

Saim Ahmed, Ahmad Taher Azar and Mohamed Tounsi
Adaptive Fault Tolerant Non-Singular Sliding Mode Control for Robotic Manipulators Based on Fixed-Time Control Law
Reprinted from: *Actuators* **2022**, *11*, 353, doi:10.3390/act11120353 151

Yongkuk Kim and SangJoo Kwon
Robust Stabilization of Underactuated Two-Wheeled Balancing Vehicles on Uncertain Terrains
with Nonlinear-Model-Based Disturbance Compensation
Reprinted from: *Actuators* **2022**, *11*, 339, doi:10.3390/act11110339 . . . . **172**

Feifan He and Qingjiu Huang
Time-Optimal Trajectory Planning of 6-DOF Manipulator Based on Fuzzy Control
Reprinted from: *Actuators* **2022**, *11*, 332, doi:10.3390/act11110332 . . . . **190**

Preface

Welcome to this Special Issue reprint titled "Modeling, Optimization and Control of Robotic Systems." As technology continues to advance at an unprecedented pace, the integration of robotics into various facets of our lives becomes increasingly prevalent. From manufacturing to healthcare, and from exploration to entertainment, robotics plays a pivotal role in shaping the future.

This compilation represents a comprehensive exploration of the multifaceted domain of robotic systems, focusing specifically on modeling, optimization, and control aspects. Through a selection of seminal works, this collection aims to provide readers with a deeper understanding of the theoretical foundations, practical applications, and cutting-edge developments in this dynamic field.

The articles included in this Special Issue cover a wide spectrum of topics, ranging from fundamental principles of robotic modeling to advanced optimization techniques and sophisticated control strategies. Contributors from academia and industry alike have shared their expertise and insights, offering valuable perspectives on the challenges and opportunities inherent in the design, analysis, and implementation of robotic systems.

Whether you are a seasoned researcher, a graduate student, or an industry professional, we trust that this compilation will serve as a valuable resource, sparking new ideas, fostering interdisciplinary collaborations, and inspiring future innovations in the realm of robotics.

We extend our sincere gratitude to the authors for their contributions, the reviewers for their rigorous evaluation, and the editorial team for their dedication and support in bringing this Special Issue reprint to fruition.

We hope that you find this collection both informative and inspiring, and that it ignites your curiosity to delve deeper into the fascinating world of modeling, optimization, and control of robotic systems.

Ahmad Taher Azar, Amjad J. Humaidi, and Ammar K. Al Mhdawi
Editors

Article

Research on Neural Network Terminal Sliding Mode Control of Robotic Arms Based on Novel Reaching Law and Improved Salp Swarm Algorithm

Jianguo Duan [1], Hongzhi Zhang [2,*], Qinglei Zhang [1] and Jiyun Qin [1]

1. Free Trade Zone Supply Chain Research Institute, Shanghai Maritime University, Shanghai 201306, China
2. Logistics Engineering College, Shanghai Maritime University, Shanghai 201306, China
* Correspondence: 202130210086@stu.shmtu.edu.cn

Abstract: Modeling errors and external disturbances have significant impacts on the control accuracy of robotic arm trajectory tracking. To address this issue, this paper proposes a novel method, the neural network terminal sliding mode control (ALSSA-RBFTSM), which combines fast nonsingular terminal sliding mode (FNTSM) control, radial basis function (RBF) neural network, and an improved salp swarm algorithm (ALSSA). This method effectively enhances the trajectory tracking accuracy of robotic arms under the influence of uncertain factors. Firstly, the fast nonsingular terminal sliding surface is utilized to enhance the convergence speed of the system and achieve finite-time convergence. Building upon this, a novel multi-power reaching law is proposed to reduce system chattering. Secondly, the RBF neural network is utilized to estimate and compensate for modeling errors and external disturbances. Then, an improved salp swarm algorithm is proposed to optimize the parameters of the controller. Finally, the stability of the control system is demonstrated using the Lyapunov theorem. Simulation and experimental results demonstrate that the proposed ALSSA-RBFTSM algorithm exhibits superior robustness and trajectory tracking performance compared to the global fast terminal sliding mode (GFTSM) algorithm and the RBF neural network fast nonsingular terminal sliding mode (RBF-FNTSM) algorithm.

Keywords: robotic arm; fast nonsingular terminal sliding mode; RBF neural network; improved salp swarm algorithm; novel multi-power reaching law; Lyapunov theorem

1. Introduction

With the development of automation and intelligent manufacturing, the application scope of robots and automation equipment is becoming increasingly extensive. As integral components of robots, robotic arms are widely utilized in various fields, such as production, manufacturing, healthcare, aviation, logistics, and agriculture [1]. Trajectory tracking of robotic arms is a crucial technique in robot control, enabling them to accurately follow a given path in space, thereby achieving high-quality manufacturing and automation operations. Currently, trajectory tracking control of robotic arms faces challenges such as strong nonlinearity, high uncertainty, and complexity. Therefore, researching high-performance trajectory tracking control strategies for robotic arms is of significant importance.

PID control has the advantages of simplicity, ease of tuning, and ease of implementation, making it a popular strategy in the field of robotic arm control [2–4]. However, PID control also suffers from the disadvantages of limited adaptability to nonlinear systems, poor robustness to parameter variations and uncertainties, and difficulty in dealing with delays and time lags. Therefore, scholars both domestically and internationally have proposed many other methods for trajectory tracking control of robotic arms, such as robust control [5], adaptive control [6], fuzzy control [7], iterative learning control [8], neural network control [9], sliding mode control [10], and backstepping control [11]. Sliding mode control is widely applied in the field of robot control due to its high tracking accuracy, strong robustness, and low requirement for system modeling. A terminal sliding mode control method was proposed by Zhao et al. [12], which can stabilize the system state to an equilibrium point within finite time without requiring precise robot dynamics models. This approach offers faster computation speed and a simpler controller structure, but the speed of convergence still needs to be improved. To address this problem, Doan et al. [13] proposed a fast terminal sliding mode control method that combines fast terminal sliding surfaces with the super-twisting control law. This combination results in smoother control torque, enabling faster and more accurate compensation for external disturbances and nonlinear elements. It ensures system stability and robustness. The method further improves the convergence speed but suffers from the singularity problem. For the singularity problem, Jin et al. [14] introduced a nonsingular terminal sliding mode control method that combines nonsingular terminal sliding surfaces with time delay estimation. It achieves fast convergence using nonsingular terminal sliding mode and implements model-free control using time delay estimation. This method solves the singularity problem, is easy to implement, and has high robustness and accuracy, but the convergence speed is relatively slow. Considering the two main issues of convergence speed and singularity, a fast nonsingular terminal sliding mode control method was proposed by Liang et al. [15]. It utilizes a second-order fast nonsingular terminal sliding mode to achieve rapid convergence, avoid singularities, and reduce chattering. Furthermore, an artificial neural network is introduced to handle model uncertainties and disturbances without the need for any prior knowledge. The method can achieve finite-time convergence with a fast convergence rate while avoiding the singularity problem.

However, sliding mode control suffers from chattering, which can degrade control performance and even lead to system instability. To address this issue, the reaching law approach is often employed to adjust and control the system states. A new exponential reaching law was proposed by Wang et al. [16], which incorporates the system state variable to relate the convergence speed with the variation of the system state. This approach enhances the dynamic performance and robustness of the system, effectively suppressing the phenomenon of oscillations. This method speeds up the convergence of the system and allows the system to approach the sliding mold surface faster, yet it may also lead to high-frequency oscillations and overshoot phenomena, resulting in degradation of control performance. To address this problem, Xia et al. [17] combined a double-power reaching law with an improved terminal sliding mode. The double-power reaching law ensures that the system can reach the sliding surface within a finite time from any initial state, while the improved terminal sliding surface ensures that position and velocity errors approximate zero. This method can balance the convergence speed and stability of the system within a certain range, ensuring faster convergence speed and effectively attenuating the jitter vibration phenomenon of the robotic arm. It achieves high tracking accuracy and a strong anti-interference ability, but it also leads to a relatively complex parameter adjustment. Additionally, Ba et al. [18] designed a composite reaching law that combines the cotangent function and the exponential reaching law. This approach shortens the reaching time to the sliding surface and reduces the velocity near the sliding surface. It makes the convergence process smoother and avoids the problem of high-frequency jittering caused by excessive speed when approaching the sliding mold surface. In order to solve the jitter problem caused by the sign function, Zhang et al. [19] designed an improved multiple-power reaching law by replacing the sgn functions with the sigmoid functions, utilizing the smoothing property of the sigmoid functions to reduce the jitter and vibration caused by the sgn functions. This method enhances the control quality and convergence speed of sliding mode control, exhibiting strong robustness and versatility.

Neural network control has the advantages of high precision, low latency, and strong adaptability, making it highly advantageous in nonlinear control, and extensive research has been conducted in this area [20]. Liu et al. [21] studied a robot neural network control system based on a genetic algorithm. The genetic algorithm is used to optimize the neural network, simplifying the network structure and improving tracking effectiveness. However, the method has high computational complexity and requires a long optimization time. He and Dong [22] proposed a fuzzy neural network learning algorithm to identify uncertain system models. This method does not require prior knowledge or a sufficient amount of observation data about uncertainties. Impedance learning is introduced to address the interaction between the robot and the environment. This control method ensures the tracking performance of the system under state constraints and uncertainties, but the design and parameter tuning of the fuzzy neural network are relatively complex. Tlijani et al. [23] presented a non-singular fast terminal sliding mode control strategy based on a wavelet neural network observer. A wavelet observer is designed using the online approximation capability of neural networks to estimate modeling errors, external disturbances, and uncertainties in joint robots. This control method can overcome the jitter vibration phenomenon and ensure the accuracy and stability of the position control of articulated robots, but the design and parameter adjustment of the observer are relatively complex and sensitive to the modeling and observation errors of the system. Several of the above methods are relatively complex; thus, Sun et al. [24] designed a neural network control method based on radial basis functions, which utilizes neural networks to approximate the unknown model of the robot and deal with the uncertainty of the system with good tracking performance and small tracking error. Compared with other neural network control methods, this method has a fast training speed and relatively simple parameter adjustment. On this basis, Fan et al. [25] developed a sliding mode controller based on RBF neural networks. This controller utilizes the sliding mode control algorithm to counteract external disturbances and employs the radial basis function neural network control algorithm to address system uncertainties. The combination of the two control methods ensures a relatively simple controller structure while improving tracking accuracy and robustness.

To address the problem of decreased trajectory tracking accuracy in robotic arms caused by modeling errors and external disturbances, this paper proposes a neural network terminal sliding mode control algorithm based on a novel reaching law and an improved salp swarm algorithm. Firstly, a fast nonsingular terminal sliding mode surface is selected to achieve finite-time convergence and avoid singularity issues. We propose a novel multi-power reaching law, replacing the sign functions with saturation functions to reduce system chattering. Secondly, considering the capability of RBF neural networks to approximate any continuous functions, we utilize RBF neural networks to estimate model uncertainties and external disturbances. An adaptive law is designed to automatically adjust the neural network weights. Furthermore, we propose an adaptive leader salp swarm algorithm to optimize the parameters of the controller, thereby improving the effectiveness of trajectory tracking control. Finally, we conduct simulations of ABB six-axis robotic arm trajectory tracking control in the Matlab environment to validate the effectiveness and reliability of the proposed control method. The main contributions of this paper are as follows:

1. A novel reaching law is proposed, which utilizes the tanh and sigmoid functions to replace the sign functions in traditional multi-power reaching law. This enables the system state to slide rapidly and accurately onto the sliding surface, suppressing oscillations and enhancing system stability and disturbance rejection capabilities.
2. An improved salp swarm algorithm is proposed, incorporating adaptive inertia weight factors and adaptive adjustment strategies to enhance convergence speed, overall performance, and solution accuracy.
3. A novel neural network terminal sliding mode controller is proposed and applied to the trajectory tracking control of an ABB robot. The superior control performance of the controller is verified through simulation and experimental validation.

The organization of this paper is as follows: Section 2 presents the dynamic model of the robot and the design of the ALSSA-RBFTSM controller. Section 3 provides the simulation and experimental results. Section 4 presents the conclusions of this paper.

2. Controller Design

2.1. Robotic Arm Dynamics Model

The dynamic model of the robotic arm can be obtained using the Lagrange method [26], as follows:

$$M(q)\ddot{q} + C(q,\dot{q})\dot{q} + G(q) + F(\dot{q}) + \tau_d = \tau \tag{1}$$

where $q \in R^{n\times 1}$ represents the joint angles, $\dot{q} \in R^{n\times 1}$ represents the joint angular velocities, $\ddot{q} \in R^{n\times 1}$ represents the joint angular accelerations, $M(q) \in R^{n\times n}$ represents the inertia matrix, $C(q,\dot{q}) \in R^{n\times n}$ represents the Coriolis and centrifugal force matrix, $G(q) \in R^{n\times 1}$ represents the gravity matrix, $F(\dot{q}) \in R^{n\times 1}$ represents the friction matrix, $\tau \in R^{n\times 1}$ represents the control input matrix, and $\tau_d \in R^{n\times 1}$ represents the external disturbance matrix.

In practice, obtaining an accurate dynamic model of a robotic arm is challenging, and modeling errors can degrade control performance and reduce trajectory tracking accuracy. Therefore, considering the modeling errors in the dynamic modeling of the robotic arm, the dynamic model can be divided into a deterministic part and an uncertain part [27]. Thus, $M(q)$, $C(q,\dot{q})$, and $G(q)$ can be represented as:

$$\begin{cases} M(q) = M_0(q) + \Delta M(q) \\ C(q,\dot{q}) = C_0(q,\dot{q}) + \Delta C(q,\dot{q}) \\ G(q) = G_0(q) + \Delta G(q) \end{cases} \tag{2}$$

The aggregate uncertainty arising from modeling errors and external disturbances can be represented as:

$$f = \Delta M(q)\ddot{q} + \Delta C(q,\dot{q})\dot{q} + \Delta G(q) + F(\dot{q}) + \tau_d \tag{3}$$

In this case, the dynamic equation can be reexpressed as:

$$M_0(q)\ddot{q} + C_0(q,\dot{q})\dot{q} + G_0(q) + f = \tau \tag{4}$$

2.2. Design of Fast Nonsingular Terminal Sliding Mode Control

Define the system tracking error as:

$$e = q - q_d \tag{5}$$

where q is the actual position vector and q_d is the desired position vector.

The FNTSM surface [28] is designed as:

$$s = \dot{e} + \alpha e + \beta |e|^\lambda sgn(e) \tag{6}$$

where $\alpha, \beta \in R$, $1 < \lambda < 2$.

The derivative of the sliding mode surface function can be obtained as:

$$\dot{s} = \ddot{e} + \alpha \dot{e} + \beta \lambda |e|^{(\lambda-1)} \dot{e} \tag{7}$$

Without considering the compound disturbance of the system, and letting $\dot{s} = 0$, the equivalent control law can be obtained as:

$$u_{eq} = M_0(q)\ddot{q}_d - M_0(q)\left[\alpha \dot{e} + \beta \lambda |e|^{(\lambda-1)} \dot{e}\right] + C_0(q,\dot{q}) + G_0(q) \tag{8}$$

The traditional multi-power reaching law [29] is as follows:

$$\dot{s} = -k_1|s|^{a_1}sgn(s) - k_2|s|^{a_2}sgn(s) - k_3|s|^{a_3}sgn(s) - k_4 s \tag{9}$$

where $k_1 > 0$, $k_2 > 0$, $k_3 > 0$, $k_4 > 0$, $a_1 > 1$, $0 < a_2 < 1$, and the value of a_3 is taken as follows:

$$a_3 = \begin{cases} \max\{a_1, |s|\}, |s| \geq 1 \\ \min\{a_2, |s|\}, |s| < 1 \end{cases} \tag{10}$$

when the system state satisfies the condition $|s| < 1$, and the reaching law is mainly influenced by $-k_2|s|^{a_2}sgn(s) - k_3|s|^{a_3}sgn(s)$. When the system state satisfies the condition $|s| \geq 1$, the reaching law is mainly influenced by $-k_1|s|^{a_1}sgn(s) - k_3|s|^{a_3}sgn(s)$. The value of a_3 ensures that the system can adaptively change the exponential parameter in the reaching law, resulting in a faster convergence rate.

Considering the chattering issue caused by the sign functions, this paper proposes improvements to the multi-power reaching law. The sigmoid function and tanh function have the advantages of continuity and fast response. As the system state approaches the sliding surface, the output of the tanh function gradually saturates, resulting in a slower convergence speed. When the system state is far from the sliding surface, the convergence speed of the sigmoid function is relatively fast. Therefore, the sigmoid function is used to replace the first sign function in the multi-power reaching law, the tanh function is used to replace the second sign function, and a nonlinear function is designed to replace the third sign function. This helps avoid the control torque chattering caused by the sign functions in sliding mode control, allowing the system to enter the sliding surface more smoothly and quickly. The designed nonlinear function is as follows:

$$f(s) = \begin{cases} sigmoid(s), |s| \geq 1 \\ tanh(s), |s| < 1 \end{cases} \tag{11}$$

The newly designed reaching law in this paper is as follows:

$$\dot{s} = -k_1|s|^{a_1}sigmoid(s) - k_2|s|^{a_2}tanh(s) - k_3|s|^{a_3}f(s) - k_4s \tag{12}$$

when the system state satisfies the condition $|s| < 1$, the reaching law is mainly influenced by $-k_2|s|^{a_2}tanh(s) - k_3|s|^{a_3}tanh(s)$, leading to a reduction in the adjustment magnitude of the system, thereby suppressing the occurrence of oscillations and vibrations. When the system state satisfies the condition $|s| \geq 1$, the reaching law is mainly influenced by $-k_1|s|^{a_1}sigmoid(s) - k_3|s|^{a_3}sigmoid(s)$, enabling the system to adjust its state more quickly and approach the sliding surface rapidly. By leveraging the characteristics of the tanh and sigmoid functions, the system exhibits a certain degree of adaptability to parameter variations and disturbances, thus enhancing its stability and reliability.

According to the reaching law, the switching control law can be obtained as follows:

$$u_{sw} = M_0(q)\left[k_1|s|^{a_1}sigmoid(s) + k_2|s|^{a_2}tanh(s) + k_3|s|^{a_3}f(s) + k_4s\right] \tag{13}$$

2.3. Design of RBF Neural Network

Let the input vector of the neural network be $x = (x_1, x_2, \cdots, x_n)^T$, the hidden layer basis function be $h = (h_1, h_2, \cdots, h_j)^T$, and the output be $y = (y_1, y_2, \cdots, y_m)^T$. The functional expression of the RBF neural network can be expressed as:

$$h_j(x) = \exp\left(\frac{\|x - c_j\|^2}{2b_j^2}\right), j = 1, 2, \cdots, m \tag{14}$$

where $c_j = (c_{j1}, c_{j2}, \cdots, c_{jn})^T$ denotes the center vector of the function, $b_j = (b_{j1}, b_{j2}, \cdots, b_{jn})^T$ denotes the bandwidth of the Gaussian basis function, and m denotes the number of network nodes in the hidden layer.

The expression for the approximation of a nonlinear function by an RBF neural network is:

$$f(x) = W^{*T}h(x) + \varepsilon \tag{15}$$

where W^* represents the ideal network weights, ε is the neural network approximation error, and it satisfies $\varepsilon \leq \varepsilon_N$.

The RBF neural network is utilized to approximate $f(x)$, and the output of the neural network is:

$$\hat{f}(x) = \hat{W}^T h(x) \tag{16}$$

where $\hat{W}$ represents the actual weights of the neural network.

Define the weight estimation error as:

$$\tilde{W} = W^* - \hat{W} \tag{17}$$

Take the derivative of the Equation (17):

$$\dot{\tilde{W}} = -\dot{\hat{W}} \tag{18}$$

Define the neural network output estimation error [30] as:

$$\begin{aligned}\tilde{f} &= f - \hat{f} \\ &= W^{*T}h(x) + \varepsilon - \hat{W}^T h(x) \\ &= \tilde{W}^T h(x) + \varepsilon\end{aligned} \tag{19}$$

In order to enhance the performance of the RBF neural network, a neural network adaptive law is introduced, allowing for adaptive updates of the neural network weights. The neural network adaptive update law designed in this study is as follows:

$$\dot{\hat{W}} = \gamma h(x) s^T \tag{20}$$

where γ is the adjustment factor to be designed.

Define the robust term as:

$$v = \varepsilon_N sgn(s) \tag{21}$$

The total control law of the system at this point is:

$$\begin{aligned}u &= u_{eq} - u_{sw} + \hat{f} - v \\ &= M_0(q)\ddot{q}_d - M_0(q)\left[\alpha\dot{e} + \beta\lambda|e|^{(\lambda-1)}\dot{e}\right] + C_0(q,\dot{q}) + G_0(q) + \hat{W}^T h - \varepsilon_N sgn(s) - \\ &\quad M_0(q)\left[k_1|s|^{a_1} sigmoid(s) + k_2|s|^{a_2} tanh(s) + k_3|s|^{a_3} f(s) + k_4 s\right]\end{aligned} \tag{22}$$

2.4. Control System Stability Analysis

2.4.1. Certificate of Necessity

Assuming that the Lyapunov function $V(x)$ is asymptotically stable, to prove that:

1. $V(x) > 0$ holds for all $x \neq 0$: since $V(x)$ is asymptotically stable, according to the definition of the Lyapunov function, there exists a positive constant a and a positive constant b, such that for all x satisfying $\|x\| > a$, there is $V(x) > b$. That is to say, for all non-zero vectors x, as long as their paradigm is greater than a, the Lyapunov function $V(x)$ is greater than b. Therefore, one can conclude that $V(x) > 0$ holds for all $x \neq 0$.
2. $V(0) = 0$: since $V(x) > 0$ holds for all $x \neq 0$, we can deduce that $V(0)$ must be equal to 0. Otherwise, if $V(0)$ is greater than 0, then there exists a small neighborhood where $V(x) > 0$. This contradicts the condition that $V(x) > 0$ holds for all $x \neq 0$.
3. $\dot{V} \leq 0$ holds for all $x \neq 0$: the derivative of the Lyapunov function $V(x)$ can represent the rate of change of the state of the system. Since $V(x)$ is asymptotically stable, by the definition of the Lyapunov function, for all x satisfying $\|x\| > a$, there is $\dot{V} \leq 0$. This implies that the Lyapunov function $V(x)$ is decreasing over the range of these x. The derivative of $V(x)$ holds for all $x \neq 0$: the derivative of $V(x)$ can represent the

rate of change of the state of the system. Also, by the definition of asymptotic stability, $\dot{V} \leq 0$ must tend to 0, i.e., $\dot{V}(0) = 0$.

In summary, if the Lyapunov function is asymptotically stable, we can obtain that $V(x) > 0$, $V(0) = 0$, and $\dot{V} \leq 0$.

2.4.2. Certificate of Sufficiency

Define the Lyapunov function [31] to be:

$$V = \frac{1}{2}s^T M_0 s + \frac{1}{2} tr\left(\tilde{W}^T \gamma^{-1} \tilde{W}\right) \tag{23}$$

Take the derivative of the Lyapunov function:

$$\begin{aligned}
\dot{V} &= s^T M_0 \dot{s} + \tfrac{1}{2} s^T \dot{M}_0 s + tr\left(\tilde{W}^T \gamma^{-1} \dot{\tilde{W}}\right) \\
&= s^T M_0 \left(\ddot{e} + \alpha \dot{e} + \beta \lambda |e|^{(\lambda-1)} \dot{e}\right) - tr\left(\tilde{W}^T \gamma^{-1} \dot{\hat{W}}\right) \\
&= s^T M_0 \left(\ddot{q} - \ddot{q}_d + \alpha \dot{e} + \beta \lambda |e|^{(\lambda-1)} \dot{e}\right) - tr\left(\tilde{W}^T \gamma^{-1} \dot{\hat{W}}\right)
\end{aligned} \tag{24}$$

Substituting Equations (4), (19) and (22) gives:

$$\begin{aligned}
\dot{V} =\ & -s^T M_0 [k_1 |s|^{a_1} sigmoid(s) + k_2 |s|^{a_2} tanh(s) + k_3 |s|^{a_3} f(s) + k_4 s] \\
& + s^T [\varepsilon - \varepsilon_N sgn(s)] - tr\tilde{W}^T \left(\gamma^{-1} \dot{\hat{W}} - s^T h(x)\right)
\end{aligned} \tag{25}$$

From the above equation, $\dot{V} \leq 0$ holds all the time; if and only if $s = 0$, then $\dot{V} = 0$. According to the Lyapunov stability theorem, if $V > 0$ and $\dot{V} \leq 0$, it can be obtained that the system is asymptotically convergent under the Lyapunov condition.

2.5. Improved Salp Swarm Algorithm

The salp swarm algorithm (SSA) is a heuristic optimization algorithm inspired by the behavioral characteristics of a marine organism called salp. The algorithm simulates the movement and propagation of a salp swarm, where individuals update their positions and velocities through information exchange and cooperation to search for the optimal solution [32]. By mimicking the biological features and collaborative behavior of salp swarms, the SSA can effectively search for the global optimum in complex optimization problems. The basic process of the SSA [33] is as follows:

Step 1: Initialize the population. Initialize the positions of the salps based on the upper and lower limits of each dimension in the search space. The positions of the salps are initialized as:

$$X_j^i = rand(N,D) \times (ub_j - lb_j) + lb_j \tag{26}$$

where $X_j^i (i = 1, 2, \ldots, N, j = 1, 2, \ldots, D)$ is the position of the i-th salp in the j-th dimension, N is the population size of the salp, D is the spatial dimension, $rand(N, D)$ is a uniform random number in the range of $[N, D]$, and ub_j and lb_j are the upper and lower bounds on the search space in the j-th dimension.

Step 2: Calculate the fitness value of each salp according to the objective function.

Step 3: Determine the initial location of the food source. Rank the adaptation values of the salps, and the location of the optimal salp is the location of the food source.

Step 4: Identify leaders and followers. The first half of the salp chain are the leaders, and the rest are the followers.

Step 5: Update the position of the salp leader as follows:

$$X_j^1 = \begin{cases} F_j + c_1((ub_j - lb_j)c_2 + lb_j), c_3 \geq 0.5 \\ F_j - c_1((ub_j - lb_j)c_2 + lb_j), c_3 < 0.5 \end{cases} \quad (27)$$

where X_j^1 is the position of the first salp leader in the j-th dimension, F_j is the position of the food source in the j-th dimension, and c_2 and c_3 are uniformly distributed random numbers between 0 and 1. c_1 is adaptively decreasing with the number of iterations. The value of c_1 is taken as follows:

$$c_1 = 2e^{-(4t/T)^2} \quad (28)$$

where t is the current iteration number, and T is the maximum number of iterations.

Step 6: Update the positions of the salp followers as follows:

$$X_j^i = \frac{1}{2}\left(X_j^i + X_j^{i-1}\right) \quad (29)$$

where $j \geq 2$, X_j^i represents the position of the i-th salp follower in the j-th dimension search area.

Step 7: Apply boundary processing to each dimension of the updated individual, and update the location of the food source based on the new globally optimal salp location after the update.

Step 8: Determine whether the termination condition is satisfied; if so, output the result. Otherwise, proceed to step 4 and continue iterating.

The SSA is similar to other heuristic algorithms and may encounter the issue of local optima, along with certain limitations in terms of optimization accuracy and solution stability. To address these problems, this study improves the SSA and proposes an adaptive leader salp swarm algorithm (ALSSA).

By introducing an adaptive inertia weight factor, the influence of food sources on the leader position undergoes adaptive changes during the update process. As the number of iterations increases, the impact of food sources gradually decreases, thereby limiting the search range, improving the accuracy and efficiency of the search, and avoiding the unrestricted search range issue in the leader position update stage of SSA. The formula for calculating the inertia weight in this paper is as follows:

$$w = w_{max} - (w_{max} - w_{min})(t/T)^2 \quad (30)$$

where w_{max} and w_{min} are the upper and lower limits of the inertia weight.

By incorporating the previous generation's salp leader position into the leader position update formula, the updated leader position is influenced not only by the previous generation's salp leader position but also by the previous generation's global best solution. This approach effectively avoids the problem of the basic algorithm getting trapped in local optima and improves the algorithm optimization accuracy. The improved salp leader position update formula is as follows:

$$X_j^i(t) = X_j^i(t-1) + \left(F_j(t-1) - X_j^i(t-1)\right) \cdot rand(0,1) \quad (31)$$

where $X_j^i(t-1)$ represents the position of the i-th salp leader in the j-th dimension of the previous generation, $F_j(t-1)$ represents the position of the food source in the previous generation, and $rand(0,1)$ denotes a uniform random number between 0 and 1.

Combining Equations (29) and (30), the new salp leader position update equation can be expressed as follows:

$$X_j^i(t) = X_j^i(t-1) + \left(w \cdot F_j(t-1) - X_j^i(t-1)\right) \cdot rand(0,1) \quad (32)$$

We introduce an adaptive adjustment strategy to dynamically decrease the number of salp leaders with an increasing iteration count while increasing the number of followers adaptively. This approach ensures a balance between global and local search throughout the entire phase, thereby improving the convergence accuracy of the algorithm. It effectively avoids the issues of early convergence to local optima and low optimization accuracy in the later stages. The updated formula for calculating the number of leaders and followers is as follows:

$$r = b_0 \left(\tan\left(-\frac{\pi t}{4T} + \frac{\pi}{4}\right) - k_0 \cdot rand(0,1) \right) \quad (33)$$

where b_0 is the coefficient to control the ratio of leaders to followers, k_0 is the perturbation deviation factor, the number of leaders is equal to rN, and the number of followers is equal to $(1-r)N$.

The objective function of ALSSA is used to minimize angular tracking errors, which is expressed as follows:

$$J = \frac{1}{n} \sum_{i=1}^{n} |e_i| \quad (34)$$

The specific meaning of this expression is as follows: for a given number of sampling points n, calculate the absolute values of the angular tracking errors $|e_i|$ at each sampling point, and then sum the absolute values of the angular tracking errors at all sampling points to obtain the value of the objective function.

In the designed controller, parameters that have a minimal impact on control performance are considered as priors and do not require adjustment. There are a total of six adjustable controller parameters, namely α, β, k_1, k_2, k_3, k_4. The precise values of these control parameters will be determined by the ALSSA method.

3. Simulation and Experimental Results

3.1. Simulation Results

To validate the effectiveness and superiority of the proposed neural network terminal sliding mode control algorithm for the robotic arms, based on a novel reaching law and an improved salp swarm algorithm, this study conducted simulation experiments using the ABB IRB120 robotic arm as the research subject in Matlab R2022b software.

The ABB IRB120 robot is a six-axis robotic arm developed by ABB, a leading robotics company. It is designed for various industrial applications, including assembly, material handling, and machine tending. The IRB120 robot offers high precision, flexibility, and compactness, making it suitable for use in small workspaces. It has a payload capacity of up to 3 kg and a reach of 580 mm, allowing it to perform tasks with precision and agility. The IRB120 robot is equipped with advanced features such as integrated vision systems and user-friendly programming interfaces, enabling easy integration and efficient operation in industrial environments. The ABB IRB120 robot is shown in Figure 1.

Denavit–Hartenberg (DH) parameters and mass parameters play crucial roles in the modeling of robotic arms, as they are essential for accurately describing the kinematic and dynamic characteristics of the arm. DH parameters describe the geometric and kinematic properties of the robotic arm, providing the geometric relationships between its joints and enabling the precise execution of desired motions. On the other hand, mass parameters describe the distribution of mass within the robotic arm, influencing its inertia properties and dynamic response, which are vital for achieving precise motion control. The DH parameters and quality parameters of the ABB IRB120 robot are shown in Tables 1 and 2.

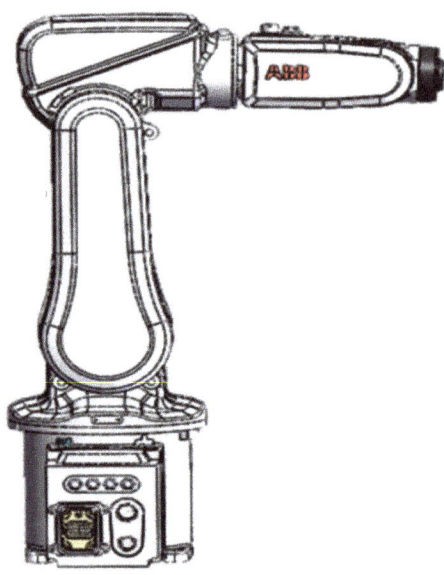

Figure 1. ABB IRB120 robot.

Table 1. The DH parameter list of the ABB IRB120 robot.

Joint	Angle θ (°)	Offset d (m)	Length a (m)	Twist α (°)
Joint 1	θ_1	0.290	0	−90
Joint 2	θ_2	0	0.270	0
Joint 3	θ_3	0	0.070	−90
Joint 4	θ_4	0.302	0	90
Joint 5	θ_5	0	0	−90
Joint 6	θ_6	0.072	0	0

Table 2. The quality parameter list of the ABB IRB120 robot.

Joint	Mass (kg)	Position of the Center of Mass (m)
Joint 1	9.28	(−0.02819, 0.00002, 0.13210)
Joint 2	3.91	(−0.00216, 0.00118, 0.39124)
Joint 3	2.94	(0.00178, −0.01867, 0.61730)
Joint 4	1.33	(0.00856, −0.22070, 0.62499)
Joint 5	0.55	(0.01133, −0.29682, 0.62287)
Joint 6	0.01	(0.01367, −0.36273, 0.61955)

Since the inertia matrix $M(q)$, the Coriolis and centrifugal matrice $C(q, \dot{q})$, and the gravitational matrix $G(q)$ of the ABB IRB120 six-axis robotic arm are too complicated, the detailed dynamics parameter matrices are not listed here. The model determination section is set to $M_0 = 0.8M$, $C_0 = 0.8C$, $G_0 = 0.8G$. The initial angles of the ABB robotic arm are $q_1(0) = q_2(0) = q_3(0) = q_4(0) = q_5(0) = q_6(0) = 0.05$. The reference trajectories are $q_{d_1} = q_{d_2} = q_{d_3} = q_{d_4} = q_{d_5} = q_{d_6} = 0.1sint$. The parameters of the sliding mode control are $\alpha = 2$, $\beta = 0.4$, $\lambda = 1.5$, $k_1 = k_2 = k_3 = k_4 = 0.5$, $a_1 = 1.2$, $a_2 = 0.2$. The joint friction is $F(\dot{q}) = 0.1\dot{q} + 0.1\text{sgn}(\dot{q})$. The external disturbance is $\tau_d = 0.5sint$. The parameter of the robust term is $\varepsilon_N = 0.1$. The parameters of the RBF neural network are $\gamma = 0.01$, $b = 10$, $c = [-1 \ -0.5 \ -0.25 \ -0.125 \ -0.0625 \ -0.03125 \ 0 \ 0.03125 \ 0.0625 \ 0.125 \ 0.25 \ 0.5 \ 1]$. The parameters of the ALSSA are $N = 30$, $T = 500$, $w_{\max} = 0.9$, $w_{\min} = 0.4$, $b_0 = 0.75$, $k_0 = 0.2$. The number of iterations to obtain the optimal solution is 29, and the optimized sliding mode control parameters are $\alpha = 2.7$, $\beta = 1.8$, $k_1 = 0.1$, $k_2 = 0.8$, $k_3 = 1.4$, $k_4 = 1.5$.

The ALSSA-RBFTSM algorithm designed in this paper is compared with the global fast terminal sliding mode (GFTSM) algorithm proposed in the literature [34] and the RBF neural network fast nonsingular terminal sliding mode (RBF-FNTSM) algorithm proposed in the literature [35]. From Figure 2, it can be seen that the GFTSM algorithm has the smallest initial control torques, but it experiences the most serious control torque jitter. The RBF-FNTSM algorithm effectively suppresses control torque jitter, but there is still a certain amount of jitter that remains. At the same time, its initial control torques increase. The ALSSA-RBFTSM algorithm demonstrates smooth control torques with little jitter, but it has the largest initial control torques. From Figure 3, it can be observed that all three control algorithms enable the robotic arm to track the desired trajectory within a certain time period. However, the GFTSM algorithm deviates from the desired trajectory at certain time intervals, while the RBF-FNTSM algorithm and the proposed algorithm in this paper remain mostly on the desired trajectory. Figure 4 demonstrates that when subjected to uncertainties such as friction and external disturbances, the position tracking errors of the proposed algorithm remain consistently at zero. In contrast, the GFTSM algorithm and the RBF-FNTSM algorithm exhibit fluctuating position tracking errors. The GFTSM algorithm is most affected, exhibiting significant fluctuations in position tracking error and poor position tracking performance. The RBF-FNTSM algorithm demonstrates a certain level of disturbance rejection capability, suppressing uncertainties to some extent, but still experiences a certain degree of position tracking error fluctuations. In comparison to the GFTSM and RBF-FNTSM algorithms, the ALSSA-RBFTSM algorithm exhibits improved performance, demonstrating better robustness and position tracking effectiveness when faced with uncertainties such as friction and external disturbances.

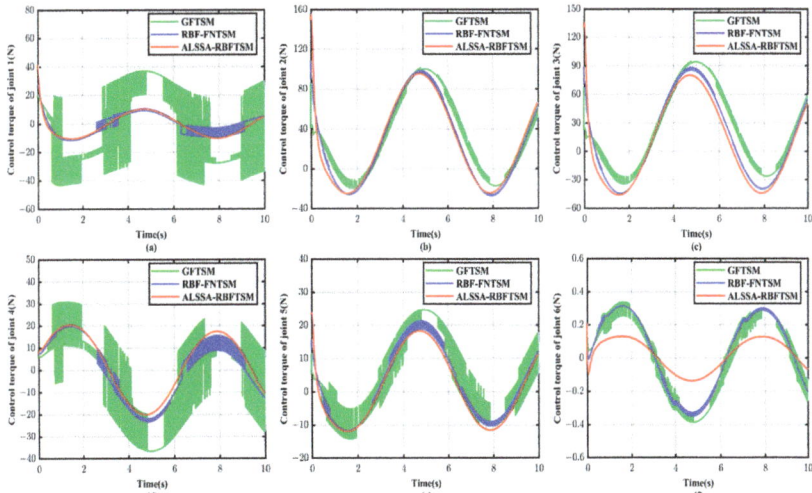

Figure 2. Control torques of different controllers. (**a**) Joint 1; (**b**) Joint 2; (**c**) Joint 3; (**d**) Joint 4; (**e**) Joint 5; (**f**) Joint 6.

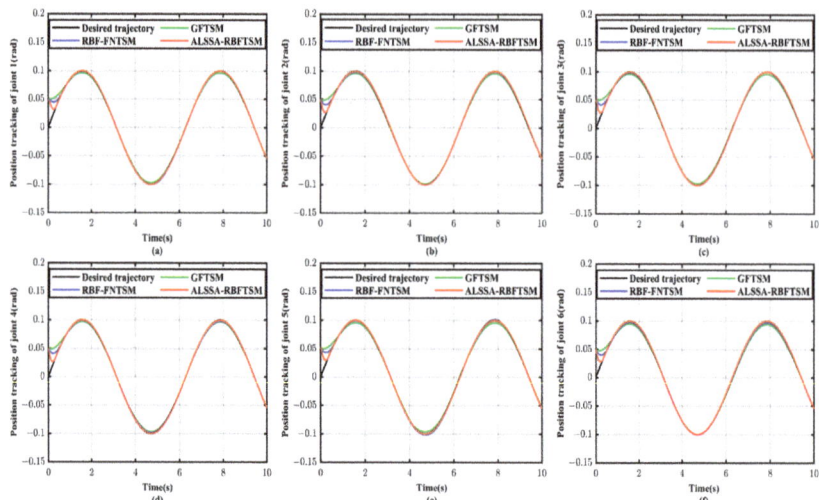

Figure 3. Position tracking of different controllers. (**a**) Joint 1; (**b**) Joint 2; (**c**) Joint 3; (**d**) Joint 4; (**e**) Joint 5; (**f**) Joint 6.

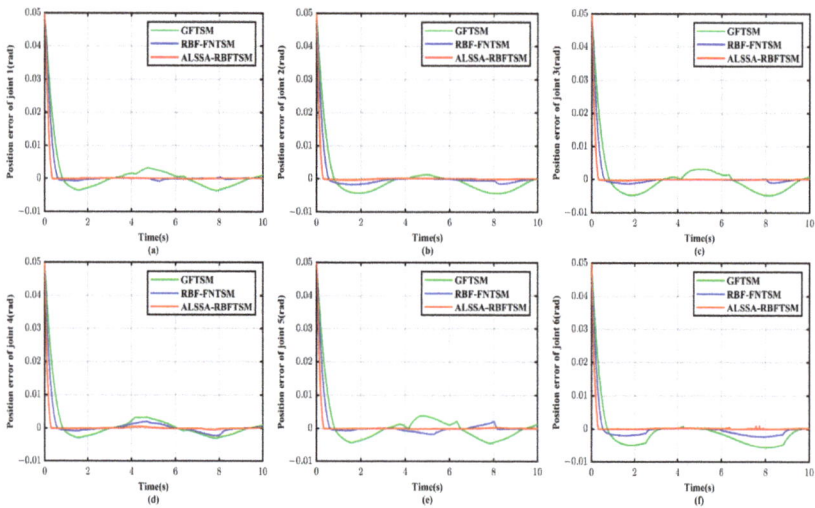

Figure 4. Position tracking errors of different controllers. (**a**) Joint 1; (**b**) Joint 2; (**c**) Joint 3; (**d**) Joint 4; (**e**) Joint 5; (**f**) Joint 6.

Figure 5 demonstrates that the velocities of all three control algorithms can effectively track the desired trajectories. The GFTSM algorithm exhibits the longest convergence time, while the RBF-FNTSM algorithm shows a slightly accelerated convergence speed. The ALSSA-RBFTSM control algorithm designed in this study demonstrates the shortest convergence time. Figure 6 shows that the velocity tracking errors of all three control algorithms converge to nearly zero, indicating a favorable control performance. The GFTSM algorithm has relatively significant fluctuations in trajectory tracking errors. The error fluctuations in the RBF-FNTSM algorithm are less noticeable. In contrast, the ALSSA-RBFTSM control algorithm designed in this study demonstrates the fastest convergence speed and the smallest tracking errors, showcasing superior steady-state characteristics.

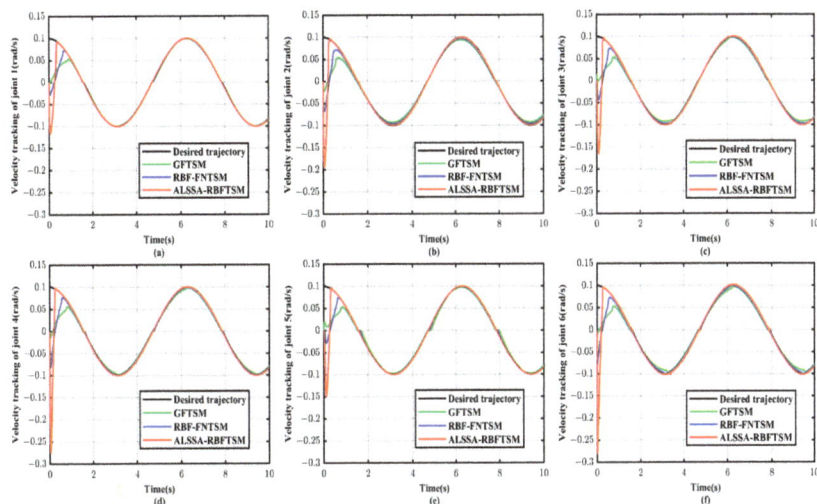

Figure 5. Velocity tracking of different controllers. (**a**) Joint 1; (**b**) Joint 2; (**c**) Joint 3; (**d**) Joint 4; (**e**) Joint 5; (**f**) Joint 6.

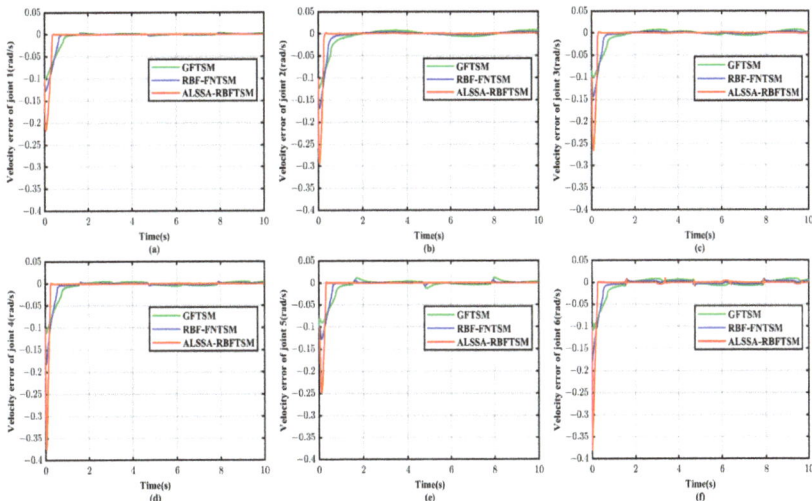

Figure 6. Velocity tracking errors of different controllers. (**a**) Joint 1; (**b**) Joint 2; (**c**) Joint 3; (**d**) Joint 4; (**e**) Joint 5; (**f**) Joint 6.

According to the results presented in Tables 3 and 4, it can be observed that the ALSSA-RBFTSM algorithm designed in this study exhibits the best control performance. It demonstrates the smallest average steady-state error and maximum steady-state error in position tracking for each joint of the robotic arm. Comparative analysis reveals that, compared to the GFTSM control algorithm, the ALSSA-RBFTSM control algorithm reduces the average steady-state error in position tracking for each joint by 97.6%, 96.5%, 99.1%, 90.7%, 95.1%, and 95.3% respectively. Furthermore, it reduces the maximum steady-state error in position tracking for each joint by 95.5%, 95.0%, 97.0%, 86.5%, 92.7%, and 83.9%, respectively. In comparison to the RBF-FNTSM control algorithm, the ALSSA-RBFTSM control algorithm reduces the average steady-state error in position tracking for each joint by 68.5%, 84.2%, 85.7%, 82.6%, 82.3%, and 87.3%, respectively. Additionally, it reduces the maximum steady-state error in position tracking for each joint by 79.4%, 85.3%, 85.5%, 79.2%, 84.8%, and 60.9%, respectively.

Table 3. Position tracking average steady-state error.

Joint	GFTSM	RBF-FNTSM	ALSSA-RBFTSM
Joint 1	1.75×10^{-3}	1.31×10^{-4}	4.13×10^{-5}
Joint 2	1.83×10^{-3}	4.10×10^{-4}	6.48×10^{-5}
Joint 3	2.38×10^{-3}	1.53×10^{-4}	2.19×10^{-5}
Joint 4	1.68×10^{-3}	9.02×10^{-4}	1.57×10^{-4}
Joint 5	2.79×10^{-3}	6.03×10^{-4}	1.07×10^{-4}
Joint 6	2.49×10^{-3}	9.10×10^{-4}	1.16×10^{-4}

Table 4. Position tracking maximum steady-state error.

Joint	GFTSM	RBF-FNTSM	ALSSA-RBFTSM
Joint 1	3.65×10^{-3}	8.07×10^{-4}	1.66×10^{-4}
Joint 2	4.43×10^{-3}	1.50×10^{-3}	2.21×10^{-4}
Joint 3	4.84×10^{-3}	9.98×10^{-4}	1.45×10^{-4}
Joint 4	3.33×10^{-3}	2.16×10^{-3}	4.49×10^{-4}
Joint 5	4.42×10^{-3}	2.12×10^{-3}	3.22×10^{-4}
Joint 6	5.65×10^{-3}	2.33×10^{-3}	9.12×10^{-4}

3.2. Experiment Results

In this section, we implement the proposed control strategy on the packaging unit of an ABB robot in the intelligent manufacturing production line in our laboratory. The intelligent manufacturing production line comprises six experimental stations: unordered screening unit, visual sorting unit, dimension detection unit, laser marking unit, assembly unit, and packaging unit. These stations utilize automation equipment and robots to carry out production tasks, reducing the requirement for manual operations and enhancing production efficiency. The ALSSA-RBFTSM algorithm designed in this paper is applied to the ABB six-axis robotic arm in the packing unit of the production line to design the robot grasping and placing test. Figures 7 and 8 illustrates the process of robot grasping and placing.

Figure 7. Trajectory tracking control for robotic arm gripping tests.

Figure 8. Trajectory tracking control for robotic arm placement tests.

The system conducted 50 grasping and placing experiments on black boxes. The success rate for grasping was 92%, while the success rate for placing was 86%. The main reason for the grasping failures is the positional deviation of the black boxes on the tray, which caused the robotic arm to misalign or have unstable grasping. The primary reason for the placing failures is the angular deviation of the lid of the yellow paper box, resulting in interference with the black boxes during the placing process. The experimental results above demonstrate that, for multiple grasping and placing tasks, the ABB robot can reliably track the trajectory, successfully completing the grasping and placing operations. The system operates smoothly during the workflow, without significant occurrences of excessive vibrations.

4. Conclusions

This paper proposes a neural network terminal sliding mode control algorithm for robotic arms, based on a reaching law and an improved salp swarm algorithm. A fast nonsingular terminal sliding surface is utilized to achieve finite-time convergence, and the traditional multi-power reaching law is improved to reduce system oscillations. An RBF neural network is employed to estimate the model uncertainties and external disturbances of the system. The improved salp swarm algorithm is utilized to optimize controller parameters, further enhancing control performance. A robust term is designed to compensate for estimation errors in the RBF neural network. The stability of the system is proven, using the Lyapunov stability theory. Simulation results demonstrate that, compared to the GFTSM control algorithm, the ALSSA-RBFTSM control algorithm reduces the average steady-state position tracking error of the robotic arm by up to 99.1% and the maximum steady-state position tracking error by up to 97.0%. Compared to the RBF-FNTSM control algorithm, the ALSSA-RBFTSM control algorithm reduces the average steady-state position tracking error by up to 87.3% and the maximum steady-state position tracking error by up to 85.5%. The experimental results show that the designed control algorithm enables the robot to stably track trajectories and complete grasping and placing tasks. The simulation and experimental results demonstrate the effectiveness and reliability of the proposed control algorithm, showcasing its excellent disturbance rejection capability and trajectory tracking performance.

Author Contributions: Conceptualization, H.Z. and Q.Z.; methodology, H.Z. and J.D.; software, H.Z.; validation, H.Z., J.D. and J.Q.; writing—original draft preparation, H.Z.; writing—review and editing, H.Z., J.D. and J.Q. All authors have read and agreed to the published version of the manuscript.

Funding: This research received no external funding.

Data Availability Statement: The data used to support the findings of this study are included within the article and are also available from the corresponding authors upon request.

Acknowledgments: We thank Haodong Li, Lei Yang, and Shanlin Li of Shanghai Maritime University for their valuable discussions and useful suggestions in this work.

Conflicts of Interest: The authors declare no conflict of interest.

References

1. Yang, Q.; Ma, X.; Wang, W.; Peng, D. Adaptive Non-Singular Fast Terminal Sliding Mode Trajectory Tracking Control for Robot Manipulators. *Electronics* **2022**, *11*, 3672. [CrossRef]
2. Kelly, R.; Haber, R.; Haber-Guerra, R.E.; Reyes, F. Lyapunov Stable Control of Robot Manipulators: A Fuzzy Self-Tuning Procedure. *Intell. Autom. Soft Comput.* **1999**, *5*, 313–326. [CrossRef]
3. Guerra, R.E.H.; Schmitt-Braess, G.; Haber, R.H.; Alique, A.; Alique, J.R. Using circle criteria for verifying asymptotic stability in PI-like fuzzy control systems: Application to the milling process. *IEE Proc.-Control Theory Appl.* **2003**, *150*, 619–627. [CrossRef]
4. Lyu, X.; Lin, Z. Design of PID control for planar uncertain nonlinear systems with input delay. *Int. J. Robust Nonlinear Control* **2022**, *32*, 9407–9420. [CrossRef]
5. Burkan, R.; Uzmay, İ. Logarithmic based robust approach to parametric uncertainty for control of robot manipulators. *Int. J. Robust Nonlinear Control* **2005**, *15*, 427–436. [CrossRef]
6. Wei, B. Adaptive Control Design and Stability Analysis of Robotic Manipulators. *Actuators* **2018**, *7*, 89. [CrossRef]
7. Raković, M.; Anil, G.; Mihajlović, Ž.; Srđjan, S.; Naik, S.; Borovac, B.; Gottscheber, A. Fuzzy position-velocity control of underactuated finger of FTN robot hand. *J. Intell. Fuzzy. Syst.* **2018**, *34*, 2723–2736. [CrossRef]
8. Yovchev, K.; Delchev, K.; Krastev, E. State Space Constrained Iterative Learning Control for Robotic Manipulators. *Asian J. Control* **2018**, *20*, 1145–1150. [CrossRef]
9. Xu, K.; Wang, Z. The design of a neural network-based adaptive control method for robotic arm trajectory tracking. *Neural Comput. Appl.* **2022**, *35*, 8785–8795. [CrossRef]
10. Wu, H.; Zhang, X.; Song, L.; Zhang, Y.; Wang, C.; Zhao, X.; Gu, L. Parallel Network-Based Sliding Mode Tracking Control for Robotic Manipulators with Uncertain Dynamics. *Actuators* **2023**, *12*, 187. [CrossRef]
11. Guo, Q.; Sun, P.; Yin, J.M.; Yu, T.; Jiang, D. Parametric adaptive estimation and backstepping control of electro-hydraulic actuator with decayed memory filter. *ISA Trans.* **2016**, *62*, 202–214. [CrossRef] [PubMed]
12. Zhao, D.; Li, S.; Gao, F. A new terminal sliding mode control for robotic manipulators. *Int. J. Control* **2009**, *82*, 1804–1813. [CrossRef]
13. Doan, Q.V.; Vo, A.T.; Le, T.D.; Kang, H.J.; Nguyen, N.H.A. A Novel Fast Terminal Sliding Mode Tracking Control Methodology for Robot Manipulators. *Appl. Sci.* **2020**, *10*, 3010. [CrossRef]
14. Jin, M.; Lee, J.; Chang, P.; Choi, C. Practical Nonsingular Terminal Sliding-Mode Control of Robot Manipulators for High-Accuracy Tracking Control. *IEEE Trans. Ind. Electron.* **2009**, *56*, 3593–3601. [CrossRef]
15. Liang, X.; Wang, H.; Zhang, Y. Adaptive nonsingular terminal sliding mode control for rehabilitation robots. *Comput. Electr. Eng.* **2022**, *99*, 107718. [CrossRef]
16. Wang, A.; Jia, X.; Dong, S. A New Exponential Reaching Law of Sliding Mode Control to Improve Performance of Permanent Magnet Synchronous Motor. *IEEE Trans. Magn.* **2013**, *49*, 2409–2412. [CrossRef]
17. Xia, Y.; Xie, W.; Ma, J. Research on trajectory tracking control of manipulator based on modified terminal sliding mode with double power reaching law. *Int. J. Adv. Robot. Syst.* **2019**, *16*, 1729881419847899. [CrossRef]
18. Ba, K.; Yu, B.; Liu, Y.; Jin, Z.; Gao, Z.; Zhang, J.; Kong, X. Fuzzy Terminal Sliding Mode Control with Compound Reaching Law and Time Delay Estimation for HDU of Legged Robot. *Complexity* **2020**, *2020*, 5240247. [CrossRef]
19. Zhang, Y.; Wang, Y.J.; Yu, J.Q. A Novel MPPT Algorithm for Photovoltaic Systems Based on Improved Sliding Mode Control. *Electronics* **2022**, *11*, 2421. [CrossRef]
20. Cruz, Y.J.; Rivas, M.; Quiza, R.; Villalonga, A.; Haber, R.E.; Beruvides, G. Ensemble of convolutional neural networks based on an evolutionary algorithm applied to an industrial welding process. *Comput. Ind.* **2021**, *133*, 103530. [CrossRef]
21. Liu, A.; Zhang, Y.; Zhao, H.; Wang, S.; Sun, D. Neural network control system of cooperative robot based on genetic algorithms. *Neural Comput. Appl.* **2020**, *33*, 8217–8226. [CrossRef]
22. He, W.; Dong, Y. Adaptive Fuzzy Neural Network Control for a Constrained Robot Using Impedance Learning. *IEEE Trans. Neural Netw. Learn. Syst.* **2018**, *29*, 1174–1186. [CrossRef] [PubMed]
23. Tlijani, H.; Jouila, A.; Nouri, K. Wavelet neural network sliding mode control of two rigid joint robot manipulator. *Adv. Mech. Eng.* **2022**, *14*, 16878132221119886. [CrossRef]
24. Sun, C.; He, W.; Ge, W.; Chang, C. Adaptive Neural Network Control of Biped Robots. *IEEE Trans. Syst. Man Cybern. Syst.* **2016**, *47*, 315–326. [CrossRef]
25. Fan, B.; Zhang, Y.; Chen, Y.; Meng, L. Intelligent vehicle lateral control based on radial basis function neural network sliding mode controller. *CAAI Trans. Intell. Technol.* **2022**, *7*, 455–468. [CrossRef]
26. Chen, Z.; Yang, X.; Liu, X. RBFNN-based nonsingular fast terminal sliding mode control for robotic manipulators including actuator dynamics. *Neurocomputing* **2019**, *362*, 72–82. [CrossRef]
27. Ahmed, S.; Azar, A.T.; Tounsi, M. Adaptive Fault Tolerant Non-Singular Sliding Mode Control for Robotic Manipulators Based on Fixed-Time Control Law. *Actuators* **2022**, *11*, 353. [CrossRef]
28. Zhang, Z.; Zhang, K.; Han, Z. Three-dimensional nonlinear trajectory tracking control based on adaptive sliding mode. *Aerosp. Sci. Technol.* **2022**, *128*, 107734. [CrossRef]

29. Chen, Y.; Tan, R.; Zheng, Y.; Zhou, Z. Sliding-Mode Control With Multipower Approaching Law for DC-Link Voltage of Z-Source Photovoltaic Inverters. *IEEE Access* **2019**, *7*, 133812–133821. [CrossRef]
30. Qu, C.; Hu, Y.; Guo, Z.; Han, F.; Wang, X. New Sliding Mode Control Based on Tracking Differentiator and RBF Neural Network. *Electronics* **2022**, *11*, 3135. [CrossRef]
31. Pham, P.C.; Kuo, Y.L. Robust Adaptive Finite-Time Synergetic Tracking Control of Delta Robot Based on Radial Basis Function Neural Networks. *Appl. Sci.* **2022**, *12*, 10861. [CrossRef]
32. Khajehzadeh, M.; Iraji, A.; Majdi, A.; Keawsawasvong, S.; Nehdi, M.L. Adaptive Salp Swarm Algorithm for Optimization of Geotechnical Structures. *Appl. Sci.* **2022**, *12*, 6749. [CrossRef]
33. Ding, L.; Ma, R.; Wu, Z.; Qi, R.; Ruan, W. Optimal Joint Space Control of a Cable-Driven Aerial Manipulator. *Comput. Model. Eng. Sci.* **2023**, *135*, 441–464. [CrossRef]
34. Fang, Q.; Mao, P.; Shen, L.; Wang, J. A global fast terminal sliding mode control for trajectory tracking of un-manned aerial manipulation. *Meas. Control* **2022**, *56*, 763–776. [CrossRef]
35. Guo, L.; Liu, W.; Li, L.; Lou, Y.; Wang, X.; Liu, Z. Neural Network Non-Singular Terminal Sliding Mode Control for Target Tracking of Underactuated Underwater Robots with Prescribed Performance. *J. Mar. Sci. Eng.* **2022**, *10*, 252. [CrossRef]

Disclaimer/Publisher's Note: The statements, opinions and data contained in all publications are solely those of the individual author(s) and contributor(s) and not of MDPI and/or the editor(s). MDPI and/or the editor(s) disclaim responsibility for any injury to people or property resulting from any ideas, methods, instructions or products referred to in the content.

Article

High-Precision Control of Industrial Robot Manipulator Based on Extended Flexible Joint Model

Siyong Xu [1], Zhong Wu [1],* and Tao Shen [2]

1 School of Instrumentation and Optoelectronic Engineering, Beihang University, Beijing 100191, China; xsyong@buaa.edu.cn
2 Beijing Institute of Electronic Engineering, Beijing 100039, China; shentao_buaa@buaa.edu.cn
* Correspondence: wuzhong@buaa.edu.cn

Abstract: High-precision industrial manipulators are essential components in advanced manufacturing. Model-based feedforward is the key to realizing the high-precision control of industrial robot manipulators. However, traditional feedforward control approaches are based on rigid models or flexible joint models which neglect the elasticities out of the rotational directions and degrade the setpoint precision significantly. To eliminate the effects of elasticities in all directions, a high-precision setpoint feedforward control method is proposed based on the output redefinition of the extended flexible joint model (EFJM). First, the flexible industrial robots are modeled by the EFJM to describe the elasticities in joint rotational directions and out of the rotational directions. Second, the nonminimum-phase EFJM is transformed into a minimum-phase system by using output redefinition. Third, the setpoint control task is transformed from Cartesian space into joint space by trajectory planning based on the EFJM. Third, a universal recursive algorithm is designed to compute the feedforward torque based on the EFJM. Moreover, the computational performance is improved. By compensating the pose errors caused by elasticities in all directions, the proposed method can effectively improve the setpoint control precision. The effectiveness of the proposed method is illustrated by simulation and experimental studies. The experimental results show that the proposed method reduces position errors by more than 65% and the orientation errors by more than 62%.

Keywords: industrial robot manipulator; setpoint control; feedforward control; nonminimum-phase system; elasticity compensation; extended flexible joint model

1. Introduction

Industrial robot manipulators have been applied in many manufacturing fields, such as assembly and welding. However, it is still a great challenge to expand robotics applications to high-precision machining processes due to the low accuracy [1]. Various feedback control methods such as PID control, sliding mode control [2], and observer-based control [3] have been adopted to improve the end effector setpoint control precision of industrial robots. However, it is difficult to achieve high-precision control with only feedback controllers owing to the complex nonlinear dynamics of industrial manipulators. Alternatively, model inversion-based feedforward control [4] is an effective approach that solves the problem by compensating the nonlinear dynamics. A nonlinear PD controller plus feedforward compensation was proposed for rigid robots to achieve the finite-time stabilization of the tracking error [5]. To improve the robustness-to-payload uncertainty, an intelligent feedforward controller using a neural network and fuzzy logic was designed for a two-link robot manipulator [6].

Nevertheless, the above feedforward control methods are based on the rigid robot model, which neglects the flexible deformations of manipulators. Actually, the flexibilities of some compliant transmission elements such as harmonic drives and cycloidal gears have significant effects on setpoint control performance [7]. In response to the problem, the flexible joint model (FJM) was proposed, which models the joint as a linear torsional spring [8].

Based on the FJM, a feedforward minimum-time position control method was proposed to avoid oscillation of a flexible robot [9]. Based on comprehensive modeling of the flexible joint and an extended generalized Maxwell friction model, an adaptive feedforward controller was designed to compensate the nonlinear dynamics of transmissions [10].

However, only the elasticities in revolute directions are considered in the FJM, which neglects the elasticities out of the rotational plane. In practice, modern industrial manipulators tend to have a slender design and lightweight materials. As a result, the flexible deformations out of the rotational plane caused by links and bearings are unneglectable, especially for high-speed and heavy-load manipulators [11]. Hence, the flexible joint model can not accurately describe a modern industrial robot. To improve the model accuracy, an extended flexible joint model (EFJM) was proposed [12] which can describe not only the elasticities in rotational planes but also the elastic deformations out of the plane. Then, the EFJM was validated on a modern industrial manipulator, and the results showed that the EFJM can greatly improve the model accuracy [13]. Thus, feedforward control based on the EFJM is a prospective way to improve the control precisions of flexible industrial manipulators.

Nevertheless, the EFJM possesses a differential nonflat characteristic, which is a great challenge for the feedforward controller design [14]. The feedforward control problem of a minimum-phase EFJM was solved by using differential algebraic equation (DAE) theory; thus, the tracking performance was improved significantly [12]. However, the EFJM is minimum phase only in special configuration. In most cases, the EFJM is a nonminimum-phase system [15]. A nonminimum-phase system possesses unstable internal dynamics; thus, the traditional feedforward control method cannot give a bounded solution [16]. To obtain a bounded feedforward input, a continuous DAE optimization solver and a discretized DAE optimization solver were proposed to solve the feedforward control problem of an EFJM with three degrees of freedom (DOFs) [17].

However, numerical optimization was adopted in the above methods due to the limitation of being nonminimum phase. Consequently, the existing methods have a heavy burden of calculation which is unacceptable for industrial robots with high DOFs. Moreover, the above methods are all based on analytic dynamic equations, which are difficult to obtain for complex manipulators. Thus, a high-precision feedforward control method with reasonable computational burden for general complex flexible industrial manipulators should be further explored.

To improve the setpoint control precision and reduce the computational burden, a new feedforward control approach based on the output redefinition of the EFJM is proposed for flexible industrial robots in this paper. Firstly, the output of the EFJM is redefined to transform the EFJM into a minimum-phase system. Thus, the limitation of the unstable internal dynamics is eliminated. Secondly, the joint trajectory is planned based on the kinematics and statics equations of the EFJM. Thus, the pose error caused by elasticity is compensated, and the setpoint problem is transformed into joint space. Finally, a universal feedforward torque computation algorithm for the EFJM is designed to reduce the calculation burden. The simulation and experimental studies demonstrate that the proposed method improves the control precision and computational efficiency remarkably.

The rest of this paper is organized as follows. In Section 2, the EFJM is introduced, and the setpoint control problem is formulated. The feedforward control method is proposed in Section 3. In Section 4, simulations and experiments are implemented. The conclusion is given in Section 5.

2. Problem Formulation
2.1. Extended Flexible Joint Model

Lightweight design has been widely adopted in modern industrial robot manipulators, which causes complex mechanical elasticity in all directions. However, the traditional flexible joint model describes the joint by using a torsional spring, which can only model the joint flexibilities in rotational directions. In view of the problem, the EFJM was proposed to describe the elasticities of modern industrial robots more accurately [12].

The extended flexible joint robot model is a lumped-parameter model consisting of a serial kinematic chain of rigid bodies. The rigid bodies are connected with extended flexible joints which consist of actuated joints and nonactuated joints. An example of an extended flexible joint is shown in Figure 1. The actuated joint consists of a motor, transmission, and a spring damping system, describing the elasticity in the rotational direction. The nonactuated joint uses a spring–damper pair to describe the elasticity out of the rotational plane caused by bearings, tools, and links. Consequently, the EFJM can describe the elasticities in all directions; thus, the model accuracy is improved significantly.

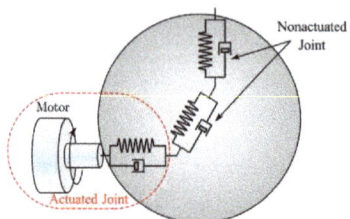

Figure 1. An example of an extended flexible joint.

Assuming the weight of the load is known, the EFJM of a robot can be obtained by using the bottom-up approach in [13]. During the modeling process, the number and location of nonactuated joints should be determined by making a compromise between model accuracy and complexity. Then, the equations of dynamics can be derived by using Lagrange equations.

$$M(q)\ddot{q} + C(q,\dot{q})\dot{q} + G(q) = \begin{bmatrix} \tau_s - F_a(\dot{q}_a) \\ \tau_e \end{bmatrix} \quad (1)$$

$$B\ddot{\theta} + \tau_s + F_m(\dot{\theta}) = \tau_c \quad (2)$$

where $q = [q_a^T, q_e^T]^T \in \mathbb{R}^{n_a+n_e}$, $q_a \in \mathbb{R}^{n_a}$, and $q_e \in \mathbb{R}^{n_e}$ are the actuated and nonactuated joint angular position vectors, respectively; $\theta = \eta^{-1}\theta_m \in \mathbb{R}^{n_a}$ and $\theta_m \in \mathbb{R}^{n_a}$ are the motor angular position vector; $\eta \in \mathbb{R}^{n_a \times n_a}$ denotes the gear ratio matrix; $F_a(\dot{q}_a) \in \mathbb{R}^{n_a}$ and $F_m(\dot{\theta}) \in \mathbb{R}^{n_a}$ are the friction torque vectors of the link side and motor side, respectively; $M(q) \in \mathbb{R}^{n \times n}$ is the inertia matrix of the robot; $C(q,\dot{q})\dot{q} \in \mathbb{R}^n$ is the Coriolis and centripetal torque vector; and $G(q) \in \mathbb{R}^n$ is the gravity torque vector, where $n = n_a + n_e$. $B = \eta^{-2}J$. $J \in \mathbb{R}^{n_a \times n_a}$ denotes the inertia diagonal matrix of the motor side. τ_c is the motor torque vector, i.e., the control input. Since the flexible deflections are small, the flexibilities are modeled by linear springs and dampers in this paper. Then, the elastic torque vectors τ_s and τ_e are expressed as:

$$\tau_s = -K_s(\theta - q_a) - D_s(\dot{\theta} - \dot{q}_a) \quad (3)$$

$$\tau_e = -K_e q_e - D_e \dot{q}_e \quad (4)$$

where $K_s, D_s \in \mathbb{R}^{n_a \times n_a}$ and $K_e, D_e \in \mathbb{R}^{n_e \times n_e}$ denote the stiffness and damping matrices in actuated and nonactuated directions, respectively. Consequently, the elasticity deformations of the manipulator are divided into two parts: elasticity deformation in the actuated direction $\theta - q$ and in the nonactuated direction q_e.

Partitioning the generalized coordinates into actuated and nonactuated coordinates, the link-side dynamics (1) can also be separated into two parts:

$$\begin{bmatrix} M_a & M_{ae} \\ M_{ae}^T & M_e \end{bmatrix} \begin{bmatrix} \ddot{q}_a \\ \ddot{q}_e \end{bmatrix} + \begin{bmatrix} C_a & C_{ae} \\ C_{ea} & C_e \end{bmatrix} \begin{bmatrix} \dot{q}_a \\ \dot{q}_e \end{bmatrix} + \begin{bmatrix} G_a \\ G_e \end{bmatrix} = \begin{bmatrix} \tau_s - F_a \\ \tau_e \end{bmatrix} \quad (5)$$

where the dependency on the generalized coordinate q and its derivate $\dot{q}$ is dropped for readability.

Obviously, the submatrices M_e, C_e, and G_e satisfy the following properties [7].

Property 1: Inertia matrix $M_e(q)$ is symmetric and positive definite, i.e., $\forall q \in \mathbb{R}^n$, $\xi \in \mathbb{R}^{n_e} : \xi^T M_e(q)\xi = \xi^T M_e^T(q)\xi \geq 0$, $\xi^T M_e(q)\xi = 0 \Leftrightarrow \xi = 0$.

Property 2: $M_e(q)$ and $C_e(q,\dot{q}) = [c_{ij}]$ satisfy the following equations:

$$\begin{bmatrix} M_a & M_{ae} \\ M_{ae}^T & M_e \end{bmatrix} \begin{bmatrix} \ddot{q}_a \\ \ddot{q}_e \end{bmatrix} + \begin{bmatrix} C_a & C_{ae} \\ C_{ea} & C_e \end{bmatrix} \begin{bmatrix} \dot{q}_a \\ \dot{q}_e \end{bmatrix} + \begin{bmatrix} G_a \\ G_e \end{bmatrix} = \begin{bmatrix} \tau_s - F_a \\ \tau_e \end{bmatrix} \quad (6)$$

Property 3: Both gravity torque and its partial derivative with respect to q are formed by trigonometric functions of the variable q. Thus, there exist positive constants M and α such that:

$$\|G_e(q)\| \leq M, \left\|\frac{\partial G_e(q)}{\partial q_e}\right\| \leq \alpha, \forall q \in \mathbb{R}^n \quad (7)$$

where $\|\cdot\|$ denotes the Euclidean norm of a vector or matrix.

Correspondingly, the reasonable assumptions are made as follows:

Assumption 1. *The damping matrix D_e in the nonactuated direction is not zero.*

Assumption 2. *The stiffness matrix of the nonactuated joint satisfies:*

$$\lambda_{min}(K_e) > \alpha \quad (8)$$

where $\lambda_{min}(K_e)$ denotes the minimum eigenvalue of K_e.

2.2. Setpoint Control Problem

Using the forward kinematics of the robot, the orientation and position of the end effector can be expressed as:

$$Z = \Gamma(q) \quad (9)$$

The objective of point-to-point feedforward control is to design a control torque τ_c such that the end effector of manipulator systems (1), (2), and (9) moves to a desired constant pose Z_f at specified time t_f from initial configuration q_0, with all elastic deformations being compensated and all closed-loop signals remaining bounded.

The EFJM is a differentially nonflat system; thus, the feedforward control input relies on the stable solution of the internal dynamics. However, from motor torque τ_c to end effector pose Z, the system is nonminimum phase in most cases, i.e., the solution of the internal dynamics may be unbounded [16]. Thus, it is difficult to compute the feedforward torque directly based on the end effector pose.

In response to the above limitations, the proposed feedforward setpoint control method consists of two steps, as shown in Figure 2. Firstly, the system output is redefined as q_a, and the reference trajectories of actuated joint positions $q_{ad}(t)$ are planned. Secondly, the nominal feedforward torque is computed by using the EFJM of the robot based on the reference actuated joint trajectories $q_{ad}(t)$. Then, the desired point-to-point motion of the end effector is accomplished indirectly.

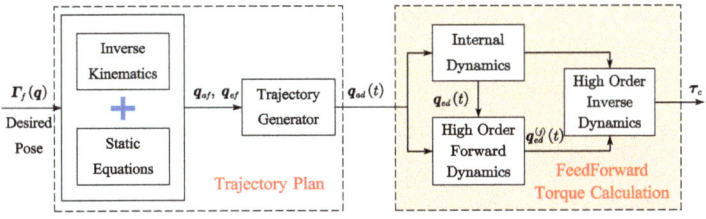

Figure 2. Procedure of proposed feedforward control method.

3. Controller Design

To achieve high-precision setpoint control of the end effector, an output-redefinition-based feedforward control method is proposed for the EFJM in this section.

Firstly, it is proven through Lyapunov theorem that the EFJM is transformed into a minimum-phase system by redefining the system output as q_a. Secondly, the reference trajectory $q_{ad}(t)$ is planned in joint space based on the kinematics and static equation of the EFJM. Thus, the pose error caused by the flexibility deformations is compensated accurately. Finally, the feedforward control torque for the EFJM is calculated by using the recursive dynamics algorithms; thus, the computational burden is further reduced.

3.1. Output Redefinition of EFJM

As mentioned above, from motor torque τ_c to end effector pose Z, the EFJM is non-minimum phase in most cases. Consequently, an unbounded solution of internal dynamics may be obtained, leading to unbounded feedforward torques. To stabilize the internal dynamics and overcome the limitation of being nonminimum phase, the system output is redefined as $y = q_a$ in this section. Then, the stability of internal dynamics is analyzed.

Differentiating the first equation of (5) twice yields:

$$M_a q_a^{(4)} + M_{ae} q_e^{(4)} + f_a = \ddot{\tau}_s \tag{10}$$

where $f_a = 2\left(\dot{M}_a q_a^{(3)} + \dot{M}_{ae} q_e^{(3)}\right) + \ddot{M}_a \ddot{q}_a + \ddot{M}_{ae} \ddot{q}_e + \ddot{N}_a + \ddot{F}_a$.

Neglect the damping of actuated joints D_s and consider the motor dynamics (2); then, the input output relationship of the EFJM is obtained.

$$y^{(4)} = -M_a^{-1}\left(K_s \ddot{q}_a + M_{ae} q_e^{(4)} + f_a\right) + M_a^{-1} K_s B^{-1}(u - \tau_s - F_m) \tag{11}$$

where $u = \tau_c$ is the system input.

Clearly, the dynamics of the unactuated joints coordinates are the internal dynamics of the EFJM.

$$M_e \ddot{q}_e + M_{ea} \ddot{q}_{ad} + C_e \dot{q}_e + C_{ea} \dot{q}_a + G_e = -K_e q_e - D_e \dot{q}_e \tag{12}$$

Let the output $q_a = q_{ad}$ and $\dot{q}_{ad} = \ddot{q}_{ad} = 0$; then, the zero dynamics of the EFJM are obtained as:

$$\ddot{q}_e = -M_e^{-1} K_e q_e - M_e^{-1}(C_e + D_e)\dot{q}_e - M_e^{-1} G_e \tag{13}$$

We can conclude from Assumption 2 [7] that system (13) has an equilibrium $q_{e0}, \dot{q}_e = 0$, which satisfies:

$$G_e(q_{e0}) + K_e q_{e0} = 0 \tag{14}$$

The Lyapunov candidate function is chosen as:

$$V = \frac{1}{2} \dot{q}_e^T M_e \dot{q}_e + P(q_e) - P(q_{e0}) \tag{15}$$

where $P(q_e)$ denotes an energy-like function which is defined as:

$$P(q_e) = \frac{1}{2}(q_e - q_{e0})^T K_e (q_e - q_{e0}) + U_e(q_e) - q_e^T G_e(q_{e0}) \tag{16}$$

where $U_e(q_e)$ means the gravitational potential energy of robot which satisfies:

$$\frac{\partial U_e(q_e)}{\partial q_e} = G_e(q_e) \tag{17}$$

Obviously, $q_e = q_{e0}$ is the stationary point of function, as the partial derivative of $P(q_e)$ w.r.t q_e is:

$$\frac{\partial P(q_e)}{\partial q_e} = K_e(q_e - q_{e0}) + G_e(q_e) - G_e(q_{e0}) = 0 \tag{18}$$

Taking the partial derivative of (18) with respect to q_e again yields:

$$\frac{\partial^2 P}{\partial q_e^2} = K_e + \frac{\partial G_e(q_e)}{\partial q_e} \tag{19}$$

According to Property 3 and the assumption $\lambda_{min}(K_e) > \alpha$, the right side of (19) is positive definite. Hence, q_{e0} is the global minimum point for $P(z_1)$. Then, we obtain $\forall q_e \in \mathbb{R}^{n_e}, \dot{q}_e \in \mathbb{R}^{n_e}, V \geqslant 0$, and $V = 0 \Leftrightarrow q_e = q_{e0}, \dot{q}_e = 0$.

The time derivative of V is:

$$\dot{V} = \dot{q}_e^T K_e(q_e - q_{e0}) + \dot{q}_e^T(G_e(q_e) - G_e(q_{e0})) + \frac{1}{2}\dot{q}_e^T \dot{M}_e \dot{q}_e + \dot{q}_e^T M_e \ddot{q}_e \tag{20}$$

According to (12) and (14), we obtain:

$$\dot{V} = -\dot{q}_e^T D_e \dot{q}_e + \frac{1}{2}\dot{q}_e^T\left(\dot{M}_e - C_e\right)\dot{q}_e - \dot{q}_e^T(K_e q_{e0} + G_e(q_{e0})) \tag{21}$$

Recalling Property 2 yields:

$$\dot{V} = -z_2^T D_e z_2 \leqslant 0 \tag{22}$$

According to Assumption 1, $\dot{V}$ is negative semi-definite if and only if $z_2 = 0$. What is more, the function V is a radially unbounded positive semi-definite function. We can conclude from the Krasovskii theorem that the equilibrium $z_1 = z_{10}, z_2 = 0$ is globally asymptotically stable. Thus, the original unstable internal dynamics are transformed into new, stable internal dynamics by choosing actuated joint position vector q_a as system out. The limitation of the nonminimum-phase EFJM can be avoided.

3.2. Trajectory Planning in Joint Space

It is obvious that the flexible deformations of unactuated joints lead to a pose error of the end effector; thus, the inverse kinematics problem of the extended flexible joint model should first be studied in trajectory planning. For convenience, assume that the robot is a six-DOFs serial joint robot manipulator and away from the singularity. Obviously, the dimension of q is larger than six; thus, the kinematic relation (9) of the EFJM is noninvertible. In order to obtain a unique solution, additional constraints on unactuated joints should be considered. In a static condition, the unactuated joint positions are determined by gravity torque; thus, the following equations should be satisfied:

$$\begin{cases} Z_f = \Gamma(q_f) \\ G_e(q_f) = -K_e q_{ef} \end{cases} \tag{23}$$

The desired joint positions q_{af} and q_{ef} can be obtained by solving the above nonlinear algebraic equations with a numerical solver which requires an initial guess. Considering the elastic deformations in nonactuated directions are small, the solution of the inverse kinematics of the rigid model can be chosen as the initial guess.

Based on the initial configuration q_0 and desired configuration q_f, the joint position reference trajectories q_{ad} and its derivatives $\dot{q}_{ad}, \ddot{q}_{ad}, q_{ad}^{(3)}$, and $q_{ad}^{(4)}$ can be planned in joint space by adopting a trajectory planning algorithm with continuous jerk profile.

$$\left[q_{ad}, \dot{q}_{ad}, \ddot{q}_{ad}, q_{ad}^{(3)}, q_{ad}^{(4)}\right] = TrajectoryPlanAlgorithm(q_{a0}, q_{af}, t_0, t_f) \tag{24}$$

Through the accurate trajectory tracking of q_{ad}, the end effector accomplishes the desired point-to-point motion. Thus, the setpoint control problem is transformed to the trajectory tracking problem in joint space.

3.3. Calculation of Feedforward Torque

According to (2) and (3), the feedforward torque can be obtained as:

$$\tau_{FF} = B\left(K_s^{-1}\ddot{\tau}_s + \ddot{q}_a\right) + \tau_s + F_m \tag{25}$$

The elastic torque vector in actuated direction τ_s and its derivatives $\dot{\tau}_s$ and $\ddot{\tau}_s$ can be expressed as:

$$\tau_s = M_a \ddot{q}_{ad} + M_{ae} \ddot{q}_{ed} + N_a + F_a \tag{26}$$

$$\dot{\tau}_s = M_a q_{ad}^{(3)} + M_{ae} q_{ed}^{(3)} + \dot{M}_a \ddot{q}_{ad} + \dot{M}_{ae} \ddot{q}_{ed} + \dot{N}_a + \dot{F}_a \tag{27}$$

$$\ddot{\tau}_s = M_a q_{ad}^{(4)} + M_{ae} q_{ed}^{(4)} + 2\dot{M}_a q_{ad}^{(3)} + 2\dot{M}_{ae} q_{ed}^{(3)} + \ddot{M}_a \ddot{q}_a + \ddot{M}_{ae} \ddot{q}_{ae} + \ddot{N}_a + \ddot{F}_a \tag{28}$$

where $N_a = C_a \dot{q}_{ad} + C_{ae} \dot{q}_{ed} + G_a$. The above equations can be calculated efficiently by using the recursive Newton–Euler algorithm (RNEA) [18] and elastic joint Newton–Euler algorithm (EJNEA) [19], respectively.

$$\tau_s = RNEA\left(q_d, \dot{q}_d, \ddot{q}_d\right) \tag{29}$$

$$\dot{\tau}_s = EJNEA_3\left(q_d, \dot{q}_d, \ddot{q}_d, q_d^{(3)}\right) \tag{30}$$

$$\ddot{\tau}_s = EJNEA\left(q_d, \dot{q}_d, \ddot{q}_d, q_d^{(3)}, q_d^{(4)}\right) \tag{31}$$

where $q_d = [q_{ad}^T, q_{ed}^T]^T$, $\dot{q}_d = [\dot{q}_{ad}^T, \dot{q}_{ed}^T]^T$, $\ddot{q}_d = [\ddot{q}_{ad}^T, \ddot{q}_{ed}^T]^T$, $q_d^{(3)} = \left[q_{ad}^{(3)T}, q_{ed}^{(3)T}\right]^T$, and $q_d^{(4)} = \left[q_{ad}^{(4)T}, q_{ed}^{(4)T}\right]^T$, and EJNEA$_3$ means the reduced version of the EJNEA, returning $\dot{\tau}_s$.

Note that the nonactuated joint angular positions q_{ed}, velocities $\dot{q}_{ed}$, accelerations $\ddot{q}_{ed}$, jerks $q_{ed}^{(3)}$, and snaps $q_{ed}^{(4)}$ are required. Since the stability of zero dynamics is ensured, q_{ed} and $\dot{q}_{ed}$ can be obtained by solving the internal dynamics (12) using numerical integration solvers based on initial condition $q_e(t_0) = q_{e0}$, $\dot{q}_e(t_0) = 0$.

Then, $\ddot{q}_{ed}$ can be obtained efficiently by solving the following linear equations:

$$\overline{M}_e \ddot{q}_e = -\left(\overline{M}_{ea} \ddot{q}_{ad} + \overline{N}_e\right) - K_e q_{ed} - D_e \dot{q}_{ed} \tag{32}$$

where $\overline{M}_e \triangleq M_e(q_{ad}, q_{ed})$, $\overline{M}_{ea} \triangleq M_{ea}(q_{ad}, q_{ed})$, and $\overline{N}_e = N_e(q_{ad}, q_{ed}, \dot{q}_{ad}, \dot{q}_{ed})$. $\overline{M}_e$ and $\overline{M}_{ea}$ are obtained using the composite rigid body algorithm (CRBA) [20]. Let $\ddot{q}_{ed} = 0$; then, $\overline{M}_{ea} \ddot{q}_{ad} + \overline{N}_e$ can be obtained through adopting the RNEA.

$$\overline{M}_{ea} \ddot{q}_{ad} + \overline{N}_e = RNEA\left(q_d, \dot{q}_d, [\ddot{q}_{ad}^T, 0]^T\right) \tag{33}$$

Similarly, $q_{ed}^{(3)}$ and $q_{ed}^{(4)}$ can be obtained by solving the following equations:

$$\overline{M}_e \dddot{q}_{ed} = -\overline{\dot{n}}_e - K_e \dot{q}_{ed} - D_e \ddot{q}_{ed} \tag{34}$$

$$\overline{M}_e q_{ed}^{(4)} = -\left(\overline{\ddot{n}}_e + \dot{\overline{M}}_e \dddot{q}_{ed}\right) - K_e \ddot{q}_{ed} - D_e \dddot{q}_{ed} \tag{35}$$

where $\bar{n}_e = \overline{\boldsymbol{M}}_e \ddot{\boldsymbol{q}}_{ed} + \overline{\boldsymbol{M}}_{ea} \ddot{\boldsymbol{q}}_{ad} + \overline{\boldsymbol{M}}_{ea} \dot{\boldsymbol{q}}_{ad} + \overline{\boldsymbol{N}}_e$. The nonlinear terms $\bar{n}_e$ and $\dot{\bar{n}}_e + \dot{\overline{\boldsymbol{M}}}_e \ddot{\boldsymbol{q}}_{ed}$ are calculated by adopting the EJNEA and EJNEA$_3$ as follows:

$$\bar{n}_e = EJNEA_3 \left(\boldsymbol{q}_d, \dot{\boldsymbol{q}}_d, \ddot{\boldsymbol{q}}_d, \begin{bmatrix} \dddot{\boldsymbol{q}}_{ad}^T, 0 \end{bmatrix}^T \right) \tag{36}$$

$$\dot{\bar{n}}_e + \dot{\overline{\boldsymbol{M}}}_e \ddot{\boldsymbol{q}}_{ed} = EJNEA \left(\boldsymbol{q}_d, \dot{\boldsymbol{q}}_d, \ddot{\boldsymbol{q}}_d, \dddot{\boldsymbol{q}}_d, \begin{bmatrix} \boldsymbol{q}_{ad}^{(4)T}, 0 \end{bmatrix}^T \right) \tag{37}$$

According to (3), the motor position $\boldsymbol{\theta}_d$ and velocity $\dot{\boldsymbol{\theta}}_d$ are derived as:

$$\boldsymbol{\theta}_d = -\boldsymbol{K}_s^{-1} \boldsymbol{\tau}_s + \boldsymbol{q}_{ad} \tag{38}$$

$$\dot{\boldsymbol{\theta}}_d = -\boldsymbol{K}_s^{-1} \dot{\boldsymbol{\tau}}_s + \dot{\boldsymbol{q}}_{ad} \tag{39}$$

By now, all required variables in (25) are known; thus, the feedforward torque calculation is completed, and the total procedure is summarized as follows:

Step 1. Solve the internal dynamics (12) using an ODE solver to obtain $\boldsymbol{q}_{ed}$ and $\dot{\boldsymbol{q}}_{ed}$;
Step 2. Compute matrices $\overline{\boldsymbol{M}}_e$ and $\overline{\boldsymbol{M}}_{ea}$ using the CRBA;
Step 3. Compute $\overline{\boldsymbol{M}}_{ea} \ddot{\boldsymbol{q}}_{ad} + \overline{\boldsymbol{N}}_e$ using the RNEA and solve (32) to obtain $\ddot{\boldsymbol{q}}_{ed}$;
Step 4. Compute $\bar{n}_e$ using the EJNEA$_3$ and solve (34) to obtain $\boldsymbol{q}_{ed}^{(3)}$;
Step 5. Compute $\dot{\bar{n}}_e + \dot{\overline{\boldsymbol{M}}}_e \ddot{\boldsymbol{q}}_{ed}$ using the EJNEA and solve (35) to obtain $\boldsymbol{q}_{ed}^{(4)}$;
Step 6. Compute $\boldsymbol{\tau}_s$, $\dot{\boldsymbol{\tau}}_s$, and $\ddot{\boldsymbol{\tau}}_s$ using the RNEA, EJNEA$_3$, and EJNEA, respectively;
Step 7. Compute $\boldsymbol{\theta}_d$ and $\dot{\boldsymbol{\theta}}_d$ using (38) and (39);
Step 8. Compute feedforward torque $\boldsymbol{\tau}_{cFW}$ using (25).

Remark 1. *The elastic deformations in nonactuated directions are compensated by solving (23), while the elasticities in actuated directions are compensated in the feedforward torque calculation algorithm. Thus, the proposed method can further improve the control precision.*

Remark 2. *It is time consuming to solve the internal dynamics (12) through numerical integration. However, the traditional stable inversion methods [17] are based on numerical optimization which needs to solve the internal dynamics repetitively. In contrast, the internal dynamics need to be solved only once in the proposed calculation algorithm since the EFJM is transformed into a minimum-phase system. Thus, the computational burden is remarkably reduced.*

Remark 3. *The proposed calculation algorithm does not require the analytic expression of the robot; thus, it can be applied to general open-chain robots easily.*

4. Simulation and Experimental Results

Considering the disturbance, noise, and the parameter uncertainties of actual manipulators, a PID feedback controller is employed in simulations and experiments to improve the robustness and to avoid the drift of tracking errors. Since only the motor side is equipped with position sensors for most industrial manipulators, the motor torque command is designed as:

$$\boldsymbol{\tau}_c = \boldsymbol{\tau}_{FF} + \boldsymbol{K}_P (\boldsymbol{\theta} - \boldsymbol{\theta}_d) + \boldsymbol{K}_D \left(\dot{\boldsymbol{\theta}} - \dot{\boldsymbol{\theta}}_d \right) + \boldsymbol{K}_I \int (\boldsymbol{\theta} - \boldsymbol{\theta}_d) dt \tag{40}$$

where $\boldsymbol{\tau}_{FF}$ is the feedforward torque, and $\boldsymbol{K}_P$, $\boldsymbol{K}_D$, and $\boldsymbol{K}_I$ are constant controller gain matrices. The reference motor trajectories $\boldsymbol{\theta}_d$ are obtained using (38).

4.1. Simulation Results

(1) Example 1: A planar robot

To validate the superiority of the proposed output-redefinition-based feedforward control approach (ORFF), simulations using the ORFF, the traditional FJM-based feedforward approach (FJMFF) [21], and the continuous DAE optimization solver (CDAEOS) [17] are carried out on a planar robot in this section. As shown in Figure 3, the EFJM of this planar robot has three rigid bodies, two actuated joints, and one nonactuated joint. The dynamic parameters of each link in this planar robot are shown in Table 1 where the link parameters include length l, inertia I, mass m, center of mass c, and joint parameters including stiffness k, damping d, and motor inertia b.

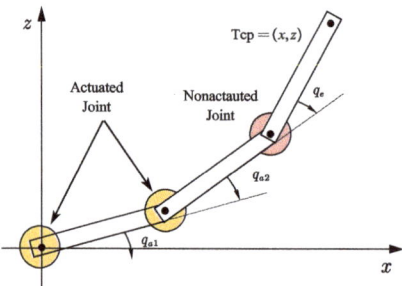

Figure 3. The EFJM of planar robot.

Table 1. Dynamic parameters of planar robot.

Link	m (kg)	I (kgm^2)	l(m)	c(m)	Joint	k(Nm/rad)	d (Nm/(rad·s^{-1}))	b (kgm^2)
1 and 2	100	0.5	1	0.5	1 and 2	5×10^5	0	100
3	200	0.7	1.4	0.7	3	5×10^5	500	-

To show the efficiency of the proposed computation algorithm clearly, the feedforward torques are solved using three methods on an Intel i5-10400 PC with 16 G RAM. The step size is selected as 1 ms in the simulation. The tip of the robot moves from $Q_0 = [0.5, 2.5]$ m to $Q_f = [0, 3]$ m in 0.5 s, 1 s, and 2 s. The execution times and setpoint control errors of the three methods are shown in Table 2.

Table 2. Solving times and control errors of the three methods in simulation, example 1.

Motion Time	0.5 s			1 s			2 s		
Method	ORFF	FJMFF	CDAEOS	ORFF	FJMFF	CDAEOS	ORFF	FJMFF	CDAEOS
Solving time (s)	0.6384	0.1680	154.0	1.209	0.2428	170.3	1.922	0.4038	129.8
Error (mm)	0.5062	0.9890	1.855	0.2510	2.644	1.344	0.02861	0.5760	0.07245

As indicated in Table 2, the setpoint control error of the proposed ORFF is significantly reduced compared with that of the FJMFF and CDAEOS under three conditions. When the moving time is 1 s, the control error of the ORFF is reduced by over 90% and 80% compared with that of the CDAEOS and FJMFF, respectively. On the other hand, the execution time of the ORFF is 4–5 times that of the FJMFF, while the execution time of the CDAEOS is much longer than that of the other two methods.

The bounded feedforward torques and nonactuated joint positions obtained by using the proposed ORFF are shown in Figure 4a. As a comparison, the feedforward torques are solved without output redefinition, and the results are shown in Figure 4b. It is obvious that the internal dynamics of the original EFJM system are unstable, and the feedforward torques are unbounded. Thus, the results in Figure 4 demonstrate that the system is transformed into a nonminimum-phase system by output redefinition.

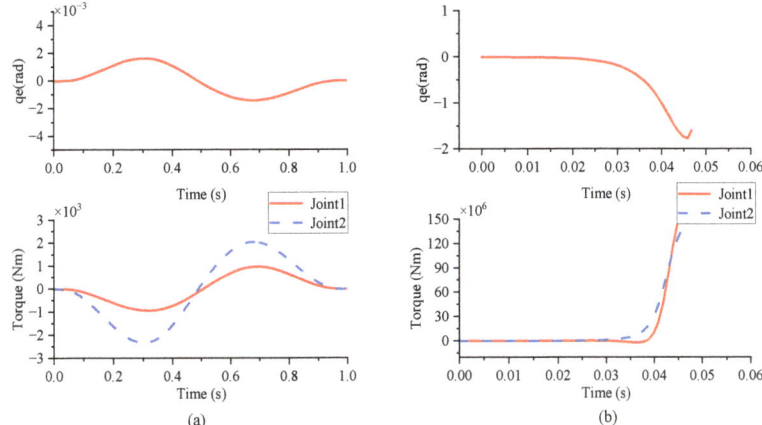

Figure 4. Nonactuated joint positions and feedforward torques: (**a**) with output redefinition; (**b**) without output redefinition.

(2) Example 2: Six DOFs Manipulator

To prove the proposed method can be applied to complex industrial manipulators, simulations are carried out on an EFORT ER7 robot with six DOFs. The dynamic parameters are shown in Table 3.

Table 3. Dynamic parameters of ER7.

Parameters	Link1	Link2	Link3
Mass (kg)	9.1366	9.4724	4.9985
Center of mass (m)	$[0.01847, -0.017, -0.070]$	$[0.1563, 0.0523, 0.0312]$	$[0.0142, 4.8 \times 10^{-3}, 0.0248]$
Inertia (kgm²)	$\begin{bmatrix} 0.1194 & 0.0009 & 0.006 \\ 0.0009 & 0.1093 & -0.0036 \\ 0.006 & -0.0036 & 0.055 \end{bmatrix}$	$\begin{bmatrix} 0.0518 & -0.0088 & -0.0415 \\ -0.0088 & 0.44 & 0.0008 \\ -0.0415 & 0.0008 & 0.4063 \end{bmatrix}$	$\begin{bmatrix} 0.0211 & 0.0027 & 2.02 \times 10^{-4} \\ 0.0027 & 0.0191 & 2.6 \times 10^{-4} \\ 2.0 \times 10^{-4} & 2.6 \times 10^{-4} & 0.0176 \end{bmatrix}$
Parameters	Link4	Link5	Link6
Mass(kg)	5.3476	1.6462	0.01
Center of mass (m)	$[-0.0132, 0.0251, -0.171]$	$[6.1 \times 10^{-4}, -0.0174, 5.3 \times 10^{-4}]$	$[1.5 \times 10^{-4}, 0, -9.8 \times 10^{-4}]$
Inertia (kgm²)	$\begin{bmatrix} 0.2390 & 0.0052 & 0.0353 \\ 0.0052 & 0.2324 & -0.0231 \\ 0.0353 & -0.0231 & 0.0205 \end{bmatrix}$	$\begin{bmatrix} 4.7 \times 10^{-3} & -2.4 \times 10^{-5} & -1.2 \times 10^{-5} \\ -2.4 \times 10^{-5} & 1 \times 10^{-3} & -1.2 \times 10^{-6} \\ -1.2 \times 10^{-5} & -1.2 \times 10^{-6} & 4.8 \times 10^{-3} \end{bmatrix}$	$\begin{bmatrix} 1.36 \times 10^{-6} & 0 & 0 \\ 0 & 1.33 \times 10^{-6} & 0 \\ 0 & 0 & 2.66 \times 10^{-6} \end{bmatrix}$

Firstly, simulations are carried out using the rigid model of ER7, where all elasticities are ignored. The traditional rigid-model-based feedforward method (RMFF) is used to control the robot, i.e., the feedforward torque τ_{FF} in (40) is computed using the rigid robot model. The parameters of the PID controller are chosen as $k_{Pj} = 100$, $k_{Dj} = 1$, and $k_{Ij} = 1$, where $j = 1, 2, \cdots, 6$. The target pose of the end effector is selected randomly in the task space, and 100-run simulations are carried out. The setpoint control root-mean-square errors (RMSEs) are shown in Table 4.

Table 4. Setpoint control RMSEs of rigid model using RMFF.

Δx(mm)	Δy(mm)	Δz(mm)	$\Delta \psi$(deg)	$\Delta \theta$(deg)	$\Delta \varphi$(deg)
9.581×10^{-4}	8.713×10^{-4}	3.015×10^{-4}	2.712×10^{-3}	7.822×10^{-3}	7.285×10^{-3}

Secondly, simulations are carried out using the flexible model of ER7 with different load levels. The EFJM of ER7 with six actuated joints and two nonactuated joints is built as shown in Figure 5. The flexible parameters are shown in Table 5, where the two nonactuated joints are denoted by joints 1Y and 3Y.

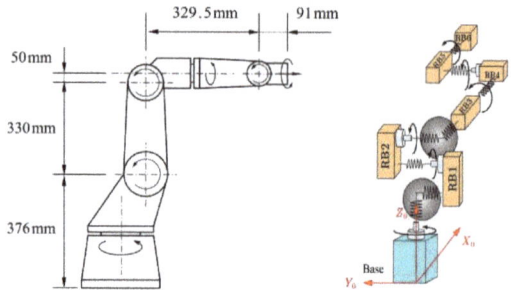

Figure 5. Geometric model and extended flexible joint model of EFORT ER7.

Table 5. Parameters of extended flexible joints of ER7.

Joint	1	1Y	2	3	3Y	4	5	6
Stiffness (Nm/rad)	36,407	226,357	17,922	13,410	56,854	146,586	139,076	7446
Damping (Nm/(rad·s^{-1}))	0	858.99	0	0	37.25	0	0	0
Inertia of motor (kgm^2)	2.047	0	2.285	0.4954	0	0.1847	0.0805	0.0288

Similarly, 100-run simulations for ER7 are carried out by selecting the target end effector pose randomly. In order to demonstrate the improved performance of the proposed method under the different load conditions, the payload of the robot is set to 0 kg, 3 kg, and 6.5 kg, respectively. Since the model is too complicated for the CDAEOS to obtain a solution in reasonable time, only the traditional RMFF and FJMFF are adopted for comparison. The step size of the feedforward torque solver is 1 ms. The average execution times of the ORFF and FJMFF are 1.3457 s and 0.2554 s, respectively. The setpoint control RMSE of the ORFF and FJMFF are shown in Table 6, where the orientation error is given in the form of a Euler angle. The control results of the first group of simulations using the proposed ORFF under 6.5 kg payload are shown in Figures 6–9. The actuated joint and nonactuated positions are shown in Figures 6 and 7, respectively. The actuated joint velocities are shown in Figure 8. It can be seen that the nonactuated joint positions are bounded, which indicates that the internal dynamics are stable. Hence, bounded control torques are obtained by using the proposed ORFF method, as shown in Figure 9.

Table 6. Setpoint control RMSEs of flexible model in simulation, example 2.

Payload	Method	Δx(mm)	Δy(mm)	Δz(mm)	$\Delta \psi$(deg)	$\Delta \theta$(deg)	$\Delta \varphi$(deg)
0 kg	RMFF	9.553×10^{-1}	7.806×10^{-1}	2.061×10^{-1}	1.192×10^{1}	8.256×10^{0}	6.531×10^{0}
	FJMFF	8.660×10^{-2}	4.815×10^{-2}	1.196×10^{-2}	3.867×10^{-1}	7.419×10^{-1}	4.289×10^{-1}
	ORFF	2.944×10^{-4}	4.506×10^{-4}	1.586×10^{-4}	2.524×10^{-3}	2.881×10^{-3}	4.379×10^{-3}
3 kg	RMFF	2.174×10^{0}	2.536×10^{0}	9.789×10^{-1}	3.829×10^{0}	1.640×10^{1}	1.881×10^{1}
	FJMFF	2.509×10^{-1}	2.211×10^{-1}	4.948×10^{-2}	1.024×10^{0}	1.930×10^{0}	1.696×10^{0}
	ORFF	8.139×10^{-4}	7.726×10^{-4}	3.249×10^{-4}	4.230×10^{-3}	6.909×10^{-3}	6.773×10^{-3}
6.5 kg	RMFF	9.553×10^{-1}	7.806×10^{-1}	2.061×10^{-1}	1.192×10^{1}	8.256×10^{0}	6.531×10^{0}
	FJMFF	1.677×10^{0}	1.595×10^{0}	5.654×10^{-1}	2.419×10^{0}	1.162×10^{1}	1.137×10^{1}
	ORFF	1.463×10^{-3}	1.643×10^{-3}	6.991×10^{-4}	4.079×10^{-3}	1.298×10^{-2}	1.260×10^{-2}

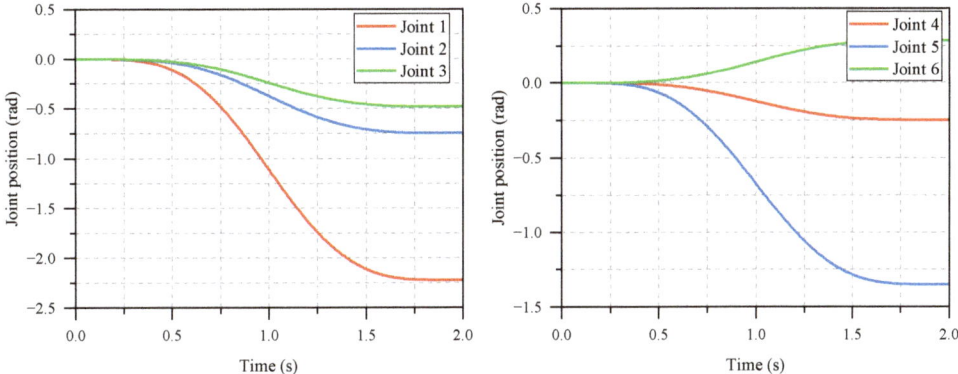

Figure 6. Actuated joint positions in first group simulation under ORFF.

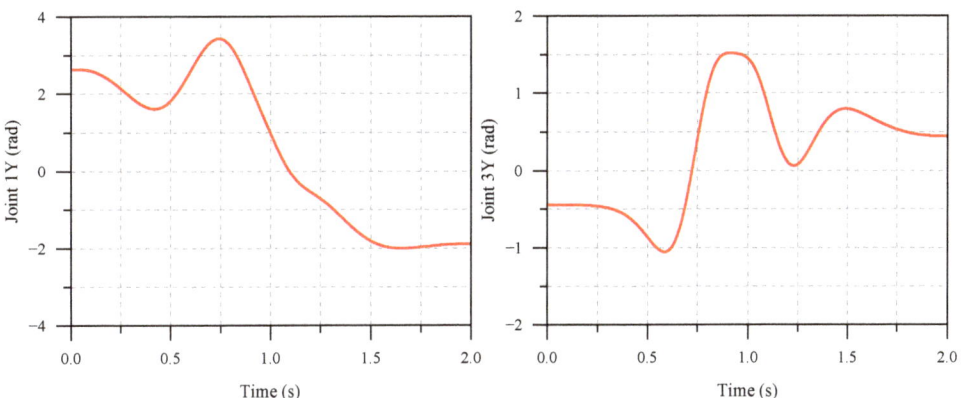

Figure 7. Nonactuated joint positions in first group simulation under ORFF.

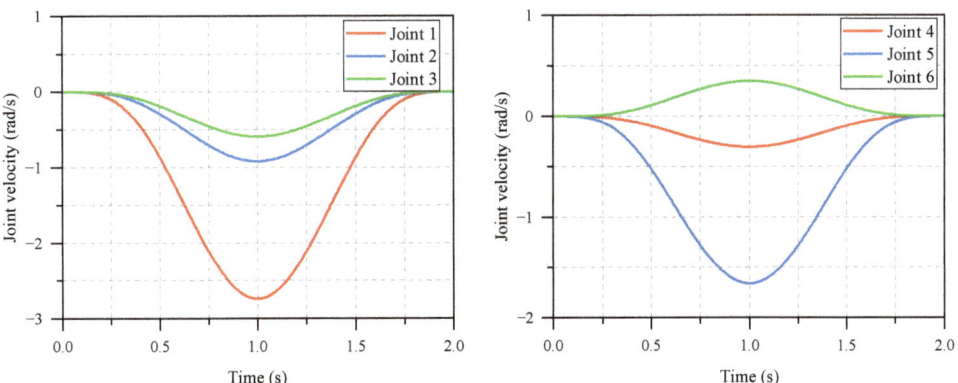

Figure 8. Actuated joint velocities in first group simulation under ORFF.

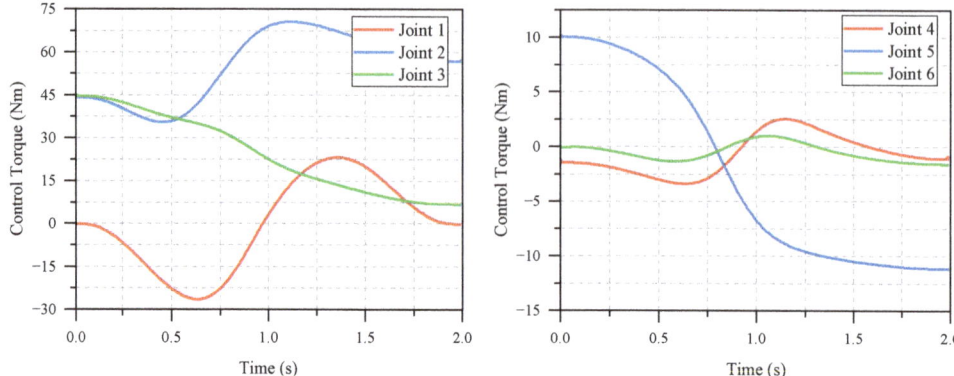

Figure 9. Control torques in first group simulation under ORFF.

As shown in Table 5, the traditional RMFF can achieve a satisfactory control accuracy for a rigid robot model. However, the control accuracy of the RMFF is greatly reduced in a flexible robot model when the effects of elasticities are considered, as shown in Table 6. Although the FJM method can improve the control accuracy, it fails to achieve satisfactory results as it can only compensate the effects of elasticities in rotational directions. In contrast, the proposed ORFF method achieves optimal control precision since it can compensate the effects of elasticities in all directions. In addition, it can be seen that the control RMSE of the flexible model using the ORFF is at the same level as the control RMSE of the rigid model using the RMFF control method. This also indicates that the pose error caused by flexibilities are compensated accurately by using the ORFF. Moreover, by comparing the control accuracy under different load conditions, it can be seen that the improvement achieved by the ORFF is more evident under high-payload conditions.

4.2. Experimental Results

To further evaluate the effectiveness of the proposed feedforward control method, experiments are carried out using a Franka Emika Panda 7-DOF Manipulator. As shown in Figure 10, the experimental platform consists of the robot, its control unit, and a workstation PC. Based on ROS, the PC can send real-time torque commands at 1 kHz to the robot.

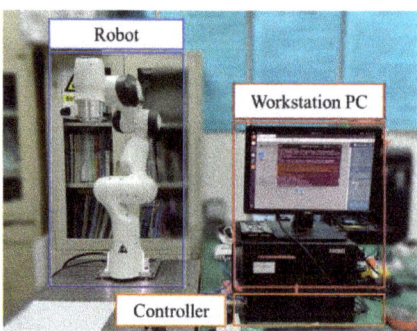

Figure 10. Experimental platform.

In order to simulate the effect of the unactuated joint, the motor position of the third joint remains fixed. Then, the dynamics of the Panda can be described by the EFJM, as shown in Figure 11. The parameters of the extended flexible joints are identified through experiments, as shown in Table 7, where the unactuated joint is denoted by joint 3Y. The dynamic parameters of the Panda have already been identified [22].

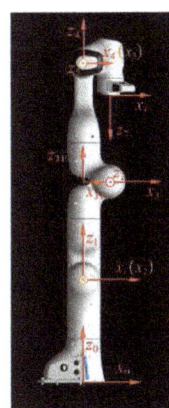 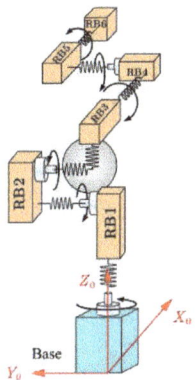

Figure 11. Parameters and the EFJM of the Franka Emika Panda.

Table 7. Parameters of extended flexible joints of the Panda.

Joint	1	2	3	3Y	4	5	6
Stiffness (Nm/rad)	14,250	14,250	14,250	14,250	9000	9000	9000
Damping (Nm/(rad·s^{-1}))	0	0	0	15	0	0	0

In experiment, 25 target points are selected randomly in Cartesian space. Then, the ORFF and FJMFF are employed to control the robot combined with the PD controller. The parameters of the PD controller are shown in Table 8. Similarly, the CDAEOS is not employed in the experiments due to its heavy computational burden. The feedforward torques are solved offline, and the average execution times of the ORFF and FJMFF are 8.2552 s and 0.9884 s, respectively. The desired trajectories of the actuated joints are generated by using a smooth planning algorithm [23], and corresponding feedforward torques are computed. The setpoint control RMSEs of the two control methods are shown in Table 9. It can be seen that the RMSE of the proposed method is reduced significantly compared with that of the FJMFF. The position RMSEs of the proposed method decrease by 65%, 81%, and 92% in the x-, y-, and z-directions, respectively, and the orientation RMSEs decrease by 62%, 64%, and 71% in the three directions, respectively.

Table 8. Parameters of PD controller in experiments.

Joint	1	2	3	4	5	6
k_P	5000	5000	4000	2500	2500	1500
k_D	30	30	30	15	15	10

Table 9. Setpoint control RMSEs of two methods in experiments.

	Δx(mm)	Δy(mm)	Δz(mm)	$\Delta \psi$(deg)	$\Delta \theta$(deg)	$\Delta \varphi$(deg)
FJMFF	1.761×10^{-1}	2.101×10^{-1}	4.962×10^{-1}	2.867×10^{-2}	3.259×10^{-2}	4.448×10^{-2}
ORFF	6.163×10^{-2}	3.831×10^{-2}	3.890×10^{-2}	1.082×10^{-2}	1.114×10^{-2}	1.271×10^{-2}

Figures 12–14 show the control results of the first group of experiments under the proposed ORFF method. Figures 12 and 13 show the actuated joint positions and velocities, respectively. The control torques using the proposed ORFF method are shown in Figure 14. It can be seen that all signals are bounded, which indicates that the nonminimum-phase EFJM is transformed into a minimum-phase system.

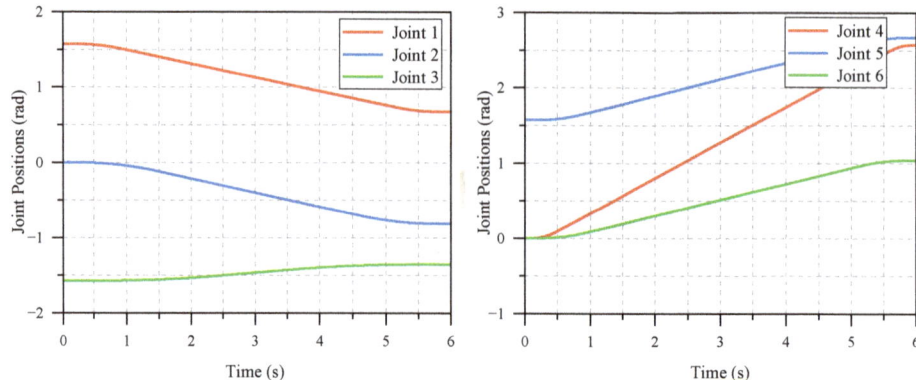

Figure 12. Actuated joint positions in first group experiment under ORFF.

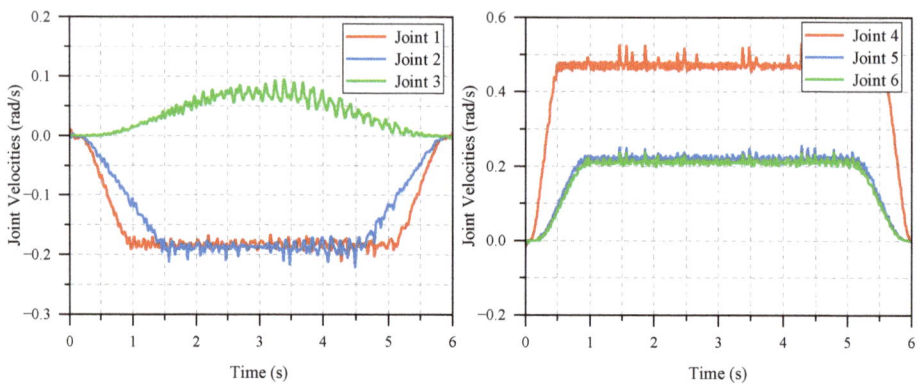

Figure 13. Actuated joint velocities in first group experiment under ORFF.

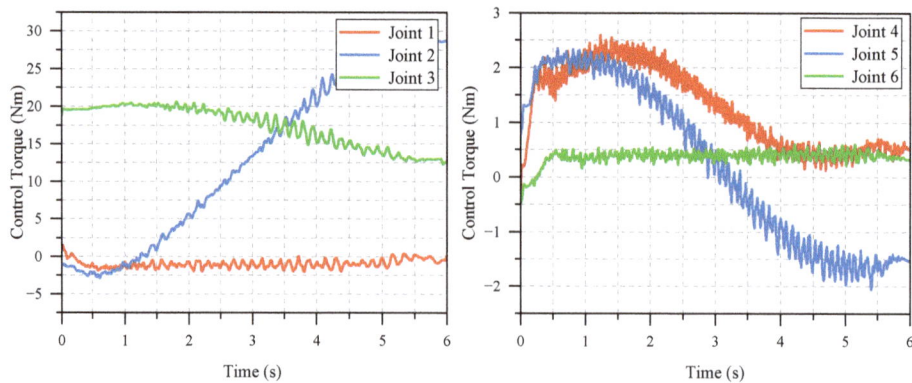

Figure 14. Control torques in first group experiment under ORFF.

Through the simulation and experimental results, it can be seen that the ORFF achieves better setpoint control performance compared with the FJMFF and CDAEOS. The excellent setpoint control performance indicates that the pose error caused by elastic deformations in all directions is compensated based on the EFJM. Compared with the FJMFF, the execution time of the ORFF is increased as the cost of significant performance improvement.

Compared with the CDAEOS, the computational burden of the ORFF is greatly reduced. In addition, the feedforward torques obtained by the ORFF are bounded in all simulations and experiments. Thus, it is indicated that the unstable internal dynamics are transformed into stable ones, which is consistent with the theoretical analysis.

Remark 4. *Although the EFJM is more complicated than the classical FJM, the dynamics model accuracy is improved significantly by using the EFJM. Consequently, the proposed ORFF based on the EFJM can improve the end effector setpoint control precision remarkably.*

5. Conclusions

In this paper, a feedforward control method based on the output redefinition of the EFJM is proposed for flexible industrial manipulators. Based on the EFJM, the pose error caused by flexibilities in actuated and nonactuated directions are compensated accurately. By output redefinition, the original nonminimum-phase EFJM is transformed into a minimum-phase system. A recursive feedforward torque computation algorithm is designed to reduce the computational burden. Simulation and experimental results indicate that the proposed method can improve the setpoint control precision significantly compared with traditional feedforward control methods. Future work will focus on extending the feedforward control method to the trajectory tracking control problem and the condition with unknown load.

Author Contributions: Conceptualization, S.X. and Z.W.; methodology, S.X.; software, S.X. and T.S.; validation, S.X.; Writing—original draft, S.X.; writing—review and editing, S.X. and Z.W. All authors have read and agreed to the published version of the manuscript.

Funding: This research was funded by the National Natural Science Foundation of China, grant number U1913206.

Data Availability Statement: The numerical and experimental data sets generated and analyzed during the current study are available from the corresponding author on reasonable request.

Conflicts of Interest: The authors declare no conflict of interest.

References

1. Kim, S.H.; Min, B. Joint Compliance Error Compensation for Robot Manipulator Using Body Frame. *Int. J Precis. Eng. Manuf.* **2020**, *21*, 1017–1023. [CrossRef]
2. Tran, D.; Truong, H.; Ahn, K.K. Adaptive Nonsingular Fast Terminal Sliding Mode Control of Robotic Manipulator Based Neural Network Approach. *Int. J. Precis. Eng. Manuf.* **2021**, *22*, 417–429. [CrossRef]
3. Kim, M.J.; Chung, W.K. Disturbance-Observer-Based PD Control of Flexible Joint Robots for Asymptotic Convergence. *IEEE Trans. Robot.* **2015**, *31*, 1508–1516. [CrossRef]
4. Mei, Z.; Chen, L.; Ding, J. Feed-Forward Control of Elastic-Joint Industrial Robot Based on Hybrid Inverse Dynamic Model. *Adv. Mech. Eng.* **2021**, *13*, 16878140211038102. [CrossRef]
5. Cruz Zavala, E.; Nuño, E.; Moreno, J.A. Robust Trajectory-Tracking in Finite-Time for Robot Manipulators Using Nonlinear Proportional-Derivative Control Plus Feed-Forward Compensation. *Int. J. Robust Nonlinear Control* **2021**, *31*, 3878–3907. [CrossRef]
6. Nho, H.C.; Meckl, P. Intelligent Feedforward Control and Payload Estimation for a Two-Link Robotic Manipulator. *IEEE/ASME Trans. Mechatron.* **2003**, *8*, 277–283. [CrossRef]
7. Sun, L.; Zhao, W.; Yin, W.; Sun, N.; Liu, J. Proxy Based Position Control for Flexible Joint Robot with Link Side Energy Feedback. *Robot. Auton. Syst.* **2019**, *121*, 103272. [CrossRef]
8. Spong, M.W. Modeling and Control of Elastic Joint Robots. *J. Dyn. Syst. Meas. Control-Trans. ASME* **1987**, *109*, 310–318. [CrossRef]
9. Consolini, L.; Gerelli, O.; Guarino Lo Bianco, C.; Piazzi, A. Flexible Joints Control: A Minimum-Time Feed-Forward Technique. *Mechatronics* **2009**, *19*, 348–356. [CrossRef]
10. Madsen, E.; Rosenlund, O.S.; Brandt, D.; Zhang, X. Adaptive Feedforward Control of a Collaborative Industrial Robot Manipulator Using a Novel Extension of the Generalized Maxwell-Slip Friction Model. *Mech. Mach. Theory* **2021**, *155*, 104109. [CrossRef]
11. Ohr, J.; Moberg, S.; Wernholt, E.; Hanssen, S.; Pettersson, J.; Persson, S.; Sander-Tavallaey, S. Identification of Flexibility Parameters of 6-Axis Industrial Manipulator Models. In Proceedings of the ISMA2006, Leuven, Belgium, 18–20 September 2006; pp. 3305–3314.
12. Moberg, S.; Hanssen, S. A DAE Approach to Feedforward Control of Flexible Manipulators. In Proceedings of the IEEE International Conference on Robotics & Automation, Rome, Italy, 10–14 April 2007; pp. 3439–3444.

13. Moberg, S.; Wernholt, E.; Hanssen, S.; Brog Rdh, T. Modeling and Parameter Estimation of Robot Manipulators Using Extended Flexible Joint Models. *J. Dyn. Syst. Meas. Control-Trans. ASME* **2014**, *136*, 031005. [CrossRef]
14. Bastos, G.; Seifried, R.; Brüls, O. Analysis of Stable Model Inversion Methods for Constrained Underactuated Mechanical Systems. *Mech. Mach. Theory* **2017**, *111*, 99–117. [CrossRef]
15. Moberg, S.; Hanssen, S. Inverse Dynamics of Flexible Manipulators. In Proceedings of the 2009 Conference on Multibody Dynamics, Warsaw, Poland, 29 June–2 July 2009; pp. 1–20.
16. Seifried, R.; Blajer, W. Analysis of Servo-Constraint Problems for Underactuated Multibody Systems. *Mech. Sci.* **2013**, *4*, 113–129. [CrossRef]
17. Moberg, S. *Modeling and Control of Flexible Manipulators*; phdMoberg370497; Linköpings University: Linköping, Sweden, 2010.
18. Luh, J.Y.; Walker, M.W.; Paul, R.P. On-Line Computational Scheme for Mechanical Manipulators. *J. Dyn. Syst. Meas. Control-Trans. ASME* **1980**, *102*, 69–76. [CrossRef]
19. Buondonno, G.; De Luca, A. Efficient Computation of Inverse Dynamics and Feedback Linearization for VSA-Based Robots. *IEEE Robot. Autom. Lett.* **2016**, *1*, 908–915. [CrossRef]
20. Walker, M.W.; Orin, D.E. Efficient Dynamic Computer Simulation of Robotic Mechanisms. *J. Dyn. Syst. Meas. Control-Trans. ASME* **1982**, *104*, 205–211. [CrossRef]
21. Ruderman, M.; Iwasaki, M. Sensorless Torsion Control of Elastic-Joint Robots with Hysteresis and Friction. *IEEE Trans. Ind. Electron.* **2016**, *63*, 1889–1899. [CrossRef]
22. Gaz, C.; Cognetti, M.; Oliva, A.; Robuffo Giordano, P.; De Luca, A. Dynamic Identification of the Franka Emika Panda Robot with Retrieval of Feasible Parameters Using Penalty-Based Optimization. *IEEE Robot. Autom. Lett.* **2019**, *4*, 4147–4154. [CrossRef]
23. Fang, Y.; Hu, J.; Liu, W.; Shao, Q.; Qi, J.; Peng, Y. Smooth and Time-Optimal S-Curve Trajectory Planning for Automated Robots and Machines. *Mech. Mach. Theory* **2019**, *137*, 127–153. [CrossRef]

Disclaimer/Publisher's Note: The statements, opinions and data contained in all publications are solely those of the individual author(s) and contributor(s) and not of MDPI and/or the editor(s). MDPI and/or the editor(s) disclaim responsibility for any injury to people or property resulting from any ideas, methods, instructions or products referred to in the content.

Article

Design and Kinematic Characteristic Analysis of a Spiral Robot for Oil and Gas Pipeline Inspections

Hongwei Yan [1,*], Pengyang Zhao [1], Canjun Xiao [2], Dengxiao Zhang [2], Shaoni Jiao [3], Haibing Pan [4] and Xi Wu [5]

1. School of Mechanical Engineering, North University of China, Taiyuan 030051, China; s202102049@st.nuc.edu.cn
2. Shanxi Honganxiang Technology Company, Yuncheng 044000, China
3. College of Mechanical and Vehicle Engineering, Taiyuan University of Technology, Taiyuan 030024, China
4. Shanxi Coal Import and Export Group Science and Technology Research Institute Co., Ltd., Taiyuan 030032, China
5. Coal Mine Electromechanical Technology Institute, Shanxi Datong University, Datong 037003, China
* Correspondence: aweigeyan@nuc.edu.cn

Abstract: This study presents a spiral pipeline robot designed for detecting and preventing oil and gas pipeline leakages. A comprehensive analysis of factors such as spiral angle, normal force, pipe material, and operating attitude is conducted based on the robot's mechanical model in a straight pipe. This in-depth investigation determines the optimal spiral angle, normal force, pipeline material, and operating attitude to enhance the robot's motion stability and traction performance. Using virtual prototype technology, the robot's traction performance is simulated under various working conditions, normal forces, and attitude angles within the pipeline. An experimental platform is established to verify the impact of deflection angle, normal force, and pipeline material on traction performance. The experimental results and simulation analysis mutually validate each other, providing a reliable reference for robot design and optimization. The spiral pipeline robot and its motion strategy proposed in this study possess both theoretical value and practical application prospects in the field of oil and gas pipeline inspection and maintenance.

Keywords: spiral pipe robot; pipeline inspection; motion characteristic; virtual prototyping technology

1. Introduction

As industrialization accelerates, nations' demand for oil and gas resources continues to grow [1]. In this context, oil and gas pipelines, serving as essential means of energy transportation, hold a pivotal strategic position and economic value in national industrial development [2]. However, over time, various defects may gradually emerge inside these pipelines, such as leakage points, pits, and corrosion [3].

Oil and gas pipeline inspections currently rely heavily on manual methods, which have limitations and are inefficient in promptly detecting pipeline leaks [4]. In recent years, pipeline robots have emerged as effective tools to improve the accuracy and efficiency of inspections and prevent pipeline leakage accidents. These specialized devices are designed for narrow spaces and offer strong adaptability and reliability [5,6]. They can be equipped with various sensors, such as ultrasonic, infrared, and magnetic flux leakage sensors, to detect defects such as leakage points, corrosion, and pits in pipelines [7]. Additionally, pipeline robots possess data analysis and storage capabilities, allowing them to process and analyze collected information in real time and provide accurate and reliable results to maintenance personnel [8].

Researchers including Shao et al. have categorized pipeline robots into three structural types: wheeled, tracked, and non-wheeled [9]. Wheeled robots refer to robots that have drive wheels installed on their main body, creating a sealed contact with the inner wall of the pipeline, allowing the robot to move within the pipeline [10,11]. Miao et al. developed a wheeled pipeline isolation and plugging robot and investigated its dynamic characteristics during the traversal of weld seams [12]. Wheeled robots can be further classified based on their mode of motion, namely direct-wheel drive and spiral drive. Spiral drive robots are characterized as having the axis of their drive wheels at a certain angle with respect to the central axis of the pipeline, resulting in a spiral trajectory along the inner wall. A spiral pipeline robot was designed by Yonsei University in South Korea, capable of operating within branch pipelines with zero curvature radius and varying diameters [13].

Tracked pipeline robots, unlike wheeled robots, feature tracks that provide a larger contact area with the pipeline. This design offers increased friction and superior traction, resulting in more reliable operation compared to wheeled robots. Zhang et al. developed a tracked pipeline inspection robot that allows for the individual speed adjustment of each track. This enables the robot to achieve posture adjustments within the pipeline and adapt to geometric constraints present in the pipeline environment [14].

Non-wheeled pipeline robots, such as snake-like robots, utilize complex motion control algorithms to navigate and operate within pipelines [15]. Gao and other researchers proposed a multi-link magnetic wheel pipeline robot that demonstrates good control performance in linear movement, turning, wall climbing, and obstacle crossing, among other aspects. This robot can adapt to various terrains effectively [16].

In certain scenarios, robots employ tethered cable connections for their operations. In other operational environments, robots utilize wireless communication methods [17]. However, wireless communication and positioning between robots and ground base stations face technical challenges in the context of buried oil and gas pipelines. The underground environment, consisting of soil, rock, concrete, and other materials, significantly weakens communication signals, reducing their transmission distance. Moreover, communication signals in underground environments may encounter reflection, refraction, and scattering within pipelines, resulting in delays, distortions, and interference. The complexity of the pipeline environment further hinders accurate signal localization [18]. To address these challenges, researchers have proposed several solutions, such as the Kalman filter, an efficient linear optimal estimation algorithm that predicts system states based on incomplete and noisy measurement data [19–21]. By integrating data from various sensors such as inertial measurement units (IMU), odometers, magnetometers, and optical sensors, the Kalman filter eliminates noise and provides accurate position and attitude estimation for robots within the pipeline [22,23]. Another solution is simultaneous localization and mapping (SLAM), a technology that enables robots to estimate their location within an unknown environment while constructing a map of that environment. SLAM assists pipeline robots in creating a map that contains pipeline geometry, running trajectories, and other relevant information. The SLAM algorithm continuously updates the robot's position within the map [24–26]. Wireless communication is also essential, and it is facilitated through radio frequency (RF) signals between robots and ground workstations. Common approaches include outdoor positioning based on relay nodes placed along a straight path [27] and utilizing the radio frequency signal of the robot within a metal pipe, eliminating the need for ground operators to possess knowledge of the pipeline map. In the latter case, a radio frequency signal transmitter and receiver capture periodic received signal fading, which is then used to establish the robot's positioning system based on the periodic signal fading [28,29].

Spiral pipeline robots have been widely utilized in specialized operations due to their simple structure and excellent performance in bending pipelines. However, these robots still face challenges related to insufficient traction and limited load capacity. To address these issues, this study presents a spiral pipeline robot designed with environmental detection and motion control capabilities. By examining multiple factors that affect the robot's traction performance, this research aims to enhance the work efficiency and safety of the spiral pipeline robot.

2. Pipeline Inspection Robot System Design

Figure 1 shows the main unit of the pipeline inspection robot. The external structure of the robot is composed of the robot spiral motion unit, the motor drive unit, the support unit, the battery box, the front detection and control unit, the rear detection and control unit and the upper unit. The robot specifications are shown in Table 1.

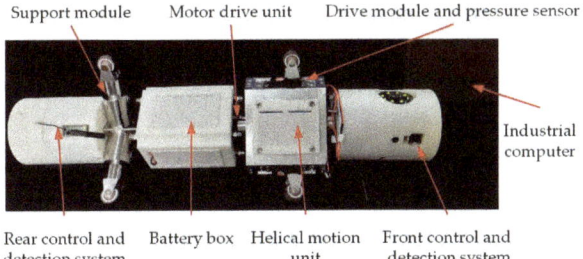

Figure 1. Pipeline inspection robot prototype.

Table 1. Main technical parameters of the pipeline inspection robot.

Technical Parameter	Parameter Value
Robot length/mm	580
Robot weight/kg	8.5 kg
Adaptive pipe diameter/mm	180–225
Maximum velocity/(m·min^{-1})	3
The minimum radius of curvature is available/mm	600

2.1. Structure Design of Pipeline Robot

Figure 2 describes the structure of a spiral motion unit, which is an engineering component designed to operate in a pipe or similar cylindrical environment. The unit consists of three drive modules that are equidistantly positioned at 120° intervals around the circumference. Each module has a built-in spring and steering gear that both connect to a wheel frame. A driving wheel is attached to this frame using specialized bolts. The steering gear is fastened to a mounting frame with bolts, and four springs are evenly placed at the base of this frame, allowing the drive module to adapt to varying pipe diameters. The spiral motion unit has three battery compartments arranged circumferentially, and the module can be connected to a drive motor module through a coupling. The spiral motion unit features driving wheels on each module that are positioned at a specific angle, known as the spiral angle, with respect to the axis of the pipeline. This orientation enables the generation of a driving force along the pipeline through a mechanism.

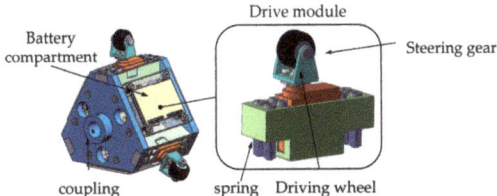

Figure 2. Schematic diagram of spiral motion unit structure.

Figure 3 illustrates the central motor module positioned at the center of the robot. The central motor is connected to the large bevel gears via the output end, while the three small bevel gears are evenly distributed circumferentially, with a separation of 120 degrees between each gear. The small bevel gears are securely affixed to the lead screw, and upon driving the large bevel gears, the three small bevel gears commence rotation. This rotational motion is transmitted to the synchronous belt and the lead screw, thereby inducing movement of the lead screw nut. By compressing the spring around the smooth rod, the screw nut propels the entire drive module along the pipe's diameter. Consequently, this motion instigates a variation in the positive pressure between the driving wheel and the inner wall of the pipe. To monitor the contact pressure between the driving wheels and the inner wall of the pipeline, pressure sensors are strategically placed between each driving module and its corresponding spring. By adjusting the spring compression of the central motor, it is possible to control the positive pressure exerted by the driving wheel, ensuring optimal performance and adaptability to various pipeline conditions.

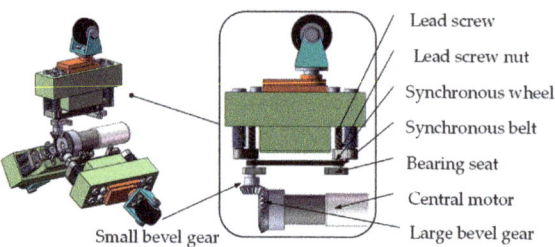

Figure 3. Structure diagram of the central motor.

The motor driving unit is a crucial component of the system and primarily consists of a stepper motor, connecting rod, round nut, and battery box. As illustrated in Figure 4, the battery housing serves as the primary support for the motor drive unit, with front and rear baffles connected by connecting rods. These rods are secured with four nuts on each side. The stepper motor is attached to one side baffle, and it powers the front and side spiral motion units to move circularly around the pipeline axis, enabling the robot to travel in a helical pattern within the pipeline. To supply the necessary power, the battery box is designed with four compartments to accommodate four lithium batteries.

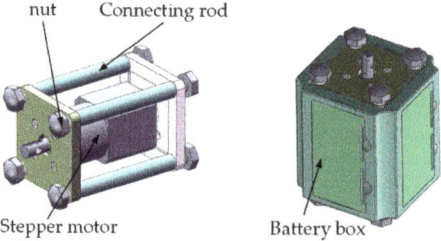

Figure 4. Structure diagram of motor drive unit with battery box.

The support module, an essential component of the system, is composed of a support wheel, lifting column, support seat, spring, and smooth bolt. Figure 5 illustrates the structure of the support module. The support seat serves as the main structural support, with three supporting units connected to the support frame by welding at 120° intervals around the circumference. The support module is designed to adapt to varying pipe diameters, ensuring that the support wheel maintains vertical contact with the inner wall of the pipe, providing effective support. Connected to the drive motor module through the rear support body, the support module can balance reverse torque generated during rotation. The support wheel is mounted on the wheel frame using child and mother bolts. The lifting column, equipped with a built-in spring, can move up and down to enable the support module to adapt to changes in pipe diameter, ensuring its effectiveness in providing the necessary support under different pipeline conditions.

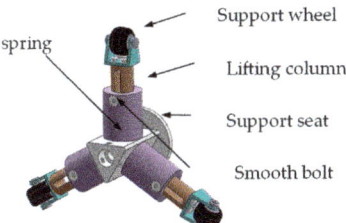

Figure 5. Schematic diagram of support unit structure.

2.2. Control System Design

Figure 6 presents the control system of the pipeline inspection robot. The robot's CPU is an STM32-F103 chip, while the console utilizes an embedded industrial computer. The pipeline inspection robot communicates with the industrial computer via wireless communication, and the robot CPU directs the robot to operate within the pipeline based on the commands provided by the operator using the industrial computer. Additionally, the robot performs defect detection and information collection functions within the pipeline.

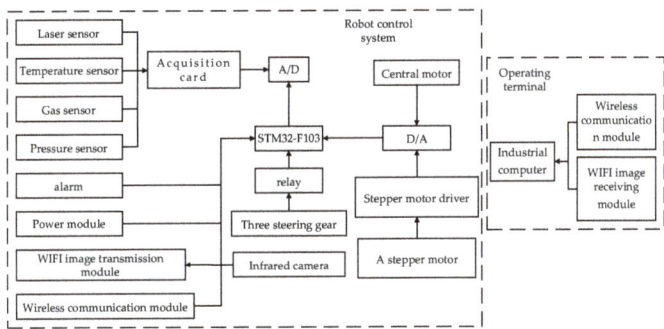

Figure 6. Control system diagram.

The robot control system encompasses the robot motion control unit, the pipeline information acquisition unit, and the wireless communication unit. The pipeline information acquisition unit collects images and environmental data from within the pipeline. Image information includes defects such as cracks, leakages, pits, and corrosion. Image acquisition is achieved through two infrared night vision cameras with autofocus capabilities, positioned at the front and rear of the robot.

The front camera rotates and continuously scans around the pipeline's axis during the robot's spiral advancement, capturing defect information in the dark pipeline environment and fulfilling the 360° detection requirements for the pipeline's inner wall. The rear camera supports the robot's navigation and positioning functions within the pipeline, continuously outputting and storing images in real time. The collected environmental information encompasses gas concentrations, pipe diameters, and pipe temperatures.

The robot motion control unit governs the deflection angle of the three steering motors and the speed of the stepper motor and the central motor, adjusting the robot's posture, speed, and bending mode while operating in the pipeline. Pressure sensors measure the pressure between the driving wheel and the pipeline's inner wall, and the error value between the current pressure and the target pressure for the specific application is calculated. This error signal serves as the output signal for PID control, directing the central motor to adjust the positive pressure in order to achieve the desired robot traction force and improve the robot's working efficiency within the pipeline.

Pipeline robots employ visual positioning methods within pipelines, utilizing images and point cloud data gathered by front and rear cameras, as well as laser ranging sensors, to ascertain the robot's position and orientation within the pipeline. The process involves several specific steps: (1) data collection: images and point cloud data are collected by the robot's cameras and laser ranging sensors; (2) feature extraction: the scale-invariant feature transform (SIFT) algorithm is employed to extract relevant features conducive to positioning, such as pipeline defects; (3) feature matching: the extracted features in the current image or point cloud data are matched with previously collected data or features in a pre-constructed map; (4) motion estimation: by matching pairs of feature points, the relative motion of the robot between two instances can be estimated; and (5) fusion and optimization: the estimated motion information is integrated into the robot's positioning system, along with data from other sensors, such as odometers and inertial navigation systems.

Wireless communication leverages radio frequency (RF) technology to facilitate data transmission between pipeline robots and ground control centers. Utilizing specific frequency bands and modulation modes, low-frequency RF signals can minimize signal attenuation in underground environments. Low-frequency signals experience relatively less loss when penetrating underground structures, thereby enhancing communication distances. In the communication between pipeline robots and ground control centers, multiple antennas are installed on both the robots and the control stations to transmit signals simultaneously across multiple channels. This can counteract, to some extent, the multipath effect (where communication signals in underground environments may reflect, refract, and scatter within the pipe) and signal attenuation (as wireless signals experience attenuation when passing through underground structures). Signal attenuation is particularly pronounced when traversing metal, water, or other high-density materials, resulting in limited communication distances. Employing relay nodes for segmental signal transmission can increase communication distances and signal coverage. In pipeline robot-to-ground communication, multiple relay nodes are deployed to enable multi-hop transmission. When direct communication is hindered by signal attenuation and environmental obstacles, signals can be transmitted sequentially through relay nodes, allowing for longer-distance and more reliable communication.

2.3. Design of PID System for Pressure Regulation

The PID control principle is shown in Figure 7. The PID control system comprises the following components: a stepper motor, a lead screw nut, a spring, and a pressure sensor. The stepper motor controls the movement of the lead screw nut by adjusting the number of steps, thereby altering the compression of the spring and generating the corresponding elastic force. Simultaneously, the pressure sensor is utilized to measure the actual level of elastic force exerted by the spring. Assuming that the spring stiffness is k, the damping coefficient is b, the lead of the screw nut is P_h, and the angle of the stepper motor is $\varphi(t)$, then the displacement $x(t)$ of the screw nut can be expressed as:

$$x(t) = \frac{P_h \cdot \varphi(t)}{2\pi} \qquad (1)$$

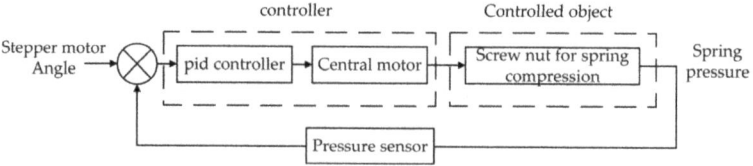

Figure 7. PID control schematic diagram.

The spring force $F(t)$ can be expressed as:

$$F(t) = k \cdot x(t) + b \cdot \dot{x}(t) \qquad (2)$$

The transfer function $G_s(s)$ of the system composed of a screw nut and a spring can be obtained by means of the Laplace transform:

$$G_s(s) = \frac{F(s)}{\theta(s)} == \left(\frac{k \cdot P_h}{2\pi} + \frac{b \cdot P_h}{2\pi} \cdot s\right) \tag{3}$$

The stepper motor transfer function is simplified to a first-order inertial system, K_m is the angle coefficient of the stepper motor, T is the time constant of the stepper motor, and the transfer function is:

$$G_m(s) = \frac{\varphi(s)}{U(s)} = \frac{K_m}{Ts+1} \tag{4}$$

The whole system transfer function is:

$$G(s) = G_s(s)G_m(s) \tag{5}$$

The transfer function of the PID controller is:

$$D(s) = K_p + \frac{K_i}{s} + K_d s \tag{6}$$

By repeatedly adjusting the parameters K_p, K_i and K_d of the three links, the PID control system with a fast response and small steady-state error can be obtained.

3. Robot Motion Characteristic Analysis and Mechanical Model Establishment

3.1. Analysis of Robot Traction Characteristics

As shown in Figure 8, in the given context, F_w represents the traction force of the robot, while F_T denotes the driving force acting on the driving wheel during the rotation process of the driving module. F_f is the lateral force generated by the side-sliding of the driving wheel as the robot spirals through the pipeline. N denotes the positive pressure of the driving wheel, and θ signifies the spiral angle. Additionally, γ represents the angle between the actual and expected running direction of the robot. The deflection stiffness coefficient of the driving wheel is represented by K_y, and the dynamic friction coefficient is denoted by μ. Φ is the sideslip rate.

$$F_f = \begin{cases} \left(1 - \frac{1}{4\Phi}\right)\mu N & \Phi > 1/2 \\ \Phi \mu N & \Phi \leq 1/2 \end{cases} \tag{7}$$

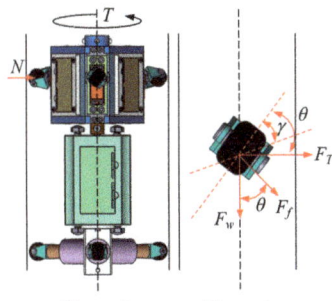

Figure 8. Traction analysis model.

The sideslip rate Φ can be expressed as:

$$\Phi = \frac{K_y \tan \gamma}{\mu N} \tag{8}$$

The sideslip force F_f can be expressed as:

$$F_f(\gamma) = \begin{cases} N\mu\left(1 - \dfrac{N\mu \cot\gamma}{4K_y}\right) & \dfrac{K_y \tan\gamma}{N\mu} > \dfrac{1}{2} \\ K_y \tan\gamma & \dfrac{K_y \tan\gamma}{N\mu} \le \dfrac{1}{2} \end{cases} \quad (9)$$

The robot can generate traction under the following conditions:

$$\begin{cases} F_T \cos\theta = F_w \sin\theta \\ F_T \sin\theta + F_w \cos\theta = W(\gamma) \\ \gamma \le \theta \end{cases} \quad (10)$$

Under ideal conditions, where the driving wheel supplies enough friction force and no slipping takes place, the traction force of the robot can be described as a function of the variables discussed earlier. Assuming that $\theta = \gamma$ (where θ is the spiral angle and γ represents the ideal angle for effective traction),

$$F_w(\theta) = \begin{cases} N\mu\left(1 - \dfrac{N\mu \cot\theta}{4K_y}\right)\cos\theta & \dfrac{K_y \tan\theta}{N\mu} > \dfrac{1}{2} \\ K_y \sin\theta & \dfrac{K_y \tan\theta}{N\mu} \le \dfrac{1}{2} \end{cases} \quad (11)$$

Based on this analysis, the traction force and spiral angle of the robot operating within the pipe are related to the positive pressure exerted by the robot, the contact between the driving wheel and the inner wall of the pipe, and the pipe material. As the spiral angle increases, the robot's traction force also increases, reaching a maximum value at an optimal angle. Beyond this point, the traction force begins to decrease gradually. Thus, it is essential to find the optimal spiral angle to maximize the traction force and ensure efficient robot performance within the pipeline.

3.2. Robot Positive Pressure Analysis in Pipeline

When it comes to pipeline operations, robots are required to not only move forward and backward, but also to rotate around the axis of the pipeline. This necessitates that the driving wheels of the robot exert appropriate normal forces against the inner wall of the pipeline while maintaining an optimal operational posture angle, as shown in Figure 9a. The posture angle, denoted as ω, is defined as the angle between the support module and the XZ plane. The total enclosed force between the driving wheels and the inner wall of the pipeline is represented by $\sum N$. The slope of the pipeline with respect to the horizontal plane is defined as τ.

$$\sum N = \begin{cases} 2mg \cos\omega \cos\tau & -60° \le \omega \le 60° \\ 2mg \cos(\omega - 120°) \cos\tau & 60° \le \omega \le 180° \\ 2mg \cos(\omega - 240°) \cos\tau & 180° \le \omega \le 300° \end{cases} \quad (12)$$

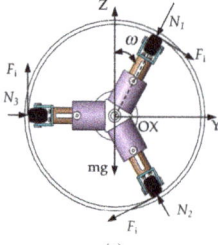

(a)

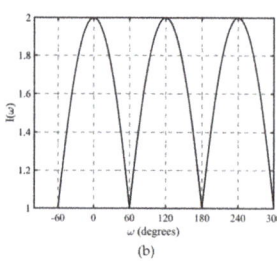

(b)

Figure 9. (a) Normal force distribution diagram. (b) Relationship between driving factor and attitude angle.

The parameter I_g is defined as the driving factor, which represents the ratio of the robot's weight to the enclosed force. It serves as a measure of the contribution of the robot's own weight to the traction force.

$$I_g = \frac{\sum N}{mg} = \begin{cases} 2\cos\omega\cos\tau & -60° \leq \omega \leq 60° \\ 2\cos(\omega - 120°)\cos\tau & 60° \leq \omega \leq 180° \\ 2\cos(\omega - 240°)\cos\tau & 180° \leq \omega \leq 300° \end{cases} \quad (13)$$

From the above equation, it can be observed that the robot's pose angle ω affects the driving factor. Therefore, in order to maximize the utilization of the driving factor and enhance the robot's traction performance, it is beneficial to increase the normal force and select the optimal pose angle. When operating in a horizontal straight pipe, as shown in Figure 9b, it is evident that the optimal pose angles for the robot are 0°, 120°, and 240°, where the robot achieves the maximum driving factor.

3.3. The Trajectory of the Robot's Spiral Motion in the Pipe

An XYZ coordinate system is established along the running direction of the robot, as illustrated in Figure 10a. As the pipeline robot moves within the pipeline, smooth movement can be achieved by ensuring that the spiral angle of the driving wheel is consistent across all driving modules. The cross-section of the pipeline robot is circular, and the parametric equation for this circle can be expressed as follows:

$$R_p = \begin{bmatrix} x \\ y \\ z \end{bmatrix} = \begin{bmatrix} R_p \cos\alpha \\ R_p \sin\alpha \\ 0 \end{bmatrix} \quad (14)$$

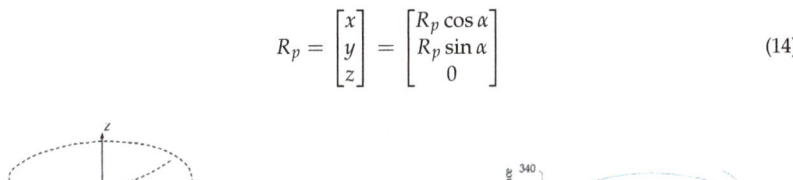

(a)   (b)

Figure 10. (a) Theoretical running trajectory of the robot within the pipeline. (b) Actual running trajectory of the robot as it moves through the pipeline.

R_p represents the radius of the circle (in mm); considering that the radius of the driving wheel can be ignored, it can be replaced by the length of the pipeline robot's driving arm. α denotes the rotation angle (in degrees) of the pipeline robot's driving arm around its center.

The spiral angle θ is formed between the driving wheel and the pipeline axis, causing the driving wheel's path along the inner wall of the pipeline to form a helical trajectory. Based on the geometric relationship, the linear displacement of the helix along the Z-axis is $R\alpha\tan\theta$, and the trajectory line $H_s(\alpha)$ of the helical motion can be expressed as follows:

$$\begin{bmatrix} H_s(\alpha) \\ 1 \end{bmatrix} = \begin{bmatrix} X \\ Y \\ Z \\ 1 \end{bmatrix} = T_Z \begin{bmatrix} R_p \\ 1 \end{bmatrix} = \begin{bmatrix} R_p \cos\alpha \\ R_p \sin\alpha \\ R_p\alpha\tan\theta \\ 1 \end{bmatrix} \quad (15)$$

$$T_Z = \begin{bmatrix} 1 & 0 & 0 & 0 \\ 0 & 1 & 0 & 0 \\ 0 & 0 & 1 & R_p \alpha \tan\theta \\ 0 & 0 & 0 & 1 \end{bmatrix} \tag{16}$$

Mathematica software was employed to validate the Hs(α) trajectory. With R_p set to 200 mm, θ at 30°, and α ranging from 0° to 360°, the actual running trajectory curve of the robot was obtained, as depicted in Figure 10b.

4. Influencing Factors and Simulation Analysis of Robot Traction Performance

A prototype model was created using ADAMS simulation software. The robot was imported into ADAMS, and its structure was simplified by retaining only the components associated with the transmission. This process led to the final establishment of the virtual prototype model for the pipeline robot.

4.1. Influence of Different Materials on Traction Performance of Robot in Straight Pipe Operation

The material used for oil pipelines is typically stainless-steel composite steel pipe, which is generally coated with an anti-corrosive layer on the inside, providing good corrosion resistance. Gas pipelines, on the other hand, are primarily made from steel, aluminum, or plastic pipes. Consequently, the traction force exerted by the pipeline robot varies depending on factors such as the transportation medium, transportation pressure, and pipe material. As demonstrated earlier, the traction force of the pipeline robot relies on the friction force between the driving wheel and the inner wall of the pipeline. This study investigates the difference in traction force for the pipeline robot under various working conditions and analyzes the magnitude of the traction force by simulating and altering its contact friction coefficient.

The traction force acting under different working conditions was simulated in ADAMS. First, the optimal spiral angle was set to 40°, and the contact force parameters between the driving wheel and the inner wall of the pipeline were established. The working condition refers to the operating state of the robot in various environments. Material 1 and Material 2 represent the materials of the driving wheel and the pipeline, respectively, and the stiffness coefficient K is 2855. The force index e is 1.1; the damping c is 0.57; the penetration depth d is 0.1; mus denotes the coefficient of static friction, while mud represents the coefficient of dynamic friction; v_s is the static translation velocity; and v_d corresponds to the friction translation velocity. Additional simulation parameters for different working conditions are presented in Table 2 below. The pipe diameter is set at 200 mm, and the robot's running time is 5 s.

Table 2. Contact parameters of robot and pipeline simulation.

Working Condition	Material 1	Material 2	Mus	Mud	v_s	v_d
1	rubber	Steel (dry)	0.3	0.25	1	10
2	rubber	Steel (wet)	0.08	0.05	1	10
3	rubber	Aluminum (dry)	0.25	0.2	1	10
4	rubber	Aluminum (wet)	0.05	0.03	1	10

In the ADAMS simulation process, the traction force of the robot in operation can be simulated by placing a tension spring between the pipeline robot and the pipeline. The tension and compression spring is positioned on the pipeline axis. One end is connected to the robot's center, and the other end is connected to the center of the vertical plane passing through the pipeline axis. The spring's stiffness coefficient is set to 800, and the damping coefficient is set to 0.5. The simulation results of traction force in a straight pipe are shown in Figure 11 below.

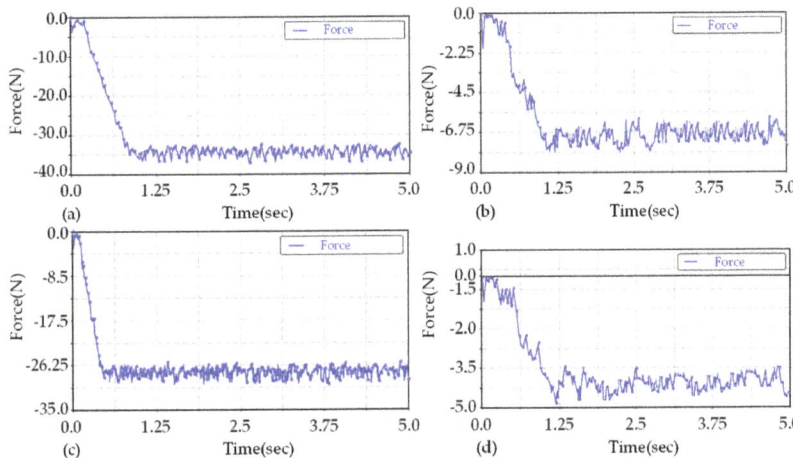

Figure 11. (a–d) Traction forces of the robot in the straight pipe under working conditions 1, 2, 3, and 4, respectively.

According to the simulation results, the tension of the tension spring in the four simulated operating conditions in the straight pipe will slip as the robot accelerates to its maximum speed. The maximum traction of the robot will fluctuate within a small range, and the traction will increase with the friction coefficient. The difference in the transportation medium within the pipe made from the same material will also impact the traction force. The tractive force of the robot running in a pipeline without a transport medium is significantly greater than that in a pipeline containing a medium.

4.2. Influence of Positive Pressure on Traction Performance of Robot Support Wheel

The pipeline robot is designed with three groups of supporting wheels, distributed at a 120-degree circumference, and each supporting wheel has a normal pressure with the inner wall of the pipeline. The appropriate normal pressure is crucial for the robot's performance. Excessive normal pressure will result in high power consumption, while insufficient positive pressure will prevent the robot's driving wheel from generating enough friction with the pipeline's inner wall. In the analysis of normal force, the pipeline was set with no medium transport, the material was plexiglass, the coefficient of static friction was 0.2, the coefficient of dynamic friction was 0.15, and the simulation time was 10 s.

The normal force of the driving wheel was set at 100 N, 110 N, 120 N, and 130 N, respectively, and the simulation results met the requirement of traction force greater than 30 N, as shown in Figure 12 below. The tractive forces were 33 N, 36 N, 38 N, and 38 N, respectively. The traction of the driving wheel increases with the increase in positive pressure. However, when the positive pressure reaches a certain value, the traction will no longer increase, because the robot's maximum load capacity has an upper limit, ultimately causing the robot to become stuck in the pipeline and unable to function normally. Consequently, the normal force should be controlled between 100 N and 120 N, ensuring that the robot can run smoothly in the pipeline while consuming less power.

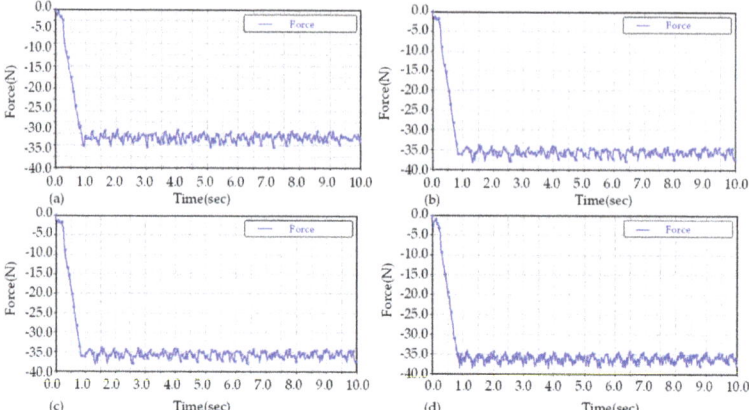

Figure 12. Tractive forces of the pipeline robot under different positive pressure settings. (**a**–**d**) Tractive forces when the positive pressures are 100 N, 110 N, 120 N, and 130N, respectively.

4.3. Analysis of the Influence of Robot Attitude Angle on the Rotation of the Support Unit

When the spiral pipeline robot travels within a pipeline, its spiral module rotates around the pipeline axis, while the support module serves to balance the counter torque generated by the spiral module. Consequently, the robot not only moves forward and backward inside the pipeline but also rotates around the pipeline axis, resulting in a change in the robot's motion posture that deviates from its initial position. The support module is distributed circumferentially at 120-degree intervals. Although deviations in the robot's motion posture do not impact its operation, it must maintain the optimal posture for entering bends as it navigates them. Furthermore, during the operation of the robot's towing cable module, posture deviations can cause the cable to become entangled, necessitating limits and corrections to the robot's posture deflection.

Based on the analysis in Section 3.2, different attitude angles affect the robot's torque. Therefore, four representative attitude angles of 0°, 30°, 60°, and 90° were selected for further examination. The simulation results are shown in Figure 13. In the 0–90° attitude angle range, the support module's rotational torque increases gradually with the rising attitude angle. When the attitude angle reaches 90°, the torque is at its maximum, and when the angle is 0°, the torque approaches zero. By adjusting the robot's attitude angle to 0 degrees and maximizing the positive pressure between the support unit and the pipeline's inner wall, the torque of the robot's support unit can be reduced, effectively restraining the support unit's rotation along the pipeline axis.

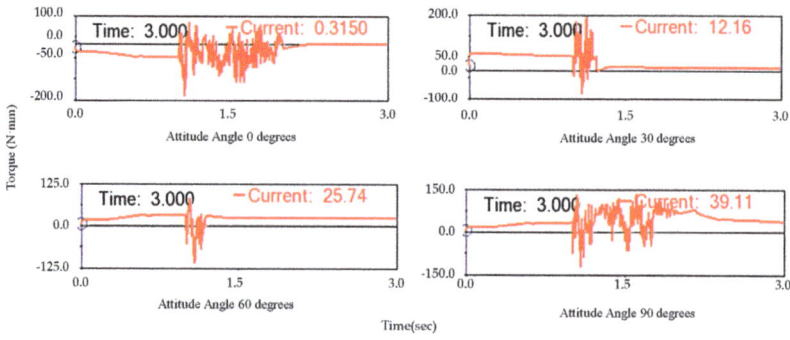

Figure 13. Robot torque of different attitude angles.

5. Traction Experiment Verification and Analysis

An experimental platform was constructed for the pipeline robot. As shown in Figure 14, one end of the spring is attached to the pipeline robot, while the other end is connected to a force sensor. The sensor remains fixed in a specific position, and the robot initiates its operation within the pipeline. This setup enables researchers to systematically analyze the performance of the robot under various conditions, optimizing its design for maximum efficiency and functionality.

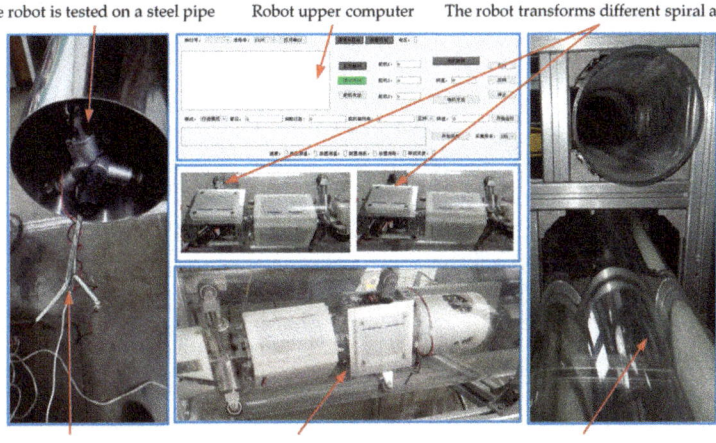

Figure 14. Robot traction experiment test environment.

In this experiment, steel and plexiglass pipes are utilized as materials. Industrial lubricating oil is applied to simulate the conditions of a medium under actual operation. During the robot's operation, when a slip occurs, the force sensor will cease data collection. The tractive force of the robot is influenced by factors such as normal force, spiral angle, pipe contact, and motor driving force. The spiral angle, pipe material, and driving wheel normal force were chosen as variables, with the peak value collected by the sensor being considered as valid data. A 42-series motor (the drive motor in the drive module of the robot) was employed as the driving motor for the robot prototype, and the torque was set at 10 Nm.

The test results are displayed in Figure 15a, and the trend of traction force variation is generally consistent with the theoretical analysis. The traction force initially increases and then decreases with the increase in the spiral angle; however, there is a significant deviation from the theoretical analysis under conditions with small spiral angles. In sections with small spiral angles, the pipe wall cannot provide sufficient friction, making it prone to slippage and unsmooth operation. As the spiral angle increases, the slippage gradually disappears.

Among the four experimental working conditions, the steel pipe (dry) has the largest friction factor, and the optimal spiral angle is approximately 40°, followed by the plexiglass pipe (dry), with its optimal spiral angle at around 50°. Therefore, the optimal spiral angle for robot traction tends to increase as the friction factor decreases. Consequently, the robot's spiral angle should be set based on different working conditions and varying spiral angles. The tractive force of running in a steel pipe (dry) is greater than that of running in a plexiglass (dry) pipe.

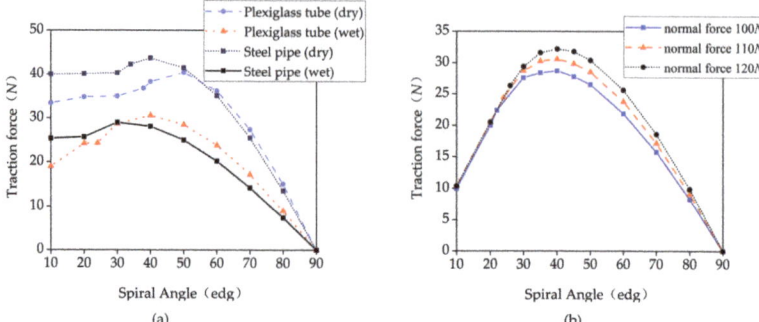

Figure 15. (**a**) Experiment involving the robot under various working conditions; (**b**) experiment with the robot operating under different normal forces.

In the steel pipe (dry) condition, the robot operates with a large traction force due to its relatively high friction factor. The higher the friction factor, the greater the traction force. In pipelines made from the same material, the tractive force of the robot's operation in a pipeline with a transport medium is significantly lower than in a pipeline without a transport medium.

In the experiment, the robot's experimental working condition was set as a plexiglass pipe, and three different values of 100 N, 110 N, and 120 N were established by adjusting the normal force of the driving wheel. The normal force was monitored using a drive wheel pressure sensor, and each peak traction was recorded as a data collection point during the test. The test results, shown in Figure 15b, exhibit the same variation trend as the simulation, although they are smaller than the simulation value. Under the same working conditions, the optimal spiral angle of the robot is approximately 40 degrees, and the optimal spiral angle does not change as the normal force increases.

6. Conclusions

(1) In this study, a spiral pipeline robot designed for oil and gas pipeline detection is presented, and a corresponding mechanical model is constructed. The robot's traction performance is investigated through dynamic simulations, and the simulation results are verified by experiments. It is found that the tractive force is closely related to the normal force, helix angle, contact between the driving wheel and the pipe, and the pipe material. In the small helix angle range, the robot is prone to skidding. As the helix angle increases, the skidding phenomenon gradually decreases, and the tractive force initially increases before decreasing. When the helix angle reaches 90°, the tractive force becomes zero.

(2) Under different working conditions, the robot's traction force displays an increasing trend with the rise in the friction coefficient, but the optimal helix angle decreases. Therefore, it is necessary to adjust the appropriate deflection angle based on the actual working condition. In pipelines of the same material, the presence or absence of a transport medium affects the tractive force, with the force in dry pipelines being significantly higher than that in pipelines containing a transport medium. The variable helix angle bending strategy enables the robot to exhibit good passing performance in bending pipes and offers better stability than a fixed helix angle bending.

(3) Under the same working conditions, the robot's traction force can be improved by adjusting the normal force of the driving wheel. The greater the normal force, the greater the traction. When the normal force changes, the optimal helix angle for traction remains at approximately 40° without significant change. Moreover, the motion stability of the robot is a critical issue affected by various factors, such as the center of gravity's position and inertial force. To enhance motion stability and traction,

the robot structure and control algorithm should be optimized, and a balance between various factors should be achieved.

Author Contributions: Equipment design and manufacturing process, H.Y.; Prototype processing and manufacturing, P.Z. and H.Y.; Control systems and software development, P.Z. and C.X.; Writing and review, H.Y. and S.J.; Simulation analysis, P.Z. and X.W.; Experimental support, D.Z. and H.P.; All authors have read and agreed to the published version of the manuscript.

Funding: This paper is part of a project that has received funding from the Fundamental Research Program of Shanxi Province: "Research on the Kinematics Characteristics of the Driving Mechanism for Leakage Blocking Repair in Multi-point Dispersed Sections of Pipelines (20210302123038)" and the special project of scientific and technological cooperation and exchange in Shanxi Province: "Intelligent equipment technology for defect detection and emergency prevention and control in dangerous source pipe" (202104041101001) and a research project supported by Shanxi Scholarship Council of China "Research on screw driven pipeline robot for leakage plugging and repairing technology "(2020–110) and North University of China Science and Technology project "Research on Circumferential Welding Robot Technology of Pipeline Internal weld" (20221817). The authors would like to express their gratitude for the support for this study. Moreover, the authors sincerely thank Professor Wu Wenge of North University of China for his critical discussion and Dr. Dahua Xie of Silicon Valley, USA for linguistic assistance during the preparation of this manuscript.

Data Availability Statement: Data are contained within the article.

Acknowledgments: This research was generously supported by the following organizations, to which we express our sincere gratitude: Shanxi Provincial Key Laboratory of Advanced Manufacturing, North University of China; Taiyuan University of Technology National and Local Joint Engineering Laboratory of Mine Fluid Control; Shanxi Datong University Coal Mine Electromechanical Technology Institute; Shanxi Coal Import and Export Group Science and Technology Research Institute Co., Ltd.; and Shanxi Honganxiang Science and Technology Co., Ltd.

Conflicts of Interest: The authors declare no conflict of interest.

References

1. Yan, H.; Wang, L.; Li, P.; Wang, Z.; Yang, X.; Hou, X. Research on Passing Ability and Climbing Performance of Pipeline Plugging Robots in Curved Pipelines. *IEEE Access* **2020**, *8*, 173666–173680. [CrossRef]
2. Li, J.; Huang, F.; Tu, C.; Tian, M.; Wang, X. Elastic Obstacle-Surmounting Pipeline-Climbing Robot with Composite Wheels. *Machines* **2022**, *10*, 874. [CrossRef]
3. Teng, X.; Jiang, X.; Ma, R. Construction of fluid-solid coupling model of flexible multibody system for pipeline robots driven by differential pressure. *Nongye Gongcheng Xuebao/Trans. Chin. Soc. Agric. Eng.* **2020**, *36*, 31–39.
4. Yin, F. Inspection Robot for Submarine Pipeline Based on Machine Vision. In Proceedings of the 2021 Asia-Pacific Conference on Image Processing, Electronics and Computers, IPEC 2021, Dalian, China, 14–16 April 2021.
5. Torajizadeh, H.; Asadirad, A.; Mashayekhi, E.; Dabiri, G. Design and manufacturing a novel screw-in-pipe inspection robot with steering capability. *J. Field Robot.* **2022**, *40*, 429–446. [CrossRef]
6. Wu, K.; Sang, H.; Xing, Y.; Lu, Y. Design of wireless in-pipe inspection robot for image acquisition. *Ind. Robot.-Int. J. Robot. Res. Appl.* **2023**, *50*, 145–161. [CrossRef]
7. Kim, H.M.; Yang, S.U.; Choi, Y.S.; Mun, H.M.; Park, C.M.; Choi, H.R. Design of back-drivable joint mechanism for in-pipe robot. In Proceedings of the IEEE/RSJ International Conference on Intelligent Robots and Systems, IROS 2015, Hamburg, Germany, 28 September–2 October 2015; pp. 3779–3784.
8. Yan, H.; Li, J.; Kou, Z.; Liu, Y.; Li, P.; Wang, L. Research on the Traction and Obstacle-Surmounting Performance of an Adaptive Pipeline-Plugging Robot. *Stroj. Vestn.-J. Mech. Eng.* **2022**, *68*, 14–26. [CrossRef]
9. Shao, L.; Wang, Y.; Guo, B.; Chen, X. A review over state of the art of in-pipe robot. In Proceedings of the 12th IEEE International Conference on Mechatronics and Automation, ICMA 2015, Beijing, China, 2–5 August 2015; pp. 2180–2185.
10. Kazeminasab, S.; Aghashahi, M.; Katherine Banks, M. Development of an Inline Robot for Water Quality Monitoring. In Proceedings of the 5th International Conference on Robotics and Automation Engineering, ICRAE 2020, Singapore, 20–22 November 2020; pp. 106–113.
11. Waleed, D.; Mustafa, S.H.; Mukhopadhyay, S.; Abdel-Hafez, M.F.; Jaradat, M.A.K.; Dias, K.R.; Arif, F.; Ahmed, J.I. An In-Pipe Leak Detection Robot with a Neural-Network-Based Leak Verification System. *IEEE Sens. J.* **2019**, *19*, 1153–1165. [CrossRef]
12. Miao, X.; Zhao, H.; Gao, B.; Ma, Y.; Hou, Y.; Song, F. Motion analysis and control of the pipeline robot passing through girth weld and inclination in natural gas pipeline. *J. Nat. Gas Sci. Eng.* **2022**, *104*, 104662. [CrossRef]

13. Lee, D.; Park, J.; Hyun, D.; Yook, G.; Yang, H.-s. Novel mechanisms and simple locomotion strategies for an in-pipe robot that can inspect various pipe types. *Mech. Mach. Theory* **2012**, *56*, 52–68. [CrossRef]
14. Zhao, W.; Zhang, L.; Kim, J. Design and Analysis of Independently Adjustable Large In-Pipe Robot for Long-Distance Pipeline. *Appl. Sci.* **2020**, *10*, 3637. [CrossRef]
15. Liljebck, P.; Pettersen, K.Y.; Stavdahl, O.; Gravdahl, J.T. A review on modelling, implementation, and control of snake robots. *Robot. Auton. Syst.* **2012**, *60*, 29–40. [CrossRef]
16. Gao, M.; Huang, M.; Tang, K.; Lang, X.; Gao, J. Design, Analysis, and Control of a Multilink Magnetic Wheeled Pipeline Robot. *IEEE Access* **2022**, *10*, 67168–67180. [CrossRef]
17. Liu, G. Data Collection in MI-Assisted Wireless Powered Underground Sensor Networks: Directions, Recent Advances, and Challenges. *IEEE Commun. Mag.* **2021**, *59*, 132–138. [CrossRef]
18. Worley, R.; Yu, Y.; Anderson, S. Acoustic Echo-Localization for Pipe Inspection Robots. In Proceedings of the 2020 IEEE International Conference on Multisensor Fusion and Integration for Intelligent Systems, MFI 2020, Karlsruhe, Germany, 14–16 September 2020; pp. 160–165.
19. Maneewarn, T.; Thung-Od, K. ICP-EKF localization with adaptive covariance for a boiler inspection robot. In Proceedings of the 7th IEEE International Conference on Cybernetics and Intelligent Systems, CIS 2015 and the 7th IEEE International Conference on Robotics, Automation and Mechatronics, RAM 2015, Siem Reap, Cambodia, 15–17 July 2015; pp. 216–221.
20. Siqueira, E.; Azzolin, R.; Botelho, S.; Oliveira, V. Sensors data fusion to navigate inside pipe using Kalman Filter. In Proceedings of the 21st IEEE International Conference on Emerging Technologies and Factory Automation, ETFA 2016, Berlin, Germany, 6–9 September 2016.
21. Wu, Y.; Mittmann, E.; Winston, C.; Youcef-Toumi, K. A practical minimalism approach to in-pipe robot localization. In Proceedings of the 2019 American Control Conference, ACC 2019, Philadelphia, PA, USA, 10–12 July 2019; pp. 3180–3187.
22. Liu, Z.; Krys, D. The use of laser range finder on a robotic platform for pipe inspection. *Mech. Syst. Signal Process.* **2012**, *31*, 246–257. [CrossRef]
23. Kheirandish, M.; Yazdi, E.A.; Mohammadi, H.; Mohammadi, M. A fault-tolerant sensor fusion in mobile robots using multiple model Kalman filters. *Robot. Auton. Syst.* **2023**, *161*, 104343. [CrossRef]
24. Ma, K.; Schirru, M.; Zahraee, A.H.; Dwyer-Joyce, R.; Boxall, J.; Dodd, T.J.; Collins, R.; Anderson, S.R. PipeSLAM: Simultaneous Localisation and Mapping in Feature Sparse Water Pipes using the Rao-Blackwellised Particle Filter. In Proceedings of the 2017 IEEE International Conference on Advanced Intelligent Mechatronics, AIM 2017, Munich, Germany, 3–7 July 2017; pp. 1459–1464.
25. Aitken, J.M.; Evans, M.H.; Worley, R.; Edwards, S.; Zhang, R.; Dodd, T.; Mihaylova, L.; Anderson, S.R. Simultaneous Localization and Mapping for Inspection Robots in Water and Sewer Pipe Networks: A Review. *IEEE Access* **2021**, *9*, 140173–140198. [CrossRef]
26. Chuang, T.-Y.; Sung, C.-C. Learning and SLAM based decision support platform for sewer inspection. *Remote Sens.* **2020**, *12*, 968. [CrossRef]
27. Wu, D.; Chatzigeorgiou, D.; Youcef-Toumi, K.; Ben-Mansour, R. Node Localization in Robotic Sensor Networks for Pipeline Inspection. *IEEE Trans. Ind. Inform.* **2016**, *12*, 809–819. [CrossRef]
28. Rizzo, C.; Kumar, V.; Lera, F.; Villarroel, J.L. RF odometry for localization in pipes based on periodic signal fadings. In Proceedings of the 2014 IEEE/RSJ International Conference on Intelligent Robots and Systems, IROS 2014, Chicago, IL, USA, 14–18 September 2014; pp. 4577–4583.
29. Rizzo, C.; Seco, T.; Espelosin, J.; Lera, F.; Villarroel, J.L. An alternative approach for robot localization inside pipes using RF spatial fadings. *Robot. Auton. Syst.* **2021**, *136*, 103702. [CrossRef]

Disclaimer/Publisher's Note: The statements, opinions and data contained in all publications are solely those of the individual author(s) and contributor(s) and not of MDPI and/or the editor(s). MDPI and/or the editor(s) disclaim responsibility for any injury to people or property resulting from any ideas, methods, instructions or products referred to in the content.

Towards Metaverse: Utilizing Extended Reality and Digital Twins to Control Robotic Systems

Tero Kaarlela [1,*], Tomi Pitkäaho [1], Sakari Pieskä [1], Paulo Padrão [2], Leonardo Bobadilla [2], Matti Tikanmäki [3], Timo Haavisto [4], Víctor Blanco Bataller [4], Niko Laivuori [4] and Mika Luimula [4]

1. Department of Industrial Management, Centria University of Applied Sciences, 84100 Ylivieska, Finland; tomi.pitkaaho@centria.fi (T.P.); sakari.pieska@centria.fi (S.P.)
2. Knight Foundation School of Computing and Information Sciences, Florida International University, Miami, FL 33199, USA; ppadraol@fiu.edu (P.P.); bobadilla@cs.fiu.edu (L.B.)
3. Probot OY, Planeettatie 6B, 90450 Kempele, Finland; matti.tikanmaki@probot.fi
4. School of ICT, Turku University of Applied Sciences, 20520 Turku, Finland; timo.haavisto@turkuamk.fi (T.H.); victor.blancobataller@turkuamk.fi (V.B.B.); niko.laivuori1@turkuamk.fi (N.L.); mika.luimula@turkuamk.fi (M.L.)
* Correspondence: tero.kaarlela@centria.fi

Abstract: Digitalization shapes the ways of learning, working, and entertainment. The Internet, which enables us to connect and socialize is evolving to become the metaverse, a post-reality universe, enabling virtual life parallel to reality. In addition to gaming and entertainment, industry and academia have noticed the metaverse's benefits and possibilities. For industry, the metaverse is the enabler of the future digital workplace, and for academia, digital learning spaces enable realistic virtual training environments. A connection bridging the virtual world with physical production systems is required to enable digital workplaces and digital learning spaces. In this publication, *extended reality–digital twin to real* use cases are presented. The presented use cases utilize extended reality as high-level user interfaces and digital twins to create a bridge between virtual environments and robotic systems in industry, academia, and underwater exploration.

Keywords: metaverse; digital twin; robotics; extended reality

1. Introduction

Digitalization shapes how we learn, work, and entertain ourselves by providing the tools for location- and time-independent presence and control of things. Gaining new knowledge, learning new skills, playing games, socializing with others, and controlling production systems is possible from anywhere by using everyday mobile devices. Advancements in digitalization and the availability of mobile devices have grown a new generation of digital natives [1,2]. Socializing, learning, and working in virtual environments are natural for the digital native generation, who have grown up using mobile devices. The metaverse is one of the latest implementations of evolving digitalization enabling the aforementioned activities in a parallel digital version of our reality [3].

In the metaverse, we can exist as avatars and learn or work similarly to in the real world, enabling a natural virtual environment for the digital native generation. Gaming and entertainment are the most popular ways to experience the metaverse; multiplayer gaming can be an immersive social event [4]. In addition to entertainment and gaming, the industry has recognized the potential of the metaverse as an enabler of the digital workplace, and the first steps have already been taken to create the industrial metaverse [5,6]. The metaverse can increase production efficiency by enabling location-independent control of the physical machinery that is required to manufacture everyday products for the consumer market.

The underwater environment is unnatural for humans, and working in the deep sea requires diving gear or remotely operated vehicles (ROVs). Due to the cold temperatures and human physics, working in the deep sea is only possible for relatively short periods to avoid hypothermia and divers' disease [7]. In addition to the harsh physical conditions, the limited underwater visibility is challenging for divers and the teleoperators of ROVs. By combining XR interfaces, the metaverse, and DTs, it is possible to remove the user from harsh underwater conditions. In addition, XR enables the provision of an enhanced and processed virtual view of the underwater environment instead of a blurry live video stream that lacks visual cues for the teleoperator.

The benefits of location and time independence enabled by the metaverse are obvious to academia [8]. In addition to learning not being bound to a specific time and place, the digital native generation that is being educated today has a different way of processing information compared to previous generations. Instead of reading books and writing essays, the digital native generation prefers to use social forums, online videos, and Google searches to gain knowledge [9]. VEs are a way for academia to attract students' interest in engineering topics, such as robotics and automation. The metaverse enables training in basic robotic skills, such as controlling the movements and creating programs for robots in a natural way, for the digital native generation. To bridge the reality gap between fully virtual experiences, DTs enable a bridge between physical robot systems and virtual training environments.

A bridge enabling bi-directional interaction is required for a metaverse user to control and monitor physical systems. The bridge is a middleware between a virtual environment and the controller of a physical system, and it enables the user to control the actuators and monitor the sensor information of the remote system. In addition, the physical characteristics of virtual and real-world systems must match to bridge the reality gap between the two [10]. Digital twins (DTs) [11] are suitable middleware, and they enable interactions between and merging of the virtual and physical worlds. DTs enable synchronized bi-directional communication between a physical system and a virtual user interface. In addition, a DT entity describes the physical characteristics of a physical system, enabling identical twins.

Extended reality (XR) is an essential enabler of the metaverse, as it provides a high-level user interface [12] for experiencing the post-reality universe. XR enables fully virtual and mixed-reality experiences by blending reality and synthetic virtual elements [13]. While the foundation for XR was laid decades ago by the pioneers in computing [14] and entertainment [15], everyday applications have been waiting for the evolution of computing, display technologies [16], and optics [17] to enable affordable and comfortable user devices to be used to experience virtual worlds.

The research questions of this publication are the following: Can DTs and XR enable the digital workplaces required by the industrial metaverse? Are virtual learning environments enabled by utilizing the aforementioned combination of technologies? This publication presents four use cases that take steps towards the metaverse by utilizing XR and DTs to control robotic systems:

- An XR interface for future industrial robotics;
- An interface for enhancing the cognitive capabilities of the teleoperator of an underwater vehicle;
- DTs that are used as robotic training tools;
- Movement toward a maritime metaverse with social communication, hands-on experiences, and DTs.

The rest of this paper is organized as follows: Section 2 provides a review of research on the topics of the metaverse, XR, DTs, and teleoperation. Section 3 describes the methods used to implement the use cases that are presented, Section 4 presents the implemented use cases, and Section 5 discusses the presented results and concludes the paper.

2. Related Research

2.1. Teleoperation

Teleoperation has been an active research topic for decades, and it has the aim of removing barriers between operators and machines [18]. For example, a barrier preventing on-site operation can be a hazardous environment or a large distance between an operator and a machine. The first teleoperation applications were unmanned torpedoes [19,20]; lives could be saved by guiding the torpedoes to their targets from a safe location.

Since then, teleoperation has been applied to various robotic applications, such as surgery, space exploration, and the handling of hazardous materials [21–26]. González et al. [27] proposed a robot teleoperation system that enabled the operator to perform industrial finishing processes by using an industrial robot. Duan et al. [28] proposed a teleoperation system for ultrasound scanning in the healthcare sector, and the proposed solution was proven safe and effective. Caiza et al. [29] introduced a teleoperated robot for inspection tasks in oil fields; the proposed system utilized a lightweight MQTT data transfer protocol that was described in detail [30].

Underwater robotics is an efficient tool for studying, monitoring, and performing coastal conservation, coral restoration, and oil rig maintenance [31–33]. The teleoperation of underwater vehicles presents various communication difficulties because of the environment's harsh and constantly changing conditions. Among these difficulties are constraints on communication bandwidth and signal quality, packet losses, propagation delay, environmental variability, and security concerns [34,35]. As described in [36], the difficulties related to human performance when controlling teleoperated systems can be divided into two categories. The first is *remote perception,* which is challenging because natural perception processing is separated from the physical environment. The second category is *remote manipulation,* which suffers from the limitations of the operator's motor skills and their capacity to maintain situational awareness. Factors affecting remote perception and manipulation are commonly listed as a limited field-of-view (FOV) and camera viewpoint, degraded orientation, depth perception, and time delays [37].

Another key challenge in developing teleoperation applications of virtual and augmented reality is the optimal design of human–robot interfaces. In other words, given a physical system and a user input device, how should a human–robot interface translate the configuration and action spaces between the user and the physical system for teleoperation? It is worth noting that the term "optimal" implies that such an interface complies with certain constraints related to user comfort, smoothness, efficiency, continuity, consistency, and the controllability and reachability of physical systems [38].

2.2. Digital Twin Concept

The concept of DT has been an active research topic since it was introduced by Grieves [11]. DTs are digital models of physical devices or systems featuring bi-directional communication and algorithms to match physical configurations between the two [10,39]. DTs enable a user to interact with the low-level functions of a physical twin. Single devices, such as a single industrial robot, or larger entities, such as smart cities or digital factories, can be twinned [40–42]. Different approaches to categorizing DTs exist: Grieves divided DTs into DT prototypes (DTPs) and DT instances (DTIs). Kritzinger divided DTs into three levels according to the level of integration: the digital model (DM), digital shadow (DS), and digital twin (DT). In this paper, we follow Kritzinger's method for categorizing DTs. Misinterpretations and misconceptions of the evolving DT concept have existed since it was presented by Grieves [43].

The glossary of the digital twin consortium defines a DT as a virtual presentation of real-world entities and processes synchronized at a specified frequency and fidelity [44]. The DT is a mature concept that was standardized by the International Organization for Standardization (ISO) in 2021 [45].

2.3. Extended Reality

XR is a top category for virtual reality (VR) and mixed reality (MR) [13]. MR can be further divided into the augmented reality (AR) and augmented virtuality (AV) subcategories. XR has been researched for decades [14,15,46], and recent advancements in computing, optics, and electronics [16,17] have enabled immersive and augmented virtual experiences by using affordable stand-alone head-mounted displays (HMDs) or everyday mobile devices [47,48]. In addition to HMDs, a user can interact with virtual objects by using handheld controllers, which enable grabbing, pointing, and touching [49]. The latest improvements in HMD sensor technology have enabled hand-tracking, thus enabling users to interact with virtual objects by using simple gestures, such as pinching and pointing [50].

The Unity game engine, which was launched as a game engine for MacOS, has become one of the most popular game engines for desktop and mobile applications [51]. The Godot engine was released under an MIT License in 2014 as an open-source alternative for Unity [52,53]. Unity and Gogot include rendering and physics engines, installable assets, and a graphical editor. The Visual Studio integrated development environment (IDE) is used to program functionalities for game objects, and the programming language is C#. In addition to C#, Godot supports Python like GDScript language programming language. The Godot engine and Unity enable XR applications to be compiled as WebXR-runtimes, which combine WebGL, HTML5, and WebAssembly [54–56]. WebXR-runtimes can be distributed on the Internet, are cybersecure and accessible, and support cross-platform devices.

Epic's Unreal Engine (UE) is a popular game engine that is utilized widely in game programming and industrial applications [57]. Functionality programming in UE supports C++ or Blueprints, and Epic provides a content store for purchasing additional assets. While Blueprints are an easy-to-use visual tool for programming, C++ enables the programming of more complex functionalities. UE supports the compilation of WebXR binaries with version 4.24, which was released on GitHub [58].

2.4. Extended Reality in Programming and Control of Robots

Since the introduction of industrial robots, the teach pendant has been and remains the most popular programming method; over 90% of industrial robots are programmed by using a teach pendant [59,60]. Programming by utilizing a teach pendant is not an intuitive way to program an industrial robot, and researchers have studied XR as an alternative programming method for industrial robots [12,61–63]. In addition to programming, XR has been studied as an interface for the teleoperation of robots. Recent cross-scientific research has utilized XR as a high-level human–machine interface for teleoperation and a DT as a middleware that enables the teleoperator to control a physical system [64]. In addition to twinning a robot arm, González et al. and Li et al. twinned the surroundings of an environment by utilizing point clouds from three-dimensional cameras [27,65].

2.5. Communication Layer

An effective communication protocol is required to synchronize the states of digital and physical twins. MQTT [30] enables efficient communication over the Internet and local networks. MQTT is one of the most popular IoT and IIoT communication protocols since it is a lightweight and efficient publisher–subscriber communication protocol [66]. The messaging consists of three participants: the publisher, the subscriber, and a broker between the two. MQTT was originally developed for resource-constrained communications, and the latest updates enable cybersecure communications; encryption of the data and authentication of the users are enabled.

2.6. Real-Time Video

Web Real-Time Communication (WebRTC) is a real-time web-based video transfer technology [67]. WebRTC is an open-source protocol that is implemented on the User Datagram Protocol (UDP) to enable low-latency video streaming. Since UDP does not natively support congestion control, a specific congestion control mechanism (GCC) was developed for WebRTC by Google. The GCC is intended to control the resolution of a video stream in proportion to the available bandwidth, thus enabling a low-latency video stream; the trade-off is the resolution. Video streaming latencies of 80 to 100 milliseconds have been measured on mobile platforms [68].

2.7. Metaverse

The metaverse, as a post-reality universe, merges physical and virtual worlds [3]. The metaverse started as a web of virtual worlds that enabled users to teleport from one virtual world to another. The evolution of virtual multi-user environments has gone through multi-user role-playing games and gaming platforms [69] to the virtual social platforms of today [70], and the ability to socialize is one of the metaverse's key strengths. Based on the seven rules defined by Parisi [71], the one and only metaverse is a free cross-platform network that is accessible to anyone. Industry 4.0 and Education 4.0 are ongoing parallel evolutions that are enabled by digitalization. As a virtual environment (VE), the metaverse is essential to both movements [2,8]. VEs enable location- and time-independent training and education for industrial companies and educational institutions. In addition, VEs are risk-free and do not have the physical limitations of classrooms [72]. Industries are adopting the metaverse by utilizing DTs as core components to connect physical and virtual systems [73]. Industries apply the metaverse for training, engineering, working, and socializing [42].

The Industrial metaverse enables physical interaction in real time, improves the visualization of cyber–physical systems (CPSs), and can be seen as a DT of the workspace [5]. According to Kang et al. [6], the industrial metaverse is still in its infancy; in particular, privacy protection issues and the design of incentive mechanisms need more attention. Nokia's CEO Pekka Lundmark stated, "The future of the metaverse is not for consumers" [74]. Nokia has classified metaverse business into three categories: the consumer, enterprise, and industrial metaverse. In fact, Nokia is expecting the industrial metaverse to lead the commercialization of the metaverse [75]. Siemens and Nvidia have expanded their partnership to enable the industrial metaverse by connecting the Xcelerator and Omniverse platforms [76]. In addition, technology companies such as Lenovo, Huawei, HTC, Tencent, and Alibaba, as well as numerous startups, are exploring how to apply the industrial metaverse in their businesses [77].

2.8. Extended Reality, Metaverse, and Digital Twins to Reality

The combination of the industrial metaverse, DTs, and robotics is still quite a new research area. The main focus of research is driven more by VR than by the metaverse. The metaverse received much publicity during and after the pandemic, and as shown above, it has received much visibility in business forecasts. VR, DTs, and robotics were studied, for example, in welding as a platform for interactive human–robot welding and welder behavior analysis [78] and in BCI as a brain-controlled robotic arm system for achieving tasks in three-dimensional environments [79].

The metaverse has enabled co-design while reducing the communication load in real-world robotic arms and the context of their digital models [80]. In addition, in metaverse-, DT-, and robotics-related studies, a basic meta-universe simulation implementation method for the scene of an industrial robot was introduced in [81], and a multi-agent reinforcement learning solution was defined to bridge the reality gap in dynamic and uncertain metaverse systems [82]. Recent advances in artificial intelligence (AI), computing, and sensing technologies have also enabled the development of some DT applications in the underwater domain, such as in intelligent path planning and autonomous vehicle prototyping [83–85].

3. Materials and Methods

This section presents the research approach and the methods used. The use cases that are presented follow a constructive research approach, aiming to solve practical problems by developing entities [86,87]. Since the research questions presented are practically relevant and the aim is to develop prototypes to create a foundation for use cases, the constructive approach supports the answering of the research questions.

The main phases were conceptualization, development, and preliminary validation. The research questions and the review of previous research led to the conceptualization of the following statement: *To enable the control of production systems by using the metaverse, DTs and XR are required.* In the development phase, prototypes based on the aforementioned conceptualization were created, and they are presented in the Section 4. Figure 1 presents the main phases and methods utilized.

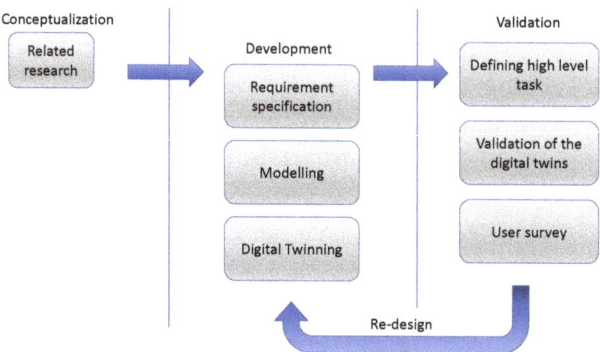

Figure 1. Methods used in the development of the presented use cases.

3.1. Requirement Specifications

The requirement specifications were drafted for the prototypes according to the IEEE Recommended Practice for Software Requirement Specifications [88] to define their functional and non-functional requirements. The functional requirements were an essential guideline during the implementation and preliminary validation phases of the prototypes. The non-functional requirements were divided into the usability, security, and performance subcategories and are presented in Table 1.

Table 1. Functional and non-functional requirements.

ID	Description	Category
F1	Digital twins of the physical robotic systems exist and enable user interaction.	Functional
F2	A user can register for the platform by using an email address.	Functional
F3	A social forum is available for the users to request help or advice on the platform's usage.	Functional
F4	Digital education material can be stored on, accessed in, and downloaded from the system by users.	Functional
F5	An extended-reality user interface is supported.	Functional
F6	Support for multiple simultaneous users.	Functional
N1	The system's focus is on robotics.	Usability
N2	Cross-platform support.	Usability
N3	Authentication of users and encryption of data	Cybersecurity
N4	Updates or upgrades of the prototype do not require end-user actions.	Usability
N5	Exercises are virtual experiences.	Usability
N6	The user can control and program physical robots.	Usability
N7	Latency of controlling a physical system of less than 250 ms.	Performance

3.2. Modeling of the Virtual Environment

An industrial-grade three-dimensional scanner was used to form three-dimensional models of larger entities, such as Centria's Robo3D Lab at Ylivieska and the harbor environment in Turku, Finland. Point clouds were imported into Blender to create digital copies of the environments by extruding features such as walls and shaping the terrains by using the point clouds as templates. Digital versions of robots, forklifts, and other production machinery were acquired from the ROS [89] and OEM manufacturer libraries. Missing items, such as custom gripper jaws and pick-and-place objects, were manually modeled by using Blender. The models contained the kinematic information of the robots' mechanic structure, and inverse kinematics were used to create virtual robot assemblies with physical constraints that were equivalent to those of physical robots. The models were also textured by utilizing Blender before exporting them to Unity. Furthermore, the final WebXR binaries were compiled by using Unity.

Regarding the prototype developed in Section 4.2, the BlueSim [90] simulator was utilized as a virtual environment to control the robot. The software-in-the-loop approach (SIL) was used to simulate the BlueROV2 hardware. A prototype was created to convert a commercial diving mask and smartphone into an HMD. The design process of a specially designed control device involved three-dimensional laser scanning, and the casing was designed by utilizing Blender.

3.3. Validation of the Prototypes

The prototypes were validated by defining high-level tasks for the robot stations. The high-level tasks were specific to the robot type in question, and if the task could not be completed, the task was failed. If the task was failed, the prototype was redesigned and developed until the task could be completed. Small groups of developers and students performed preliminary validations of the use cases. The high-level tasks that were defined are described in Section 4.

After the preliminary validation, piloting and a user survey were conducted to collect user feedback. The feedback collection was conducted as an online survey since it was easy to distribute to the students that participated in lectures online. In addition, online surveys are easy to complete, and it is possible to automatically summarize their results [91].

3.4. Cybersecurity Assessment

In the use cases that are presented, the methods for assessing cybersecurity were authorization, authentication, encryption, and vulnerability scans [92]. Authentication and authorization services were implemented on a cloud server. Encryption was implemented by using CA certificates on data transfers between the robot, the cloud server, and the client device. The cloud server was periodically scanned to detect vulnerable software on the server. The methods for solving the detected cybersecurity issues were reconfiguring and updating vulnerable software components.

4. Implementation and Validation of Use Cases

In this section, the implementations of the use cases are presented. All of the presented use cases provide additional functionality over traditional virtual representations. First, we will present Probot's implementation of DT and XR to teleoperate an arm robot installed on a mobile platform. The second use case presents FIU's testbed for controlling and twinning an ROV. Furthermore, a unique method for translating a teleoperator's body movements to control commands for an ROV is presented. Centria's implementation of a virtual robotic training platform is presented in the third use case. In addition to enabling the user to teleoperate connected physical robots, multiuser capability and social aspects of the metaverse are presented. The fourth use case presents the TUAS social VR platform, which enables training and education in robotic aspects in the maritime sector. In addition to twinning the robots, harbor machines, such as forklifts, are included.

4.1. Probot's Extended-Reality Interface for Future Industrial Robotics

Over the last decade, the amount of data collected in industrial processes has significantly increased. Furthermore, the application of new technologies, such as drones, mobile robots, and service robots, requires advanced user interfaces for control. Probot developed advanced user interfaces to provide solutions for presenting data from industrial processes and to control advanced robots by utilizing XR and DTs.

In the MIMIC project [93], an eight-month project funded by the RIMA [94], a DT of an arm robot installed on a mobile robot was created. The DT enabled the user to teleoperate a mobile manipulator by using a VR user interface and a specially developed glove that tracked the position of the user's hand and sensed the positions of the user's fingers. The aforementioned data were translated into the control commands for the manipulator. VE was implemented by using the Unreal Engine, and the communication layer was based on a custom socket-based protocol. Figure 2 presents the prototype's setup.

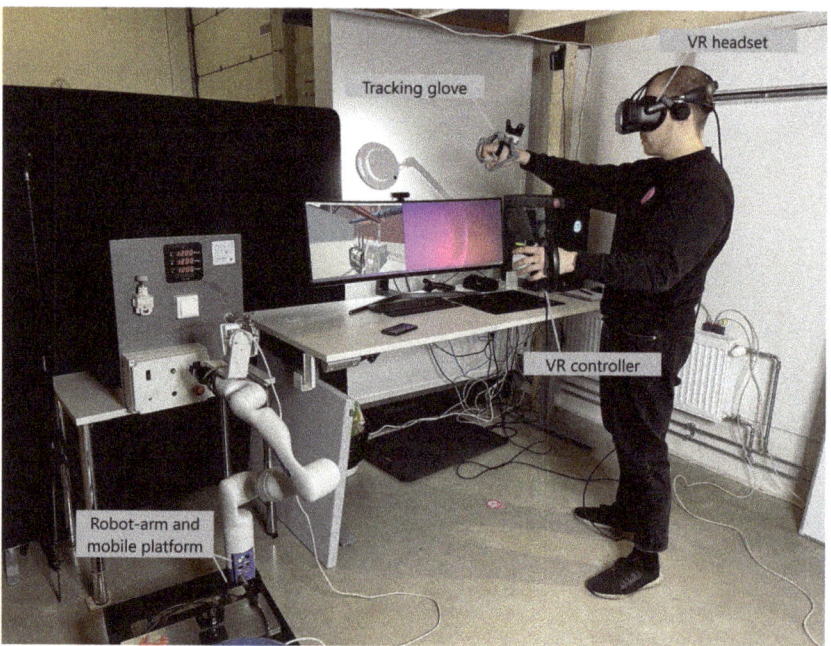

Figure 2. The setup of the MIMIC demonstration.

The focus during research and development was on user comfort and the efficiency of the teleoperation. Probot developed two control methods for teleoperating the robot: ghost and direct control. In ghost control, the user set the target position for the ghost robot and enabled movement with the controller button. After the target was validated as collision-free and within the joint limits, the target was commissioned for the physical robot. In direct control, the physical robot instantly followed the DT's movements in near-real time. Figure 3 shows a view of the VR user interface for teleoperation.

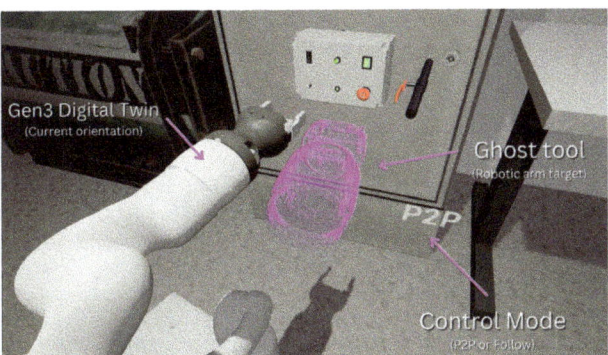

Figure 3. The DT view of the demonstration of teleoperation in MIMIC.

To validate the system and to compare the two control methods, Probot arranged testing sessions. During the testing, employees who were familiar with robot teleoperation and XR utilized the developed prototype to grasp and manipulate objects. During the preliminary validation, it was noted that the direct control method posed latency issues related to constantly sending position messages between the DT and the physical robot. The latency caused delays in the control and had a negative impact on the user experience. Furthermore, if the user controlled the DT at a high velocity, the positions of the digital and physical twins did not match.

The ghost control method minimized the data transfers between the DT and the physical robot. Furthermore, the ghost control mode enabled the DT to validate the trajectories before they were committed to the physical robot. While the direct control method enabled a natural way to move the robot by using the DT, the aforementioned latency and in-position control loop issues resulted in a poor user experience. The participants in the testing demonstration agreed that the ability to accurately set the robot's position before committing to physical robots in the ghost control mode enabled more accurate and comfortable control of the manipulator compared to direct control.

4.2. FIU's Robotics Testbed for Teleoperation in Environments with Sensing and Communication Challenges

In our recent work [95], we introduced an optimization-based framework for designing human–robot interfaces that comply with user comfort and efficiency constraints. Additionally, we proposed a new approach to teleoperating a remotely operated underwater vehicle, which involved capturing and translating movements of the human body into control commands for the ROV.

The VE in this use case was the BlueSim [90] simulator, which was compiled by using the Godot engine [52,53]. The communication layer between the simulator and the real environment enabled the connection of the virtual and physical ROVs. A software-in-the-loop (SIL) approach was used to simulate the BlueROV2 hardware for testing and refinement during our development work. Figure 4 presents the virtual and physical environments and the communication layer between the DT and the physical ROV. A customized smartphone case was created to capture and translate body movements into ROV control commands to turn a commercial diving mask and smartphone into an HMD. The design process involved a three-dimensional laser scanner that extracted the mask's point cloud data, which were then used to design the casing in 3D-CAD SolidWorks.

To access orientation and pressure data from the smartphone's inertial measurement unit (IMU), we utilized the Sensorstream IMU+GPS application [96], which streamed the data to the UDP port of the teleoperator's workstation. In addition, an application based on OpenCV was created to process the virtual underwater video stream and send only black-and-white images for the teleoperator to save bandwidth. Finally, a Python script was developed to receive this sensor data stream and translate it into directional commands for the ROV and up-and-down commands for the ROV camera. Figure 4 presents the current development of a DT for the BlueROV2 [97], an open-source ROV platform for underwater navigation and exploration. On the virtual side, we used a high-fidelity model of a simulated BlueROV2 in a simulated pool. On the physical side, we will use the real BlueROV2 in FIU's testbed.

To validate our system's feasibility, usability, and performance, we created a prototype as a proof of concept; we conducted a study with human subjects by using the prototype to send commands to an ROV that was simulated in a virtual environment. Figure 5 presents the experimental procedure, which involved three tasks. Firstly, users were given a simulated scenario of an empty pool and were allowed 3 min to become accustomed to the HMD and simulator. Secondly, users were presented with an RGB video stream from the front camera of the simulated robot, and they needed to locate a cubic shape in the pool by directing the camera toward it. Because the underwater environment presented significant limitations in terms of data communication and because humans possess an innate skill for interpreting and comprehending meaning and shapes, even in low-quality images, the third task provided users with a black-and-white video stream of the pool and asked them to locate an oval shape. This time, the oval shape was located in one corner of the pool, while the cubic shape was located in another.

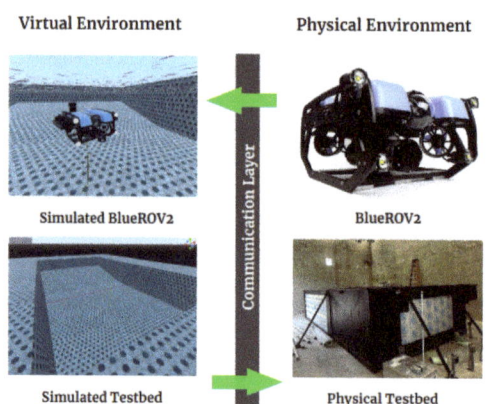

Figure 4. Virtual and physical underwater environments for enabling digital twinning applications.

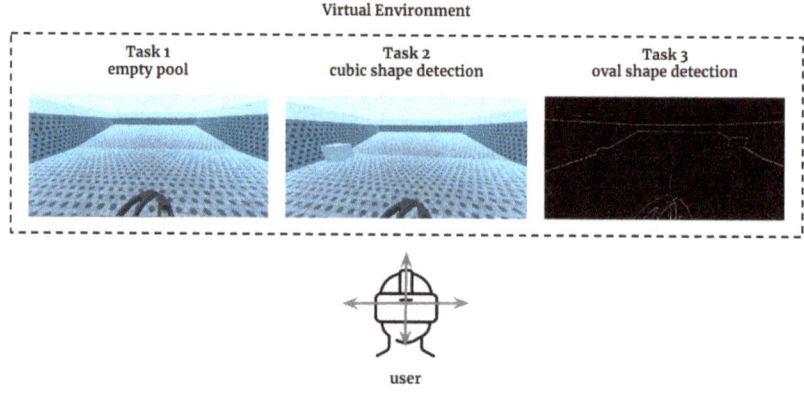

Figure 5. Experimental setup: The RGB video stream was first displayed on the user's HMD for familiarization with the virtual environment (task 1) and then displayed for task 2, and a modified video stream was provided for teleoperation task 3 [95].

User feedback was collected after the experiments. The users reported that it would be more comfortable to use the custom HMD if the distance between the eyes and the smartphone was increased. This would allow for a better field of view and reduce eye strain. Furthermore, our experiments indicated that slow communication, which resulted in laggy image updates on the smartphone screen, could significantly increase the time it took to complete tasks. This was because users needed to wait for the images to be updated before proceeding with their tasks.

4.3. Centria's Extended Reality as a Robotic Training Tool

Centria created an online platform for education and training in robotics. The platform enabled students to learn robotics by reading online materials, watching instructional videos, and conducting practical exercises. Currently, collaborative and industrial robot types are available on the platform for students to practice their robotic skills. Students can conduct exercises by reserving a free time slot for a specific robot type and accessing the provided link at a specific time to access the virtual user interface and the DT of the robot. XR training scenarios are implemented by using the Unity game engine, and the digital models of the robots and environments were created by using Blender. To enable cross-platform compatibility, runtimes are compiled as WebXR binaries that are available online and accessible using mobile or desktop devices.

The bi-directional communication layer that synchronizes the states of digital and physical twins is based on the MQTT communication protocol, which runs on Websockets [98]. XR web applications utilize a Websocket to publish and subscribe to MQTT topics on the cloud server's MQTT broker. The communication layer enables the monitoring and control of the robots that are connected to the platform. The joint and cartesian positions of each articulated robot and the mobile robot's spatial x, y, and z locations are published on the message broker on the cloud server. The method for controlling the robots is similar to the ghost control described earlier in Section 4.1.

WebRTC provides a near-real-time video stream of the physical robots to the user. The cloud server manages the congestion control to maintain the low latency of the video stream, while the actual video stream data are cast directly to clients. In the Robo3D Lab, a local server is set up to host the WebRTC clients that are streaming the video and to connect the cameras to the platform. Figure 6 presents the architecture of the cloud-based platform.

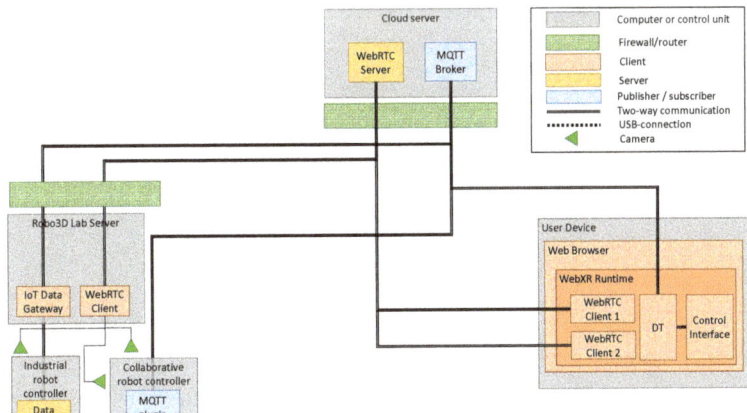

Figure 6. The architecture of Centria's online platform [99].

DTs on the platform enable the user to interact with physical robots by moving a robot's TCP. The DTs are based on three-dimensional models of robots, including a kinematic model created by using Blender. In Unity, inverse and forward kinematic algorithms based on the Jacobian matrix and the Denavit–Hartenberg convention are used to calculate the joint positions based on the requested tool-center-point (TCP) position and to calculate the TCP position based on the joint values [100,101]. The algorithm for validating the trajectories for articulated arm robots is presented in pseudocode in Algorithm 1. In addition to kinematic limitations, the DTs utilize the Unity physics engine to calculate and validate only collision-free trajectories.

A user can join the platform in immersive mode by using a VR headset or in desktop mode by using a desktop computer or a mobile device. In VR mode, handheld controllers are used to interact with the VE; in desktop mode, two virtual joysticks are provided to interact with the environment. Each of the users is presented as an avatar in the virtual environment. To enable a multi-user system, the spatial locations of the avatars are centrally synchronized among the players. Synchronization of the avatars' locations is implemented by utilizing the communication layer described in the previous section.

The feedback collection was conducted during a "construction robotics" course. The participating students were a group of ten students studying at the University of Oulu. The students had no prior experience in controlling or programming robots. The feedback for pre-defined questions in the form of "yes or no" options was collected after conducting online lectures and teleoperating the robots on the platform. Sixty percent of the students considered the platform suitable for learning the basics and programming of robots. Seventy percent considered the platform suitable for monitoring remote robot cells, and all considered the platform suitable for debugging existing robot programs. Figure 7 presents the XR robotic training environment.

Algorithm 1 Inverse Kinematics.

Require: requested position, requested pose, lower and higher thresholds for joint values, τ_L and τ_H, respectively.
    counter = 0
    while counter < 100 **do**
        calculate Jacobian inverse matrix;
        calculate joint angles and position deviation;
        if joint angles < τ_L OR joint angles > τ_H OR position deviation > 1e-3 **then**
            counter++;
        else
            move physical twin;
            break;
        end if
    end while

Figure 7. Multi-user XR robotic training session with a video stream of a physical robot.

4.4. TUAS VR Social Platform

Turku University of Applied Sciences developed a metaverse technology called the TUAS VR Social Platform, which combines several- or multi-user environments into a unified, seamless platform that enables the visualization of big data and remote control solutions. This platform consists of features for social communication, hands-on experience, and DT integration [102]. Social communication and hands-on experience enable collaborative training in the maritime sector, such as in operating forklifts in harbor environments, as presented in Figure 8.

The multi-user environments that have been developed can also consist of DTs with specific functionalities that can be integrated into the platform. The customizable application programming interface (API) support of the platform enables the coupling of the DTs with physical machinery and equipment, thus providing access to the functionality of physical systems. In the design of the TUAS VR Social Platform, the data privacy protection concerns highlighted by Kang et al. [6] were taken into account. The platform provides identity, authenticity, and authority services for industrial training, planning, and operations, such as in the teleoperation of systems. Figure 8 presents the log-in screen and the VE.

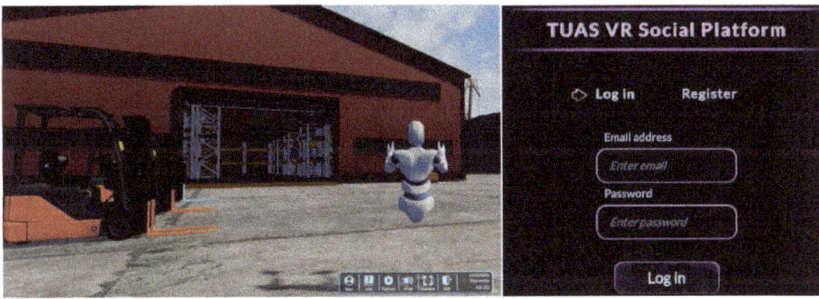

Figure 8. Multi-user environments enabling collaborative training and user validation.

In the teleoperation prototype, we aimed to create a self-contained system for teleoperating robots by using VR as the user interface based on previous work on this type of system [103]. Creating a DT of a physical robot is essential for providing a realistic user experience. A low-latency communication layer between the digital and physical twins was implemented by using the MQTT protocol. WebRTC enabled the streaming of the video of the physical robot to the VE with low latency.

To create the VE, the Turku University of Applied Sciences robotics laboratory was scanned by utilizing a laser scanner to enable a matching virtual environment for an unmanned ground vehicle (UGV). The system's control was developed to support cross-platform VR controllers and position updating of the DT by using an accelerometer. The digital models and texturing of the DT were improved. In addition, object distance detection was implemented in this phase by utilizing a robot's camera to pick up an object with the robot arm during teleoperation. The simplified architecture of the TUAS platform is presented in Figure 9.

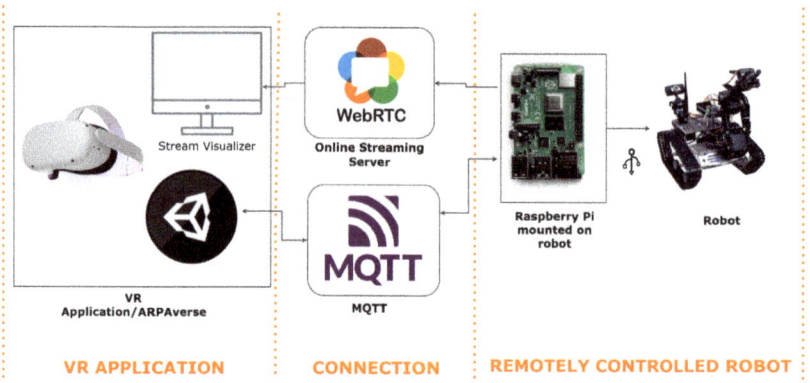

Figure 9. Architecture of the TUAS VR Social Platform.

The implemented teleoperation application comprises a physical robot, a VR user interface, and a DT connecting the two. The application was designed to be modular, thus enabling the merging of parts of the solution into already existing projects. The developed features mentioned above were merged into the industrial metaverse environment by adding the DTs of the robots and the laboratory into the existing metaverse environment.

This implementation allows any user of this collaborative training environment to take control of a physical robot and to move the robot around the laboratory by utilizing the feedback and control of the DT and the live video stream from the physical environment. At the end of this first pilot case, we validated the system by utilizing high-level gripping and moving tasks to prove the low latency of teleoperation and video streaming. Figure 10 presents the virtual environment for teleoperation and the VR devices utilized.

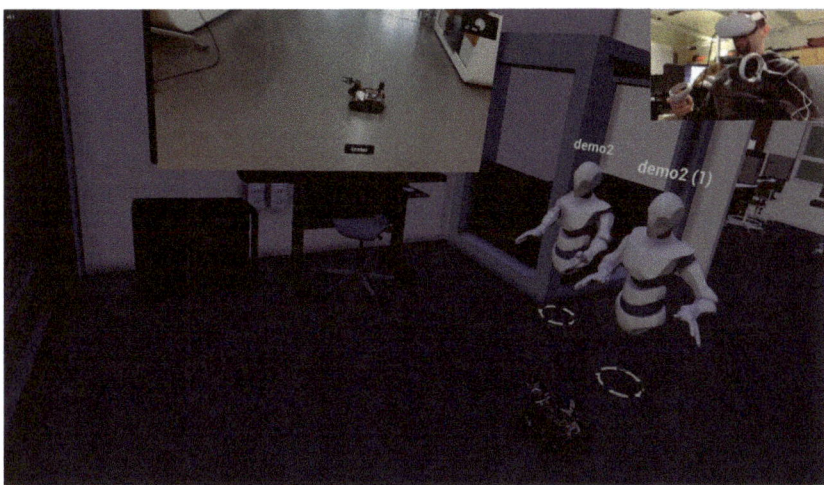

Figure 10. Visualization of the teleoperation of the robot, the video stream of the physical laboratory, the VR headset, and the smart gloves.

To ascertain our system's usability, usefulness, and effectiveness, staff members of the research group piloted the developed system and provided feedback on its usability. A high-level task was defined for the teleoperated robot to validate the DT. The defined task required the user to pick up a cardboard cube and place it in a different location by using the robot arm.

The test was considered successful if the users could complete the task, which would indicate that the system was accurate, effective, and usable. In addition to the control efficiency and latency, the video stream's latency was evaluated. According to the user feedback, the latencies observed did not significantly affect the user experience. Approximately seventy percent of users reported that the system was usable and precise enough for the teleoperation of a UGV and robot arm. The piloting users suggested the addition of a diagram of each controller's button function in the VE and the improvement of the DT's accuracy for larger movements. The feedback was taken into account to improve the DT in the future.

5. Discussion

This paper presented the implementations of four DTs that enable the control of physical systems by using XR technologies. All use cases were *extended reality–digital twin to real* implementations where data validation and two-way data transmission between the twins were implemented as part of the process. Our study showed that remotely connected systems that enable an industrial metaverse can be built by using currently available tools.

The first use case showed an implementation of robot trajectory programming by utilizing a combination of VR and a haptic glove. A DT of a mobile robot equipped with a robot arm was controlled in a VR environment. The second use case was an implementation of a DT for ROVs controlled in VR. The VR was implemented by using a designed and manufactured HMD based on a smartphone. The ROV could be controlled by following a person's head movements, and an enhanced live stream of the ROV was displayed on the HMD. Both use cases enabled a realistic and natural way for the teleoperator to control the devices by using the user's head movements or finger tracking. By using these high-level control interfaces, users can interact with the environment by utilizing DTs.

The third and fourth use cases were implementations of a multi-agent VR environment with multiple DTs connected to mobile, collaborative, and industrial robots. Users could teleoperate physical robots in a VR environment. In addition, the use cases enabled social interaction and collaborative training. These use cases enabled location- and time-independent training and collaboration, making them more realistic and natural than single-user virtual environments.

The research questions set for the work are the following: Can DTs and XR enable the digital workplaces required by the industrial metaverse? Are virtual learning environments enabled by utilizing the aforementioned combinations of technologies?

With the achieved results, it was proven that digital workplaces, which are required by the industrial metaverse, can be implemented by using DTs and XR—to some extent. Depending on the nature of the work and the operator's experience level, other ways of working, such as audio control, may be more flexible and faster. However, it must be noted that different ways of working have pros and cons; e.g., audio control is vulnerable to noise and raises severe concerns related to safety and cybersecurity. Additional haptic devices can make the experience more real with the feedback provided by the real world.

At its current stage, the proposed system is suitable for virtual learning and training. Through the experience that has been gained, it is possible that the proposed systems can be used in industrial use cases, assuming that users are comfortable and familiar with the systems and knows their restrictions. The new generation of digital natives might find these systems to be natural ways of interacting with the physical world.

6. Conclusions

In this publication, four use cases that utilized XR and DTs to control robotic systems were presented and discussed to answer the research questions. In conclusion, the usefulness of DTs and XR depends greatly on the nature of the work and the operator's experience level. It must be noted that virtual learning by utilizing DTs is a natural learning method, especially for the digital native generation. In some cases, other methods, such as voice control, are more feasible for controlling systems.

The proposed approach can be further enhanced for user-assisted autonomous systems. With additional modules that enable them to learn, such as reinforcement learning, the proposed systems can learn various skills, such as robotized assembly or machining. Such systems can offer alternative methods for operators to perform tasks more efficiently. Although the presented use cases were small-scale demonstrations, the use cases can be replicated and scaled for more complex and physically larger systems.

In the future, more comprehensive feedback from users is required; in this paper, only small groups of developers and students participated in the piloting and surveys. By exposing the systems to larger audiences, they can be improved to meet the demanding requirements of real industrial applications. Studies that differentiate among utility, usability, and user experience in industrial environments provide feedback on systems' feasibility. In addition, an automated online feedback system that is integrated into the platform can enable comprehensive feedback collection.

Author Contributions: Conceptualization, T.K., P.P., V.B.B., and M.T.; methodology, T.K. and V.B.B.; software, T.K, P.P., V.B.B., and M.T.; validation T.K., P.P., V.B.B., and M.T.; investigation, T.K.; data curation, T.K. and T.P.; writing—original draft preparation, T.K., N.L., T.H., V.B.B., and M.T.; writing—review and editing, T.P. and S.P.; visualization, T.K, V.B.B., N.L., and M.T.; supervision, S.P., L.B. and M.L.; project administration, T.K. All authors have read and agreed to the published version of the manuscript.

Funding: This research was funded by the European Research Council (ERC) under the European Union's Horizon 2020 Research and Innovation Program (grant agreements n° 825196 and n° 824990). Support was also received through the NSF grants IIS-2034123 and IIS-2024733, the U.S. Department of Homeland Security grant 2017-ST-062000002, and the Finnish Ministry of Education and Culture under the research profile for funding for the project "Applied Research Platform for Autonomous Systems" (diary number OKM/8/524/2020).

Institutional Review Board Statement: Not applicable.

Informed Consent Statement: Not applicable.

Data Availability Statement: Not applicable.

Conflicts of Interest: The authors declare no conflict of interest.

References

1. Rideout, V.; Foehr, U.; Roberts, D. GENERATION M2 Media in the Lives of 8- to 18-Year-Olds. 2010. Available online: https://files.eric.ed.gov/fulltext/ED527859.pdf (accessed on 13 April 2023).
2. Lee, H.J.; Gu, H.H. Empirical Research on the Metaverse User Experience of Digital Natives. *Sustainability* **2022**, *14*, 14747. [CrossRef]
3. Mystakidis, S. Metaverse. *Encyclopedia* **2022**, *2*, 486–497. [CrossRef]
4. Barnes, A. Metaverse in Gaming: Revolution in Gaming Industry with Next-Generation Experience. 2023. Available online: https://www.datasciencecentral.com/metaverse-in-gaming-revolution-in-gaming-industry-with-next-generation-experience/ (accessed on 13 April 2023).
5. Lee, J.; Kundu, P. Integrated cyber-physical systems and industrial metaverse for remote manufacturing. *Manuf. Lett.* **2022**, *34*, 12–15. [CrossRef]
6. Kang, J.; Ye, D.; Nie, J.; Xiao, J.; Deng, X.; Wang, S.; Xiong, Z.; Yu, R.; Niyato, D. Blockchain-based Federated Learning for Industrial Metaverses: Incentive Scheme with Optimal AoI. In Proceedings of the 2022 IEEE International Conference on Blockchain (Blockchain), Espoo, Finland, 22–25 August 2022; pp. 71–78. [CrossRef]
7. Francis, T.; Pearson, R.; Robertson, A.; Hodgson, M.; Dutka, A.; Flynn, E. Central nervous system decompression sickness: Latency of 1070 human cases. *Undersea Biomed. Res.* **1988**, *15*, 403–417. [PubMed]
8. Miranda, J.; Navarrete, C.; Noguez, J.; Molina-Espinosa, J.M.; Ramírez-Montoya, M.S.; Navarro-Tuch, S.A.; Bustamante-Bello, M.R.; Rosas-Fernández, J.B.; Molina, A. The core components of education 4.0 in higher education: Three case studies in engineering education. *Comput. I Electr. Eng.* **2021**, *93*, 107278. [CrossRef]
9. Prensky, M. Digital Natives, Digital Immigrants. 2001. Available online: https://www.marcprensky.com/writing/Prensky%20-%20Digital%20Natives,%20Digital%20Immigrants%20-%20Part1.pdf (accessed on 15 April 2023).
10. Kritzinger, W.; Karner, M.; Traar, G.; Henjes, J.; Sihn, W. Digital Twin in manufacturing: A categorical literature review and classification. *IFAC-PapersOnLine* **2018**, *51*, 1016–1022. [CrossRef]
11. Grieves, M. *Origins of the Digital Twin Concept*; Florida Institute of Technology: Melbourne, FL, USA, 2016; Volume 8, [CrossRef]
12. Burdea, G. Invited review: The synergy between virtual reality and robotics. *IEEE Trans. Robot. Autom.* **1999**, *15*, 400–410. [CrossRef]
13. Milgram, P.; Kishino, F. A Taxonomy of Mixed Reality Visual Displays. *IEICE Trans. Inf. Syst.* **1994**, *E77-D*, 1321–1329.
14. Sutherland, I.E. A Head-Mounted Three Dimensional Display. In Proceedings of the Fall Joint Computer Conference, Part I, New York, NY, USA, 9–11 December 1968; AFIPS'68 (Fall, part I), pp. 757–764. [CrossRef]
15. Heilig, M.L. Sensorama Simulator. U.S. Patent 3050870A, 10 January 1961.
16. Kawamoto, H. The history of liquid-crystal display and its industry. In Proceedings of the 2012 Third IEEE History of Electro-Technology Conference (HISTELCON), Pavia, Italy, 5–7 September 2012; pp. 1–6. [CrossRef]
17. Howlett, E.M. Wide Angle Color Photography Method and System. U.S. Patent 4406532A, 27 September 1983.
18. Siciliano, B.; Khatib, O. *Springer Handbook of Robotics*; Springer: Berlin/Heidelberg, Germany, 2007.
19. Wilson, E.; Evans, C.J. Method of Controlling Mechanism by Means of Electric or Electromagnetic Waves of High Frequency. U.S. Patent 663400A, 4 December 1900.
20. Hammond, J.H.; Purington, E.S. A History of Some Foundations of Modern Radio-Electronic Technology. *Proc. IRE* **1957**, *45*, 1191–1208. [CrossRef]
21. Ferrell, W.R.; Sheridan, T.B. Supervisory control of remote manipulation. *IEEE Spectr.* **1967**, *4*, 81–88. [CrossRef]
22. Sheridan, T. Teleoperation, telerobotics and telepresence: A progress report. *Control. Eng. Pract.* **1995**, *3*, 205–214. [CrossRef]
23. Goertz, R.C. Fundamentals of general-purpose remote manipulators. *Nucleon. (U.S.) Ceased Publ.* **1952**, *10*, 36–42.
24. Kim, W.; Liu, A.; Matsunaga, K.; Stark, L. A helmet mounted display for telerobotics. In Proceedings of the Digest of Papers. COMPCON Spring 88 Thirty-Third IEEE Computer Society International Conference, San Francisco, CA, USA, 29 February–3 March 1988; pp. 543–547. [CrossRef]
25. Marescaux, J. Nom de code: « Opération Lindbergh ». *Ann. Chir.* **2002**, *127*, 2–4. [CrossRef] [PubMed]
26. Laaki, H.; Miche, Y.; Tammi, K. Prototyping a Digital Twin for Real Time Remote Control Over Mobile Networks: Application of Remote Surgery. *IEEE Access* **2019**, *7*, 20325–20336. [CrossRef]
27. González, C.; Solanes, J.E.; Muñoz, A.; Gracia, L.; Girbés-Juan, V.; Tornero, J. Advanced teleoperation and control system for industrial robots based on augmented virtuality and haptic feedback. *J. Manuf. Syst.* **2021**, *59*, 283–298. [CrossRef]
28. Duan, B.; Xiong, L.; Guan, X.; Fu, Y.; Zhang, Y. Tele-operated robotic ultrasound system for medical diagnosis. *Biomed. Signal Process. Control* **2021**, *70*, 102900. [CrossRef]
29. Caiza, G.; Garcia, C.A.; Naranjo, J.E.; Garcia, M.V. Flexible robotic teleoperation architecture for intelligent oil fields. *Heliyon* **2020**, *6*, e03833. [CrossRef] [PubMed]
30. IBM. Transcript of IBM Podcast. 2011. Available online: https://www.ibm.com/podcasts/software/websphere/connectivity/piper_diaz_nipper_mq_tt_11182011.pdf (accessed on 22 February 2022).

31. Terracciano, D.S.; Bazzarello, L.; Caiti, A.; Costanzi, R.; Manzari, V. Marine Robots for Underwater Surveillance. *Curr. Robot. Rep.* **2020**, *1*, 159–167. [CrossRef]
32. Quattrini Li, A.; Rekleitis, I.; Manjanna, S.; Kakodkar, N.; Hansen, J.; Dudek, G.; Bobadilla, L.; Anderson, J.; Smith, R.N. Data correlation and comparison from multiple sensors over a coral reef with a team of heterogeneous aquatic robots. In Proceedings of the International Symposium on Experimental Robotics, Nagasaki, Japan, 3–8 October 2016; Springer: Berlin/Heidelberg, Germany, 2016; pp. 717–728.
33. Shukla, A.; Karki, H. Application of robotics in offshore oil and gas industry—A review Part II. *Robot. Auton. Syst.* **2015**, *75*, 508–524. [CrossRef]
34. Zereik, E.; Bibuli, M.; Mišković, N.; Ridao, P.; Pascoal, A. Challenges and future trends in marine robotics. *Annu. Rev. Control* **2018**, *46*, 350–368. [CrossRef]
35. Domingues, C.; Essabbah, M.; Cheaib, N.; Otmane, S.; Dinis, A. Human-robot-interfaces based on mixed reality for underwater robot teleoperation. *IFAC Proc. Vol.* **2012**, *45*, 212–215. [CrossRef]
36. Chen, J.Y.C.; Haas, E.C.; Barnes, M.J. Human Performance Issues and User Interface Design for Teleoperated Robots. *IEEE Trans. Syst. Man, Cybern. Part C (Appl. Rev.)* **2007**, *37*, 1231–1245. [CrossRef]
37. Becerra, I.; Suomalainen, M.; Lozano, E.; Mimnaugh, K.J.; Murrieta-Cid, R.; LaValle, S.M. Human Perception-Optimized Planning for Comfortable VR-Based Telepresence. *IEEE Robot. Autom. Lett.* **2020**, *5*, 6489–6496. [CrossRef]
38. Hauser, K. Design of Optimal Robot User Interfaces. In Proceedings of the Workshop on Progress and Open Problems in Motion Planning, 2014 IEEE International Conference on Robotics and Automation (ICRA), Hong Kong, China, 31 May–7 June 2014.
39. Rosen, R.; von Wichert, G.; Lo, G.; Bettenhausen, K.D. About The Importance of Autonomy and Digital Twins for the Future of Manufacturing. *IFAC-PapersOnLine* **2015**, *48*, 567–572.
40. Gomez, F. AI-Driven Digital Twins and the Future of Smart Manufacturing. 2021. Available online: https://www.machinedesign.com/automation-iiot/article/21170513/aidriven-digital-twins-and-the-future-of-smart-manufacturing (accessed on 8 April 2023).
41. Lv, Z.; Qiao, L.; Mardani, A.; Lv, H. Digital Twins on the Resilience of Supply Chain Under COVID-19 Pandemic. *IEEE Trans. Eng. Manag.* **2022**, 1–12. [CrossRef]
42. Nokia Oyj. How Digital Twins Are Driving the Future of Engineering. 2021. Available online: https://www.nokia.com/networks/insights/technology/how-digital-twins-driving-future-of-engineering/ (accessed on 8 April 2023).
43. Grieves, M. Excerpt from Forthcoming Paper Intelligent Digital Twins and the Development and Management of Complex Systems the "Digital Twin Exists ONLY after There Is A Physical Product" Fallacy. 2021. Available online: https://www.researchgate.net/publication/350822924_Excerpt_From_Forthcoming_Paper_Intelligent_Digital_Twins_and_the_Development_and_Management_of_Complex_Systems_The_Digital_Twin_Exists_ONLY_After_There_Is_A_Physical_Product_Fallacy (accessed on 15 April 2023).
44. Digital Twin Consortium. Glossary of Digital Twins. 2021. Available online: https://www.digitaltwinconsortium.org/glossary/glossary.html#digital-twin (accessed on 15 April 2023).
45. *ISO 23247-1:2021*; Automation Systems and Integration—Digital Twin Framework for Manufacturing—Part 1: Overview and General Principles. International Organization for Standardization: Geneva, Switzerland, 2000.
46. Krueger, M.W. Responsive Environments. In Proceedings of the National Computer Conference, New York, NY, USA, 13–16 June 1977; AFIPS'77, pp. 423–433. [CrossRef]
47. Qadri, M.; Hussain, M.; Jawed, S.; Iftikhar, S.A. Virtual Tourism Using Samsung Gear VR Headset. In Proceedings of the 2019 International Conference on Information Science and Communication Technology (ICISCT), Karachi, Pakistan, 9–10 March 2019; pp. 1–10. [CrossRef]
48. Perla, R.; Gupta, G.; Hebbalaguppe, R.; Hassan, E. InspectAR: An Augmented Reality Inspection Framework for Industry. In Proceedings of the 2016 IEEE International Symposium on Mixed and Augmented Reality (ISMAR-Adjunct), Merida, Mexico, 19–23 September 2016; pp. 355–356. [CrossRef]
49. Maereg, A.; Atulya, N.; David, R.; Emanuele, S. Wearable Vibrotactile Haptic Device for Stiffness Discrimination during Virtual Interactions. *Front. Robot. AI* **2017**, *4*, 42. [CrossRef]
50. Neamoniti, S.; Kasapakis, V. Hand Tracking vs. Motion Controllers: The effects on Immersive Virtual Reality Game Experience. In Proceedings of the 2022 IEEE International Symposium on Multimedia (ISM), Naples, Italy, 5–7 December 2022; pp. 206–207. [CrossRef]
51. Datta, S. Top Game Engines To Learn in 2022. 2022. Available online: https://blog.cloudthat.com/top-game-engines-learn-in-2022/ (accessed on 8 April 2023).
52. Linietsky, J.; Manzur, A. Godot Engine. 2022. Available online: https://github.com/godotengine/godot (accessed on 13 April 2023).
53. Thorn, A. *Moving from Unity to Godot*; Springer: Berlin/Heidelberg, Germany, 2020.
54. Hickson, I.; Hyatt, D. HTML 5. 2008. Available online: https://www.w3.org/TR/2008/WD-html5-20080122/ (accessed on 13 April 2023).
55. Khan, M.Z.; Hashem, M.M.A. A Comparison between HTML5 and OpenGL in Rendering Fractal. In Proceedings of the 2019 International Conference on Electrical, Computer and Communication Engineering (ECCE), Cox'sBazar, Bangladesh, 7–9 February 2019; pp. 1–6. [CrossRef]

56. Unity Technologies. WebAssembly Is Here! Available online: https://blog.unity.com/technology/webassembly-is-here (accessed on 13 April 2023).
57. Peters, E.; Heijligers, B.; Kievith, J.; Razafindrakoto, X.; Oosterhout, R.; Santos, C.; Mayer, I.; Louwerse, M. Design for Collaboration in Mixed Reality Technical Challenges and Solutions. In Proceedings of the 2016 8th International Conference on Games and Virtual Worlds for Serious Applications (VS-GAMES), Barcelona, Spain, 7–9 September 2016. [CrossRef]
58. Epic Games Inc. Accessing Unreal Engine Source Code on GitHub. 2022. Available online: https://www.unrealengine.com/en-US/ue-on-github (accessed on 16 April 2023).
59. Zhang, F.; Lai, C.Y.; Simic, M.; Ding, S. Augmented reality in robot programming. *Procedia Comput. Sci.* **2020**, *176*, 1221–1230. [CrossRef]
60. Abbas, S.M.; Hassan, S.; Yun, J. Augmented reality based teaching pendant for industrial robot. In Proceedings of the 2012 12th International Conference on Control, Automation and Systems, Jeju, Republic of Korea, 17–21 October 2012; pp. 2210–2213.
61. Shu, B.; Arnarson, H.; Solvang, B.; Kaarlela, T.; Pieskä, S. Platform independent interface for programming of industrial robots. In Proceedings of the 2022 IEEE/SICE International Symposium on System Integration (SII), Narvik, Norway, 9–12 January 2022; pp. 797–802. [CrossRef]
62. Togias, T.; Gkournelos, C.; Angelakis, P.; Michalos, G.; Makris, S. Virtual reality environment for industrial robot control and path design. *Procedia CIRP* **2021**, *100*, 133–138. [CrossRef]
63. Lotsaris, K.; Gkournelos, C.; Fousekis, N.; Kousi, N.; Makris, S. AR based robot programming using teaching by demonstration techniques. *Procedia CIRP* **2021**, *97*, 459–463. [CrossRef]
64. Kaarlela, T.; Padrao, P.; Pitkäaho, T.; Pieskä, S.; Bobadilla, L. Digital Twins Utilizing XR-Technology as Robotic Training Tools. *Machines* **2023**, *11*, 13. [CrossRef]
65. Li, X.; He, B.; Wang, Z.; Zhou, Y.; Li, G.; Jiang, R. Semantic-Enhanced Digital Twin System for Robot–Environment Interaction Monitoring. *IEEE Trans. Instrum. Meas.* **2021**, *70*, 7502113. [CrossRef]
66. Alkhafajee, A.R.; Al-Muqarm, A.M.A.; Alwan, A.H.; Mohammed, Z.R. Security and Performance Analysis of MQTT Protocol with TLS in IoT Networks. In Proceedings of the 2021 4th International Iraqi Conference on Engineering Technology and Their Applications (IICETA), Najaf, Iraq, 21–22 September 2021; pp. 206–211. [CrossRef]
67. Jansen, B.; Goodwin, T.; Gupta, V.; Kuipers, F.; Zussman, G. Performance Evaluation of WebRTC-based Video Conferencing. *ACM Sigmetrics Perform. Eval. Rev.* **2018**, *45*, 56–68. [CrossRef]
68. Eltenahy, S.; Fayez, N.; Obayya, M.; Khalifa, F. Comparative Analysis of Resources Utilization in Some Open-Source Videoconferencing Applications based on WebRTC. In Proceedings of the 2021 International Telecommunications Conference (ITC-Egypt), Alexandria, Egypt, 13–15 July 2021; pp. 1–4. [CrossRef]
69. Dionisio, J.D.N.; III, W.G.B.; Gilbert, R. 3D Virtual Worlds and the Metaverse: Current Status and Future Possibilities. *ACM Comput. Surv.* **2013**, *45*, 1–38. [CrossRef]
70. Mystakidis, S.; Berki, E.; Valtanen, J.P. Deep and Meaningful E-Learning with Social Virtual Reality Environments in Higher Education: A Systematic Literature Review. *Appl. Sci.* **2021**, *11*, 2412. [CrossRef]
71. Parisi, T. The Seven Rules of the Metaverse. 2021. Available online: https://medium.com/meta-verses/the-seven-rules-of-the-metaverse-7d4e06fa864c (accessed on 7 April 2023).
72. Kaarlela, T.; Pieskä, S.; Pitkäaho, T. Digital Twin and Virtual Reality for Safety Training. In Proceedings of the 2020 11th IEEE International Conference on Cognitive Infocommunications (CogInfoCom), Mariehamn, Finland, 23–25 September 2020; pp. 115–120. [CrossRef]
73. What Is the Industrial Metaverse—And Why Should I Care? 2022. Available online: https://new.siemens.com/global/en/company/insights/what-is-the-industrial-metaverse-and-why-should-i-care.html (accessed on 7 April 2023).
74. Lundmark, P. The Real Future of the Metaverse Is Not for Consumers. 2022. Available online: https://www.ft.com/content/af0c9de8-d36e-485b-9db5-5ee1e57716cb (accessed on 8 April 2023).
75. Nokia OYj. Metaverse Explained. 2023. Available online: https://www.nokia.com/about-us/newsroom/articles/metaverse-explained/ (accessed on 9 April 2023).
76. Siemens. Siemens and NVIDIA to Enable Industrial Metaverse. 2022. Available online: https://press.siemens.com/global/en/pressrelease/siemens-and-nvidia-partner-enable-industrial-metaverse (accessed on 9 April 2023).
77. MA, SI. Metaverse to Usher in Golden era of Innovation. 2022. Available online: http://www.chinadaily.com.cn/a/202212/19/WS639fba52a31057c47eba5047.html (accessed on 9 April 2023).
78. Wang, Q.; Jiao, W.; Wang, P.; Zhang, Y. Digital Twin for Human-Robot Interactive Welding and Welder Behavior Analysis. *IEEE/CAA J. Autom. Sin.* **2021**, *8*, 334–343. [CrossRef]
79. Jeong, J.H.; Shim, K.H.; Kim, D.J.; Lee, S.W. Brain-Controlled Robotic Arm System Based on Multi-Directional CNN-BiLSTM Network Using EEG Signals. *IEEE Trans. Neural Syst. Rehabil. Eng.* **2020**, *28*, 1226–1238. [CrossRef]
80. Han, D.; Mulyana, B.; Stankovic, V.; Cheng, S. A Survey on Deep Reinforcement Learning Algorithms for Robotic Manipulation. *Sensors* **2023**, *23*, 3762. [CrossRef]
81. Wang, Y.; Wang, C.; Zhang, H. Industrial Robotic Intelligence Simulation in Metaverse Scenes. In Proceedings of the 2022 China Automation Congress (CAC), Xiamen, China, 25–27 November 2022; pp. 1196–1201. [CrossRef]
82. Shi, H.; Liu, G.; Zhang, K.; Zhou, Z.; Wang, J. MARL Sim2real Transfer: Merging Physical Reality with Digital Virtuality in Metaverse. *IEEE Trans. Syst. Man, Cybern. Syst.* **2023**, *53*, 2107–2117. [CrossRef]

83. Yang, J.; Xi, M.; Wen, J.; Li, Y.; Song, H.H. A digital twins enabled underwater intelligent internet vehicle path planning system via reinforcement learning and edge computing. *Digit. Commun. Netw.* 2022, in press. [CrossRef]
84. Yang, M.; Wang, Y.; Wang, C.; Liang, Y.; Yang, S.; Wang, L.; Wang, S. Digital twin-driven industrialization development of underwater gliders. *IEEE Trans. Ind. Inform.* **2023**, 1–11. [CrossRef]
85. Barbie, A.; Pech, N.; Hasselbring, W.; Flögel, S.; Wenzhöfer, F.; Walter, M.; Shchekinova, E.; Busse, M.; Türk, M.; Hofbauer, M.; et al. Developing an Underwater Network of Ocean Observation Systems With Digital Twin Prototypes—A Field Report From the Baltic Sea. *IEEE Internet Comput.* **2022**, *26*, 33–42. [CrossRef]
86. Lukka, K. *The Constructive Research Approach*; Publications of the Turku School of Economics and Business Administration: Turku, Finland, 2003; pp. 83–101.
87. Kasanen, E.; Lukka, K.; Siitonen, A. The constructive approach in management accounting research. *J. Manag. Account. Res.* **1993**, *5*, 243–264.
88. IEEE Std 830-1998; IEEE Recommended Practice for Software Requirements Specifications. IEEE: Piscataway, NJ, USA, 1998; pp. 1–40. [CrossRef]
89. Messmer, F.; Hawkins, K.; Edwards, S.; Glaser, S.; Meeussen, W. Universal Robot. 2019. Available online: https://github.com/ros-industrial/universal_robot (accessed on 8 April 2023).
90. Galvani, W.; Pereira, P. Bluesim. 2023. Available online: https://github.com/bluerobotics/bluesim (accessed on 13 April 2023).
91. Singh, A.; Taneja, A.; Mangalaraj, G. Creating online surveys: Some wisdom from the trenches tutorial. *IEEE Trans. Prof. Commun.* **2009**, *52*, 197–212. [CrossRef]
92. NIST. Guide to Enterprise Telework, Remote Access, and Bring Your Own Device (BYOD) Security. 2016. Available online: https://csrc.nist.gov/publications/detail/sp/800-46/rev-2/final (accessed on 15 April 2023).
93. RIMA. MIMIC (2OC). 2022. Available online: https://community.rimanetwork.eu/6682/MIMIC-2OC (accessed on 17 April 2023).
94. RIMA. RIMA Robotics for Inspection and Maintenance. 2022. Available online: https://rimanetwork.eu/ (accessed on 17 April 2023).
95. Padrao, P.; Fuentes, J.; Kaarlela, T.; Bayuelo, A.; Bobadilla, L. Towards Optimal Human-Robot Interface Design Applied to Underwater Robotics Teleoperation. *arXiv* **2023**, arXiv:2304.02002.
96. Lorenz, A. Sensorstream IMU+GPS. 2023. Available online: https://play.google.com/store/apps/details?id=de.lorenz_fenster.sensorstreamgps (accessed on 21 February 2023).
97. Bluerobotics Inc. BlueROV2. 2023. Available online: https://bluerobotics.com/store/rov/bluerov2/ (accessed on 2 February 2023).
98. The WebSocket Protocol. 2011. Available online: https://www.rfc-editor.org/rfc/rfc6455.html (accessed on 8 April 2023).
99. Kaarlela, T.; Arnarson, H.; Pitkäaho, T.; Shu, B.; Solvang, B.; Pieskä, S. Common Educational Teleoperation Platform for Robotics Utilizing Digital Twins. *Machines* **2022**, *10*, 577. [CrossRef]
100. Craig, J.J. *Introduction to Robotics: Mechanics and Control*; Pearson: London, UK, 2022.
101. Nicolescu, A.; Ilie, F.M.; Tudor George, A. Forward and inverse kinematics study of industrial robots taking into account constructive and functional parameter's modeling. *Proc. Manuf. Syst.* **2015**, *10*, 157.
102. Luimula, M.; Haavisto, T.; Pham, D.; Markopoulos, P.; Aho, J.; Markopoulos, E.; Saarinen, J. The use of metaverse in maritime sector—A combination of social communication, hands on experiencing and digital twins. In Proceedings of the AHFE (2022) International Conference, New York, NY, USA, 24–28 July 2022; AHFE Open Access, Volume 31. [CrossRef]
103. Blanco Bataller, V. Control Remoto de un Brazo Robótico Utilizando Realidad Virtual. Bachelor's Thesis, Universitat Politècnica de València, Valencia, Spain, 2021. Available online: https://riunet.upv.es/handle/10251/176778 (accessed on 17 April 2023).

Disclaimer/Publisher's Note: The statements, opinions and data contained in all publications are solely those of the individual author(s) and contributor(s) and not of MDPI and/or the editor(s). MDPI and/or the editor(s) disclaim responsibility for any injury to people or property resulting from any ideas, methods, instructions or products referred to in the content.

Article

Development of a Deformable Water-Mobile Robot

Changlong Ye, Yang Su, Suyang Yu * and Yinchao Wang

School of Mechatronics Engineering, Shenyang Aerospace University, Shenyang 110136, China; changlye@163.com (C.Y.); su_yang9866@163.com (Y.S.); wangyinchao2008@126.com (Y.W.)
* Correspondence: yu_suyang@163.com

Abstract: This article proposes a deformable water-mobile robot that can be used for rescue work. The robot body adopts an open-motion chain structure with two degrees of freedom, including two drive modules and one main control module. The three modules are connected through deformation joints, and each drive module is equipped with an underwater thruster. The robot can obtain a triangle, linear shape, curved shape, and U-shape through deformation and have three types of motion: linear shape motion, U-shaped motion, and curved shape motion. In the linear shape, a multi-island genetic algorithm was used to optimize the structural parameters with the minimum resistance and the maximum volume. Floating state analysis was conducted in the U-shape, and the structural parameters were reasonably designed. By experimenting with the robot prototype on water, the robot can achieve oscillating, linear, U-shaped, and horizontal rotary motion, has an automatic adjustment function, and effective buoyancy meets the required requirements.

Keywords: water-mobile robot; deformable; genetic algorithm

Citation: Ye, C.; Su, Y.; Yu, S.; Wang, Y. Development of a Deformable Water-Mobile Robot. *Actuators* **2023**, *12*, 202. https://doi.org/10.3390/act12050202

Academic Editors: Ahmad Taher Azar, Amjad J. Humaidi and Ammar K. Al Mhdawi

Received: 13 April 2023
Revised: 10 May 2023
Accepted: 11 May 2023
Published: 12 May 2023

Copyright: © 2023 by the authors. Licensee MDPI, Basel, Switzerland. This article is an open access article distributed under the terms and conditions of the Creative Commons Attribution (CC BY) license (https://creativecommons.org/licenses/by/4.0/).

1. Introduction

The number of people killed due to water disasters has increased in recent years. It is vital to quickly reach the target location and successfully rescue people in the water. At present, manual rescue not only slows response time, but during the rescue of people in distress, due to the complexity and danger of the environment, the rescuers may have safety problems. Many companies and universities at home and abroad have researched water-mobile robots to meet the various needs of water work. With the comprehensive current research status, the water-mobile robot can be divided into traditional and non-traditional hull structures according to the structure. The traditional hull structure is mainly based on the common hull type modification, such as eVe-1 developed by Kim et al. This unmanned boat is a catamaran configuration [1]. Le developed a U-shaped unmanned boat based on the catamaran structure to perform water rescue missions [2]. Zong et al. developed a special trimaran based on the hull structure. This boat was fitted with T-shaped sails to improve sailing performance [3]. Goulon et al. developed an unmanned boat on the water called HARLE, equipped with a fisheries science echosounder for aquatic surveys [4]. Makhsoos et al. developed a water robot called Morvarid by using solar energy as a new source of energy [5]. Morge et al. developed a compact sailboat to take full advantage of wind energy, simplifying traditional sailboats' structure and increasing flexibility [6]. Johnston et al. developed a wave-driven unmanned boat called AutoNaut, which can propel the body forward with alternating waves on the water [7,8]. For non-traditional hull structures, researchers from various countries have mainly used bionics to conduct relevant research [9–13]. Nad et al. developed a water robot consisting of four thrusters. This robot moves more flexibly [14]. Inoue et al. developed a robot called Quince. This robot has various detection devices to detect conditions such as body temperature [15]. Huang et al. developed a buoyancy-supported water strider robot based on the locomotor ability of water striders to achieve water walking capability [16].

The robots of Kim [1] and Zong [3] use a multi-hull structure for traditional hull structures. Such robots increase overall flexibility and stability but have a single structure and large size. The U-shaped unmanned boat developed by Le [2] can achieve rescue but has a high forward resistance due to its structure. Waterborne devices developed by Makhsoos [5], Morge [6], and Johnston [7,8] have been better developed in the energy direction. However, none of these studies proposed a suitable structure in terms of rescue. For non-hull structures, none of such bionic robots developed by Nad [14], Inoue [15], and Huang [16] have water rescue as their main application scenario.

For the above problems, a deformable water-mobile robot is designed in this paper [17]. This robot can reduce the resistance by deformation. The linear shape and U-shape of the robot are used as the main motion form. The robot was optimized by linear shape simulation and U-shaped floating state analysis to find the optimal size solution. Through experiments, it is verified that the deformable water-mobile robot can achieve the corresponding functions.

2. Robot Structure

2.1. Functional Requirements of Robots

According to the characteristics of the water rescue task, the robot needs to enter the working environment quickly and reach the target location quickly, and return safely after stably carrying the fallen person. As shown in Figure 1a, the robot designed in this article can be thrown directly into the water and enter the water environment smoothly. The robot is triangular when thrown, and the triangular structure is stable to resist the impact of falling water. As shown in Figure 1b, the robot can be unfolded into a linear form, which can quickly complete the adjustment of the upper and lower positions of the thrusters and quickly reach the target site. As shown in Figure 1c, the robot can take advantage of its structural characteristics to turn into a curved shape when turning, which can reduce the minimum turning radius. As shown in Figure 1d, the robot turns into a U-shape after reaching the target location and wraps the person up by differential steering to play the role of buoyancy support and return safely.

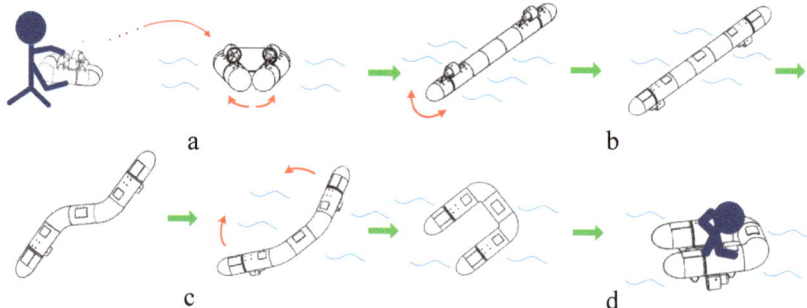

Figure 1. Schematic diagram of robot functions. (**a**) Throwing state diagram; (**b**) The linear shape diagram of the robot; (**c**) The curved shape diagram of the robot; (**d**) U-shape diagram of the robot.

2.2. Principle of Configuration

In nature, water snakes are flexible and quick when swimming in water. They can bend their bodies to smoothly pass through various complex water environments, which is exactly the mobility characteristics needed for water-mobile robots. Based on the characteristics of biological water snakes, a new water-mobile robot with a three-link, two-drive joint open kinematic chain configuration was designed. The body includes a front segment (1), a middle segment (3), and a rear segment (4). The ends of the middle segment are connected to the front and rear segments by the deformable segment (2), respectively. The front and rear segments are fixed to the thruster (5). The schematic diagram and structural diagram of the mechanism are shown in Figures 2 and 3.

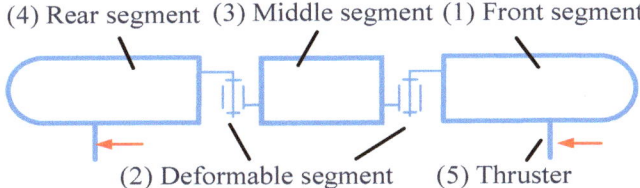

Figure 2. Sketch of robot mechanism.

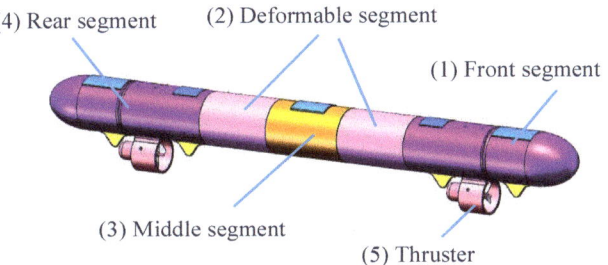

Figure 3. Robot structure diagram.

Many current water-mobile robots with rescue aspects are U-shaped, as in reference [2], but the shape of such robots is immutable during movement. The robot in this article has a linear shape when it reaches the target location and a U-shape when it returns. Under the same structural parameters, the drag analysis is performed for the linear shape in this article and the U-shape in reference [2]. Water drag can be calculated as Equation (1) [18]:

$$F_d = \frac{1}{2} \rho_f v_d^2 \, A \, C_D \tag{1}$$

where F_d is the water drag, ρ_f is the density of water, v_d is the robot's speed, A is the cross-sectional area of the robot, and C_D is the drag coefficient of the robot.

When the structural parameters of the two shapes are the same, assuming that the density of water and the robot's speed is certain, the two shapes' cross-sectional area and drag coefficient are obviously different. The cross-sectional area and drag coefficient of the linear shape are smaller than those of the U-shape, so the water drag in the linear shape will be smaller.

2.3. Structural Design of Robots

As shown in Figure 4, the middle segment includes a middle segment shell, with a middle hatch cover (9) set at the top of the middle segment shell, a middle segment sealed chamber (14) inside the middle segment shell, and line pipelines (10) set on both sides of the middle segment sealed chamber. The middle part of the middle segment sealed chamber is the controller chamber (13).

The deformable segment (2) includes a sealing tube (8), an upper base (17), a flanged shaft (18), a bearing (19), a coupling (21), a bracket (22), a steering gear (20), and a lower base (23). The sealing tube provides a sealing connection between the two rotating sub-joints. The flange shaft (18) is bolted to one end of the upper base (17) through its flange, and the outer circular surface of the shaft section of the flanged shaft is coaxially set with the bracket (22) through the bearing (19). The shaft section of the flange protrudes from the bearing section and is connected to the steering gear output shaft (20) by a coupling (21). The steering gear is bolted to one end of the lower base (23), the other end of the steering gear seat is hinged to the middle segment shell of the middle segment (3), and the steering gear (20) is connected to the controller via a wire.

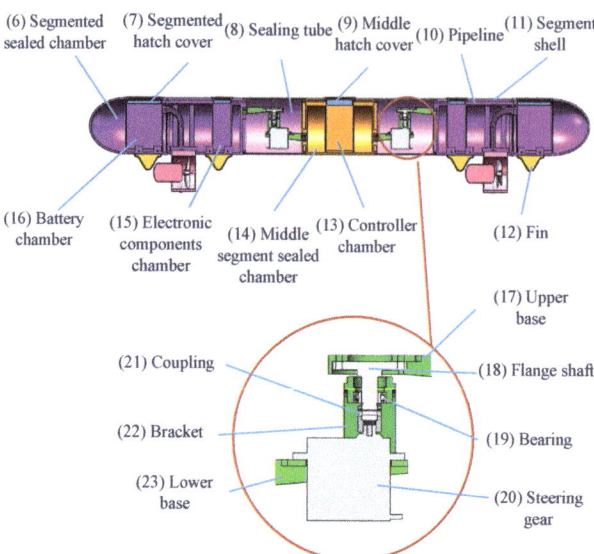

Figure 4. Robot sectional view.

The front segment of the body (1) has the same structure as the rear segment, including the segmented shell (11). A segmented hatch cover (7) is mounted on the segmented shell, and a segmented sealed chamber (6) is formed inside the segmented shell. The section of the segmented shell is shaped to resemble a rotary bullet. The segmented sealed chamber is divided into an electronic component chamber (15) and an embedded battery chamber (16), and the electronic component chamber is located near the middle segment (3). A battery is installed in the embedded battery chamber, and an electronic component chamber has a built-in electronic governor connecting the battery to the chassis thruster (5). The bottom of the segmented shell (11) has fins (12) and thruster mounts mounted by bolts, and the thruster mounts have chassis thrusters mounted on them. The two thrusters are propelled in the same direction.

Firstly, the staff threw the robot in a triangular state into the water. The staff presses the unfolding button, the front and rear segments of the body rotate in opposite directions, and both act simultaneously on the middle segment of the body to complete the unfolding action. After unfolding, it changes from a triangular state to a linear state when the front and rear segments' chassis thrusters (5) are in the same line. After throwing in a triangular posture, the underwater thruster may be exposed to the air. As the robot becomes a linear shape, it is designed with an offset center of mass. Its special counterweight structure thrusters can be automatically submerged in the water to enter the movement preparation phase.

Based on the relative position of the robot and the target point, the robot chassis thruster (5) is controlled to drive rapidly in a linear state in the direction of the target point. If the robot drifts in the direction midway, the staff presses the adjustment lever of the controller to control the steering gear (20) at the deformable segment (2) to work. The steering gear drives the front segment and rear segment (4) to rotate so that the robot transforms into a curved shape for direction adjustment, thus changing the relative position of the two chassis thrusters in a non-linear state, and the two chassis thrusters do not share the same thrust direction to achieve the purpose of motion steering.

After reaching the target point, the staff presses the U-shaped button of the operator, and the steering gear at the deformable segment works and drives the front and rear segments to rotate, deforming the robot into a U-shaped state. Currently, the front and rear segments are in a non-collinear parallel state of the chassis thrusters for the differential motion to achieve the robot's attitude adjustment to avoid directional drift until the stable return to the safety zone.

3. Shape Optimization Analysis

3.1. Force Analysis

In this article, the force analysis of the robot is performed while in the manned state. Due to the presence of the human itself discharging the volume of water, the buoyancy force of the water to the human is F_1. The robot discharges the volume of water, the buoyancy force of the water to the robot is F_2, $m_1 g$ is the weight of the human, and $m_2 g$ is the weight of the robot, as shown in Figure 5.

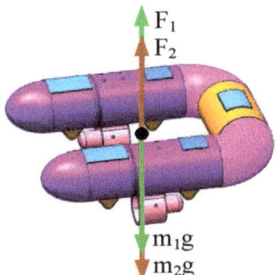

Figure 5. Schematic diagram of the forces on the water-mobile robot.

Buoyancy can be calculated as Equation (2):

$$F_f = \rho_f\, g\, V_f \qquad (2)$$

where F_f is the robot's buoyancy, g is gravity's acceleration, and V_f is the volume of discharged water.

People on the water can displace about 80–90% of their volume. This article is designed to be able to rescue 75 kg adults as the goal, excluding the buoyancy of the human displacement volume. The load-bearing weight is reduced by about eight times. The robot requires a minimum effective load-bearing volume of about 0.0019 m^3 and an effective load-bearing capacity of 1.9 kg.

3.2. Fluid Dynamics Control Equations and Turbulence Models

When a robot moves in the water environment, the fluid as a continuous medium should follow three major laws: the law of conservation of mass, conservation of momentum, and conservation of energy. This article develops the mathematical model using the CFD method [19]. People for hydrodynamic analysis are usually assumed to be incompressible, so only consider satisfying the mass and momentum conservation equations.

Menter optimized using the standard k-ω model and proposed the SST k-ω turbulence model. The SST k-ω turbulence model has higher accuracy and credibility, so the SST k-ω turbulence model is chosen as the CFD numerical simulation calculation model in this article. The control equations for the SST k-ω turbulence models are presented in the literature [19].

3.3. Determination of Objective Function and Constraint Conditions

Because the robot designed in this article is a three-segment robot, to ensure the overall stability of the robot, the bow and stern adopt a consistent external structure. Huapan et al. [20] showed that the sailing drag of semi-ellipsoid and semi-ellipse is less, so the bow and stern both use the semi-ellipsoid structure, and the linear shape control parameters are shown in Figure 6.

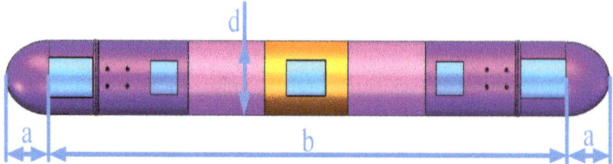

Figure 6. Linear shape control parameters.

The equation of the curve of the semi-ellipse can be calculated as Equation (3) [20]:

$$y = \pm \frac{d}{2a}\sqrt{a^2 - x^2} \qquad (3)$$

The volume of the body can be calculated as Equation (4):

$$V = \pi d^2 \left(\frac{a}{3} + \frac{d}{4}\right) \qquad (4)$$

where d is the maximum cross-sectional diameter, b is the length of the middle section of the body, a is the length of the semi-ellipse, and x is the distance from the point on the long axis to the vertex of the ellipse.

In this article, a rectangular computational domain of 4 m × 2 m × 2 m is established with the middle of the robot as the origin, a dense grid is used near the surface of the robot, and the final grid number of the whole basin is about 1 million cells. To make the robot move at a speed of 0.7 m/s when the size structure is optimal, set the water flow velocity for this speed for the robot drag simulation calculation. The fluid medium is set to liquid water and air, the inlet condition of the flow field is set to velocity inflow, the outlet is pressure outlet, and both the robot surface and the flow field boundary are set to a stationary wall with zero roughness.

In this article, the robot's size is optimized to improve the robot's overall performance. On the one hand, the optimization makes the robot as large as possible, which generates more buoyancy and leaves more space to carry various electronic devices. On the other hand, it makes the drag force as small as possible to achieve an energy-efficient design. In this article, to meet the robot's functional requirements to prevent the control parameters from being too small or too large and leading to an unreasonable design, the relevant dimensions should be limited to determine the upper and lower limits of each parameter. The optimization objectives, as well as the constraints, are as follows:

$$\text{Objective} \begin{cases} \text{Minimize : Drag} \\ \text{Maximize : Volume} \end{cases} \qquad (5)$$

$$\text{Constraints} \begin{cases} 45 \leq a \leq 135 \\ 750 \leq b \leq 1200 \\ 50 \leq d \leq 275 \end{cases} \qquad (6)$$

3.4. Simulation Analysis

Under the constraint of the feasible domain, the 3D surface plots of the independent and dependent variables (drag) are derived using Matlab simulation software. The interrelationships between the respective independent and dependent variables are obtained, as shown in Figure 7. Figure 7a represents the surface plot of the relationship between the independent variables a and b and the drag when d = 90. Figure 7b represents the surface plot of the relationship between the independent variables a and d and the drag when b = 1000. Figure 7c represents the surface plot of the relationship between the independent variables b and d and the drag when a = 25.

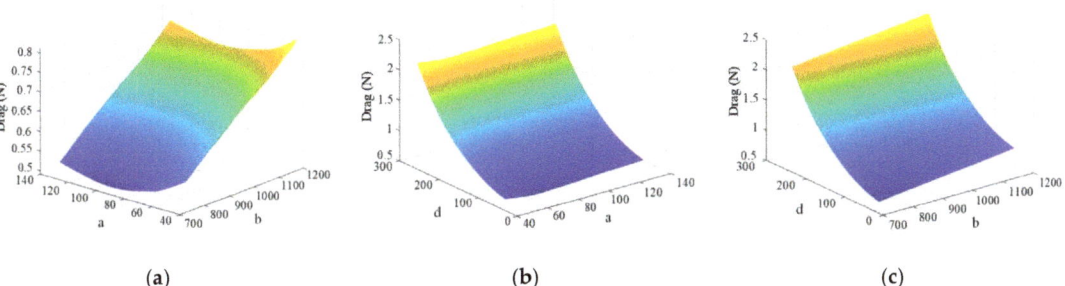

Figure 7. (**a**) a Surface graph of the relationship between b and drag; (**b**) a Surface graph of the relationship between d and drag; (**c**) b Surface graph of the relationship between d and drag.

The figure above shows the size of the three parameters a, b, and d directly affecting drag. The change in the value of d has a significantly larger effect on the drag value than the change in the values of a and b. The range of d variation is the most sensitive to the effect of drag.

With the objective function equation of volume above, the 3D surface plots of the independent and dependent variables (volume) are simulated using Matlab simulation software under the constraint range. Figure 8a represents the surface plot of the relationship between the independent variables a and b and the volume when d = 90. Figure 8b represents the surface plot of the independent variables a and d versus volume when b = 1000. Figure 8c represents the surface plot of the independent variables b and d versus volume when a = 125.

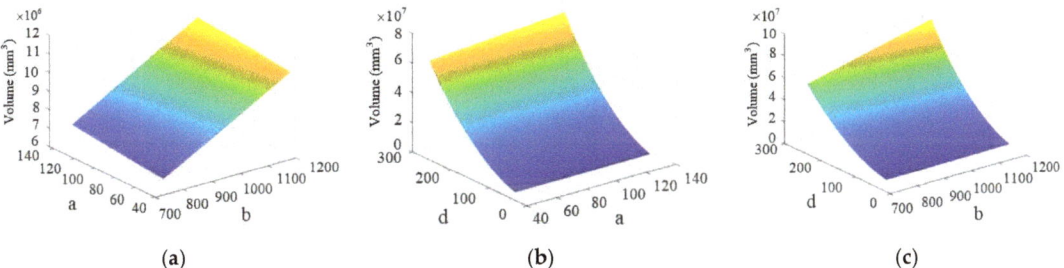

Figure 8. (**a**) a Surface graph of the relationship between b and volume; (**b**) a Surface graph of the relationship between d and volume; (**c**) b Surface graph of the relationship between d and volume.

The figure above shows the size of the three parameters a, b, and d directly affecting the volume. The changes in the values of b and d have a significantly larger effect on the volume taken than the value of a. It can be seen in Figure 8c that when the value of d is small, the change in the value of b does not have a significant effect on the volume. As the value of d increases, the value of b becomes more influential on the volume. The degree of effect of d is larger than that of b. The range of variation of d is most sensitive to the volume effect.

According to the above objective function and constraints, the volume maximum and drag minimum are simultaneously used as optimization objectives to find the optimal solution. The optimization design platform is established, and the optimization flow chart is shown in Figure 9. First, set the initial values of the 3D model control parameters. The initial values of each parameter are set as follows: a = 90, b = 1000, and d = 100. The model is then meshed, and the drag and volume values are calculated. The optimization component is then used to regenerate the control parameter values based on the obtained drag and volume and repeat the above steps until the optimal solution is found.

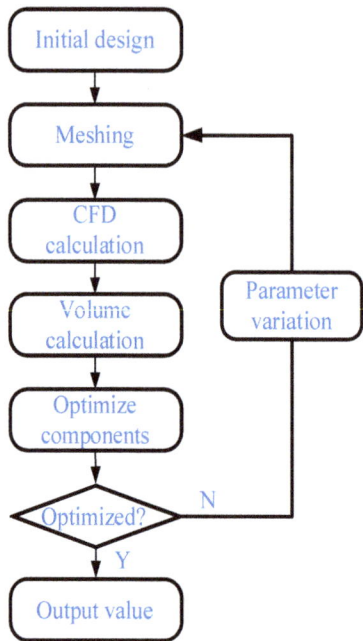

Figure 9. Optimization flow chart.

Optimization is performed according to the parameters given above. The values of the parameters are continuously changed in the optimization, and the drag values obtained from the iterative calculations are extracted. In this article, a multi-island genetic algorithm is chosen as the optimization method to find the optimal solution and avoid getting a locally optimal solution [21–23]. The population size of the genetic algorithm is chosen as 10, the number of evolutionary generations is 10, the crossover probability is 1, the variation probability is 0.01, and the migration probability is 0.01, which is calculated 1000 times. The feasible solutions for volume and drag are shown in Figure 10:

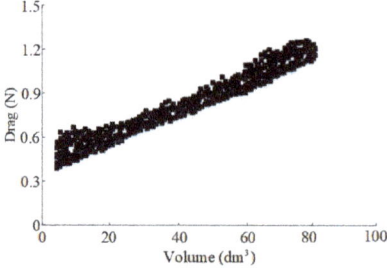

Figure 10. Set of feasible solutions for drag and volume.

The above figure shows the calculation results obtained with the minimum drag and the maximum volume simultaneously as the optimization objectives. For a robot to increase its volume, it must reduce some of its drag. Similarly, if a robot profile with optimal drag performance is sought, then the requirement for a volumetric target needs to be reduced. No matter how the shape of the rotary body changes at a certain volume value, it will not be less than a certain drag value. The minimum drag value increases approximately linearly with the volume increase. Based on the required volume size of the robot, select the optimized values for the combination of design parameters as shown in Table 1:

Table 1. Parameter optimization results.

Parameter Name	Initial Value	Optimization Value
a (mm)	90	103
b (mm)	1000	1100
d (mm)	100	96
Volume (mm^3)	8,796,459	8,956,103
Drag (N)	0.512	0.455

The above table shows that the volume of the initial design is 8,796,459 mm^3, the drag is 0.512 N, the optimized volume is 8,956,102 mm^3, and the drag is 0.455 N. The optimized water-mobile robot has 11.1% less drag and 1.8% more volume. As shown in Figure 11, the wave generated by the initial size and the optimized size are shown.

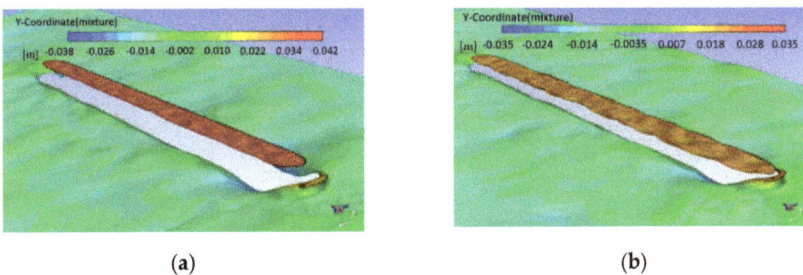

Figure 11. (a) Initial wave height; (b) Optimized wave height.

As can be seen from the figure, the waves generated around the optimized size are significantly smaller than the initial size, and the wave height is reduced by 16.7%. The optimized wave amplitude of the body likewise reflects the effective improvement of the body drag [24].

4. U-Shaped Floating State Analysis

The robot needs to become U-shaped when it reaches the target location, and this form structure is less prone to tipping and has a larger lateral moment of inertia [25]. The U-shaped body size has a great effect on its smoothness. Angular tilt occurs when the forces on the left and right sides of the lateral and longitudinal surfaces are not balanced. Reasonable design of the left and right module spacing can balance the lateral and longitudinal smoothness. Analyze the impact of the movement of small-weight objects on the small tilt angles on both sides separately. As shown in Figure 12, the shape control parameters of this shape include lateral spacing k_1 and longitudinal spacing k_2.

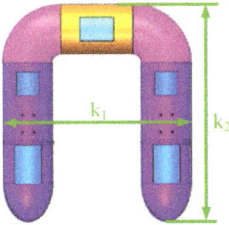

Figure 12. U shape control parameter diagram.

4.1. Center of Gravity Calculation

In the linear shape, the coordinate system is established with the midpoint at the bottom of the robot's midsection as the origin O, the direction pointing to the thruster as the X-axis, the vertical direction as the Z-axis, and the Y-axis perpendicular to the XOZ plane as shown in Figure 13.

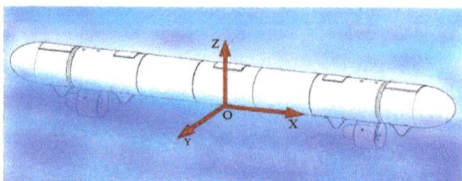

Figure 13. Linear three-dimensional coordinate diagram.

In the U-shape, the coordinate system is established with the midpoint at the bottom of the robot's midsection as the origin O, the direction pointing to the thruster as the Y-axis, the vertical direction as the Z-axis, and the X-axis perpendicular to the YOZ surface as shown in Figure 14.

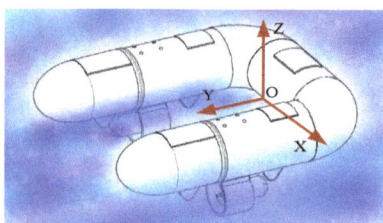

Figure 14. U-shaped 3D coordinate diagram.

Each part of the robot is in the O-XYZ coordinate system. The mass of the robot is W and contains n masses. The mass point's mass is m_i, and the position of each mass point is (x_i, y_i, z_i). The position of the center of gravity can be calculated as Equations (7)–(9):

$$x_G = \frac{\sum_{i=1}^{n} m_i x_i}{W} \tag{7}$$

$$y_G = \frac{\sum_{i=1}^{n} m_i y_i}{W} \tag{8}$$

$$z_G = \frac{\sum_{i=1}^{n} m_i z_i}{W} \tag{9}$$

When the robot is in the linear shape state, the center of gravity coordinates of the robot is (0, 0, 37.4). In the U-shaped state, the coordinates of the robot's center of gravity are (0, K, 37.4), and K is the value associated with k_1.

4.2. Buoyancy Center Calculation

The derivation process of the buoyancy center calculation is in Appendix A. When the robot is in a linear shape, the X and Y directions are symmetrical, so x = 0 and y = 0, and the buoyancy center coordinates are (0, 0, 21.3). In the U-shaped state, the x-direction is symmetric with x = 0, and the buoyancy center coordinates are (0, K, 21.3). The center of gravity position is higher than the buoyancy center position in both linear shape state and U-shaped state.

4.3. Floating State Analysis

The tilt angle resulting from the weight movement is influenced by the parameters k_1 and k_2 in the lateral and longitudinal plane, respectively. Since the total length of the body remains unchanged, the two parameters are related by the following Equation, and at this time, the control parameter is only one variable, k_1.

$$k_1 + 2k_2 = 1412 \tag{10}$$

When in the lateral plane, move the p-weight object from point A to point A_1 along the lateral horizontal direction. As shown in Figure 15, the robot's center of gravity moves from the original point G_{H0} to point G_{H1}. The body produces a lateral tilt, and the waterline moves from W_0L_0 to W_1L_1.

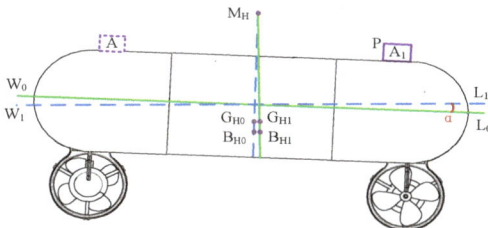

Figure 15. Schematic diagram of lateral movement.

After the object moves, the robot will have a lateral angle tilt, and the derivation process is shown in Appendix B.

At the longitudinal plane, the p-weight object is moved from point B to point B_1 along the longitudinal horizontal direction, as shown in Figure 16.

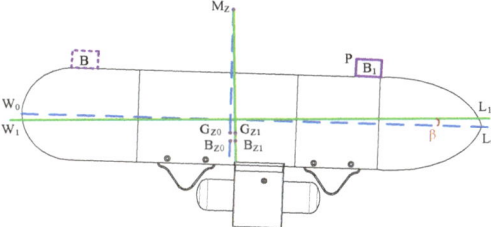

Figure 16. Schematic diagram of longitudinal movement.

After the object is moved, the robot will have a longitudinal angle tilt, and the derivation process is shown in Appendix C.

When the p-weight object is 0.3 kg, the image of k_1 against the lateral tilt angle α and the longitudinal tilt angle β is obtained, as shown in Figure 17.

The above figure shows that when the moving weight is certain, with the increase of k_1, the overall tendency of the lateral tilt angle decreases, and the overall tendency of the longitudinal tilt angle increases. When k_1 is about 0.5 mm, the two curves cross, and the lateral and longitudinal inclination angles are equal. When k_1 is less than 0.5 mm, the trend of decreasing the lateral tilt angle is more drastic, and the longitudinal tilt angle also shows a slow decreasing trend. When k_1 is larger than 0.5 mm, the decreasing lateral tilt angle trend is more moderate, and the increasing longitudinal tilt angle trend is more drastic. Considering the actual needs, the final choice of k_1 is 0.4 mm.

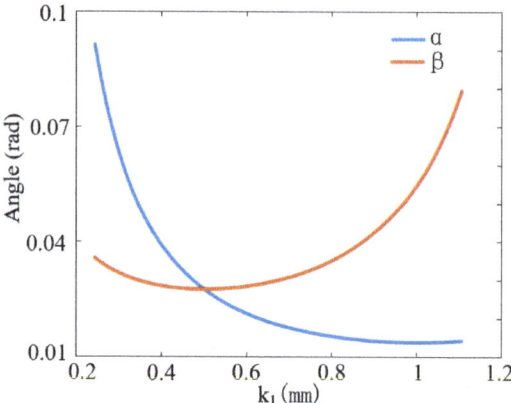

Figure 17. Diagram of the influence of parameter k_1 on inclination angle.

5. Robot Prototype Experiment

5.1. Robot Prototype

In this article, platform test experiments of the robot were conducted on the water to verify the effectiveness of the robot prototype functions based on whether the robot can achieve the corresponding motion by experimenting with the effective load-carrying capacity, the automatic adjustment function, and different motion states. The model number of the remote control is FOSS FS-i6, the model number of the receiver is FS-iA6, the model number of the thruster is T60, the model number of the electronic governor is SHARK-50A, the model number of the servo is S9177SV, and the model number of the gyroscope angle sensor is WT901WIFI. The technical data of the experimental prototype are shown in Table 2, and the schematic diagram of each attitude of the solid prototype after assembly is shown in Figure 18.

Table 2. Robot function prototype parameters.

Parameter Name	Optimization Value
Size (mm)	1306 × 96 × 168
Weight (kg)	3.5
Movement speed (m/s)	0.678
Control range (m)	500
Effective bearing capacity (kg)	3–4

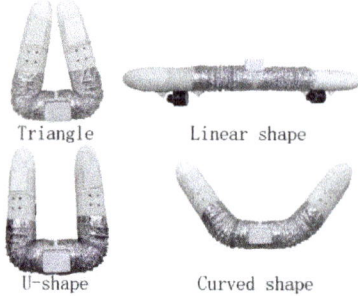

Figure 18. Schematic diagram of the pose of the experimental robot prototype.

5.2. Bearing Capacity Test Experiment

Experiment on the effective load-carrying capacity of the experimental robot prototype. When the robot is in U-shape, the dumbbell piece is used to simulate the actual weight, and the weight is bound to the front and rear segments to imitate the human arm, and this state can enclose the weight and play the role of buoyancy support. When the weight is 3 kg, the horizontal surface reaches the state shown in Figure 19, and the robot is about to miss the horizontal surface. The robot sinks underwater when the weight is added to 4 kg. The effective load-carrying capacity is 3–4 kg, which meets the initial performance index requirements.

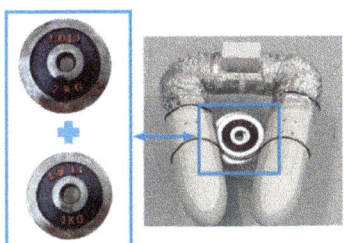

Figure 19. The effective load-carrying capacity test diagram.

5.3. Robot-Throwing Expansion Experiment

The staff threw the robot in the triangle state into the water and pressed the button of the handheld operator to convert the triangle into a linear shape. The front and rear segments of the body rotate in opposite directions, and the middle segment of the body is relatively fixed to complete the unfolding experiment, as shown in Figure 20.

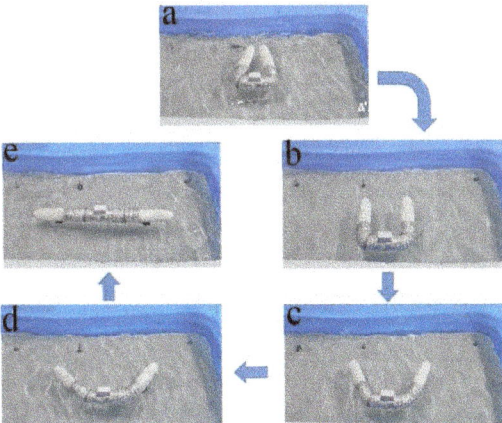

Figure 20. Throwing unfolding experiment. (**a**) Triangular shape of the robot; (**b**) U-shape of the robot; (**c**) Curved shape of the robot 1; (**d**) Curved shape of the robot 2; (**e**) Linear shape of the robot.

5.4. Automatic Attitude Adjustment Experiment

Since the robot can be thrown to the surface at will, it is important to ensure that the robot can automatically adjust so that the thrusters remain underwater. During the adjustment process, when the robot is tilted at a certain angle, a recovery torque is generated to return the robot to a positive floating state. The vertical submerged state of the thruster is set to $0°$, and the vertical exposure of the thruster to air is set to $-180°$. Theoretically, the recovery torque is 0 for robot tilt angles of $0°$ and $-180°$. Experimentation on the functional prototype of the robot when the thruster is −180°. The effect is shown in Figure 21A, and the real-time data of the robot tilt angle is shown in Figure 21B.

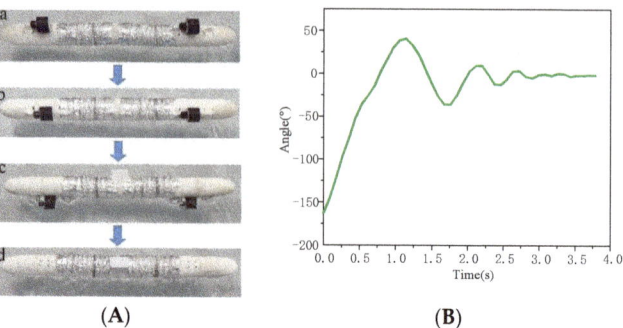

(A)   (B)

Figure 21. (**A**) Automatic adjustment experiment effect diagram. (**a**) Robot tilt angle of −180° diagram; (**b**) Robot tilt angle of −120° diagram; (**c**) Robot tilt angle of −60° diagram; (**d**) Robot tilt angle of 0° diagram; (**B**) Real-time data diagram of robot tilt angle.

When the tilt angle is −180°, the recovery moment is 0. However, in the actual situation, the left and right forces of the robot on the water surface cannot be perfectly balanced. As shown above, the thrusters can be automatically submerged in real situations.

5.5. Oscillating Motion Experiment

Due to the special structural form of robots, they can rely on their own structural characteristics for swinging motion. Figure 22 shows the motion of the robot in the swing state. The remote control controls the steering gear to make the rear segment swing from 0 to 40°. The robot moves flexibly during the swing state and has low motion noise.

Figure 22. Swing experiment. (**a**) t = 0 s; (**b**) t = 1 s; (**c**) t = 1.5 s.

5.6. Direct Flight Motion Test

Conduct experiments on linear-shaped and U-shaped direct sailing movements on the water. Only longitudinal thrust is applied to the robot to ensure straight navigation of the robot, and the ground angle is put in the pool as a position reference. Figure 23 shows the direct sailing movements state of the robot.

The robot starts from a standstill, and observing the position of the reference object and the robot shows that the motion trajectory is straight, which indicates that the robot has a good stability of motion posture on the water surface.

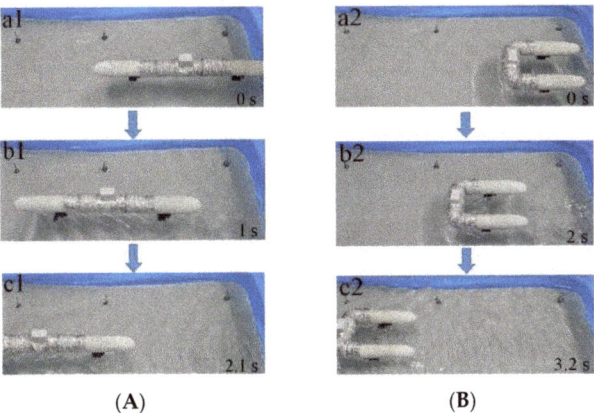

Figure 23. Direct sailing movement. (**A**) Direct sailing movement in linear shape. (**a1**) t = 0 s; (**b1**) t = 1 s; (**c1**) t = 2.1 s; (**B**) Direct sailing movement in U-shape. (**a2**) t = 0 s; (**b2**) t = 2 s; (**c2**) t = 3.2 s.

5.7. Horizontal Rotary Motion Experiment

In the U-shape, the rotation speed of the left and right propellers is adjusted so there is a certain difference in their output power, and the robot will appear to steer, as shown in Figure 24A. When the remote control controls the steering gear at the deformable section of the robot, the front and back segments swing opposite to 55° and turn into a curved shape. Under the action of the thruster, the motion trajectory is also horizontal rotary, as shown in Figure 24B.

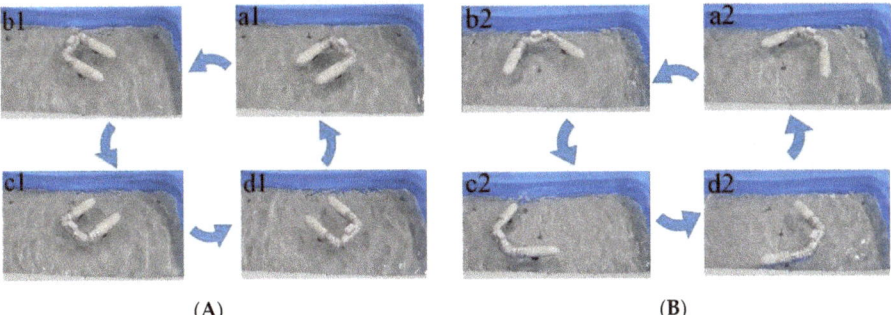

Figure 24. (**A**) U-shaped horizontal rotation motion. (**a1**) Rotate 0° horizontally; (**b1**) Rotate 90° horizontally; (**c1**) Rotate 180° horizontally; (**d1**) Rotate 270° horizontally; (**B**) Curved shape horizontal rotation motion. (**a2**) Rotate 0° horizontally; (**b2**) Rotate 90° horizontally; (**c2**) Rotate 180° horizontally; (**d2**) Rotate 270° horizontally.

In the U-shape, the robot can achieve slewing motion under the action of thrust and bow moment when there is a certain deviation between the left and right propeller speed. In the U-shape, when the propeller speed is the same, and the output power is equal, the robot can also achieve rotary motion, which aligns with the general rule of horizontal rotary motion of water-mobile robots.

6. Conclusions

A deformable water-mobile robot is proposed for the specific needs of water rescue equipment. The robot has a two-degree-of-freedom chain structure that can be deformed to respond to different work requirements. The robot has a two-degrees-of-freedom chain structure that can be deformed to respond to different work requirements. Compared with the traditional U-shaped water-mobile robot, this robot can quickly reach the target location by morphing into a linear shape. An optimization design platform is established in linear shape to optimize the robot's shape parameters based on a multi-island genetic algorithm with the objectives of minimum drag and maximum volume. Additionally, the floating state analysis was carried out in U-shaped to get the best shape structure. Finally, the robot prototype was experimented on the water surface. The robot's effective load-carrying capacity meets the design requirements and can be deployed smoothly after throwing. The thruster can automatically sink underwater according to its adjustment function, which is better for achieving different movement functions. A deformable water-mobile robot is proposed to solve the current life-saving equipment structure of a single, large water drag and other shortcomings. Subsequently, it is necessary to introduce dynamics models, add precise control systems, and cooperate with vision and other systems for autonomous navigation control.

Author Contributions: Conceptualization, C.Y.; methodology, all authors.; software, Y.S.; validation, S.Y. and Y.W.; formal analysis, Y.S.; investigation, S.Y.; resources, C.Y.; data curation, Y.W.; writing—original draft preparation, Y.S.; writing—review and editing, S.Y.; visualization, Y.W.; supervision, C.Y.; project administration, C.Y.; funding acquisition, C.Y. All authors have read and agreed to the published version of the manuscript.

Funding: Liaoning Provincial Natural Science Foundation, grant number: 20180520033. Tundamental research funds for National Natural Science Foundation of China: 52005349. Liaoning Provincial Education Department Fund-"Seedling Raising" Project for Young Scientific and Technological Talents: JYT2020136.

Data Availability Statement: Not applicable.

Conflicts of Interest: The authors declare no conflict of interest.

Appendix A

This article uses the segmentation method to calculate the position coordinates of the robot's buoyancy center. Parallel to the coordinate plane YOZ, a thin slice is taken in part below the draft line, and its thin microvolume can be calculated as Equation (A1):

$$dV_f = A_s dx \tag{A1}$$

The static moment of the thin film microvolume to the coordinate plane can be calculated as Equations (A2)–(A4):

$$dM_{yoz} = x_a A_s dx \tag{A2}$$

$$dM_{xoz} = y_a A_s dx \tag{A3}$$

$$dM_{yox} = z_a A_s dx \tag{A4}$$

The coordinates of the center of buoyancy can be calculated as Equations (A5)–(A7):

$$x_B = \frac{M_{yoz}}{V_f} \tag{A5}$$

$$y_B = \frac{M_{xoz}}{V_f} \tag{A6}$$

$$z_B = \frac{M_{yox}}{V_f} \tag{A7}$$

Appendix B

When the object moves, the robot tilts at a lateral angle. The buoyancy center B_{H0} will make a circular motion with the point of steady center M_H as the center and the radius H_{BM} as the steady lateral center. The lateral stability center radius H_{BM} can be calculated as Equation (A8) [26]:

$$H_{BM} = \frac{I_H}{V_f} \tag{A8}$$

where I_H is the lateral moment of inertia.

The high H_{GM} of lateral stability in this state can be calculated as Equation (A9):

$$H_{GM} = H_{BM} - H_{BG} \tag{A9}$$

The cross-tilt angle α of the robot after the lateral movement of the weight p can be calculated as Equation (A10):

$$\alpha = \arctan\left(\frac{p\, k_1}{\Delta H_{GM}}\right) \tag{A10}$$

where Δ is the discharge volume.

Appendix C

When the object moves, the robot tilts at a longitudinal angle. The longitudinal stability center radius Z_{BM} can be calculated as Equation (A11) [26]:

$$Z_{BM} = \frac{I_Z - A_W\, x_f^2}{V_f} \tag{A11}$$

where I_Z is the longitudinal moment of inertia, A_W is the waterline surface area at Z from the base plane, and x_f is the longitudinal coordinate of the waterline surface area A_W shape center at Z from the base plane.

The high Z_{GM} of longitudinal stability can be calculated as Equation (A12):

$$Z_{GM} = Z_{BM} - Z_{BG} \tag{A12}$$

The longitudinal inclination angle β of the robot after the longitudinal movement of the weight p can be calculated as Equation (A13):

$$\beta = \arctan\left(\frac{p\,(1412 - k_1)}{2\, \Delta\, Z_{GM}}\right) \tag{A13}$$

References

1. Kim, T.; Choi, J.; Lee, Y.; Choi, H.-T. Development of a Multi-Purpose Unmanned Surface Vehicle and Simulation Comparison of Path Tracking Methods. In Proceedings of the 2016 13th International Conference on Ubiquitous Robots and Ambient Intelligence (URAI), Xi'an, China, 19–22 August 2016; pp. 447–451.
2. Le, Y. Research on Waterjet Propulsion and Navigation Control of Unmanned Vehicles. Master's Thesis, Zhejiang University, Hangzhou, China, 2019.
3. Zong, Z.; Sun, Y.; Jiang, Y. Experimental Study of Controlled T-Foil for Vertical Acceleration Reduction of a Trimaran. *J. Mar. Sci. Technol.* **2019**, *24*, 553–564. [CrossRef]
4. Goulon, C.; Le Meaux, O.; Vincent-Falquet, R.; Guillard, J. Hydroacoustic Autonomous Boat for Remote Fish Detection in LAkE (HARLE), an Unmanned Autonomous Surface Vehicle to Monitor Fish Populations in Lakes. *Limnol. Oceanogr. Methods* **2021**, *19*, 280–292. [CrossRef]
5. Makhsoos, A.; Mousazadeh, H.; Mohtasebi, S.S.; Abdollahzadeh, M.; Jafarbiglu, H.; Omrani, E.; Salmani, Y.; Kiapey, A. Design, Simulation and Experimental Evaluation of Energy System for an Unmanned Surface Vehicle. *Energy* **2018**, *148*, 362–372. [CrossRef]
6. Morge, A.; Pelle, V.; Wan, J.; Jaulin, L. Experimental Studies of Autonomous Sailing with a Radio Controlled Sailboat. *IEEE Access* **2022**, *10*, 134164–134171. [CrossRef]

7. Johnston, P.; Pierpoint, C. Deployment of a Passive Acoustic Monitoring (PAM) Array from the AutoNaut Wave-Propelled Unmanned Surface Vessel (USV). In Proceedings of the OCEANS 2017, Aberdeen, UK, 19–22 June 2017; pp. 1–4.
8. Poole, M.; Johnston, P. Autonomous surveying of shallow coastal waters for clean seas and shorelines: Coastal monitoring of water quality. *Hydro Int.* **2017**, *21*, 24–27.
9. Wang, K.; Ma, Y.; Shan, H.; Ma, S. A Snake-Like Robot with Envelope Wheels and Obstacle-Aided Gaits. *Appl. Sci.* **2019**, *9*, 3749. [CrossRef]
10. Nguyen, Q.V.; Chan, W.L. Development and flight performance of a biologically-inspired tailless flapping-wing micro air vehicle with wing stroke plane modulation. *Bioinspir. Biomim.* **2018**, *14*, 016015. [CrossRef] [PubMed]
11. Picardi, G.; Laschi, C.; Calisti, M. Model-Based Open Loop Control of a Multigait Legged Underwater Robot. *Mechatronics* **2018**, *55*, 162–170. [CrossRef]
12. Yang, W.; Zhang, W. A Worm-Inspired Robot Flexibly Steering on Horizontal and Vertical Surfaces. *Appl. Sci.* **2019**, *9*, 2168. [CrossRef]
13. Yan, J.; Yang, K.; Liu, G.; Zhao, J. Flexible driving mechanism inspired water strider robot walking on water surface. *IEEE Access* **2020**, *8*, 89643–89654. [CrossRef]
14. Nađ, Đ.; Mišković, N.; Mandić, F. Navigation, Guidance and Control of an Overactuated Marine Surface Vehicle. *Annu. Rev. Control.* **2015**, *40*, 172–181. [CrossRef]
15. Inoue, T.; Shiosawa, T.; Takagi, K. Dynamic Analysis of Motion of Crawler-Type Remotely Operated Vehicles. *IEEE J. Ocean. Eng.* **2013**, *38*, 375–382. [CrossRef]
16. Huang, H.; Sheng, C.; Wu, G.; Shen, Y.; Wang, H. Stroke Kinematics Analysis and Hydrodynamic Modeling of a Buoyancy-Supported Water Strider Robot. *Appl. Sci.* **2020**, *10*, 6300. [CrossRef]
17. Changlong, Y.; Rui, W.; Yingxin, S.; Bing, W.; Biao, T.; Borui, Z.; Linglong, G.; Jiaqi, F. A Snake-Like Surface Rescue Robot and Its Control Method. CN Patent 111874185 A, 2 February 2022.
18. Wang, M.; Tian, Y.; Yang, S.; Wang, P. Study on the Calculation Method of Water Inflow Velocity of Loose Rock Landslide. *Sustainability* **2022**, *14*, 12767. [CrossRef]
19. Anderson, J.D. Basic Methods of computational fluid dynamics. In *Fundamentals and Applications of Computational Fluid Dynamics*, 1st ed.; Songping, W., Zhaomiao, L., Eds.; Machinery Industry Press: Beijing China, 2019; pp. 149–193.
20. Huapan, X.; Zifan, F.; Chen, Z.; Kongde, H.; Weihua, Y.; Hongzhu, D. Research on structural resistance characteristics of underwater streamline body and its application. *J. Three Gorges Univ.* **2013**, *35*, 92–96.
21. Song, B.; Lyu, D.; Jiang, J. Optimization of Composite Ring Stiffened Cylindrical Hulls for Unmanned Underwater Vehicles Using Multi-Island Genetic Algorithm. *J. Reinf. Plast. Compos.* **2018**, *37*, 668–684. [CrossRef]
22. Pang, Y.; Wamg, Y.; Yang, Z.; Gao, T. Myring type rotary hull direct sailing drag calculation and boat type optimization. *J. Harbin Eng. Univ.* **2014**, *35*, 1093–1098.
23. Peng, D. Research on Multi-Objective Optimal Design of Three-Body Combined Autonomous Underwater Vehicle Based on Parameterization. Master's Thesis, South China University of Technology, Guangzhou, China, 2020.
24. Cheng, X.; Feng, B.; Liu, Z.; Chang, H. Hull Surface Modification for Ship Resistance Performance Optimization Based on Delaunay Triangulation. *Ocean. Eng.* **2018**, *153*, 333–344. [CrossRef]
25. Zhang, W.; Li, Y.; Liao, Y.; Jia, Q.; Pan, K. Hydrodynamic Analysis of Self-Propulsion Performance of Wave-Driven Catamaran. *J. Mar. Sci. Eng.* **2021**, *9*, 1221. [CrossRef]
26. Vasilescu, M.-V.; Dinu, D. Influence of Flettner Balloon, Used as Wind Energy Capturing System, on Container Ship Stability. In *E3S Web of Conferences, Proceedings of the 9th International Conference on Thermal Equipments, Renewable Energy and Rural Development (TE-RE-RD 2020), Constanta, Romania, 26–27 June 2020*; EDP Sciences: Les Ulis, France, 2020; Volume 180, p. 02004. [CrossRef]

Disclaimer/Publisher's Note: The statements, opinions and data contained in all publications are solely those of the individual author(s) and contributor(s) and not of MDPI and/or the editor(s). MDPI and/or the editor(s) disclaim responsibility for any injury to people or property resulting from any ideas, methods, instructions or products referred to in the content.

Article

Parallel Network-Based Sliding Mode Tracking Control for Robotic Manipulators with Uncertain Dynamics

Honggang Wu [1], Xinming Zhang [1,2,*], Linsen Song [1], Yufei Zhang [3], Chen Wang [1], Xiaonan Zhao [3] and Lidong Gu [1,*]

[1] School of Mechanical and Electrical Engineering, Changchun University of Science and Technology, Changchun 130022, China; 2019200078@mails.cust.edu.cn (H.W.); songlinsen@cust.edu.cn (L.S.); wangc@cust.edu.cn (C.W.)
[2] School of Mechatronic Engineering and Automation, Foshan University, Foshan 528225, China
[3] School of Computer Science and Technology, Changchun University of Science and Technology, Changchun 130022, China; 2019200107@mails.cust.edu.cn (Y.Z.); zhaoxn@cust.edu.cn (X.Z.)
* Correspondence: zxm@cust.edu.cn (X.Z); gulidong@cust.edu.cn (L.G.)

Abstract: Robot dynamics model uncertainty and unpredictable external perturbations are important factors that influence control accuracy and stability. To accurately compensate for the dynamics model in sliding mode control (SMC), a new parallel network (PCR) is proposed in this paper. The network parallelizes the radial basis function and convolutional neural network, which gives it the advantage of making full use of one-dimensional data fitting results and two-dimensional data feature information, realizing the deep learning of multidimensional data and improving the model's compensation accuracy and anti-interference ability. Meanwhile, based on the integration of adaptive control techniques and gradient descent, a new weight update algorithm is designed to realize the online learning of PCR networks under loss-free functions. Then, a new sliding mode controller (PCR-SMC) is established. The model-free intelligent control of the robot is accomplished without knowledge of the predetermined upper bounds. Additionally, the stability analysis of the control system is proved by the Lyapunov theorem. Lastly, robot tracking control simulations are performed on two trajectories. The results demonstrate the high-precision tracking performance of this controller in comparison with the RBF-SMC controller.

Keywords: parallel network; PCR-SMC controller; uncertainty compensation; trajectory tracking

1. Introduction

Robotic manipulators are multi-input and -output nonlinear systems with an uncertain model, due to payload changes, friction, external disturbances [1], etc. Therefore, it is difficult to acquire accurate knowledge of robotic systems, resulting in the inability to design a universal and accurate motion controller [2,3], however rapid the development of robot technology or the complexity of work tasks. The focus of much engineering' research is to design a controller that is suitable for uncertain robotic model systems [4]. Mainstream control methods include proportional integral derivative control [5], adaptive control [6], neural network control [7], and sliding mode control (SMC) [8].

Among the above methods, the SMC algorithm has a special nonlinear control, known as a variable structure controller. It is insensitive to the uncertainty of inherent parameters and has high robustness to external disturbances [9]. If the control system has many unknown parameters, the SMC design becomes complicated, and its performance degrades. Meanwhile, the SMC method is prone to the chatter phenomenon in the control process [10]. Therefore, to obtain a high-performance SMC, much intelligent control research has been conducted, such as combining intelligent control with a neural network [11,12]. The fusion of computational intelligence methods and robotics can improve the accuracy, reliability, efficiency, cost-effectiveness, and competitiveness of systems.

The radial basis function neural network (RBFNN) has the advantages of simple structure and strong generalization ability [13]. The intelligent RBFNN method and SMC integration can considerably reduce chattering and improve the control performance by approximating the system model in real time [14]. Yin et al. [15] proposed an adaptive terminal SMC strategy using an RBFNN, which achieved model-free and chatter-free high-precision tracking control for stone-carving robot manipulators. Fang et al. [16] combined an RBFNN with a brain emotional nesting network and applied it to the robot's object grasping task. Chen et al. [17] designed a fixed-time fractional sliding mode controller, which improved the convergence speed and control accuracy in the trajectory tracking control field of unmanned aerial vehicles. However, an RBF neural network has a fixed-structure problem. To improve the control system's performance, Ye et al. [18] combined two controllers (the fuzzy neural network and compensation controllers) and verified their feasibility for robot control. Yen et al. [19] designed robust controllers through sliding mode control techniques, RBFNN models, and adaptive algorithms. This method effectively improved the tracking control accuracy by independently compensating for joint uncertainty. Wang et al. [20] improved the input of an RBFNN using a nearest-neighbor clustering algorithm, and then applied it to the uncertainty compensation of robotic systems.

However, RBF neural networks and their variants can only handle one-dimensional data. To overcome this limitation, using a CNN has allowed for new prospects in the field of system identification and control [21]. Yao and Chen [22] proposed a deep CNN-SMC controller. The simulation of the 5DOF system showed that the controller had high robustness and a high response tracking control effect. Zhou et al. [23] compensated for the uncertainty of the robot control system by using a CNN. The gradient descent method was used for weight learning. By combining it with the fractional-order terminal SMC, the control performance of the rigid robot was effectively improved. The CNN-SMC controller realized the processing of multidimensional data and real-time compensation of the model; however, it ignores real-time one-dimensional data feedback. In recent years, scholars in different fields combined a CNN and an RBFNN, producing excellent research results. Hemalakshmi et al. [24] used a hybrid serial CNN-RBF model to improve the classification accuracy of retinal fundus images. Hong et al. [25] connected a CNN and an RBFNN in a series and used it for 24-h wind power prediction. Sideratos et al. [26] proposed a series network structure (RBF-CNN model) for power system load forecasting. Compared with existing load forecasting methods, the proposed model had higher forecasting performance. The combination of a CNN and an RBF has produced high performance in other fields; however, it still suffers from the drawback that it can only handle one-dimensional data. How to realize the parallel processing of one- and two-dimensional data using a neural network for application to a control system is a new research direction.

In the above methods, an RBF and its improved method are used to approximate the dynamic model online, and the input is one-dimensional feedback data; a CNN and its improved scheme can estimate the dynamic model online, and its input is mainly two-dimensional history data. How to realize the parallel combination of two neural networks, taking into account the full utilization of the feature information of one-dimensional data and two-dimensional data, has not yet been reported. Therefore, a new sliding mode controller (PCR-SCM) using parallel neural networks is proposed, and then applied to the trajectory tracking control of two-link robots. The PCR network is a combination of a CNN and an RBF to achieve its parallel computation, and the weight adaptive online learning algorithm is designed. Briefly, the main contributions of this paper are as follows:

1. In this paper, we study the data mining capability of a CNN and the infinite approximation characteristics of an RBFNN. Additionally, a new PCR network is proposed. This network fully integrates information from different dimensional data, realizing the synchronization of data fitting and time series prediction.

2. A weight learning method for PCR networks in real-time control systems is designed, which integrates gradient descent and adaptive techniques, realizing the online learning of the PCR network's weight.
3. A new PCR-SMC controller is proposed and applied to the trajectory tracking control of a two-link robot. Simulations are conducted on two trajectories to verify that the controller has superior control performance in comparison with the RBF-SMC controller.

The organization of this paper is as follows: Section 2 presents the rigid robot dynamics model; Section 3 shows our design for the PCR-SMC controller, as well as proposes the adaptive weight online learning algorithm; Section 4 presents the simulation results; lastly, the conclusion and future research direction are given in Section 5.

2. Preliminaries
2.1. Robot Dynamic Model

The n-link robot is analyzed using the Lagrange method, and the closed dynamic model is shown in Equation (1) [27,28].

$$M_r(\theta)\ddot{\theta} + C_r(\theta, \dot{\theta})\dot{\theta} + G_r(\theta) + d(t) = \tau(t), \tag{1}$$

where $\theta \in R^n$ represents the joint angles, $\dot{\theta} \in R^n$ represents the angular velocities, and $\ddot{\theta} \in R^n$ represents the angular acceleration. $\tau \in R^n$ is the driving torque of the joints, $M_r(\theta) \in R^n$ is the symmetric positive definite inertia matrix, $C_r(\theta, \dot{\theta}) \in R^n$ is the Coriolis and centrifugal force matrix, $G_r(\theta) \in R^n$ represents the gravitational force vector, and $d(t) \in R^n$ is the external disturbances vector. θ, τ, $d(t)$, and $G_r(\theta)$ are the $n \times 1$ vectors, and $M_r(\theta)$ and $C_r(\theta, \dot{\theta})$ are the $n \times n$ matrices [29]. The n-link mechanism model of the robot is shown in Figure 1.

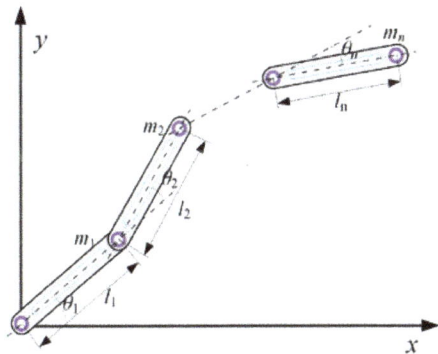

Figure 1. The model of n-link robotic manipulator.

Property 1 [30,31]. $M_r(\theta) - 2C_r(\theta, \dot{\theta})$ *is a skew symmetric matrix, and if the variable is* $\xi \in R^n$, *it satisfies Equation (2).*

$$\xi^T(M_r(\theta) - 2C_r(\theta, \dot{\theta}))\xi = 0. \tag{2}$$

Property 2 [32]. $M_r(\theta)$ *is a symmetric positive definite matrix of* $n \times n$ *and bounded; if* ψ_1 *and* ψ_2 *are positive numbers, it satisfies Equation (3).*

$$\psi_1\|x\|^2 \leq x^T M_r(\theta)x \geq \psi_2\|x\|^2 \,\forall x \in R^n. \tag{3}$$

Compared with the actual model, the established dynamic system model based on the theoretical structure of the robotic manipulator will have errors in the calculation process. Therefore, the actual dynamic model is established in Equation (4).

$$M_{r0}(\theta)\ddot{\theta} + C_{r0}(\theta,\dot{\theta})\dot{\theta} + G_{r0}(\theta) = \tau + f_r(\theta,\dot{\theta},t), \tag{4}$$

where $M_{r0}(\theta)$, $C_{r0}(\theta,\dot{\theta})$, and $G_{r0}(\theta)$ are the nominal values of $M_r(\theta)$, $C_r(\theta,\dot{\theta})$, and $G_r(\theta)$, respectively. $f_r(\theta,\dot{\theta},t) = -\Delta M_r(\theta) - \Delta C_r(\theta,\dot{\theta}) - \Delta G_r(\theta) - d(t)$ is the uncertain part of the model, where $\Delta M_r(\theta) = M_r(\theta) - M_{r0}(\theta)$, $\Delta C_r(\theta,\dot{\theta}) = C_r(\theta,\dot{\theta}) - C_{r0}(\theta,\dot{\theta})$, and $\Delta G_r(\theta) = G_r(\theta) - G_{r0}(\theta)$, are assumed to have upper bounds. However, in some practical engineering problems, it is easy to choose a larger estimated value for the upper bound. As a result, the control gain is large, which affects the control accuracy and performance. Therefore, it may be a better solution to study model-free control methods that do not require prior knowledge of the upper bound.

2.2. Sliding Mode Control

Under the feedback of the discontinuous state control law function, the control output of an SMC can be continuously switched between two smooth states, which has the characteristics of not requiring an accurate model and being insensitive to parameter changes [33,34]. In this paper, according to the control model's state feedback error, the function of the sliding surface is used, as shown in Equation (5) [33,35]. The robot's ideal target trajectory vectors are θ_d and $\dot{\theta}_d$. The robot's actual output trajectory vectors are θ and $\dot{\theta}$. The angular tracking error is $e = [e_1, e_2, \cdots, e_n]^T$, and the angular velocity tracking error is $\dot{e} = [\dot{e}_1, \dot{e}_2, \cdots, \dot{e}_n]^T$.

$$Sr = \dot{e} + \Lambda e, \tag{5}$$

where $\Lambda = \Lambda^T > 0$.

According to Equations (1) and (5), the dynamic model error expression is shown in Equation (6).

$$M_r(\theta)\dot{S}r = f(\theta) - C_r(\theta,\dot{\theta})Sr + d(t) - \tau, \tag{6}$$

where $f(\theta) = M_r(\theta)(\ddot{\theta}_d + \Lambda\dot{e}) + C_r(\theta,\dot{\theta})(\dot{\theta}_d + \Lambda e) + G_r(\theta)$ is the model's basic information, which is a nonlinear function about θ, $\dot{\theta}$, θ_d, $\dot{\theta}_d$, and $\ddot{\theta}_d$.

The design control rate is shown in Equation (7).

$$\tau = \overline{f}(\theta) + K_e Sr, \tag{7}$$

where $\overline{f}(\theta)$ is the theoretical nominal value of $f(\theta)$ for nominal model control. Equation (8) is obtained by substituting Equation (7) into Equation (6).

$$M_r(\theta)\dot{S}r = -(K_e + C_r)Sr + \widetilde{f}(\theta) + d(t), \tag{8}$$

where $\widetilde{f}(\theta) = f(\theta) - \overline{f}(\theta)$. The Lyapunov function [36] is defined as $V = \frac{1}{2}Sr^T M_r(\theta) Sr$, and its derivative is shown in Equation (9).

$$\dot{V} = Sr^T M_r \dot{S}r + \frac{1}{2}Sr^T \dot{M}_r Sr. \tag{9}$$

Equation (10) is obtained by substituting Equation (8) into Equation (9).

$$\dot{V} = -Sr^T K_e Sr + \frac{1}{2}Sr^T(\dot{M}_r - 2C_r)Sr + Sr^T \eta, \tag{10}$$

where $\eta = \tilde{f}(\theta) + d(t)$.

According to the dynamic model's oblique symmetry properties, $Sr^T\left(\dot{M}_r - 2C_r\right)Sr = 0$ and $\dot{V} = Sr^T\eta - Sr^T K_e Sr$ are obtained. The estimation error and disturbance of model information affect the control accuracy and stability. Therefore, in the absence of an accurate dynamic model and accurate judgment of disturbance, researching model approximation and disturbance compensation algorithms is an effective way to achieve high-performance model-free control.

3. Design of PCR-SMC Controller

3.1. Overall Design

A new PCR-SMC controller is proposed in this paper, and its principle is shown in Figure 2. This controller uses a CNN and an RBFNN to parallel trajectory information of different dimensions, so that it can compensate for the robot uncertainty model online and improve the control performance of robot trajectory tracking.

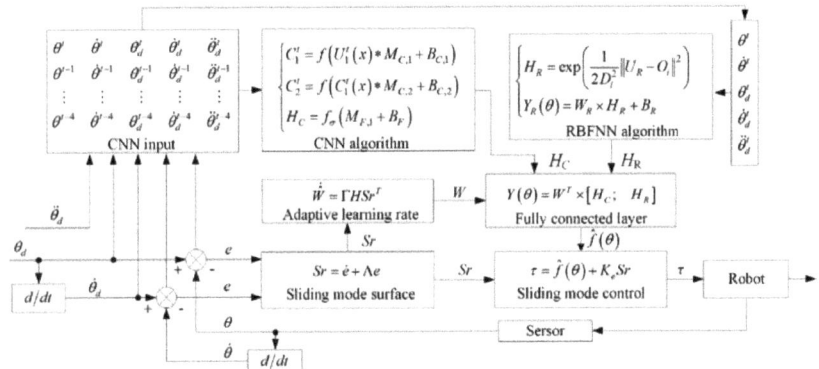

Figure 2. Schematic of the PCR-SMC controller.

In Figure 2, the errors e and $\dot{e}$ are the inputs, and the control torque τ of each joint is the output of the PCR-SMC controller. The input of an RBFNN is composed of five kinds of trajectory information, which are the expected angle θ_d, expected angular velocity $\dot{\theta}_d$, expected angular acceleration $\ddot{\theta}_d$, actual angle θ, and actual angular velocity $\dot{\theta}$. The input of the CNN is the information of the trajectory being retraced. $\hat{f}(\theta)$ is the calculation result of the dynamic model identified online by the PCR network, and it participates in trajectory tracking sliding mode control.

3.2. Design of PCR Network

A CNN has the advantages of convolution calculation, local perception, and weight sharing, and it can quickly extract features during data processing. Therefore, its application scenarios gradually penetrate into the field of intelligent industry, which requires a rapid response [37,38]. An RBFNN has the advantages of fast convergence speed, strong robustness, simple structure, and good approximation ability, and it is often used in the field of real-time control [39].

The PCR network structure is designed as shown in Figure 3. In the PCR network, the parallel calculation of an RBFNN and a CNN is performed, and then the calculation results are recomposed into a new network hidden layer; finally, the results are calculated through the output layer. The establishment of the network model and the design of the weight learning algorithm are described in detail below.

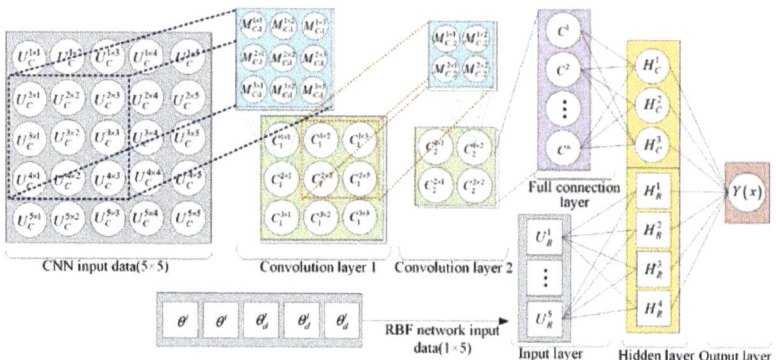

Figure 3. Structure of PCR network.

3.2.1. Convolutional Neural Network

Trajectory information constantly generates changes during the joint motion. Including θ_d, $\dot{\theta}_d$, $\ddot{\theta}_d$, θ, and $\dot{\theta}$, this information affects the system approach and control stability. Therefore, the two-dimensional data of four backtracking moments are selected as the CNN input matrix, with a size of 5 × 5, as shown in Equation (11).

$$U_C = \begin{bmatrix} \theta^t & \dot{\theta}^t & \theta_d^t & \dot{\theta}_d^t & \ddot{\theta}_d^t \\ \theta^{t-1} & \dot{\theta}^{t-1} & \theta_d^{t-1} & \dot{\theta}_d^{t-1} & \ddot{\theta}_d^{t-1} \\ \vdots & \vdots & \vdots & \vdots & \vdots \\ \theta^{t-4} & \dot{\theta}^{t-4} & \theta_d^{t-4} & \dot{\theta}_d^{t-4} & \ddot{\theta}_d^{t-4} \end{bmatrix}. \quad (11)$$

The calculation model of the convolutional layer is shown in Equation (12).

$$C_i^t = f_\sigma(\sigma_C^t) = f(U_C^t(x)*M_{C,i} + B_C), i = 1, 2, \cdots, M_{C,num}, \quad (12)$$

where M_C represents the convolution kernel, and $M_{C,num}$ represents the number of M_C. B_C is the bias, f_σ is the ReLU function, and its partial derivatives are shown in Equations (13) and (14).

$$f_\sigma(\sigma_C) = max(0, \sigma_C). \quad (13)$$

$$\dot{f}_\sigma(\sigma_c) = \begin{cases} 0 & \sigma_C \leq 0 \\ 1 & \sigma_C > 0 \end{cases}. \quad (14)$$

The output H_C of the fully connected layer is shown in Equation (15).

$$H_{C,i} = f_\sigma(\sigma_F) = f_\sigma(M_{F,i}C_i + B_F), \quad (15)$$

where M_F represents the weight of the full connection layer, B_F represents the bias, and f_σ selects the sigmoid function.

3.2.2. RBF Neural Network

In the PCR network, the dynamic variables $U_R = \left[\theta^{t-1}, \dot{\theta}^{t-1}, \theta_d^{t-1}, \dot{\theta}_d^{t-1}, \ddot{\theta}_d^{t-1}\right]$ of the dynamic model are selected as the input vector of the RBFNN. The nonlinear approximation of the model is realized through a Gaussian hidden layer and output layer [40,41]. The output result H_R of the Gaussian hidden layer is shown in Equation (16).

$$H_{R,i} = exp\left(-\frac{\|U_R - O_i\|^2}{2D_i^2}\right), \quad (16)$$

where O_i is the center point vector, and D_i is the width of the Gaussian.

The hidden layer vector H of the PCR network consists of two kinds of information, which are the result H_C of the CNN and the result H_R of the RBFNN. The output of the PCR network is shown in Equation (17).

$$Y(x) = W^T \times H, \quad (17)$$

where $H = [H_C; H_R]$, and $W = [W_1, W_2, \ldots, W_m]^T$ is the weight of the PCR network output layer.

3.2.3. Weight Update of PCR Network

Gradient descent is a commonly used weight update algorithm in a neural network. The mean square error $E = 1/2(Y_d - Y)^2$ is used as the loss function. The weight gradient is defined as the partial derivative of the loss function, as shown in Equation (18).

$$\Delta W_t = \partial E(W, Y, H)/\partial W = (Y_d - Y)H_t. \quad (18)$$

The weight update is shown in Equation (19).

$$W_t = W_{t-1} - \mu \Delta W_t, \quad (19)$$

where μ is the learning rate.

The PCR network output is used to compensate for an important parameter of the controller, and the loss function cannot be obtained during the system operation. As a result, conventional methods cannot be used for the weight update. To realize the online learning of weight, the adaptive algorithm and the gradient descent are combined. According to Equation (5) and the Lyapunov stability principle [36], the adaptive learning rate of the output layer of the PCR network is designed as shown in Equation (20).

$$\dot{\hat{W}} = \Gamma H Sr^T, \quad (20)$$

where $\Gamma = \Gamma^T > 0$ is the fixed coefficient, and Sr is the sliding mode surface output.

According to the combined features of the PCR network's hidden layer and the adaptive learning rate, the initial weight update gradient of the CNN can be obtained as $\Delta W_C = \dot{\hat{W}}_C - W_C$. Then, the gradient values of each layer in the CNN are calculated by gradient backpropagation. The gradient calculation model of the fully connected layer is shown in Equation (21).

$$\Delta M_F = H_C(1 - H_C)(W_C)^T \Delta W_C. \quad (21)$$

According to the weight gradient calculated using the above formula, the fully connected layer weight can be updated as shown in Equation (22).

$$M_F = M_F - \mu \times \Delta M_F. \quad (22)$$

In the PCR network structure, the input vector of the fully connected layer is obtained by reducing the dimension of the last convolutional layer. Therefore, the learning gradient $\Delta M_{C,2}$ model of the convolution kernel is shown in Equation (23).

$$\Delta M_{C,2} = \dot{f}_\sigma(\sigma_F)(M_F)^T \Delta M_F, \quad (23)$$

where $\dot{f}_\sigma(\sigma_F) = C_2(1 - C_2)$ is the partial derivative of the sigmoid function, and C_2 is the input data of the second convolution layer; the vector form of ΔM_F needs to be converted to matrix form. According to the convolution kernel weight gradient $\Delta M_{C,2}$, a new convolution kernel can be calculated as shown in Equation (24).

$$M_{C,2} = C_2 \times \Delta M_{C,2}. \quad (24)$$

The weight gradient $\Delta M_{C,1}$ of the previous convolution kernel can be calculated through the gradient backpropagation algorithm, as shown in Equation (25).

$$\Delta M_{C,1} = \Delta M_{C,2} \times rot180(M_{C,2}) \times \dot{f}_\sigma(\sigma_C), \quad (25)$$

where $rot180(M_{C,2})$ means that the matrix $M_{C,2}$ is flipped 180°. $\dot{f}_\sigma(\sigma_C)$ is the derivative of the ReLU function in the convolutional layer. Given the convolution kernel weight gradient $\Delta M_{C,1}$, the convolution kernel $M_{C,1}$ can be updated, as shown in Equation (26).

$$M_{C,1} = U_C(x) \times \Delta M_{C,1} \quad (26)$$

The weight of the PCR network is combined with the adaptive technology and the gradient descent algorithm to realize the online update of the network weight.

3.3. Controller Design

In practical engineering applications, accurate robot dynamic models do not exist, and nominal models are often used for robot trajectory tracking control. However, different nominal models may affect the transformation laws of system errors and degrade control performance. Therefore, the PCR network is used for the online approximation of the dynamic model and compensation for external disturbances, thus achieving model-free control.

The control rate of the PCR-SMC controller is designed as shown in Equation (27).

$$\tau = \hat{f}(\theta) + K_e Sr, \quad (27)$$

where $f(\theta)$ is composed of the robot dynamics model $(M_r\ddot{q}_r + C_r\dot{q}_r + G_r + f_r)$ and external disturbance $d(t)$; $\hat{f}(\theta)$ is the online approximation of $f(\theta)$ by the PCR network.

Submitting the control rate (Equation (27)) of the controller and the adaptive rate (Equation (20)) of the neural network into Equation (8) yields

$$M_r \dot{S}r = -(C_r + K_e)Sr + \tilde{W}^T H, \quad (28)$$

and we have

$$M_r \dot{S}r = -(C_r + K_e)Sr + \zeta_1, \quad (29)$$

where $\zeta_1 = \tilde{W}^T H$, $\tilde{W} = W - \hat{W}$.

Proof. The Lyapunov function is shown in Equation (30) [36].

$$L = \frac{1}{2}Sr^T M_r Sr + \frac{1}{2}tr\left(\tilde{W}^T F^{-1} \tilde{W}\right), \quad (30)$$

where $F = F^T > 0$ is the fixed coefficient. □

Deriving Equation (30), we can obtain Equation (31).

$$\dot{L} = Sr^T M_r \dot{S}r + \frac{1}{2} Sr^T \dot{M}_r Sr + tr\left(\tilde{W}^T F^{-1} \dot{\tilde{W}}\right). \tag{31}$$

Submitting the control rate (Equation (27)) and the neural network's adaptive rate (Equation (20)) into Equation (31) yields

$$\dot{L} = -Sr^T K_e Sr + \frac{1}{2} Sr^T \left(\dot{M}_r - 2C_r\right) Sr + tr\tilde{W}^T \left(F^{-1}\dot{\tilde{W}} + HSr^T\right). \tag{32}$$

According to the oblique symmetry characteristic (Equation (2)) of the robot dynamics model, Equation (32) becomes

$$\dot{L} = -Sr^T K_e Sr + tr\tilde{W}^T \left(F^{-1}\dot{\tilde{W}} + HSr^T\right), \tag{33}$$

where $\tilde{W} = W - \hat{W}$; the ideal weight W is a constant, an $\dot{\tilde{W}} = 0 - \dot{\hat{W}} = -\Gamma HSr^T$. According to the operational property of the trace of the matrix $Sr^T \tilde{W}^T H = tr\left(\tilde{W}^T HSr^T\right)$, which transforms Equation (33), we can obtain

$$\dot{L} = -Sr^T K_e Sr. \tag{34}$$

According to Equation (34), the Lyapunov function is $L \geq 0$, and its derivative is $\dot{L} \leq 0$. According to the LaSalle invariance principle, when $t \to 0$, $r \to 0$, $e \to 0$ and $\dot{e} \to 0$. This shows that the control system is asymptotically stable.

4. Numerical Simulation

4.1. Simulation Model and Parameter Setting

This paper organizes numerical simulations for the PCR-SMC controller in the trajectory tracking task of a two-link robot, and the robot is widely used to verify the control algorithm's performance [42]. The theoretical model of robot dynamics is shown in Equation (35).

$$M_r(\theta)\ddot{\theta} + C_r(\theta,\dot{\theta})\dot{\theta} + G_r(\theta) + d(t) = \tau(t), \tag{35}$$

where $\theta = [\theta_1 \ \theta_2]^T$, $\tau = [\tau_1 \ \tau_2]^T$, and the inertia matrix is M_r; the centrifugal force, Coriolis force matrix $C_r(\theta,\dot{\theta})$, and gravity matrix $G_r(\theta)$ are shown in Equations (36)–(38), respectively, where m_i is the mass of link i ($m_1 = 0.5$kg, and $m_2 = 1.5$kg), and l_i is the length of link i ($l_1 = 1$m and $l_2 = 0.8$m) [43,44]. θ_i and $\dot{\theta}_i$ represent the angle and angular velocity of link i, respectively; g = 9.81 m/s².

$$M_r(\theta) = \begin{bmatrix} Z_1 + Z_2 + 2Z_3\cos\theta_2 & Z_2 + Z_3\cos\theta_2 \\ m_2 l_2^2 + m_2 l_1 l_2 \cos\theta_2 & m_2 l_2^2 \end{bmatrix}, \tag{36}$$

$$C_r(\theta,\dot{\theta}) = \begin{bmatrix} -Z_3\dot{\theta}_2\sin\theta_2 & -Z_3\left(\dot{\theta}_1 + \dot{\theta}_2\right)\sin\theta_2 \\ Z_3\dot{\theta}_1\sin\theta_2 & 0 \end{bmatrix}, \tag{37}$$

$$G_r(\theta) = \begin{bmatrix} Z_4\cos(\theta_1 + \theta_2) + Z_5\cos\theta_1 \\ Z_4\cos(\theta_1 + \theta_2) \end{bmatrix}, \tag{38}$$

where $Z_1 = (m_1 + m_2)l_1^2$, $Z_2 = m_2 l_2^2$, $Z_3 = m_2 l_1 l_2$, $Z_4 = m_2 l_2 g$, and $Z_5 = (m_1 + m_2)l_1 g$.

The parameters of SMC are set as follows: $K_e = [24, 0; 0, 24]$, $\Lambda = [13, 0; 0, 13]$, and $\Gamma = [20, 0; 0, 20]$. Table 1 gives the parameters of the PCR network structure. The input of RBFNN is $U_R = \left[\theta^{t-1}, \dot{\theta}^{t-1}, \theta_d^{t-1}, \dot{\theta}_d^{t-1}, \ddot{\theta}_d^{t-1}\right]$. The input data of CNN are composed of the two-dimensional information of joint trajectories in the past five iterations, as shown in Equation (11). In addition, the RBF-SMC controller is a contrast control algorithm, and its network structure is 5–7–1. The parameters of the RBFNN part of the PCR-SMC and RBF-SMC controllers are set identically.

Table 1. Parameters of PCR network.

Parameters	Value
Number of convolution kernels ($M_{C,num}$)	2
Size ($M_{C,1}$)	2×2
Size ($M_{C,2}$)	3×3
Learning rate (μ)	0.005
Number of hidden layers (H)	7

4.2. Simulation Results and Analysis

Case 1. The control performance of the PCR-SMC controller is verified in a normal trajectory and compared with the RBF-SMC controller. The desired trajectory is shown in Equation (39) [45].

$$\theta_d(t) = \begin{bmatrix} 1.25 - (7/5)e^{-t} + (7/20)e^{-4t} \\ 1.25 + e^{-t} - (1/4)e^{-4t} \end{bmatrix}. \tag{39}$$

The initial values of the joint angle are $\theta_1(0) = 0.3$ and $\theta_2(0) = 1.9$, and the angular velocity is 0. During the 20 s simulation, random disturbance is added, and the amplitude is set to 0.1, which is used to simulate the external disturbance in the actual working condition. In addition, to effectively judge the response speed, convergence ability, and stability of the control algorithm, the externally changing load disturbance is added during the simulation for 5–10 s, as shown in Equation (40) [46]. After 15 s, the fixed load disturbance is added as $[-15; -10]$ [47].

$$\begin{bmatrix} -2.14\cos(10t) + 2 \\ 4.15\sin(20t - \pi/4) \end{bmatrix}. \tag{40}$$

Figures 4–7 show the trajectory tracking simulation results and absolute errors. The estimated performance of the PCR network is shown in Figure 8, and the output control torque is shown in Figure 9. Both the PCR-SMC and RBF-SMC controllers have obvious convergence trends before applying the load. However, the tracking error of the RBF-SMC controller is larger than that of the PCR-SMC controller. After 5 s, a continuously varying load is applied. The tracking error of the RBF-SMC controller has a large oscillation, while the PCR-SMC controller has strong anti-interference ability, and the control error is in a small interval. After 15 s, the fixed load is applied, and the control torque and network output gradually converge to a new value. The control output and trajectory tracking process of the PCR-SMC controller are more stable. This shows that the PCR-SMC controller has strong control stability and superior control performance to the RBF-SMC controller.

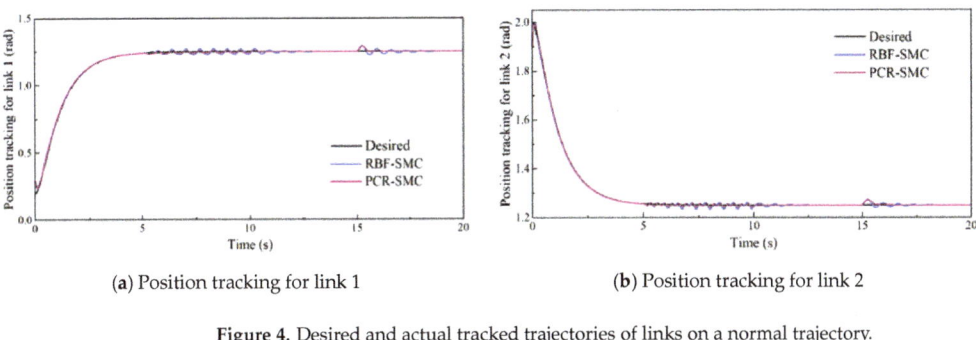

(a) Position tracking for link 1

(b) Position tracking for link 2

Figure 4. Desired and actual tracked trajectories of links on a normal trajectory.

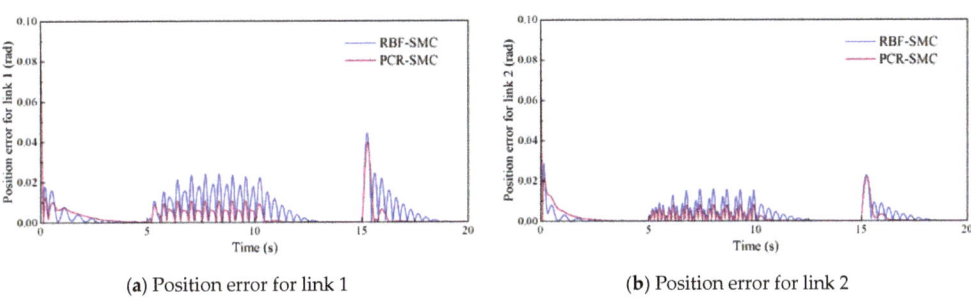

(a) Position error for link 1

(b) Position error for link 2

Figure 5. Trajectory tracking absolute error on a normal trajectory.

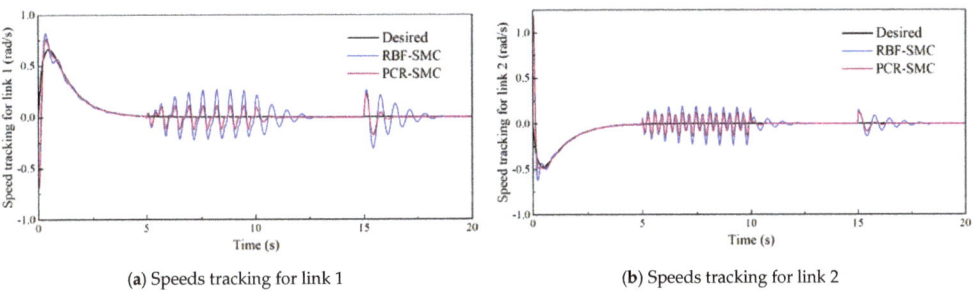

(a) Speeds tracking for link 1

(b) Speeds tracking for link 2

Figure 6. Desired and actual tracking speeds of links on a normal trajectory.

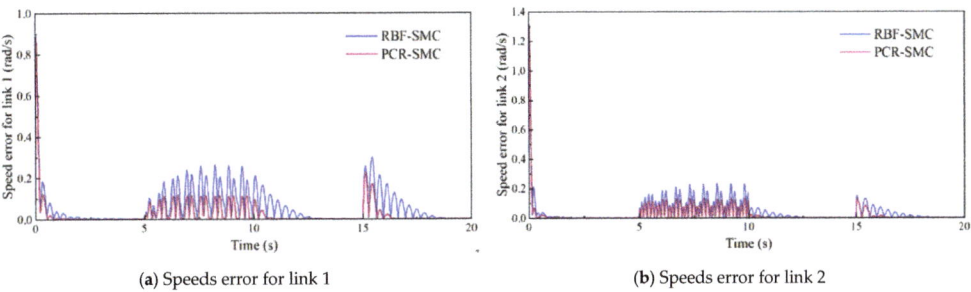

(a) Speeds error for link 1

(b) Speeds error for link 2

Figure 7. Speed tracking absolute error on a normal trajectory.

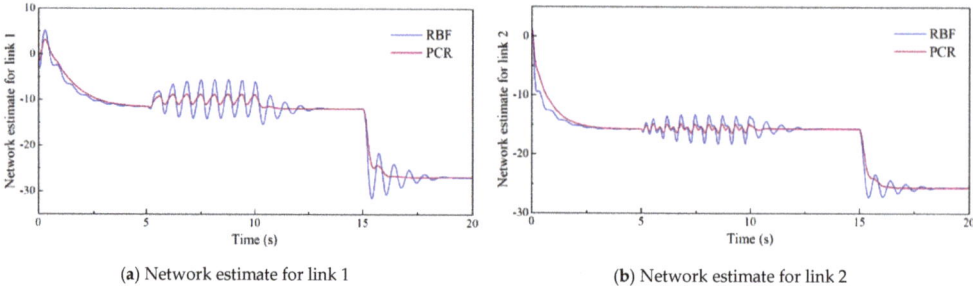

(a) Network estimate for link 1 (b) Network estimate for link 2

Figure 8. Network estimation output on a normal trajectory.

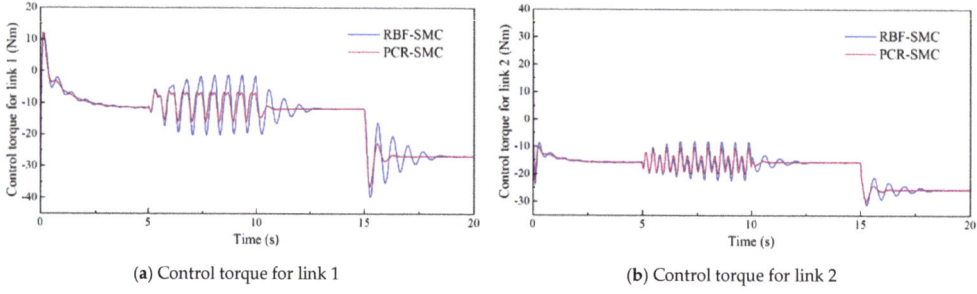

(a) Control torque for link 1 (b) Control torque for link 2

Figure 9. Control torque on a normal trajectory.

Tables 2–4 show the mean absolute error (MAE) and standard deviation (SD) of the tracking results, including the overall control process (0–20 s), the control of variable disturbances (5–10 s), and the control of fixed disturbances (15–20 s). The MAE evaluates the tracking accuracy, and the SD evaluates the tracking stability of the trajectory. By analyzing the simulation results in the tables, we determined that the PCR-SMC controller reduces the trajectory tracking error and improves stability compared with the RBF-SMC method.

Table 2. Overall tracking error (0–20 s).

Error		PCR-SMC		RBF-SMC	
		Link 1	Link 2	Link 1	Link 2
Position error	MAE	0.0039	0.0031	0.0066	0.0041
	SD	0.0135	0.0130	0.0153	0.0134
Speed error	MAE	0.0215	0.0241	0.0501	0.0366
	SD	0.0366	0.0941	0.1014	0.1050

Table 3. Tracking error with variable disturbance (5–10 s).

Error		PCR-SMC		RBF-SMC	
		Link 1	Link 2	Link 1	Link 2
Position error	MAE	0.0054	0.0037	0.0117	0.0064
	SD	0.0061	0.0043	0.0135	0.0078
Speed error	MAE	0,0517	0.0663	0.1131	0.0969
	SD	0.0661	0.1361	0.0761	0.1157

Table 4. Tracking error with fixed interference (15–20 s).

Error		PCR-SMC		RBF-SMC	
		Link 1	Link 2	Link 1	Link 2
Position error	MAE	0.0018	0.0012	0.0050	0.0023
	SD	0.0064	0.0038	0.0094	0.0046
Speed error	MAE	0.0109	0.0065	0.0420	0.0184
	SD	0.0369	0.0741	0.0202	0.0337

Case 2. The starfish-shaped trajectory is a more complex robot trajectory, which can further verify the effectiveness and stability of the PCR-SMC controller. The starfish-shaped trajectory model is shown in Equation (41).

$$\begin{bmatrix}(0.8+0.2\times sin(5t))\times cos(t+4\pi/3)\\(0.8+0.2\times sin(5t))\times sin(t+4\pi/3)\end{bmatrix}. \quad (41)$$

The initial values of θ and $\dot{\theta}$ are set to 0, and the others are the same as those in Case 1. The tracking results of the starfish trajectory at the robot's end-effector are shown in Figure 10. Figures 11 and 12 show the trajectory tracking results of the links. The model uncertainty approximation results based on the neural network are shown in Figure 13. The PCR-SMC controller has high tracking accuracy, and the output of the PCR network is more stable, showing better control performance. The effectiveness and versatility of the PCR-SMC controller are fully verified.

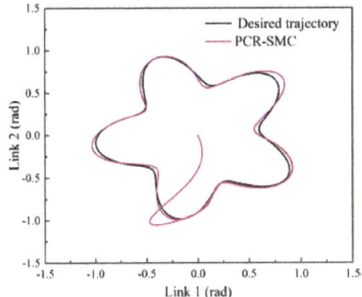

(a) Trajectory tracking for PCR-SMC controller

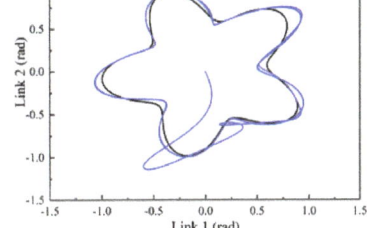

(b) Trajectory tracking for RBF-SMC controller

Figure 10. Robot end-effector trajectory tracking results.

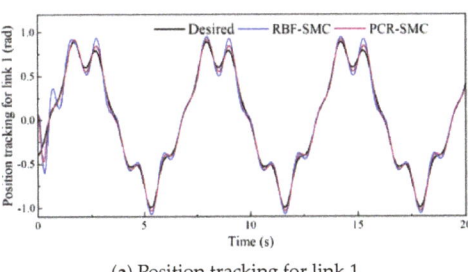

(a) Position tracking for link 1

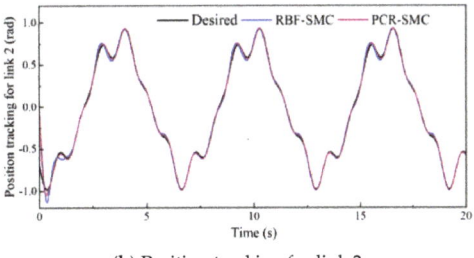

(b) Position tracking for link 2

Figure 11. Desired and actual tracked trajectories of links on a starfish-shaped trajectory.

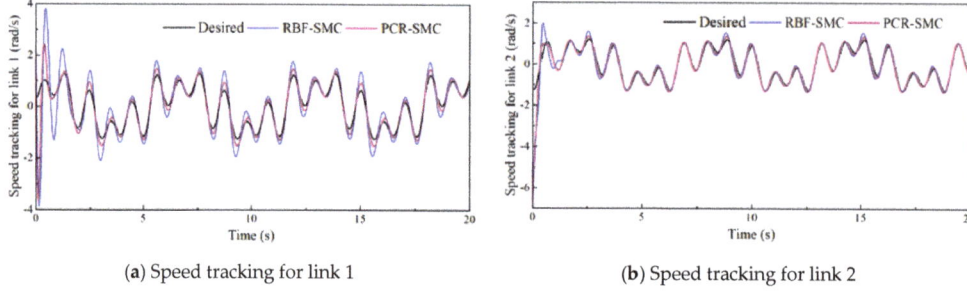

(a) Speed tracking for link 1 (b) Speed tracking for link 2

Figure 12. Desired and actual tracking speeds of links on a starfish-shaped trajectory.

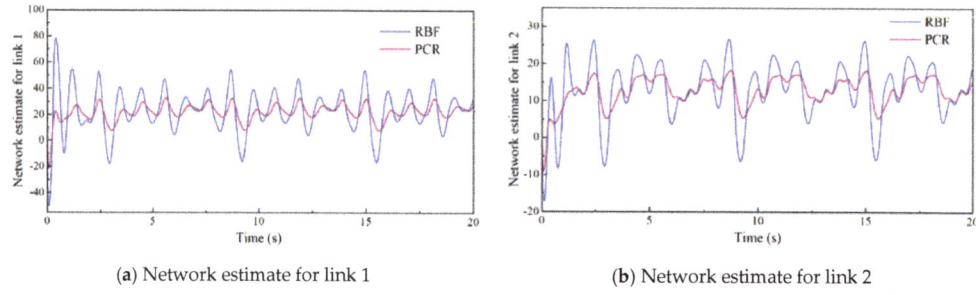

(a) Network estimate for link 1 (b) Network estimate for link 2

Figure 13. Network estimation output on a starfish-shaped trajectory.

From the simulation results of the above two trajectory tracking control methods (see Figures 8 and 13), we determined that, in the online approximation process of system model uncertainty, the output of the PCR network can converge rapidly, and the process is more stable, compared with the RBFNN. This shows that the feature value extracted by the CNN in the historical trajectory data is an important parameter for system model identification. Historical feature information is reasonably used, and it can effectively improve the identification accuracy and control stability of the dynamic model, improving the system's control performance.

The simulation results of the PCR-SMC controller proposed in this study were compared with other controllers, and the comparison results are shown in Table 5. In the case of varying load and fixed load interference, the proposed PCR-SMC controller achieved excellent control results and demonstrated excellent competitiveness.

Table 5. Controller comparison results.

Controller	Robot Type	Maximum Error	MAE	External Interference
PCR-SMC controller	2DOF	0.1 rad	0.0039 rad	Varying and fixed load
Adaptive controller [28]	2DOF	Near 0.2 rad	-	No
RFISMSC [35]	2DOF	0.1 rad	-	No
AISMC-TDE [45]	2DOF	Near 0.43 rad	0.0149 rad	Varying load
Adaptive controller [47]	2DOF	Near 0.4 rad	-	Fixed load
Robust control system [48]	2DOF	0.28 rad	-	No
HOSMC [49]	2DOF	Near 0.7 rad	-	Lower load

5. Conclusions

This paper proposed a new PCR-SMC controller and applied it to the trajectory tracking control problem of a two-link robot. We considered factors affecting trajectory tracking accuracy, including mechanical model uncertainties and external disturbances. The effective approximation and compensation of the model was realized by constructing a PCR network. Meanwhile, a new online learning algorithm was designed, by integrating adaptive control and the gradient descent method. The online learning mechanism can effectively adjust the connection weight of PCR network in real time, and the stability of the control system was proven by Lyapunov's theory. The simulation was performed with normal and starfish-shaped trajectories. The results showed that the PCR-SMC controller effectively reduced the trajectory tracking errors on both trajectories, compared with the RBF-SMC controller. This shows that the PCR-SMC controller has higher tracking accuracy, strong stability to model uncertainty and external disturbance, and excellent control performance.

In future work, we will further improve the control performance of the sliding mode controller based on the PCR network by compensating for the uncertainty of the dynamic model, and enriching the controller's application field.

Author Contributions: Conceptualization, H.W. and L.G.; methodology, H.W. and C.W.; software, H.W.; validation, Y.Z. and C.W.; resources, X.Z. (Xinming Zhang); writing—original draft preparation, H.W. and Y.Z.; writing—review and editing, X.Z. (Xinming Zhang) and L.S.; supervision, X.Z. (Xiaonan Zhao); project administration, L.S.; funding acquisition, L.G. and X.Z. (Xiaonan Zhao). All authors have read and agreed to the published version of the manuscript.

Funding: This work was supported by the Key Research and Development Project of Jilin Province Science and Technology Development Plan, grant number 20200401098GX. The Jilin Provincial Department of Education Science and Technology Project, grant number JJKH20220778KJ.

Informed Consent Statement: Not applicable.

Data Availability Statement: The data used to support the findings of this study are included within the article and are also available from the corresponding authors upon request.

Conflicts of Interest: The authors declare no conflict of interest.

References

1. Yu, X.; He, W.; Li, H.; Sun, J. Adaptive fuzzy full-state and output-feedback control for uncertain robots with output constraint. *IEEE Trans. Syst. Man Cybern. Syst.* **2020**, *51*, 6994–7007. [CrossRef]
2. Ghafarian, M.; Shirinzadeh, B.; Al-Jodah, A.; Das, T.K. Adaptive fuzzy sliding mode control for high-precision motion tracking of a multi-DOF micro/nano manipulator. *IEEE Robot. Autom. Lett.* **2020**, *5*, 4313–4320. [CrossRef]
3. Sharma, R.; Kumar, V.; Gaur, P.; Mittal, A.P. An adaptive PID like controller using mix locally recurrent neural network for robotic manipulator with variable payload. *ISA Trans.* **2016**, *62*, 258–267. [CrossRef] [PubMed]
4. Malik, A.A.; Masood, T.; Bilberg, A. Virtual reality in manufacturing: Immersive and collaborative artificial-reality in design of human-robot workspace. *Int. J. Comput. Integr. Manuf.* **2020**, *33*, 22–37. [CrossRef]
5. Wei, B. Adaptive control design and stability analysis of robotic manipulators. *Actuators* **2018**, *7*, 89. [CrossRef]
6. Tang, F.; Niu, B.; Wang, H.; Zhang, L.; Zhao, X. Adaptive fuzzy tracking control of switched MIMO nonlinear systems with full state constraints and unknown control directions. *IEEE Trans. Circuits Syst. II Express Briefs* **2022**, *69*, 2912–2916. [CrossRef]
7. Galvan-Perez, D.; Yañez-Badillo, H.; Beltran-Carbajal, F.; Rivas-Cambero, I.; Favela-Contreras, A.; Tapia-Olvera, R. Neural Adaptive Robust Motion-Tracking Control for Robotic Manipulator Systems. *Actuators* **2022**, *11*, 255. [CrossRef]
8. Chen, L.; Yan, B.; Wang, H.; Shao, K.; Kurniawan, E.; Wang, G. Extreme-learning-machine-based robust integral terminal sliding mode control of bicycle robot. *Control. Eng. Pract.* **2022**, *121*, 105064. [CrossRef]
9. Hu, H.; Bei, S.; Zhao, Q.; Han, X.; Zhou, D.; Zhou, X.; Li, B. Research on Trajectory Tracking of Sliding Mode Control Based on Adaptive Preview Time. *Actuators* **2022**, *11*, 34. [CrossRef]
10. Xu, C.Z. Research on Intelligent Backstepping Sliding Mode Control of Nonlinear Robots. Doctoral Dissertation, Huaqiao University, Quanzhou, China, 2012.
11. Zhao, T.; Liu, J.; Dian, S.; Guo, R.; Li, S. Sliding-mode-control-theory-based adaptive general type-2 fuzzy neural network control for power-line inspection robots. *Neurocomputing* **2020**, *401*, 281–294. [CrossRef]
12. Yang, Z.Y.; Wu, J.; Mei, J.P. Motor-mechanism dynamic model based neural network optimized computed torque control of a high speed parallel manipulator. *Mechatronics* **2007**, *17*, 381–390. [CrossRef]

13. Gao, H.; Xiong, L. Research on a hybrid controller combining RBF neural network supervisory control and expert PID in motor load system control. *Adv. Mech. Eng.* **2022**, *14*, 16878132221109994. [CrossRef]
14. Cheng, X.; Liu, H.; Lu, W. Chattering-suppressed sliding mode control for flexible-joint robot manipulators. *Actuators* **2021**, *10*, 288. [CrossRef]
15. Yin, F.C.; Ji, Q.Z.; Wen, C.W. An adaptive terminal sliding mode control of stone-carving robotic manipulators based on radial basis function neural network. *Appl. Intell.* **2022**, *52*, 1–18. [CrossRef]
16. Fang, W.; Chao, F.; Lin, C.M.; Zhou, D.; Yang, L.; Chang, X.; Shen, Q.; Shang, C. Visual-guided robotic object grasping using dual neural network controllers. *IEEE Trans. Ind. Inform.* **2020**, *17*, 2282–2291. [CrossRef]
17. Chen, D.; Zhang, J.; Li, Z. A novel fixed-time trajectory tracking strategy of unmanned surface vessel based on the fractional sliding mode control method. *Electronics* **2022**, *11*, 726. [CrossRef]
18. Ye, T.; Luo, Z.; Wang, G. Adaptive sliding mode control of robot based on fuzzy neural network. *J. Ambient. Intell. Humaniz. Comput.* **2020**, *11*, 6235–6247. [CrossRef]
19. Yen, V.T.; Nan, W.Y.; Van Cuong, P. Robust adaptive sliding mode neural networks control for industrial robot manipulators. *Int. J. Control. Autom. Syst.* **2019**, *17*, 783–792. [CrossRef]
20. Wang, D.H.; Zhang, S.J. Improved neural network-based adaptive tracking control for manipulators with uncertain dynamics. *Int. J. Adv. Robot. Syst.* **2020**, *17*, 1729881420947562. [CrossRef]
21. Zhang, C.; Huang, Q.; Zhang, C.; Yang, K.; Cheng, L.; Li, Z. ECNN: Intelligent Fault Diagnosis Method Using Efficient Convolutional Neural Network. *Actuators* **2022**, *11*, 275. [CrossRef]
22. Yao, X.; Chen, Z. Sliding mode control with deep learning method for rotor trajectory control of active magnetic bearing system. *Trans. Inst. Meas. Control.* **2019**, *41*, 1383–1394. [CrossRef]
23. Zhou, M.; Feng, Y.; Xue, C.; Han, F. Deep convolutional neural network based fractional-order terminal sliding-mode control for robotic manipulators. *Neurocomputing* **2020**, *416*, 143–151. [CrossRef]
24. Hemalakshmi, G.R.; Santhi, D.; Mani, V.R.S.; Geetha, A.; Prakash, N.B. Classification of retinal fundus image using MS-DRLBP features and CNN-RBF classifier. *J. Ambient. Intell. Humaniz. Comput.* **2021**, *12*, 8747–8762. [CrossRef]
25. Hong, Y.Y.; Rioflorido, C.L.P.P. A hybrid deep learning-based neural network for 24-h ahead wind power forecasting. *Appl. Energy* **2019**, *250*, 530–539. [CrossRef]
26. Sideratos, G.; Ikonomopoulos, A.; Hatziargyriou, N.D. A novel fuzzy-based ensemble model for load forecasting using hybrid deep neural networks. *Electr. Power Syst. Res.* **2020**, *178*, 106025. [CrossRef]
27. Liu, J. *Robot Control System Design and Matlab Simulation: Basic Design Method*; Press of Tsinghua University: Beijing, China, 2016; pp. 20–35.
28. Liu, A.; Zhao, H.; Song, T.; Liu, Z.; Wang, H.; Sun, D. Adaptive control of manipulator based on neural network. *Neural Comput. Appl.* **2021**, *33*, 4077–4085. [CrossRef]
29. Lu, P.; Huang, W.; Xiao, J.; Zhou, F.; Hu, W. Adaptive Proportional Integral Robust Control of an Uncertain Robotic Manipulator Based on Deep Deterministic Policy Gradient. *Mathematics* **2021**, *9*, 2055. [CrossRef]
30. Yu, X.; Zhang, S.; Fu, Q.; Xue, C.; Sun, W. Fuzzy Logic Control of an Uncertain Manipulator with Full-State Constraints and Disturbance Observer. *IEEE Access* **2020**, *8*, 24284–24295. [CrossRef]
31. Nohooji, H.R. Constrained neural adaptive PID control for robot manipulators. *J. Frankl. Inst.* **2020**, *357*, 3907–3923. [CrossRef]
32. Özyer, B. Adaptive fast sliding neural control for robot manipulator. *Turk. J. Electr. Eng. Comput. Sci.* **2020**, *28*, 3154–3167.
33. Feng, H.; Song, Q.; Ma, S.; Ma, W.; Yin, C.; Cao, D.; Yu, H. A new adaptive sliding mode controller based on the RBF neural network for an electro-hydraulic servo system. *ISA Trans.* **2022**, *129*, 472–484. [CrossRef] [PubMed]
34. Zhang, F.; Xiao, H.; Zhang, Y.; Gong, G. Distributed Drive Electric Bus Handling Stability Control Based on Lyapunov Theory and Sliding Mode Control. *Actuators* **2022**, *11*, 85. [CrossRef]
35. Zhang, X.; Xu, W.; Lu, W. Fractional-order iterative sliding mode control based on the neural network for manipulator. *Math. Probl. Eng.* **2021**, *2021*, 1–12. [CrossRef]
36. Gao, L.; Xiong, L.; Lin, X.; Xia, X.; Liu, W.; Lu, Y.; Yu, Z. Multi-sensor fusion road friction coefficient estimation during steering with lyapunov method. *Sensors* **2019**, *19*, 3816. [CrossRef]
37. Gabdullin, N.; Madanzadeh, S.; Vilkin, A. Towards end-to-end deep learning performance analysis of electric motors. *Actuators* **2021**, *10*, 28. [CrossRef]
38. Abdou, M.A. Literature review: Efficient deep neural networks techniques for medical image analysis. *Neural Comput. Appl.* **2022**, *34*, 5791–5812. [CrossRef]
39. Ding, S.; Zhao, H.; Zhang, Y.; Xu, X.; Nie, R. Extreme learning machine: Algorithm, theory and applications. *Artif. Intell. Rev.* **2015**, *44*, 103–115. [CrossRef]
40. Van Cuong, P.; Nan, W.Y. Adaptive trajectory tracking neural network control with robust compensator for robot manipulators. *Neural Comput. Appl.* **2016**, *27*, 525–536. [CrossRef]
41. Nadeem, F.; Alghazzawi, D.; Mashat, A.; Fakeeh, K.; Almalaise, A.; Hagras, H. Modeling and predicting execution time of scientific workflows in the grid using radial basis function neural network. *Clust. Comput.* **2017**, *20*, 2805–2819. [CrossRef]
42. Yang, X.; Sun, W.; Dong, H.; Wu, X. Adaptive Prescribed Performance Fuzzy Control for n-Link Flexible-Joint Robots Under Event-Triggered Mechanism. *Int. J. Fuzzy Syst.* **2022**, *25*, 1019–1033. [CrossRef]

43. Feng, Y.; Yu, X.; Man, Z. Non-singular terminal sliding mode control of rigid manipulators. *Automatica* **2002**, *38*, 2159–2167. [CrossRef]
44. Nojavanzadeh, D.; Badamchizadeh, M. Adaptive fractional-order non-singular fast terminal sliding mode control for robot manipulators. *IET Control. Theory Appl.* **2016**, *10*, 1565–1572. [CrossRef]
45. Wang, H.; Fang, L.; Song, T.; Xu, J.; Shen, H. Model-free adaptive sliding mode control with adjustable funnel boundary for robot manipulators with uncertainties. *Rev. Sci. Instrum.* **2021**, *92*, 065101. [CrossRef] [PubMed]
46. Zhang, X.; Shi, R. Adaptive Fractional-Order Nonsingular Fast Terminal Sliding Mode Control for Manipulators. *Complexity* **2021**, *2021*, 1–13. [CrossRef]
47. Liu, Q.; Li, D.; Ge, S.S.; Ji, R.; Ouyang, Z.; Tee, K.P. Adaptive bias RBF neural network control for a robotic manipulator. *Neurocomputing* **2021**, *447*, 213–223. [CrossRef]
48. Chang, Z.; Hao, L.; Yan, Q.; Ye, T. Research on manipulator tracking control algorithm based on RBF neural network. *J. Phys. Conf. Ser.* **2021**, *1802*, 032072. [CrossRef]
49. Lin, C.J.; Sie, T.Y.; Chu, W.L.; Yau, H.T.; Ding, C.H. Tracking control of pneumatic artificial muscle-activated robot arm based on sliding-mode control. *Actuators* **2021**, *10*, 66. [CrossRef]

Disclaimer/Publisher's Note: The statements, opinions and data contained in all publications are solely those of the individual author(s) and contributor(s) and not of MDPI and/or the editor(s). MDPI and/or the editor(s) disclaim responsibility for any injury to people or property resulting from any ideas, methods, instructions or products referred to in the content.

Article

Design and Coverage Path Planning of a Disinfection Robot

Pengjie Xu, Xinyi Chen and Qirong Tang *

The Laboratory of Robotics and Multibody System, School of Mechanical Engineering, Tongji University, Shanghai 201804, China
* Correspondence: qirong.tang@tongji.edu.cn

Abstract: Eliminating pathogen exposure is an important approach to control outbreaks of epidemics such as COVID-19 (coronavirus disease 2019). To deal with pathogenic environments, using disinfection robots is a practicable choice. This research formulates a 3D (three-dimensional) spatial disinfection strategy for a disinfection robot. First, a disinfection robot is designed with an extensible control framework for the integration of additional functions. The robot has eight degrees of freedom that can handle disinfection tasks in complex 3D environments where normal disinfection robots lack the capability to ensure complete disinfection. An ingenious clamping mechanism is designed to increase flexibility and adaptability. Secondly, a new coverage path planning algorithm targeted at the spraying area is used. This algorithm aims to achieve an optimal path via the rotating calipers algorithm after transformation between a 2D (two-dimensional) array and 3D space. Finally, the performance of the designed robot is tested through a series of simulations and experiments in various spaces that humans usually live in. The results demonstrate that the robot can effectively perform disinfection tasks both in computer simulation and in reality.

Keywords: COVID-19; disinfection robot; coverage path planing; extensible control framework

---

Citation: Xu, P.; Chen, X.; Tang, Q. Design and Coverage Path Planning of a Disinfection Robot. *Actuators* **2023**, *12*, 182. https://doi.org/10.3390/act12050182

Academic Editors: Ahmad Taher Azar, Amjad J. Humaidi and Ammar K. Al Mhdawi

Received: 6 March 2023
Revised: 27 March 2023
Accepted: 8 April 2023
Published: 24 April 2023

Copyright: © 2023 by the authors. Licensee MDPI, Basel, Switzerland. This article is an open access article distributed under the terms and conditions of the Creative Commons Attribution (CC BY) license (https://creativecommons.org/licenses/by/4.0/).

1. Introduction

The outbreak of COVID-19 has caused an unprecedented global threat to public health and the economy. Although the spread of some new variants has led to a situation of low death rates worldwide, improving the configuration of healthcare facilities to better respond to the status quo is still urgent. Moreover, when facing the challenges of unknown contagious diseases, reducing or eliminating exposure is always one of the crucial ways to maintain health. Traditional methods of exposure elimination, such as manual disinfectant spraying, are restricted by the availability of operators in terms of work time and concentration. Disinfection robotic systems available for remote control represent a practical and reasonable tool to fulfill various anti-epidemic purposes. Disinfection or sterilization robots can remain unhindered by peak hours or terrible operating conditions and carry out their duties all day long to prevent pathogenic attacks [1].

Many researchers in automation and engineering have also actively responded to this conception. Since the onset of the pandemic, MIT and Boston Dynamics have begun to cooperate in the design of patient interaction robots in order to reduce the frontline virus exposure of healthcare personnel [2]. The use of ultraviolet (UV) light is especially noticed because its energy is sufficient to destroy the DNA or RNA of any microorganism, and UV lights have been installed on many experimental mobile robots in an environment to be sanitized [3]. These robots utilize annotated points of interest on the map to scan the area and automatically reach the location to perform specific disinfection tasks. However, limited by the characteristics of UV light and their operating distance, these robots can only execute on-ground tasks. In a previous study [4], an intelligent disinfection robotic system was developed to enable robots to spray disinfectants in operating theaters or patients' rooms, based on the results of controlled experiments and the requirements for hospital disinfection. A key feature of this research is the application of a novel CLO_2 disinfection technology to sterilize bacteria and viruses in the air and on surfaces. Another noteworthy feature is that this robot is also based on a mobile platform, by which the disinfection abilities are severely curtailed in 3D space, such as on table tops, door handles, elevator buttons, and other regular locations that humans usually touch [5,6]. There are additional applications for disinfection robots. For example, SOMATIC is a commercial cleaning robot that can perform approximately eight hours of cleaning work each time it runs. It can even open doors and ride elevators to move around the building. The service range of this robot includes airports, casinos, office spaces, and other places such as large restrooms [7]. The designed robot is compared with two typical disinfection robots as listed in Table 1.

Table 1. Robots used for disinfection.

Related Works	Paper [2]	Paper [3]	Our robot
Disinfection method	ultraviolet light	spraying	spraying
Disinfection range	open-sided 3D space	open-sided 2D space	3D space
Degrees of freedom	5	3	8
Robot			

In order to better accomplish disinfection tasks, reasonable planning of the spraying path is a key element of the designed robot. We can convert this problem into a coverage path problem in 3D space. The coverage path planning (CPP) algorithm is a popular topic and has been substantially studied. It is applied for underwater or land inspection, unmanned aerial vehicles, milling, floor cleaning, painting, and medical tasks [8]. Both offline and online CPP algorithms have been previously proposed. For example, Han [9] proposed a complete CPP obstacle avoidance algorithm for underwater gliders in the sea, with shorter path planning and economized energy supply. Only three years have passed since the outbreak of COVID-19, so few researchers have performed in-depth studies on the disinfection path problem. Among them, Hong [10] designed a path planning model to acquire an optimal path based on the map and the robot's current location; however, the setting is restricted to conference rooms. Another study [11] investigated how the robotic path can be optimized to achieve the maximum UV-irradiation performance based on environmental geometry. Bähnemann et al. presented a path planner for low-altitude terrain coverage in known environments with unmanned rotary-wing micro aerial vehicles [12]. In this research, the algorithm was applied in conference rooms and was tested to verify the accuracy, cost, and efficiency of the robotic execution of disinfection tasks.

In line with the above studies, the objective of the present research is to design a disinfection robot that can provide effective zero-contact disinfection services for common environments in 3D space. The main characteristics of this research that differ from the existing studies are as follows.

(1) This research provides a unique design of robotic architecture from software to hardware. A key feature of our robot is that it is endowed with eight DoFs (degrees of freedom) to conduct disinfection tasks in common 3D environments based on the integration of a mobile platform, a manipulator, and the designed disinfection instrument.
(2) According to the characteristics of the designed robot, a CPP algorithm is used for disinfection in 3D space. In contrast to [9,11], the particularities are taken as the factors in the disinfection strategy.
(3) Mechanical design, multisensor data fusion, control systems, path planning, spraying disinfection, and other technologies are adopted to conduct a series of simulations and experiments to verify the performance of the robot and the proposed algorithm.

The remainder of this research is structured as follows. The second section explains the design of the disinfection robot in detail; the third section describes the proposed CPP algorithm; the fourth section verifies the performance of the robot and the proposed algorithm with two numerical examples and an experiment; and the fifth section, i.e., the conclusion, summarizes the results and outlines future work. The patents obtained based on this research are listed in the sixth section.

2. Robot Design

2.1. Function Analysis and Design

According to the requirements of COVID-19 prevention, the disinfection robot should have flexibility in 3D space that traditional robots lack. Namely, the robot should be able to correct its end-effector pose based on the specific disinfection demands and be able to smoothly adapt to various application scenarios. Remote control is also a prerequisite for dealing with unique working conditions. Therefore, power supply, communication, storage performance, and other corresponding modules of the robot should be taken into consideration. The specific requirements are listed as follows:

1. The width of the robot should be less than 1.2 m to move through elevators, bedroom doors, and other similar scenarios;
2. The spraying height should be around 1.6 m to cover most common environments;
3. The manipulator should have ample DoFs (operability and flexibility in 3D space) to access any corner that humans can touch;
4. One charge should enable a working duration of 6 h for the robot, and the robot should be able to work at different voltage values to fit different disinfection instruments;
5. The gripper should be a general part to fit different disinfection instruments;
6. The hardware and software of the robot should be extensible to achieve multifunctional integration.

2.2. Gripper Design

As one of the key components of the robot, a flexible gripper is designed to grip the spraying disinfection instruments. The gripper consists of two modules, namely the fixed and the motion modules. The fixed module comprises a fixed base body, a guide seat, and a fixed seat. The motion module comprises clamping jaws, a guide seat, and a drive plate. More definitions of the corresponding structures are shown in Figure 1.

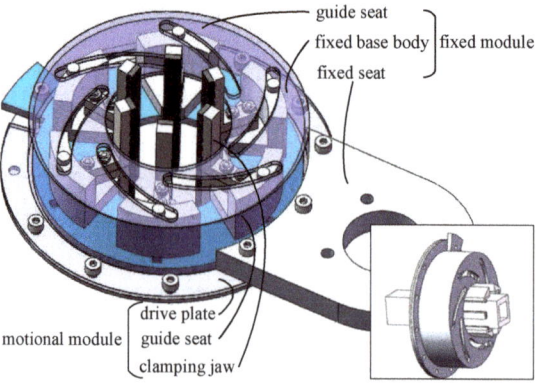

Figure 1. Structure of the gripper.

Clamping jaws are installed on the guide seat along its circumference in the radial direction in a guiding way, while the guide seat and the drive plate are fixed to the base body so that each clamping jaw can extend to clamp or retract to release an object in the radial direction when the guide seat and the drive plate can rotate relatively. The design of the clamping mechanism is simple in structure, enabling convenient adjustment of the clamping range; the clamping jaws can also be replaced to accommodate different shapes, as shown in the subgraph of Figure 1 (bottom right). The mechanical principle of the gripper can be seen in the accompanying video.

2.3. The Robotic System

To achieve the above-mentioned functions, a mobile manipulator needs to be installed to operate the spraying disinfection instruments. The mobile manipulator consists of a UR5, a serial-chain manipulator that is mounted on a nonholonomic mobile platform with two DoFs, as shown in the Figure 2. The robot should support the weights of all modules up to 50 kg and be able to move freely across a flat surface. The left and the right motors of the mobile platform are driven by 12-volt batteries. The function of the manipulator is to conduct disinfection operations in 3D space via the disinfection instrument, which is composed of a compressed air device, a thin pipe, a nozzle, a gripper, etc. The nozzle can be controlled by an electric valve with an IO interface. In order to fix the disinfection instruments to the end of the manipulator tightly and suitably for different applications, the gripper is installed on the flange of the UR5. With USB hubs, functional extension can be achieved by linking to different external sensors.

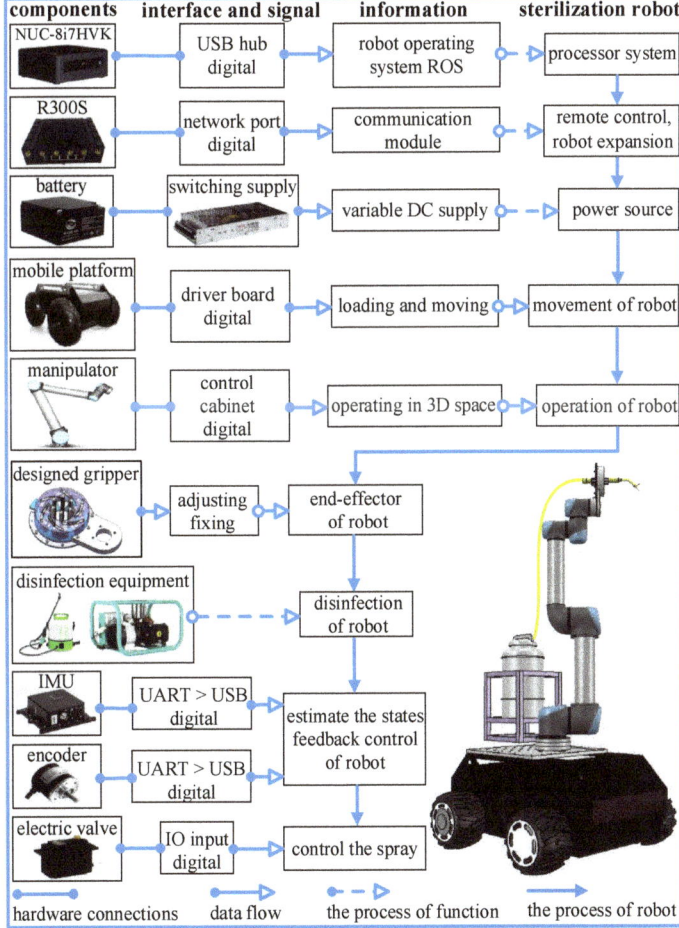

Figure 2. The designed disinfection robot system.

The software design of the disinfection robot is based on the robot operating system (ROS 1) [13]. The communication network uses a TCP/IP protocol to facilitate telecommunication with the upper computer or other intelligent robots [14]. An Intel NUC (i7-8559, 16GB RAM) works as a local computer, while the motion and control functions are encapsulated as ROS packages and executed in the NUC. The super potential of the robot is achieved by reserving ample computing power and interfaces for function extensions, such as for image processing and machine learning. Compared to various other disinfection robotic systems, this robotic system incorporates its operational parameters and various functionalities into its hardware and software structures (see more details in Figure 2).

2.4. Kinematic Analysis

The robot has eight DoFs (two in the mobile platform and six in the manipulator) to conquer difficulties and realize the desired disinfection motions. Before the kinematic analysis, one can use $P_g = [x_g, y_g, z_g, \alpha_g, \beta_g, \gamma_g]^T$ to describe the motions of the robot in the world frame (Σ_g), where the first three elements in P_g represent the position, and α_g, β_g, and γ_g are used to specify the orientations in the triplet of roll, pitch, and yaw (RPY) angles, respectively [15]. In order to achieve better spraying, the motions along the x_g and y_g directions are achieved by a mobile platform. The UR5 manipulator aims to realize the rest of the absolute motion in the world frame or absolute motion in the frame of the mobile platform. The desired joint-space trajectories can be obtained based on inverse kinematics [16].

One more thing should be noted: we deployed an underactuated system for the mobile platform. The DoFs of the mobile platform can be denoted as $q_p = [q_l \ q_r]^T$. The velocities constrainted between $p_p = [{}^g x_p \ {}^g y_p \ {}^g \gamma_p]^T$ and the intermediate variables $h_p = [v \ \omega]^T$ are expressed as in [17],

$$\dot{p} = A(p) \cdot h_p = \begin{bmatrix} \cos(\theta_p) & \sin(\theta_p) & 0 \\ 0 & 0 & 1 \end{bmatrix}^T \cdot h_p, \tag{1}$$

where h_p represents the linear and angular velocities of the mobile platform, A is a 3×2 transformation matrix, and θ_p is the joint angle of mobile platform.

In order to obtain a solution in joint space, the inverse kinematics of the mobile platform can be written as,

$$\dot{q}_p = J_p \cdot h_p = \begin{bmatrix} 1/r & W/r \\ 1/r & -W/r \end{bmatrix} \cdot h_p, \tag{2}$$

where J_p is a Jacobian matrix, and r and W are the wheel radius and rear tracks of the mobile platform, respectively.

The motions $[\alpha_g, \beta_g, {}^m \gamma_p]^T$ need to be realized by the manipulator, where ${}^m \gamma_p$ is the relative motion in the mobile platform frame (Σ_p). Hence, inverse kinematics are used for the manipulator to solve the joint variables according to $p_m = [{}^p \alpha_m, {}^p \beta_m, z_g, \alpha_g, \beta_g, {}^p \gamma_m]^T$. The kinematic models of UR5 and their solutions have been sufficiently explored in an abundance of studies [18]. In this research, iterative methods are applied for the detailed computation of UR5 [19,20]. Moreover, the proposed kinematics model of the manipulator is based on but not limited to UR5.

Furthermore, knowledge of spray distribution is required to generate a motion trajectory. The nozzle starts from the origin of the 3D surface, which is a protruding point if the surface is unfolded. It can be assumed that the spray particles form a cone and that the distribution pattern is roughly circular when the nozzle is perpendicular to the starting point (Σ_s), as shown in Figure 3. The kinematic parameters of the nozzle include the spray angle (θ_s) and the spray radius (R_s). The rate of spray impacts the element division of the disinfection area. In order to make the function of disinfection applicable, a reasonable margin of safety is defined, which can also be used to determine the effect of spraying.

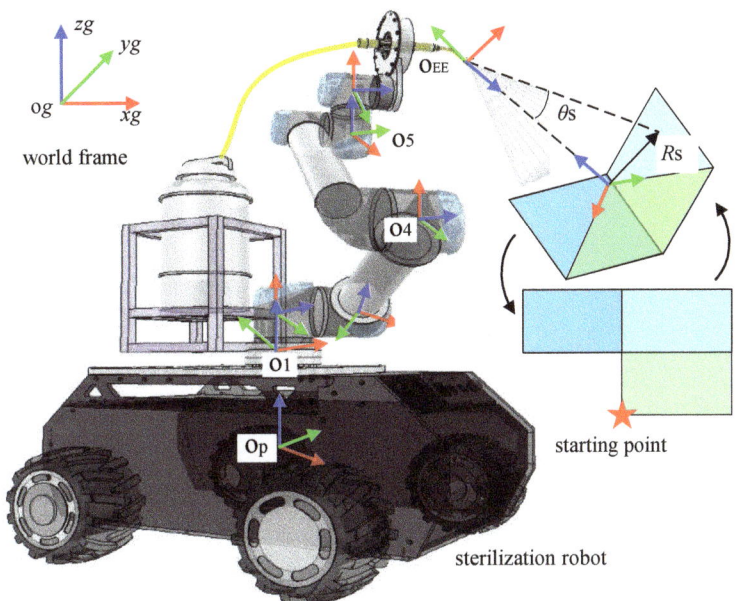

Figure 3. Kinematic analysis of the disinfection robot.

3. Coverage Path Planning

CPP is an important part of the robotic disinfection project. All common environmental areas should be marked and traversed, and the planned path can be obtained by connecting the nodes. Then, the robot follows this path to conduct the disinfection task, ensuring that all possible blind spots are covered with the minimal consumption of disinfectant. The scheme of the proposed CPP algorithm is shown in Figure 4.

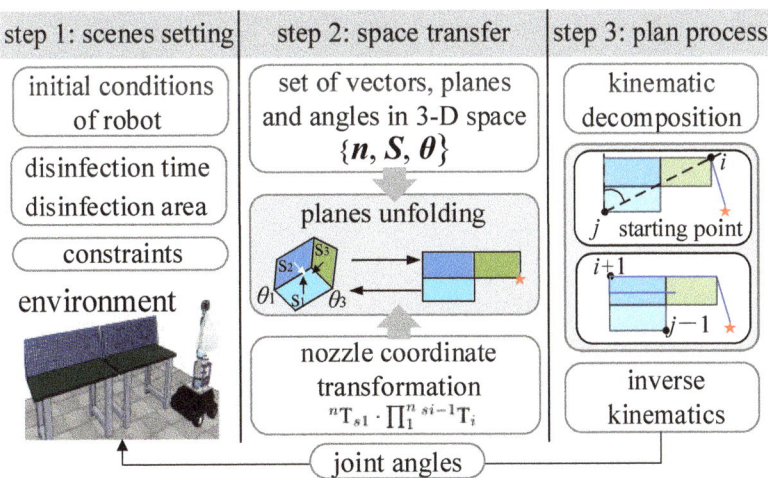

Figure 4. Scheme of coverage path planning.

3.1. Space Transfer

In contrast to traditional path planning methods, each of the areas in the selected environment should be disinfected. Here, space transfer is considered, converting square pixels in 3D space into 2D arrays so that all areas are covered adequately. Each pixel (s_i) is regarded as an element for set S in 2D space, as shown in Figure 3. Set $n = \{n \mid \vec{n}_{s1}, \vec{n}_{s2}, \ldots, \vec{n}_{sn}\}$ is defined as the normal vectors of each unfolded plane, and set $p = \{p \mid p_1, p_2, \ldots, p_n\}$ represents the vertices of each array in the unfolded plane. Based on set S, the set of angles between two planes is $\theta = \{\theta_{12}, \theta_{13}, \ldots, \theta_{nn}\}$. In practice, the initial and terminal points of the nozzle should be considered and noted as p_i and p_t.

Let ^iT_n be a 4×4 homogeneous transformation matrix between the coordinate systems from point p_i to p_n. Therefore,

$$^iT_n = {^iT_1} \cdot {^1T_2} \ldots {^{n-1}T_n}, \qquad (3)$$

The geometric parameters can be obtained with defined sets.

After the above process, the CPP algorithm can be viewed as a sequence of robot configurations by which each array is visited at least once. Each array should be evaluated to determine whether or not it is basically reachable by the robot based on its kinematic capability. If the spray does not fully cover the meshed grid, one can tag the corresponding arrays as unreachable, based on which the relative pose and the path are optimized. In summary, after this step, every array will be assigned a corresponding robot configuration. Collision detection and 'reachable'-oriented redundant configuration control are explicitly considered in the CPP algorithm. Thus, the actual coverage path may be lower than estimated in this preprocessing step.

Once the entire surface is covered, the final spray trajectory is obtained and rendered as an input to the end effector to request motion execution on the desired surface.

3.2. Coverage Path Planning

Figure 4 explains how to support the robot with the end effector to get close to the most reachable pixels in its current pose. The optimization problem of the end-effector path can be formulated as a path planning problem, the goal of which is to obtain the minimum path with the corresponding constraints and the robot configurations. After preprocessing, a path sequence (P) can be found to cover the unfolded plane (the initial and terminal points are included) within the minimum time. Based on the CPP algorithm with the rotating caliper algorithm, an unfolding plan can be introduced as $Q = \{V, E\}$, where $V = \{1, 2, \ldots, n\}$ is the set of vertices, and $E = \{(1,2), \ldots, (n,1)\}$ is the set of edges. Then, the nozzle, as defined by the search pattern, follows a path to cover the area (Q), where each point in the path will be reached by the nozzle moving in straight lines. All points in the path can be denoted as $P = \{p \mid p_i, p_1, p_2, \ldots, p_n, p_t\}$.

Using rotating calipers, antipodal pairs i and j $(i, j \in V)$ are two points on the surface of a polygon that are exactly opposite each other. The idea of the method is to compute all the antipodal pairs, find the best path for each antipodal pair, and then select the path with the lowest cost in combination with the takeoff and landing points [8]. The caliper is roated clockwise until it touches the edge then, it is rotated counter-clockwise until it touches a second edge. An $angle()$ function is then defined to compute the angle swept out by a line as it rotates from its position parallels. Next, both options are measured to determine the minimum width of the formed polygon. In application, one can define vertex i close to the initiation point. Then, the algorithm performs a sequence of decisions and procedures that do not depend on the number of vertices. Based on the antipodal pair and optimized angle, a path can be computed by the $2Dpath()$ function using a back-and-forth pattern. Finally, the plan (S) should be folded in 3D space based on an inverse kinematic solution using Equation (3). More details about its implementation are shown in Algorithm 1.

Algorithm 1 Coverage path planning algorithm

Input:
normal vectors of unfolded plane
$n = \{n \mid \vec{n}_{s1}, \vec{n}_{s2}, \ldots, \vec{n}_{sn}\}$;
the sizes of each unfolded plane $S = \{s \mid s_1, s_2, \ldots, s_n\}$;
plane angle $\theta = \{\theta_{12}, \theta_{13}, \ldots, \theta_{nn}\}$;
vertices of unfold plan $p = \{p \mid p_1, p_2, \ldots, p_n\}$;
safety margin h and spray radius R_s;
antipodal pair (i, j);

Output:
waypoints p in 3D space;

1: space transfer with n, S, θ using Equation (3);
2: define the rotation angle function $angle()$ in clockwise direction;
3: define the distance function $dist()$ between two points by using Euclidean distance formula;
4: define the back and forth path function $2Dpath()$ based on antipodal pair (i, j) and optimized angle;
5: **if** $angle(i, j) < angle(j, i)$ **then**
6:    $k \leftarrow j; l \leftarrow i$;
7: **else**
8:    $k \leftarrow i; l \leftarrow j$;
9: $\phi \leftarrow angle(k, l) - \pi$;
10: $\varphi_k \leftarrow angle(k-1, k) - \pi$; $\varphi_l \leftarrow angle(l-1, l) - \phi$;
11: **if** $\varphi_k < \varphi_l$ **then**
12:    $m \leftarrow k - 1; n \leftarrow l$;
13: **else**
14:    $m \leftarrow l - 1; n \leftarrow k$;
15: **if** $dist(k, l) < dist(m, n)$ **then**
16:    $p = 2Dpath(k, k+1)$;
17: **else**
18:    $p = 2Dpath(m+1, m)$;
19: calculate the waypoints in 3D space based on inverse solution of Equation (3);
20: calculate the joint angle of mobile platform using Equation (1);
21: calculate the joint angle of manipulator in numerical iteration method with motions $\begin{bmatrix} ^p\alpha_m, {}^p\beta_m, z_g, \alpha_g, \beta_g, {}^p\gamma_m \end{bmatrix}^T$.

4. Simulation and Experiment

The application of the designed disinfection robot and the proposed CPP algorithm is verified in this section. For the disinfection test in 3D space, we assume that the spray is uniformly distributed, and the sanitizing agents are sprayed into the appointed area every second. Since pathogens can easily be found in common environments (especially on tables and door handles that are frequently touched by humans), the estimated best spraying effect can be achieved by aiming the geometric center point of the spray nozzle at least once. Two simulations and one experiment are carried out to verify the feasibility of the robot and the proposed algorithm. The first simulation focuses on the rationality and capability of path planning for key points in diverse scenarios. The second simulation aims to verify the feasibility of the robot via a disinfection task in a simulation environment. Here, the robot is aimed to disinfect a workbench in a simulation, as shown in Figure 5. For the experiment, the scenario is identical to that in the second simulation. The experimental objective is to test the practical and theoretical performance of the robot. Corresponding videos are provided as supplementary material for this research.

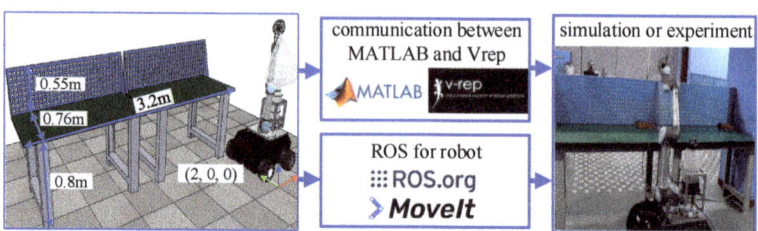

Figure 5. Scheme of the simulation and experiment.

4.1. Simulation and Experimental Settings

Vrep and MATLAB are used as tools for the simulations due to their close-to-physical environments and data processing abilities. The simulation process is conducted as follows. The proposed algorithm runs in MATLAB, and the implementation, and the feedback of the data are performed in Vrep with dynamic properties. First, the data and the algorithm are processed in MATLAB. Secondly, the communication for ROS nodes is established through the programming interface of the application. Then, defined outputs are continuously implemented, while the data results of the proposed algorithm are updated. Within the cosimulation with MATLAB and Vrep, the physical engine and the simulation steps are selected as Bullet (a physical engine) 2.73 and 50 ms, respectively.

For the experiment, the whole control system architecture is realized based on ROS1. A distributed multicomputer communication network for the multirobot system is adopted using the TCP/IP protocol [14]. The ROS master runs on a remote computer (i7-8700 CPU and 8GB RAM), with which the operator can control the robot in a noninfectious environment. For the robot, an Intel NUC (i7-8559 CPU and 16GB RAM) is used as a local workstation. The control function based on the proposed CPP algorithm is integrated and executed in the local workstation. The communication between the mobile platform and the manipulator (UR5) is based on a feature package named ROS MoveIt. They can be connected using twisted pairs. The specific operations of the simulation and the experiment are shown in Figure 5.

To better illustrate the disinfection of the robot and the proposed algorithm, the experimental area is divided into two categories: horizontal groups and vertical groups. We should also point out that a future version of the motion planner will include other parameters such as irregular regions and moving objects. The kinematic and dynamic parameters of the disinfection robot are listed in Table 2.

Table 2. Physical parameters of the designed disinfection robot.

	Size (L * W * H)	Weight	Load
Mobile platform	0.88m * 0.68m * 0.45 m	60 kg	100 kg
Manipulator	Weight : [2.58 1.55 1.20 0.52 0.41 0.09] (kg)		
	a_{DH} : [0 0.61 0.57 0 0 0] (m)		
	d_{DH} : [0.12 0 0 0.16 0.12 0.09] (m)		
	α_{DH} : [$\pi/2$ 0 0 $\pi/2$ $-\pi/2$ 0] (rad)		
	θ_{DH} : [0 $-\pi/2$ 0 $-\pi/2$ 0 0] (rad)		
Gripper	Weight	Clamping range	Clamping shape
	0.45 kg	0 ~ 60 mm	Arbitrary

The experimental process can be summarized in three steps. First, all the features of motion and path planning are packed as ROS packages. Secondly, communication tests and ROS nodes are initialized. Finally, the ROS packages of motion and path planning are executed with other necessary ROS nodes on either the local or master computers.

4.2. Validation of the CPP Algorithm

For this simulation, the scenarios are diversified, including standard, arbitrary, and concave polygons, while the antipodal pair (i, j) is randomly selected. The size of scenarios varies from 4 m to 20 m and is used to describe the unfolded shapes of the disinfection areas as much as possible. Since the nozzle is assumed to spray uniformly, the scanning radius is defined as 0.5 m in the simulation.

Figure 6 shows the results of the CPP algorithm, in which the black solid line represents the disinfection area, and the solid circles are the initial and terminal points. Some of the points are determined by calculation, while the rest are randomly selected. The lines are the end coverage paths, which are the final results after planning. Based on the proposed algorithm, the path covers every corner to ensure the full disinfection of the surfaces; key points in this path are important for the robot's motion. It can be observed that the proposed algorithm achieves the minimum redundant paths in all environments when they complete the same amount of coverage tasks. This observation is consistent with the results of the theoretical analyses in the third section.

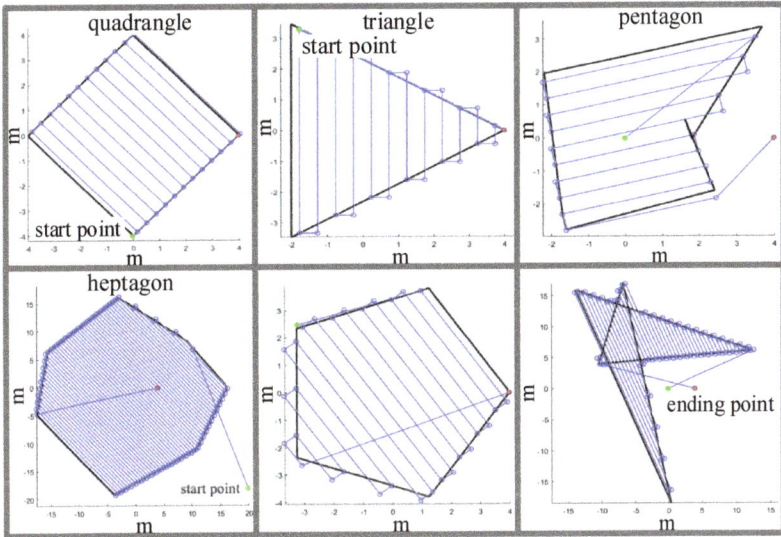

Figure 6. Coverage path planning in different environments.

4.3. Validation for Robot Disinfection in Simulation

To demonstrate the applicability of the robot and the proposed algorithm for epidemic prevention, a coverage path task is performed on a workbench. The overall size of the workbench is 3 m × 0.8 m × 1.5 m (length, width, and height, respectively). These parameters are input into the algorithm as scene setting. The initial generalized coordinates of the robot and the workbench are given in the left subfigure of Figure 5. All the initial values of joints ($\dot{q}$) are defined as zeros.

Figure 7 shows snapshots of the simulated disinfection. The snapshot at t = 5 s (top left) shows the nozzle as it begins to spray the workbench. The snapshot at t = 20 s (top right) depicts the robot as it is nearly finished spraying the first workbench. The snapshot at t = 50 s (bottom left) shows the robot as it begins to disinfect the second workbench. The snapshot at t = 80 s (bottom right) represents the accomplished disinfection. More details of the simulation can be found in the attached video. First, the robot and the proposed algorithm achieve path coverage in 3D space, and the nozzle follows a trajectory planned by the proposed algorithm. Secondly, it is feasible and in accordance with the motion plan mentioned in the third section. The end effector can easily track the trajectory of the relatively complex and mobile platform. On one hand, if we remove the data of the path of the end effector as the key point, the CPP algorithm is more practical and more easily implemented. On the other hand, the higher the altitude of the mobile platform, the larger the path losses and the more robot hovering energy required. Thirdly, the nozzle is flexible to operate due to real-time communication, execution, and feedback between MATLAB and Vrep with minimal time delay.

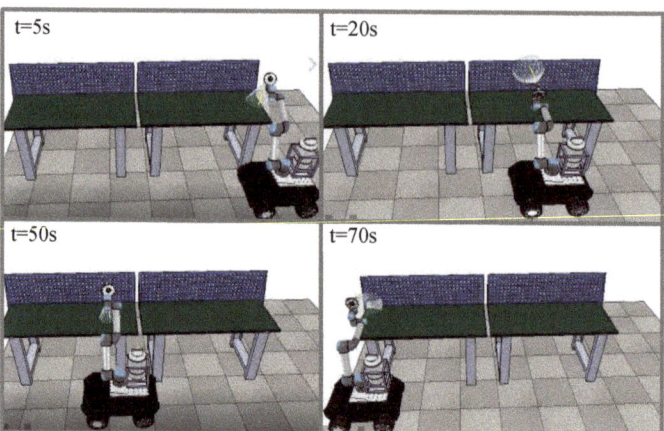

Figure 7. Disinfection in the simulation environment.

In order to express the performance of the end effector, the posture along the x_p^e, y_p^e, and z_p^e directionsis presented in Figure 8; the trajectories are smooth during the whole simulation. At the beginning, the robot adjusts its height and direction to stay in a reasonable range within the workbench. Hence, the trajectory on the z_p^e axis changes regularly. During the disinfection process, the trajectory is regular and smooth. The joint trajectories of UR5 are shown in Figure 9, with a similar regularity in joint space. The disinfection robot has fewer constraints on its movement compared to the situation in the first simulation. Therefore, the algorithm can choose among a wide variety of trajectories, enabling separate evaluation of its capability. The goal of this simulation is to evaluate the disinfection performance of the optimized trajectory planning method described in the previous sections.

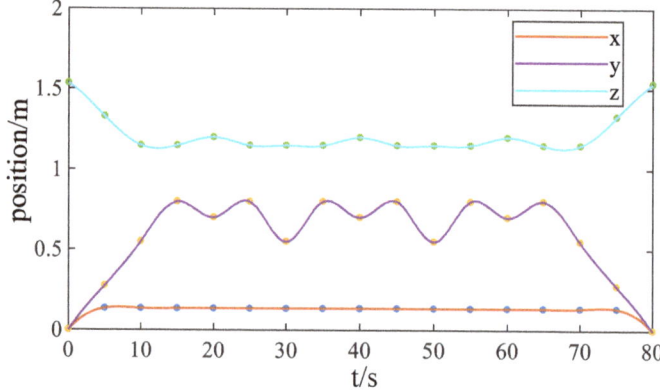

Figure 8. Posture of the nozzle along the x_p^e, y_p^e, and z_p^e directions.

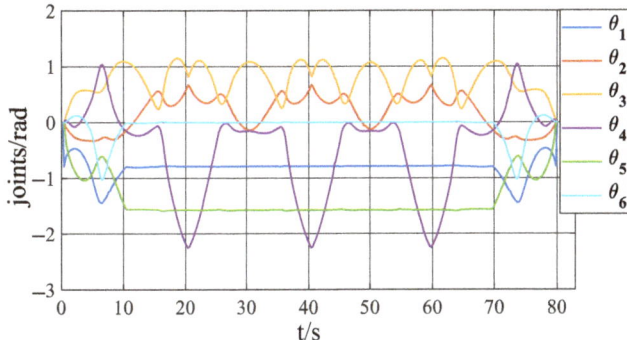

Figure 9. Joints of the manipulator in the simulation.

4.4. Experimental Validation of Robot Disinfection

In order to reproduce the properties of the disinfection robot in a physical environment, the configuration and parameters of the experiment are identical to those in the simulation. Figure 10 shows snapshots of the experimental disinfection. The snapshot at t = 5 s (the top left) shows the nozzle as it begins to spray on the workbench. The snapshot at t = 20 s (the top right) shows the robot as it is nearly finished spraying on the first workbench. The snapshot at t = 50 s (the bottom left) shows the robot as it begins to disinfect the second workbench. The snapshot at t = 70 s (the bottom right) represents the accomplished disinfection. More details of the experiment can be found in the attached video.

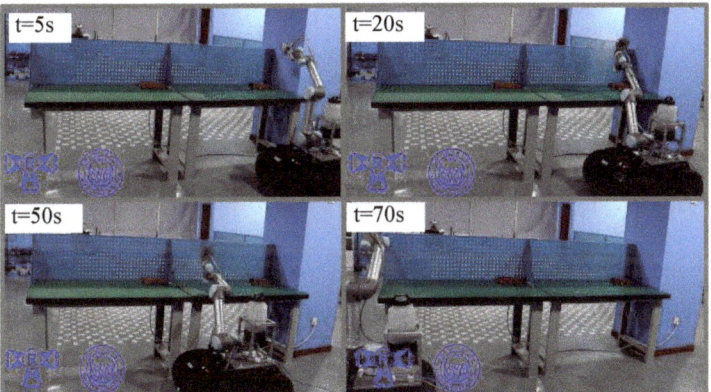

Figure 10. Disinfection in the experimental environment.

In this experiment, the robot and the proposed algorithm can achieve path coverage in real-world 3D space. Validation is conducted by seeking optimal trajectories on the horizontal and vertical surfaces, as shown in Figure 10. In order to express the performance of the end effector, the posture along the x_g, y_g, and z_g directionsis recorded in Figure 11; the trajectories are similar to those in the simulation. At the beginning, the robot adjusts its height and direction to stay in a reasonable range within the workbench. Hence, the trajectory on the z_g axis changes less smoothly. During the disinfection process, the trajectories are regular and smooth. The joint trajectories of UR5 are shown in Figure 12 with a similar regularity in joint space. The characteristics of the spray nozzle in the experiment have more influence on the performance parameters, such as actual wireless communication, spray homogenization, and thickness. We should also point out that this algorithm can handle a variety of surfaces in 3D space that humans usually touch. The results prove that the proposed disinfection robot is more suitable for spraying tasks in 3D space than regular (move-based) disinfection robots.

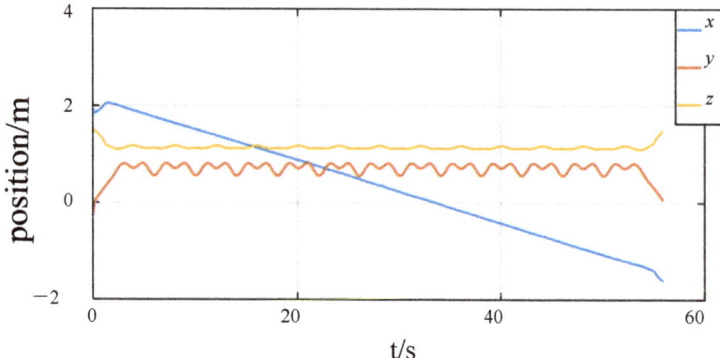

Figure 11. Posture of the end effector in the x_g, y_g, and z_g directions.

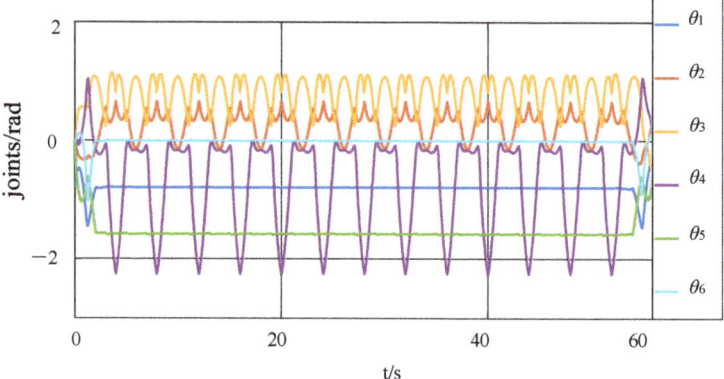

Figure 12. Joints of the manipulator in the experiment.

5. Conclusions

This research proposes an intelligent disinfection robotic system for the disinfection of common environments that humans often access. The robotic system utilizes multiple technologies, including a structural design, communication system, disinfection instrument framework, ROS1 and CPP, etc. The mobile manipulator can grant the disinfection robot more flexibility than common disinfection robots based on a mobile platform, enabling the determination of optimized trajectories that, although slightly complex, result in a better disinfection effect. Planning a feasible path is an important component of this study, for which the CPP algorithm is used to generate a rational coverage path in 3D environments. Simulations and an experiment were conducted to verify the feasibility and effectiveness of the robotic system. The proposed disinfection strategy enables the robot to automatically complete disinfection tasks throughout any target environment, thereby ensuring human safety and reducing labor required for manual disinfection. For future research, the robot can be made more intelligent and multifunctional, and more common environmental scenarios should be verified.

6. Patents

Qirong Tang, Xinyi Chen, Pengjie Xu. clamping mechanism and clamping device. Invention patent CN202111405539.1, 2022.12.27.

Qirong Tang, Xinyi Chen, Pengjie Xu. A clamping mechanism and a clamping device. Practical patent CN202122900939.1, 2022.4.9.

Author Contributions: Conceptualization, methodology, validation, and writing: P.X.; Software, validation, and data curation: X.C.; Provided the research direction, and guidance on the methodology and routes, help improving the polish work and so on: Q.T. All authors have read and agreed to the published version of the manuscript.

Funding: This work is supported by the Innovative Projects (No. 2021-JCJQ-LB-010-11). Meanwhile, this work is also partiallysupported by the Fundamental Research Funds for the Central Universities, the "National High Level Overseas Talent Plan" project and the "National Major Talent Plan" project (No. 2022-JCJQ-ZQ-079). It is also partially sponsored by the project (No. JCKY2022110C133), the project of Shanghai Key Laboratory of Spacecraft Mechanism (No. 18DZ2272200), as well as the project of Space Structure and Mechanism Technology Laboratory of China Aerospace Science and Technology Group Co., Ltd. (YY-F805202210015). All these supports are highly appreciated.

Institutional Review Board Statement: Not applicable.

Informed Consent Statement: Not applicable.

Data Availability Statement: Not applicable.

Conflicts of Interest: The authors declare no conflict of interest.

References

1. Yang, G.; Nelson, B.; Murphy, R.; Choset, H.; Mcnutt, M. Combating COVID-19 the role of robotics in managing public health and infectious diseases. *Sci. Robot.* **2020**, *5*, 1–2. [CrossRef] [PubMed]
2. Zemmar, A.; Lozano, A.; Nelson, B. The rise of robots in surgical environments during COVID-19. *Nat. Mach. Intell.* **2020**, *2*, 566–572. [CrossRef]
3. Tamantini, C.; Luzio, F.; Cordella, F.; Pascarella, G.; Zollo, L. A robotic health-care assistant for covid-19 emergency: A proposed solution for logistics and disinfection in a hospital environment. *IEEE Robot. Autom. Mag.* **2021**, *28*, 71–81. [CrossRef]
4. Zhao, Y.; Huang, H.; Chen, T.; Chiang, P.; Weng, W. A smart sterilization robot system with chlorine dioxide for spray disinfection. *IEEE Sensors J.* **2021**, *21*, 22047–22057. [CrossRef]
5. Boyce, J. Modern technologies for improving cleaning and disinfection of environmental surfaces in hospitals. *Antimicrob. Resist. Infect. Control.* **2016**, *5*, 112–123. [CrossRef] [PubMed]
6. Ortega, R.; Astolfi, A.; Bastin, G.; Rodriguez, H. Stabilization of food-chain systems using a port-controlled Hamiltonian description. In Proceedings of the 2000 American Control Conference, Chicago, IL, USA, 28–30 June 2000; pp. 2245–2249.
7. SOMATIC: Higher Quality Cleaning. 8 April 2021. Available online: http://getsomatic.com (accessed on 7 April 2023).
8. Gomez, J.V.; Melchor, M.; Lozada, J.H. Optimal coverage path planning based on the rotating calipers algorithm. In Proceedings of the 2017 International Conference on Mechatronics, Electronics and Automotive Engineering, Morelos, Mexico, 26–29 November 2017; pp. 140–144.
9. Han, G.; Zhou, Z.; Zhang, T.; Wang, H.; Guizani, M. Ant-colony-based complete-coverage path-planning algorithm for underwater gliders in ocean areas with thermoclines. *IEEE Trans. Veh. Technol.* **2020**, *69*, 8959–8971. [CrossRef]
10. Hong, H.; Shin, W.; Jieun, O.; SunWoo, L.; TaeYoung, K.; WooSub, L.; JongSuk, C.; Suh, S.; Kim, K. Standard for the quantification of a sterilization effect using an artificial intelligence disinfection robot. *Sensors* **2021**, *21*, 7776. [CrossRef]
11. Tiseni, L.; Chiaradia, D.; Gabardi, M.; Solazzi, M.; Frisoli, A. UV-C mobile robots with optimized path planning: Algorithm design and on-field measurements to improve surface disinfection against sars-cov-2. *IEEE Robot. Autom. Mag.* **2021**, *25*, 59–70. [CrossRef]
12. Bähnemann, R.; Lawrance, N.; Chung, J.J.; Pantic, M.; Siegwart, R.; Nieto, J. Revisiting Boustrophedon Coverage Path Planning as a Generalized Traveling Salesman Problem. In *Field and Service Robotics: Results of the 12th International Conference*; Springer: Singapore, 13 January 2021; pp. 277–290.
13. Ren, Y.; Sosnowski, S.; Hirche, S. Fully distributed coordinated cooperation for networked uncertain mobile manipulators. *IEEE Trans. Robot.* **2020**, *36*, 984–1003. [CrossRef]
14. Marino, A.; Pierri, F. A two stage approach for distributed cooperative manipulation of an unknown object without explicit communication and unknown number of robots. *Robot. Auton. Syst.* **2018**, *103*, 122–133. [CrossRef]
15. Li, K.; Boonto, S.; Nuchkrua, T. On-line self tuning of contouring control for high accuracy robot manipulators under various operations. *Int. J. Control. Autom. Syst.* **2020**, *18*, 1818–1828. [CrossRef]
16. Chen, L.; Yang, Q.; Li, C.; Ma, G. Euler-Lagrange system, formation control, mobile robots, multi-agent systems, multi-robot systems. *Int. J. Control. Autom. Syst.* **2021**, *19*, 1740–1750. [CrossRef]
17. Azzabi, A.; Nouri, K. Design of a robust tracking controller for a nonholonomic mobile robot based on sliding mode with adaptive gain. *Int. J. Adv. Robot. Syst.* **2021**, *18*, 1–18. [CrossRef]

18. Ferraguti, F.; Landi, C.; Costi, S.; Bonfè, M.; Fantuzzi, C. Safety barrier functions and multi-camera tracking for human-robot shared environment. *Robot. Auton. Syst.* **2020**, *124*, 1–19. [CrossRef]
19. Kebria, P.; Al-Wais, S.; Abdi, H.; Nahavandi, S. Kinematic and dynamic modelling of UR5 manipulator, In Proceedings of the 2016 IEEE International Conference on Systems, Man, and Cybernetics (SMC), Budapest, Hungary, 9–12 October 2016; pp. 9–12.
20. Weyrer, M.; Brandsttter, M.; Husty, M. Singularity avoidance control of a non-holonomic mobile manipulator for intuitive hand guidance. *Robotics* **2019**, *8*, 14. [CrossRef]

Disclaimer/Publisher's Note: The statements, opinions and data contained in all publications are solely those of the individual author(s) and contributor(s) and not of MDPI and/or the editor(s). MDPI and/or the editor(s) disclaim responsibility for any injury to people or property resulting from any ideas, methods, instructions or products referred to in the content.

Article

Electromechanical Coupling Dynamic and Vibration Control of Robotic Grinding System for Thin-Walled Workpiece

Yufei Liu [1,2], Dong Tang [1,2] and Jinyong Ju [1,2,*]

1 School of Artificial Intelligence, Anhui Polytechnic University, No. 8, Beijing Middle Road, Wuhu 241000, China
2 School of Mechanical Engineering, Anhui Polytechnic University, No. 8, Beijing Middle Road, Wuhu 241000, China
* Correspondence: junjy@ahpu.edu.cn

Abstract: The robotic grinding system for a thin-walled workpiece is a multi-dimensional coupling system composed of a robot, a grinding spindle and the thin-walled workpiece. In the grinding process, a dynamic coupling effect is generated, while the thin-walled workpiece stimulates elastic vibration; the grinding spindle, as an electromechanical coupling actuator, is sensitive to the elastic vibration in the form of load fluctuations. It is necessary to investigate the electromechanical coupling dynamic characteristics under the vibration coupling of the thin-walled workpiece as well as the vibration control of the robotic grinding system. Firstly, considering the dynamic coupling effect between the grinding spindle and thin-walled workpiece, a dynamic model of the grinding spindle and thin-walled workpiece coupling system is established. Secondly, based on this established coupling dynamic model, the vibration characteristics of the thin-walled workpiece and the electromechanical coupling dynamic characteristics of the grinding spindle are investigated. Finally, a speed adaptive control system for the grinding spindle is designed based on a fuzzy PI controller, which can achieve a stable speed for the grinding spindle under vibration coupling and has a certain suppression effect on the elastic vibration of the thin-walled workpiece at the same time.

Keywords: robotic grinding system; thin-walled workpiece; dynamic model; electromechanical coupling dynamic; vibration control

1. Introduction

High surface finishes are usually required for manufactured components with functional surfaces [1]. Due to the surface quality of the workpieces produced by rough processing, casting and printing are not sufficient for functional applications, so some post-processing by grinding or a similar process is usually needed to improve the surface quality and mechanical properties [2,3]. There are different surface-finishing processes for different workpiece requirements, such as burnishing, which is also known as roller burnishing, and ball burnishing, grinding, shot peening and traditional hand polishing [1,4,5], as well as some non-conventional manufacturing technologies, such as laser polishing, electrochemical machining, linear friction welding and electro-discharge machining [6–9].

For a certain period of time, many finishing processes operational in the industrial field mainly relied on traditional handmade or conventional machine tool processing; it can be seen that the existing polishing modes, whether the traditional manual mode or unconventional mode, display a working efficiency and working space that are not conducive to the flexibility necessary for machining production, especially for large-scale and complex structures. In recent years, the automation and intelligence of the manufacturing process have been an irresistible trend to adapt to the requirements of the processing environment, working space and related flexibility [10,11]. Compared with the machining equipment within these existing polishing modes, a robot conveys the advantages of higher flexibility, a larger workspace and a lower cost, which is, obviously, especially appropriate for the machining of large structures with complex shapes, such as aerospace structures, high-speed rail bodies and wind blades. In recent years, robotic grinding has attracted increasing attention from industry [11–14]. However, the lower stiffness of the robotic grinding system in the machining process, which is mainly caused by the articulated links and flexible joints, easily stimulates the coupling vibration, which has remained an essential issue affecting the stability of robotic machining, especially for the thin-walled workpiece [12,13].

To improve the machining stability and surface quality, some scholars studied the influence of the process parameters on the surface quality of polishing [5–7,15,16] as well as the working stiffness optimization and machining accuracy compensation through posture optimization [17–20]. Moreover, research indicated that support fixtures are essential to ensure the stability of the milling process, affecting the surface and deflection of the workpiece [21–24]. However, this is a challenge for the support fixtures of a complex workpiece, particularly regarding flexible structures, for which the local stiffness of the part is affected and may even result in an additional deformation that amplifies the cutting instability. On the other hand, it is known that the machining chatter also has an important influence on the machining surface quality, so some optimization approaches and control strategies of robotic machining chatter were also proposed [25–28]. These optimization methods mainly focus on the machining spindle unit.

As shown in Figure 1, the robotic grinding system is a multi-dimensional coupling system composed of the robot, the grinding spindle and the workpiece, and there is a complex dynamic coupling effect between the subsystems. It should be pointed out that the robotic machining process is a dynamic process, and the dynamics of the system have a decisive influence on the polishing quality and stability. Some researchers have investigated the dynamic characteristics and control strategies of the robotic machining system [29–32]; however, these studies mainly focus on the robot body separately, while the dynamic coupling effect in the system is not fully considered. In the grinding process, the force interaction between the grinding spindle and the workpiece is generated by the grinding wheel, and the thin-walled workpiece, which has a lower stiffness, stimulates the time-varying elastic vibration under the moving grinding force [33–36]. On the other hand, the grinding spindle is a typical electromechanical coupling unit, in which the electromagnetic parameters are coupled with the mechanical parameters [37]. According to the schematic diagram shown in Figure 1, the stator converts the input electric energy into a rotating magnetic field, and the interaction between the stator magnetic field and the rotating magnetic field produces a driving torque that can drive the rotor. In this case, the dynamic interaction force and elastic vibration of the thin-walled workpiece significantly affect the dynamic characteristics of the grinding spindle [26,38,39]. There is a dynamic coupling effect between the spindle and the thin-walled workpiece.

Considering the influence of the machining parameters and structural parameters, some research has been conducted on the dynamic characteristics' analysis and the optimization design of the motorized spindle unit [40–43]. However, this research is mainly carried out for the motorized spindle separately, while the dynamic coupling effect of the workpiece is not fully considered, especially the elastic vibration of the thin-walled workpiece, which will significantly affect the grinding force. In fact, according to the electromechanical coupling principle of the robotic grinding system, the elastic vibration stimulated by the thin-walled workpiece has an important influence on the dynamic response characteristics of the grinding spindle. Reciprocally, the dynamic responses and grinding force of the grinding spindle further affect the elastic vibration of the thin-walled workpiece, which leads to a complex dynamic coupling effect between the grinding spindle and the thin-walled workpiece. It is necessary to reveal the electromechanical coupling dynamic characteristics of the grinding spindle and thin-walled workpiece coupling system, which is the basis of the vibration suppression of the robotic grinding system.

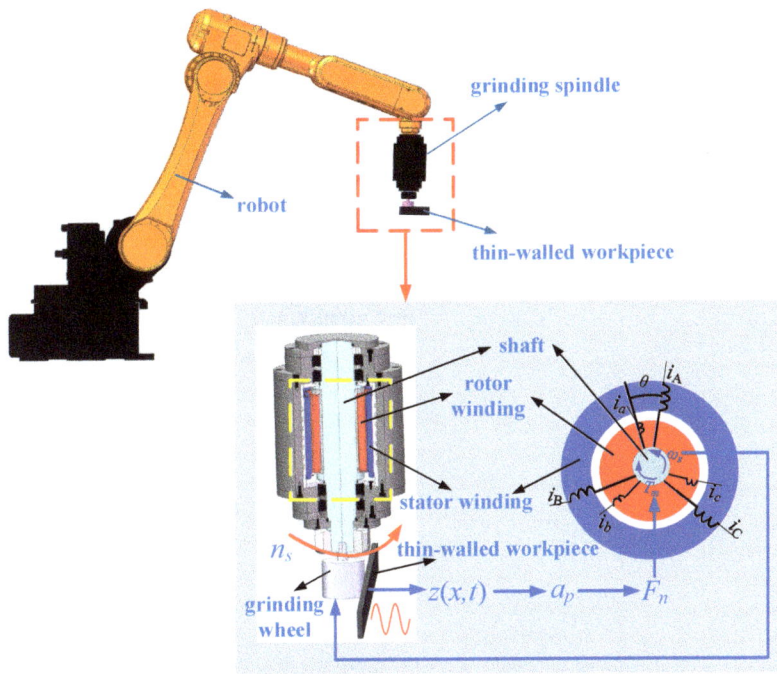

Figure 1. Composition diagram and coupling relationship of robotic grinding system for thin-walled workpiece.

On the other hand, elastic thin-walled workpieces are typical flexible structures, and their vibration control has always been the focus of attention. There has been a lot of research on the vibration control of flexible structures, the most representative of which is the active control strategy based on intelligent materials, such as piezoelectric intelligent actuators [44–46], magnetorheological intelligent actuators [47,48], etc. In this case, the flexible structure becomes an intelligent structural system. However, this method is based on intelligent actuators that inevitably change the structure form, which is difficult to implement for robotic grinding processing conditions. Some studies were also conducted to suppress the chatter of the robotic machining system through machining posture optimization [49,50], auxiliary support [22,23,51], etc. Based on the dynamic coupling effect between the grinding spindle and the thin-walled workpiece, this paper attempts to realize the vibration suppression of the thin-walled workpiece through adaptive control of the grinding spindle in the machining process.

In this paper, the core goal is to reveal the electromechanical coupling dynamic characteristics of the robotic grinding system, by considering the vibration coupling effect of the thin-walled workpiece, and, according to the dynamic coupling mechanism, the speed adaptive control of the grinding spindle as well as the vibration suppression of the thin-walled workpiece are carried out. The manuscript is organized as follows. In Section 2, the dynamic model of the coupling system is established. In Section 3, the electromechanical coupling dynamic characteristics of the robotic grinding system are analyzed based on the established coupling dynamic model. In Section 4, a speed adaptive control system for the grinding spindle is designed based on a fuzzy PI controller. In Section 5, the paper is concluded with a brief summary.

2. Dynamic Model of the Coupling System

According to the coupling relationship of the robotic grinding system, as shown in Figure 1, and considering the vibration coupling effect of the thin-walled workpiece, the dynamic model of the coupling system is established, as shown in Figure 2.

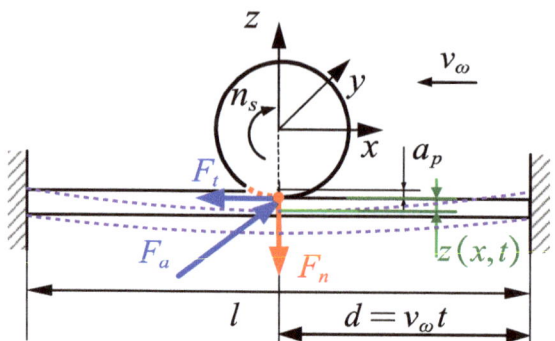

Figure 2. Dynamic model of the coupling system.

As shown in Figure 2, the grinding force can be quadratically decomposed into grinding components in the x, y and z directions along the grinding wheel, namely, tangential grinding force F_t, axial grinding force F_a and normal grinding force F_n. Among these grinding components, the normal component F_n is the main parameter in the constant force grinding. As shown in Figure 1 and according to the coupling relationship between the grinding spindle and the thin-walled workpiece, which has been indicated in the previous analysis, the elastic vibration of the thin-walled workpiece directly causes fluctuation of the grinding depth a_p as well as the grinding force, influencing the dynamic characteristics and stability of the robotic grinding system in an important way. Therefore, this paper focuses on the effect of normal component F_n and investigates the dynamic coupling relationship between the grinding spindle and the thin-walled workpiece, which can provide a theoretical basis for the subsequent control of the grinding system.

In order to analyze the coupling behavior between the grinding spindle and the thin-walled workpiece, an Euler–Bernoulli beam is used to characterize the thin-walled workpiece, and the transverse vibration $z(x,t)$ of the thin-walled workpiece is mainly considered. To establish the vibration equation of the thin-walled workpiece, the moving grinding force can be expressed as the δ function of F_n.

$$f(x,t) = F_n \delta(x - v_\omega t) \tag{1}$$

where v_ω is the grinding feed speed, and F_n is the normal component of grinding force. In general, F_n is 1.5~3 times of F_t, which is specifically related to the abrasive particles and the workpiece materials [52,53]. Referring to the material properties, hardened steel is selected, F_n/F_t is $1/0.49 = 2.04$, which can be rounded to 2; thus, it can be defined that F_n is 2 times of F_t in this paper.

In general, the grinding force is related to the workpiece material, tool material, machining parameter, machining temperature and other factors, and, of these factors, the machining parameter is the most important factor affecting machining force. Meanwhile, according to the cutting theory, there is an exponential relationship between the grinding force, which can be determined by the machining parameters and characterized with empirical formulas, and the different grinding materials and grinding conditions; the correlation coefficient is different [54,55]. To study the electromechanical coupling dynamic characteristics of the robotic grinding system, the grinding parameters and grinding conditions in this paper refer to the surface grinding conditions in the literature [53]; in this case, the grinding force can be defined as

$$F_n = 28282 \times (a_{p0})^{0.86}(n_s r)^{-1.06}(v_w)^{0.44} \quad (2)$$

According to the empirical formula, the grinding force is a constant mean value when the machining parameters are given. Considering the dynamic coupling effect of the thin-walled workpiece, the transverse vibration $z(x,t)$ of the thin-walled workpiece directly causes the fluctuation of grinding depth a_p, and, in this case, the grinding force can be further expressed as

$$F_n = 28282 \times (a_{p0} - z(x,t))^{0.86}(n_s r)^{-1.06}(v_w)^{0.44} \quad (3)$$

where a_{p0} denotes the ideal grinding depth, n_s denotes the output speed of the grinding spindle, and r is the radius of the grinding wheel. Equation (3) directly represents the coupling effect between the transverse vibration of the thin-walled workpiece and the grinding force.

The generalized force F_i in the modal coordinates can be described as

$$F_i(t) = \int_0^l f(x,t)\phi_i(x)dx = F_n \int_0^l \delta(x - v_w t)\phi_i(x)dx = F_n \phi_i(v_w t) \quad (4)$$

where $\phi_i(x)$ is the ith mode shape function of the thin-walled workpiece.

Considering the fixed constraints at both ends of the thin-walled workpiece, the modal function can be described as [45]

$$\phi_i(x) = \cosh\beta_i x - \cos\beta_i x - \frac{\cosh\lambda_i - \cos\lambda_i}{\sinh\lambda_i - \sin\lambda_i}(\sinh\beta_i x - \sin\beta_i x) \quad (5)$$

where $\lambda_i = \beta_i l$, and β_i satisfies.

$$\omega_i = \beta_i^2 \sqrt{\frac{EI}{\rho A}} = \left[\left(i + \frac{1}{2}\right)\frac{\pi}{l}\right]^2 \sqrt{\frac{EI}{\rho A}} (i = 3,4,5,\cdots) \quad (6)$$

where l is the length, E is the elastic modulus, I is the moment of inertia of the section, ρ is the density, and A is the cross-sectional area of the workpiece.

The vibration equation of the thin-walled workpiece in the form of the generalized coordinates under the grinding condition can be obtained as

$$\ddot{q}_i + \omega_i^2 q_i = \frac{F_i}{M_i} = \frac{\phi_i(v_w t)}{M_i} F_n \ (i = 1,2,3,\cdots) \quad (7)$$

where M_i is the mass of the ith mode and can be expressed as

$$M_i = \int_0^l \rho A \phi_i^2(x)dx \quad (8)$$

According to the Duhame integral [45], the solution can be obtained as

$$q_i(t) = \frac{F_n}{M_i \omega_i}\int_0^t \phi_i(v_w \tau)\sin\omega_i(t-\tau)d\tau + q_{i0}\cos\omega_i t + \frac{\dot{q}_{i0}}{\omega_i}\sin\omega_i t \quad (9)$$

where q_{i0} and $\dot{q}_{i0}$ represent the initial displacement and initial velocity in generalized coordinate form, respectively.

According to the principle of mode superposition [56], the vibration equation of the thin-walled workpiece can be expressed as

$$z(x,t) = \sum_{i=1}^{\infty} \phi_i(x) q_i(t)$$
$$= \sum_{i=1}^{\infty} \frac{F_n}{M_i \omega_i} \phi_i(x) \left[\int_0^t \phi_i(v_\omega \tau) \sin \omega_i (t-\tau) d\tau + q_{i0} \cos \omega_i t + \frac{\dot{q}_{i0}}{\omega_i} \sin \omega_i t \right] \quad (10)$$

It can be seen from Equation (10) that there is an intuitive coupling relationship between the elastic vibration of the thin-walled workpiece and grinding force. On this basis, the dynamic characteristics of the grinding spindle under vibration coupling can be further analyzed. In the subsequent solving process, the mode superposition term takes the first three orders.

According to the electromechanical dynamics method, the electromechanical coupling dynamic model of the grinding spindle can be established. Based on the electromechanical coupling relationship shown in Figure 1, there are seven generalized coordinates in the system, namely, the electromagnetic system contains six generalized coordinates, including stator current i_A, i_B, i_C and rotor current i_a, i_b, i_c, while the mechanical system contains a generalized coordinate, namely, the angular velocity of the grinding spindle ω_s, as shown in Table 1.

Table 1. Generalized coordinates of the grinding spindle.

Generalized Coordinates	Electromagnetic Subsystem						Mechanical Subsystem
	Stator			Rotor			
	$j=1$	$j=2$	$j=3$	$j=4$	$j=5$	$j=6$	$j=7$
$\tilde{\zeta}_j$	-	-	-	-	-	-	θ
$\dot{\tilde{\zeta}}_j$	i_A	i_B	i_C	i_a	i_b	i_c	ω_s
Q_j	u_A	u_B	u_C	u_a	u_b	u_c	T_L

In this paper, the electromechanical coupling dynamic equation of grinding spindle is established by the Lagrange method [57]. The Lagrangian–Maxwell equation of the system can be described as

$$\frac{d}{dt}\left(\frac{\partial L}{\partial \dot{\tilde{\zeta}}_j}\right) - \frac{\partial L}{\partial \tilde{\zeta}_j} + \frac{\partial F_R}{\partial \dot{\tilde{\zeta}}_j} = Q_j \quad (11)$$

where $\tilde{\zeta}_j$ and Q_j are the generalized coordinates and generalized force of the grinding spindle, respectively, as shown in Table 1; F_R is the system dissipation; and L denotes the Lagrangian function of the system and can be described as

$$L = T - V \quad (12)$$

where T and V denote the kinetic energy and elastic potential energy of the spindle system of the spindle system, respectively.

The kinetic energy of the spindle system includes the magnetic energy of the electromagnetic system and the kinetic energy of the mechanical system and can be described as

$$T = W + E_k = \frac{1}{2}\sum_m \sum_n L_{mn} i_m i_n + \frac{1}{2} J \omega_s^2 \quad (13)$$

where $m, n = A, B, C, a, b, c$; W is the kinetic energy of the electromagnetic system; E_k is the kinetic energy of the mechanical system; L_{mn} is the mutual inductance between winding m and winding n (when $m = n$, it is self-inductance); and the rest are mutual inductance. J is the moment of inertia of the system, and ω_s is the angular velocity of the grinding spindle.

To simplify the analysis, the elastic potential energy of the spindle system can be ignored, as it defines $V = 0$.

For the grinding spindle unit, the system dissipation includes the electromagnetic system dissipation F_e and the mechanical system dissipation F_m, which can be expressed as

$$F_R = F_e + F_m = \frac{1}{2}R_s\left(i_A{}^2 + i_B{}^2 + i_C{}^2\right) + \frac{1}{2}R_r\left(i_a{}^2 + i_b{}^2 + i_c{}^2\right) + \frac{1}{2}R_\omega \omega_s{}^2 \quad (14)$$

where R_s is the stator resistance, R_r is the rotor resistance, and R_ω is the viscous damping coefficient of spindle.

The motion equation of the mechanical system is

$$J\frac{d\omega_s}{dt} + R_\omega \omega_s = T_L - L_{ms}\left[\begin{array}{c}(i_A i_a + i_B i_b + i_C i_c)\sin\theta + (i_A i_b + i_B i_c + i_C i_a)\sin(\theta + \tfrac{2}{3}\pi) \\ + (i_A i_c + i_B i_a + i_C i_b)\sin(\theta - \tfrac{2}{3}\pi)\end{array}\right] \quad (15)$$

where ω_s is the angular velocity of the rotor winding and conveys the relationship with the spindle speed as $\omega_s = \frac{2\pi n_s}{60}$; T_L is the load torque, which is related to the grinding force $T_L = \frac{1}{2}F_n r$; L_{ms} is the mutual inductance of the stator winding; and θ is the angle between the stator winding and the rotor winding, namely, the Angular displacement of the spindle rotor.

It can be seen from Equations (10) and (15) that there is a direct coupling relationship between the transverse vibration $z(x,t)$ of the thin-walled workpiece, the grinding force F_n and the spindle speed n_s. Based on this, the electromechanical coupling dynamic characteristics of the grinding spindle under vibration coupling can be analyzed.

3. Dynamic Characteristics of the Coupling System

It can be seen that Equation (15) is a typical electromechanical coupling dynamic equation, and its analytical solution is difficult to obtain. In order to analyze the vibration characteristics of the thin-walled workpiece and the dynamic response characteristics of the mechanical and electrical coupling of the grinding spindle under vibration coupling, MATLAB Simulink software is used to build the dynamic simulation model of the coupling system of the grinding spindle and thin-walled workpiece (Figure 3). As shown in Figure 3, the dynamics simulation model consists of three modules, namely, the grinding spindle unit dynamics solving module, grinding force solving module and thin-walled parts dynamics solving module. The spindle speed obtained from the spindle unit module is input to the grinding force solving module, the grinding excitation is calculated and applied to the thin-walled parts dynamics solving module, the vibration displacement of the elastic thin-walled parts is obtained and input to the grinding force solving module, and the grinding force is input to the grinding spindle dynamics solving module. Thus, in this case, the coupling characteristics of the system dynamics can be analyzed. The grinding spindle is driven by an Ac asynchronous motor, and in order to simplify the solution process and focus on analyzing the coupling relationship of the system, the relatively small influence of the viscous damping of the spindle drive system is ignored during the simulation analysis. The related parameters of the dynamic simulation model are shown in Table 2. During the simulation, the initial displacement q_{i0} and initial velocity $\dot{q}_{i0}$ in generalized coordinate form are assigned as 0.001 and 0, respectively.

Figure 4 shows the vibration response of the thin-walled workpiece under the grinding condition. It can be seen that the thin-walled workpiece shows obvious vibration in the grinding process and exhibits dynamic time-varying characteristics for moving grinding loads that vary with their grinding point, and the amplitude near the midpoint is the largest, which is obviously different from the ideal situation ignoring the elastic vibration of the thin-walled workpiece.

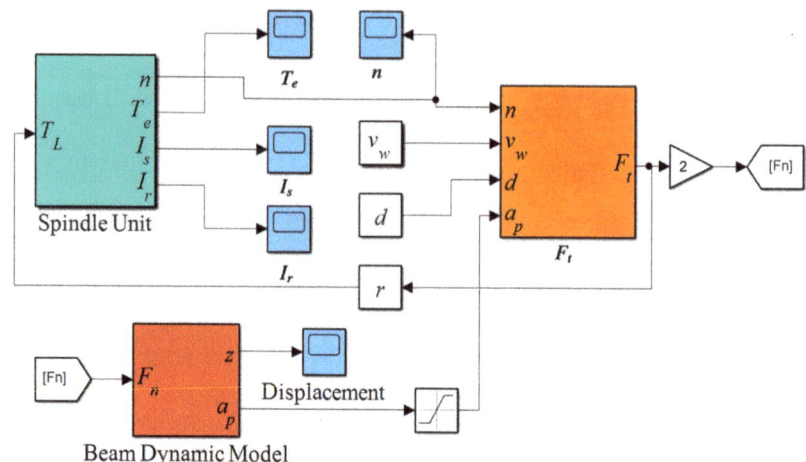

Figure 3. Dynamic simulation model of the coupling system.

Table 2. Parameters of dynamic simulation model.

Parameter	Value
Diameter of grinding wheel d	0.35 m
Speed of grinding wheel n	1500 r/min
Grinding depth a_{p0}	0.05 mm
Feed speed v_w	0.05 m/s
Length of beam l	0.5 m
Width of beam b	0.02 m
Height of beam h	0.002 m
Density of beam ρ	7850 kg/m^2
Elastic modulus of beam E	2.1×10^{11} Pa
Rated power P_N	3000 W
Rated voltage U	380 V
Power Frequency f	50 Hz
Resistance of stator winding R_s	1.7980 Ω
Resistance of rotor winding R_r	1.5880 Ω
Mutual inductance of the stator winding L_{ms}	0.2580 H
Moment of inertia J	0.0067 Nm^2
Number of magnetic poles n_p	2

According to the above analysis, the elastic vibration of the thin-walled workpiece has an important influence on the fluctuations of the grinding depth and grinding force, which will affect the dynamic response characteristics of the grinding spindle directly. In order to analyze the electromechanical coupling dynamic characteristics of the grinding spindle with the vibration coupling of the thin-walled workpiece, the output speed, electromagnetic torque and rotor current waveforms of the grinding spindle are shown in Figures 5–7, respectively. In the simulation process, the load begins to be applied at 1 s. Under the grinding load starting from 1 s, the spindle speed decreases while the electromagnetic torque and rotor current increase correspondingly, and this trend keeps a balance with the load torque. At the same time, the electromechanical coupling dynamic response characteristics of the grinding spindle are obviously different from the ideal constant load situation, when ignoring the vibration coupling, specifically the vibration coupling that enhances the fluctuations of the output speed, electromagnetic torque and rotor current. The results demonstrate the electromechanical coupling dynamic response characteristics of the grinding spindle under the vibration coupling of the thin-walled workpiece, which causes certain errors for the dynamic analysis and subsequent control, ignoring the vibration coupling effect of the thin-walled workpiece.

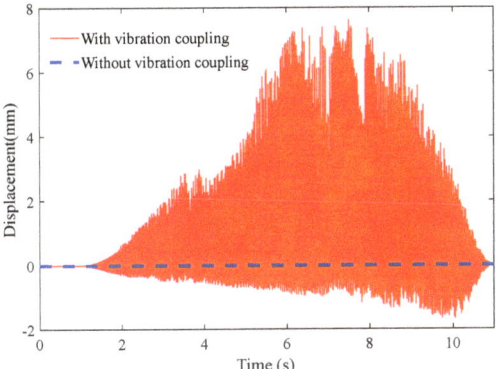

Figure 4. Vibration response of thin-walled workpiece in the grinding process.

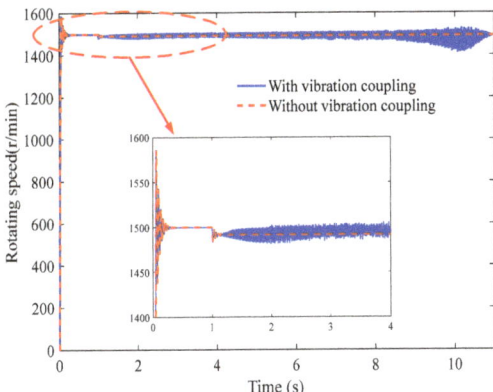

Figure 5. Speed characteristic curves of the grinding spindle with vibration coupling of thin-walled workpiece.

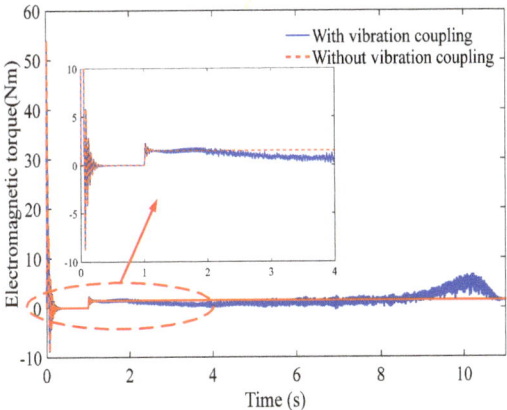

Figure 6. Electromagnetic torque curves of the grinding spindle with vibration coupling of thin-walled workpiece.

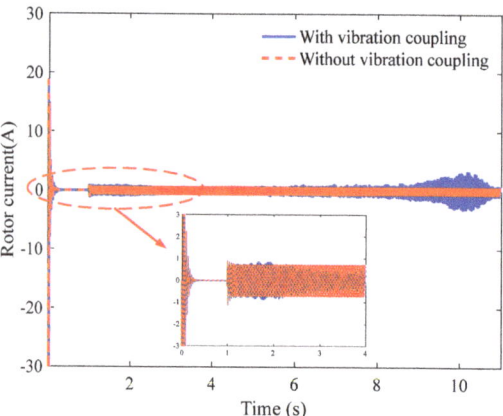

Figure 7. Rotor current curves of the grinding spindle with vibration coupling of thin-walled workpiece.

4. Speed Adaptive Control of Grinding Spindle

According to the above analysis, in the grinding process, the thin-walled workpiece exhibits elastic vibration, while the grinding spindle conveys speed fluctuations. In other words, there is a certain coupling relationship between the elastic vibration and the speed fluctuations. In this section, according to the coupling relationship, a speed adaptive control system of the grinding spindle is designed based on the fuzzy PI controller to realize disturbance suppression of the speed fluctuations of the grinding spindle and the elastic vibration of the thin-walled workpiece.

The designed speed adaptive control system is shown in Figure 8. The design of the proposed fuzzy adaptive PI control strategy is composed of the combination of a fuzzy controller and a PI controller, which is more flexible and stable compared with a traditional PI control. The fuzzy adaptive PI controller takes error e and error change rate ec as input variables and Δk_p and Δk_i as output variables. The fuzzy domains of e and ec are $[-3,3]$, and the membership function is shown in Figure 9. The membership function is shown in Figure 10. The fuzzy subsets of the input and output language variables Δk_p and Δk_i are negative large, negative medium, negative small, zero, positive small, middle and above board, which are denoted by NB, NM, NS, Z, PS, PM and PB, respectively. The fuzzy rules of Δk_p and Δk_i are shown in Tables 3 and 4, respectively, which are obtained from previous engineering experience and experiments. The output surfaces of Δk_p and Δk_i obtained from this rule are shown in Figures 11 and 12, respectively. As can be seen from Figures 11 and 12, Δk_p and Δk_i are obtained by the joint action of e and ec, and the surface is close to continuous and changes smoothly, which indicates that the designed fuzzy adaptive PI controller has good dynamic performance.

Figure 13 shows the adaptive control effect of the grinding spindle speed under the coupling vibration of the thin-walled workpiece; it can be seen that the designed fuzzy adaptive PI controller can realize the stability of the grinding spindle speed under vibration coupling, which can quickly adjust the speed to an ideal constant speed and improve the robustness of the grinding system. At the same time, it can be seen from Figure 14 that the vibration of the thin-walled workpiece under speed adaptive control is relatively attenuated, which indicates that the designed fuzzy adaptive PI controller also has a certain suppression effect on the elastic vibration of the thin-walled workpiece with a reduction in vibration amplitude of about 38.5%.

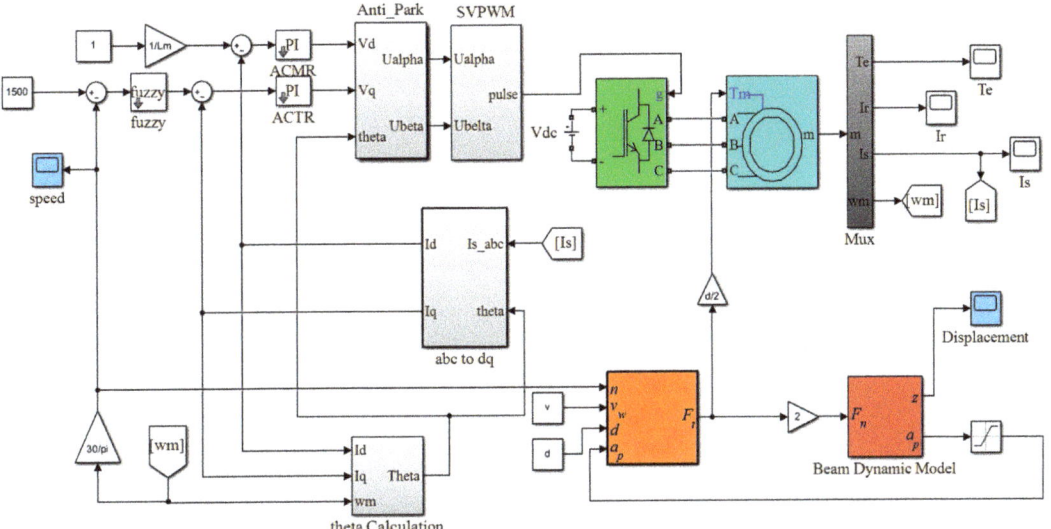

Figure 8. Speed adaptive control system of grinding spindle under vibration coupling.

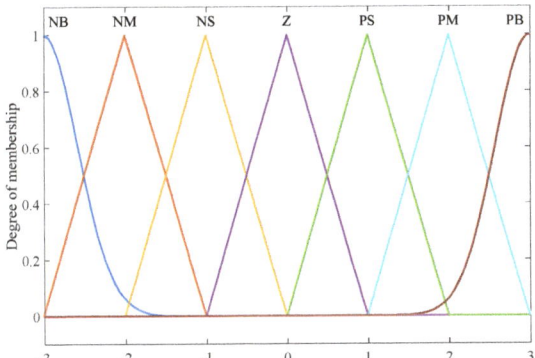

Figure 9. Membership functions of input variables *e* and *ec*.

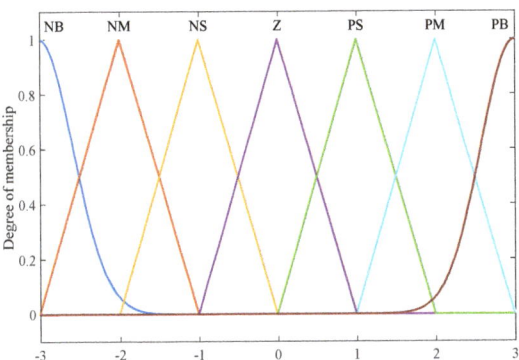

Figure 10. Membership functions of output variables Δk_p and Δk_i.

Table 3. Fuzzy control rules of ΔK_p.

e	ec						
	NB	NM	NS	Z	PS	PM	PB
NB	PB	PB	PM	PM	PS	Z	Z
NM	PB	PB	PM	PS	PS	Z	NS
NS	PM	PM	PM	PS	Z	NS	NS
Z	PM	PM	PS	Z	NS	NM	NM
PS	PS	PS	Z	NS	NS	NM	NM
PM	PS	Z	NS	NM	NM	NM	NB
PB	Z	Z	NM	NM	NM	NB	NB

Table 4. Fuzzy control rules of ΔK_i.

e	ec						
	NB	NM	NS	Z	PS	PM	PB
NB	NB	NB	NM	NM	NS	Z	Z
NM	NB	NB	NM	NS	NS	Z	Z
NS	NB	NM	NS	NS	Z	PS	PS
Z	NM	NM	NS	Z	PS	PM	PM
PS	NM	NS	Z	PS	PS	PM	PB
PM	Z	Z	PS	PS	PM	PB	PB
PB	Z	Z	PS	PM	PM	PB	PB

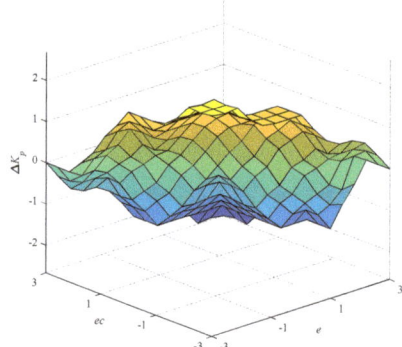

Figure 11. Input–output relation diagram of ΔK_p.

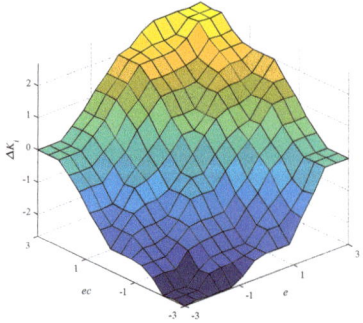

Figure 12. Input–output relation diagram of ΔK_i.

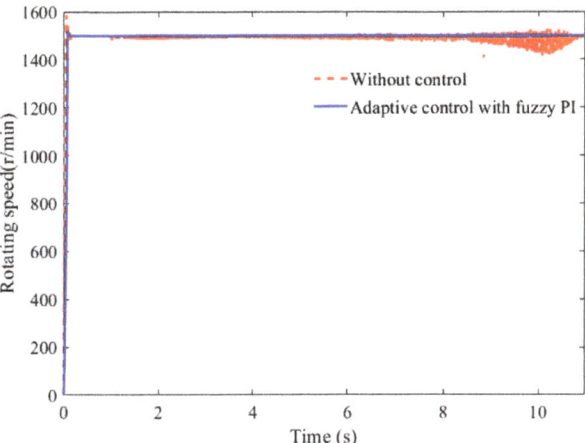

Figure 13. Adaptive control of grinding spindle speed under vibration coupling with thin-walled workpiece.

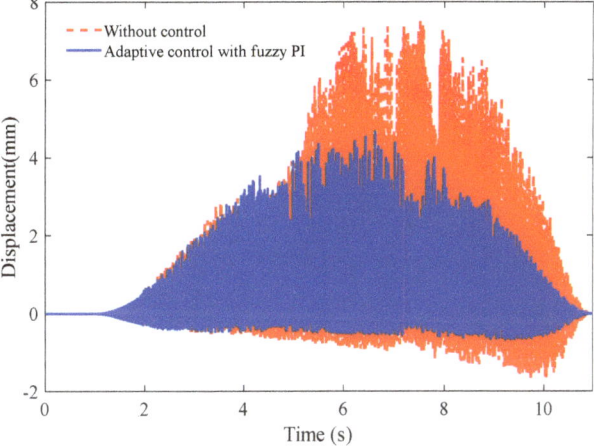

Figure 14. Vibration suppression effect of thin-walled workpiece under speed adaptive control of grinding spindle.

In order to further verify the results obtained in this paper, a virtual prototype for experimental verification is conducted. We combined the control strategy and the virtual prototype model of the elastic thin-walled workpiece in ADAMS to build a co-simulation experimental system, in which the output grinding force of the control system is applied to the elastic thin-walled workpiece. At the same time, the vibration displacement of the elastic thin-walled workpiece is feedback to the control system, to verify the control effect. The virtual prototype model of the elastic thin-walled workpiece and the constructed co-simulation experimental system are shown in Figures 15 and 16, respectively, and the co-simulation experimental results of the speed control of the grinding spindle and the vibration control of the elastic thin-walled workpiece are shown in Figures 17 and 18, respectively. The co-simulation results of the virtual prototype can also verify the effectiveness of the control strategy proposed in this paper.

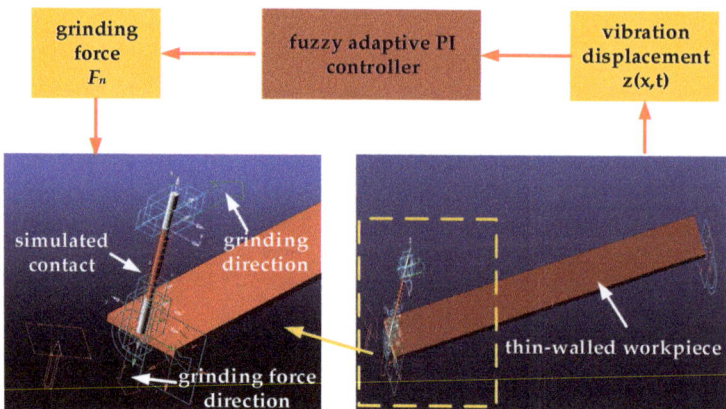

Figure 15. The schematic diagram of co-simulation experiment based on virtual prototype.

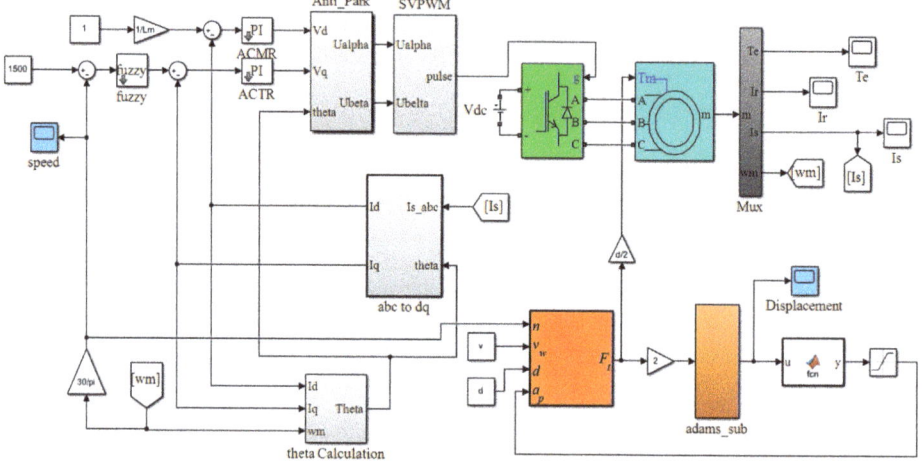

Figure 16. The co-simulation experimental model of the adaptive control strategy.

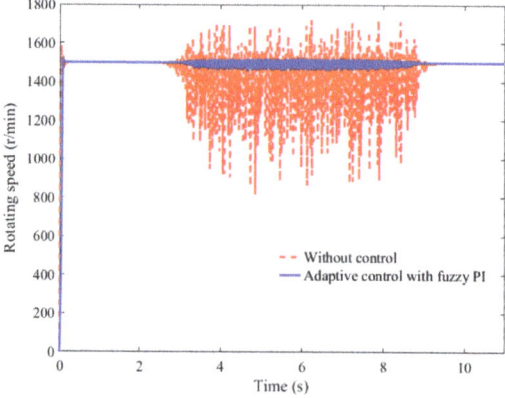

Figure 17. Speed control results of grinding spindle in the co-simulation experiment.

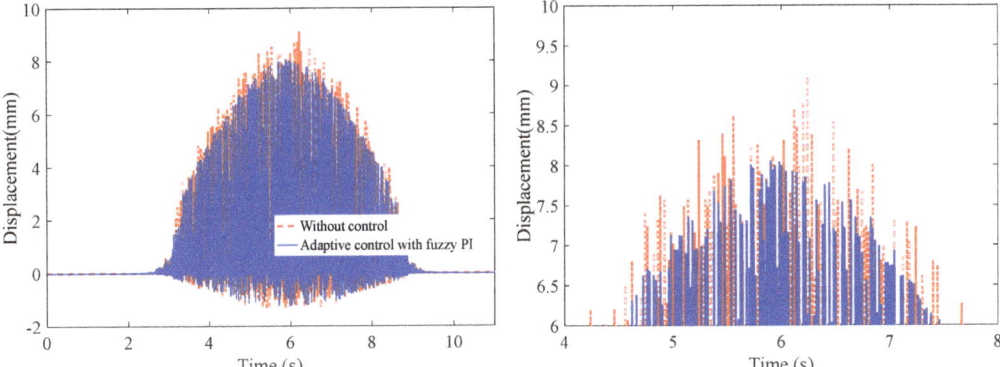

Figure 18. Vibration control results of elastic thin-walled workpiece in the co-simulation experiment: (**left**) global; (**right**) locally enlarged.

5. Conclusions

This paper established the dynamic model of the grinding spindle and thin-walled workpiece coupling system, and the electromechanical coupling dynamic characteristics of the coupling system are revealed, which have guiding significance for the vibration control of the robotic grinding system. The conclusions can be obtained as follows:

(1) the thin-walled workpiece has obvious vibration in the grinding process and exhibits dynamic time-varying characteristics for moving grinding loads that vary with the grinding point, which directly cause fluctuations of the grinding depth and grinding force and affect the dynamic response characteristics of the grinding spindle;

(2) the electromechanical coupling dynamic response characteristics of the grinding spindle with the vibration coupling of thin-walled workpiece are obviously different from the ideal constant load condition, ignoring the vibration coupling of thin-walled workpiece, specifically the vibration coupling that obviously enhances the response fluctuations of the output speed, electromagnetic torque and rotor current; thus, ignoring the vibration coupling effect of the thin-walled workpiece causes certain errors for the dynamic analysis and subsequent control;

(3) the proposed speed adaptive control of the grinding spindle based on the fuzzy PI controller can realize the stability of the grinding spindle speed under vibration coupling and has a certain suppression effect on the elastic vibration of the thin-walled workpiece, with a reduction in vibration amplitude of about 38.5%.

Author Contributions: Conceptualization, Y.L.; methodology, Y.L. and J.J.; software, Y.L. and D.T.; validation, Y.L. and D.T.; formal analysis, Y.L. and D.T.; investigation, Y.L., J.J. and D.T.; writing, Y.L. and D.T.; project administration, Y.L. and J.J.; funding acquisition, Y.L. and J.J. All authors have read and agreed to the published version of the manuscript.

Funding: This research was funded by the National Natural Science Foundation of China (No. 51805001), the Wuhu Science and Technology Project (No. 2022yf57 and No. 2022jc25), the Anhui Provincial Natural Science Foundation (No. 1908085QE193), the Natural Science Research Project of Higher Education of Anhui Province (No. KJ2019A0147), and a project funded by the China Postdoctoral Science Foundation (No. 2017M612060), Anhui Polytechnic University and the Jiujiang District Industrial collaborative Innovation Special Fund Project (2021cyxtb1).

Data Availability Statement: The data used in this article can be made available upon reasonable request. Please contact the first author, Y.L. (liuyufeiahpu@126.com).

Conflicts of Interest: The authors declare no conflict of interest.

References

1. Rodriguez, A.; López De Lacalle, L.N.; Pereira, O.; Fernandez, A.; Ayesta, I. Isotropic finishing of austempered iron casting cylindrical parts by roller burnishing. *Int. J. Adv. Manuf. Technol.* **2020**, *110*, 753–761. [CrossRef] [PubMed]
2. Pérez-Ruiz, J.D.; Marin, F.; Martínez, S.; Lamikiz, A.; Urbikain, G.; Lacalle, L. Stiffening near-net-shape functional parts of Inconel 718 LPBF considering material anisotropy and subsequent machining issues. *Mech. Syst. Signal Process.* **2022**, *168*, 108675. [CrossRef]
3. Jimenez, A.; Bidare, P.; Hassanin, H.; Tarlochan, F.; Dimov, S.; Essa, K. Powder-based laser hybrid additive manufacturing of metals: A review. *Int. J. Adv. Manuf. Technol.* **2021**, *114*, 63–96. [CrossRef]
4. Duan, Q.Q.; Wang, B.; Zhang, P.; Yang, K.; Zhang, Z.F. Improvement of notch fatigue properties of ultra-high CM400 maraging steel through shot peening. *J. Mater. Res.* **2017**, *32*, 1–9.
5. Rodriguez, A.; Calleja, A.; Lacalle, L.; Pereira, O.; Laye, J. Burnishing of fsw aluminum Al–Cu–Li components. *Metals* **2019**, *9*, 260. [CrossRef]
6. Ukar, E.; Lamikiz, A.; Lacalle, L.; Pozo, D.D.; Arana, J.L. Laser polishing of tool steel with co2 laser and high-power diode laser. *Int. J. Mach. Tools Manuf.* **2010**, *50*, 115–125. [CrossRef]
7. González, H.; Pereira, O.; Fernández-Valdivielso, A.; López de Lacalle, L.N.; Calleja, A. Comparison of flank super abrasive machining vs. flank milling on inconel®718 surfaces. *Materials* **2018**, *11*, 1638. [CrossRef]
8. Klocke, F.; Schmitt, R.; Zeis, M.; Heidemanns, L.; Kerkhoff, J.; Heinen, D.; Klink, A. Technological and economical assessment of alternative process chains for blisk manufacture. *Procedia CIRP* **2015**, *35*, 67–72. [CrossRef]
9. González, H.; Calleja, A.; Pereira, O.; Ortega, N.; López de Lacalle, L.N.; Barton, M. Super abrasive machining of integral rotary components using grinding flank tools. *Metals* **2018**, *8*, 24. [CrossRef]
10. Lu, Y.; Xu, X.; Wang, L. Smart manufacturing process and system automation: A critical review of the standards and envisioned scenarios. *J. Manuf. Syst.* **2020**, *56*, 312–325. [CrossRef]
11. Rodriguez, A.; González, M.; Pereira, O.; de Lacalle, L.N.L.; Esparta, M. Edge finishing of large turbine casings using defined multi-edge and abrasive tools in automated cells. *Int. J. Adv. Manuf. Technol.* **2021**, 1–11. [CrossRef]
12. Mohammadi, Y.; Ahmadi, K. Chatter in grinding with robots with structural nonlinearity. *Mech. Syst. Signal Process.* **2022**, *167*, 108523. [CrossRef]
13. Kim, S.H.; Nam, E.; Ha, T.I.; Hwang, S.H.; Lee, J.H.; Park, S.H.; Min, B.K. Robotic Machining: A Review of Recent Progress. *Int. J. Precis. Eng. Manuf.* **2019**, *2*, 1629–1642. [CrossRef]
14. Corral, J.; Pinto, C.; Campa, F.J.; Altuzarra, O. Surface location error of a parallel robot for routing processes. *Int. J. Adv. Manuf. Technol.* **2013**, *67*, 1977–1986. [CrossRef]
15. Aviles, R.; Albizuri, J.; Ukar, E.; Lamikiz, A.; Aviles, A. Influence of laser polishing in an inert atmosphere on the high cycle fatigue strength of aisi 1045 steel. *Int. J. Fatigue* **2014**, *68*, 67–79. [CrossRef]
16. Rodríguez, A.; López De Lacalle, L.N.; Fernández, A.; Braun, S. Elimination of surface spiral pattern on brake discs. *J. Zhejiang Univ. Sci. A* **2014**, *15*, 53–60. [CrossRef]
17. Guo, Y.J.; Dong, H.Y.; Ke, Y.L. Stiffness-oriented posture optimization in robotic machining applications. *Robot. Comput.-Integr. Manuf.* **2015**, *35*, 69–76. [CrossRef]
18. Lee, J.H.; Kim, S.H.; Min, B.K. Posture optimization in robotic drilling using a deformation energy model. *Robot. Comput.-Integr. Manuf.* **2022**, *78*, 102395. [CrossRef]
19. Chen, C.; Peng, F.; Yan, R.; Li, Y.; Wei, D.; Fan, Z.; Tang, X.; Zhu, Z. Stiffness performance index based posture and feed orientation optimization in robotic milling process. *Robot. Comput.-Integr. Manuf.* **2019**, *55*, 29–40. [CrossRef]
20. Zargarbashi, S.; Khan, W.; Angeles, J. Posture optimization in robot-assisted machining operations. *Mech. Mach. Theory* **2012**, *51*, 74–86. [CrossRef]
21. Hintze, W.; Wenserski, R.V.; Junghans, S.; Junghans, S.; Mller, C. Finish machining of Ti6Al4V SLM components under consideration of thin walls and support structure removal. *Procedia Manuf.* **2020**, *48*, 485–491. [CrossRef]
22. Wan, M.; Dang, X.B.; Zhang, W.H.; Yang, Y. Chatter suppression in the grinding process of the weakly-rigid workpiece through a moving fixture. *J. Mater. Process. Technol.* **2022**, *299*, 117293. [CrossRef]
23. Guo, Y.; Dong, H.; Wang, G.; Ke, Y. Vibration analysis and suppression in robotic boring process. *Int. J. Mach. Tools Manuf.* **2016**, *101*, 102–110. [CrossRef]
24. Wang, G.; Dong, H.; Guo, Y.; Ke, Y. Chatter mechanism and stability analysis of robotic boring. *Int. J. Adv. Manuf. Technol.* **2017**, *91*, 411–421. [CrossRef]
25. Corral, J.; Pinto, C.; Campa, F.J.; Altuzarra, O. Dynamic behavior verification of a lightweight machine for routing. *Int. J. Adv. Manuf. Technol.* **2016**, *86*, 1151–1163. [CrossRef]
26. Cao, H.; Bing, L.; He, Z. Chatter stability of milling with speed-varying dynamics of spindles. *Int. J. Mach. Tools Manuf.* **2012**, *52*, 50–58. [CrossRef]
27. Shi, J.; Jin, X.; Cao, H. Chatter stability analysis in micro-milling with aerostatic spindle considering speed effect. *Mech. Syst. Signal Process.* **2022**, *169*, 108620. [CrossRef]
28. Wang, C.; Zhang, X.; Liu, Y.; Cao, H.; Chen, X. Stiffness variation method for milling chatter suppression via piezoelectric stack actuators. *Int. J. Mach. Tools Manuf.* **2018**, *124*, 53–66. [CrossRef]

29. Cen, L.; Melkote, S.N. CCT-based mode coupling chatter avoidance in robotic grinding. *J. Manuf. Process.* **2017**, *29*, 50–61. [CrossRef]
30. Chen, C.; Peng, F.; Yan, R.; Fan, Z.; Li, Y.; Wei, D. Posture-dependent stability prediction of a grinding industrial robot based on inverse distance weighted method. *Procedia Manuf.* **2018**, *17*, 993–1000. [CrossRef]
31. Nguyen, V.; Johnson, J.; Melkote, S. Active vibration suppression in robotic grinding using optimal control. *Int. J. Mach. Tools Manuf.* **2020**, *152*, 103541. [CrossRef]
32. Yuan, L.; Sun, S.; Pan, Z.; Ding, D.; Gienke, O.; Li, W. Mode coupling chatter suppression for robotic machining using semi-active magnetorheological elastomers absorber. *Mech. Syst. Signal Process.* **2019**, *117*, 221–237. [CrossRef]
33. Liu, D.; Luo, M.; Zhang, Z.; Hu, Y.; Zhang, D. Operational modal analysis based dynamic parameters identification in grinding of thin-walled workpiece. *Mech. Syst. Signal Process.* **2022**, *167*, 108469. [CrossRef]
34. Wang, X.; Song, Q.; Liu, Z. Dynamic model and stability prediction of thin-walled component milling with multi-modes coupling effect. *J. Mater. Process. Technol.* **2020**, *288*, 116869. [CrossRef]
35. Ma, J.; Li, Y.; Zhang, D.; Zhao, B.; Wang, G.; Pang, X. Dynamic response prediction model of thin-wall workpiece-fixture system with magnetorheological damping in milling. *J. Manuf. Process.* **2022**, *74*, 500–510. [CrossRef]
36. Tian, W.; Ren, J.; Zhou, J.; Wang, D. Dynamic modal prediction and experimental study of thin-walled workpiece removal based on perturbation method. *Int. J. Adv. Manuf. Technol.* **2018**, *94*, 2099–2113. [CrossRef]
37. Meng, J.; Chen, X.; He, Y. Electromechanical coupling Dynamic modeling of High speed motorized spindle's motor-spindle subsystem. *J. Mech. Eng.* **2007**, *43*, 160–165. [CrossRef]
38. Cao, H.; Holkup, T.; Altintas, Y. A comparative study on the dynamics of high speed spindles with respect to different preload mechanisms. *Int. J. Adv. Manuf. Technol.* **2011**, *57*, 871–883. [CrossRef]
39. Zhang, S.J.; Yu, J.J.; To, S.; Xiong, Z.W. A theoretical and experimental study of spindle imbalance induced forced vibration and its effect on surface generation in diamond turning. *Int. J. Mach. Tools Manuf.* **2018**, *133*, 61–71. [CrossRef]
40. Hou, Y.L.; Li, C.H.; Zhang, Q. Investigation of structural parameters of high speed grinder spindle system on dynamic performance. *Int. J. Mater. Prod. Technol.* **2012**, *44*, 92–114. [CrossRef]
41. Xi, S.; Cao, H.; Chen, X. Dynamic modeling of spindle bearing system and vibration response investigation. *Mech. Syst. Signal Process.* **2019**, *114*, 486–511. [CrossRef]
42. Jia, W.; Gao, F.; Li, Y.; Wu, W.W.; Li, Z.W. Nonlinear dynamic analysis and chaos prediction of grinding motorized spindle system. *Shock. Vib.* **2019**, *2019*, 1–10. [CrossRef]
43. Guo, M.; Jiang, X.; Ding, Z.; Wu, Z.P. A frequency domain dynamic response approach to optimize the dynamic performance of grinding machine spindles. *Int. J. Adv. Manuf. Technol.* **2018**, *98*, 2737–2745. [CrossRef]
44. Karagiannis, D.; Clayton, G.; Nataraj, C. Boundary control of harmonic disturbances on flexible cantilever beams using piezoelectric patch actuators. *J. Vib. Control* **2016**, *22*, 3916–3929. [CrossRef]
45. Qiu, Z.; Wang, T.; Zhang, X. Sliding mode predictive vibration control of a piezoelectric flexible plate. *J. Intell. Mater. Syst. Struct.* **2020**, *32*, 65–81. [CrossRef]
46. Abdeljaber, O.; Avci, O.; Inman, D. Active vibration control of flexible cantilever plates using piezoelectric materials and artificial neural networks. *J. Sound Vib.* **2016**, *363*, 33–53. [CrossRef]
47. Jiang, X.; Zhao, G.; Lu, W. Vibration suppression of complex thin-walled workpiece based on magnetorheological fixture. *Int. J. Adv. Manuf. Technol.* **2020**, *106*, 1043–1055. [CrossRef]
48. Ma, J.; Zhang, D.; Wu, B.; Luo, M.; Chen, B. Vibration suppression of thin-walled workpiece machining considering external damping properties based on magnetorheological fluids flexible fixture. *Chin. J. Aeronaut.* **2016**, *29*, 1074–1083. [CrossRef]
49. Xiong, G.; Ding, Y.; Zhu, L. Stiffness-based pose optimization of an industrial robot for five-axis milling. *Robot. Comput.-Integr. Manuf.* **2019**, *55*, 19–28. [CrossRef]
50. Janez, G.; Timi, K.; Karl, G.; Miran, B. Accuracy improvement of robotic machining based on robot's structural properties. *Int. J. Adv. Manuf. Technol.* **2020**, *108*, 1309–1329. [CrossRef]
51. Shen, N.; Guo, Z.; Li, J.; Tong, L.; Zhu, K. A practical method of improving hole position accuracy in the robotic drilling process. *Int. J. Adv. Manuf. Technol.* **2018**, *96*, 2973–2987. [CrossRef]
52. Yin, C.; Zhou, Z. *Concise and Quick Reference Manual of Machining Process*; Chemical Industry Press: Beijing, China, 2017.
53. Li, B.M.; Zhao, B.; Li, Q. *Abrasives, Abrasive Tools and Grinding Techniques*; Chemical Industry Press: Beijing, China, 2015.
54. Wang, D.; Fan, H.; Xu, D.; Zhang, Y. Research on grinding force of ultrasonic vibration-assisted grinding of C/SiC composite materials. *Appl. Sci.* **2022**, *12*, 10352. [CrossRef]
55. Zhang, D.K.; Li, C.; Jia, D.; Zhang, Y. Investigation into engineering ceramics grinding mechanism and the influential factors of the grinding force. *Int. J. Control Autom.* **2014**, *7*, 19–34. [CrossRef]
56. Singiresu, S.R. *Mechanical Vibration*, 5th ed.; Pearson Education Inc.: New York, NY, USA, 2011.
57. Wen, X.; Qiu, J.; Tao, J. *Analytical Dynamics of Electromechanical Systems and Applications*; Science Press: Beijing, China, 2007.

Disclaimer/Publisher's Note: The statements, opinions and data contained in all publications are solely those of the individual author(s) and contributor(s) and not of MDPI and/or the editor(s). MDPI and/or the editor(s) disclaim responsibility for any injury to people or property resulting from any ideas, methods, instructions or products referred to in the content.

Article

Disturbance-Observer-Based Dual-Position Feedback Controller for Precision Control of an Industrial Robot Arm

Namhyun Kim, Daejin Oh, Jun-Young Oh and Wonkyun Lee *

School of Mechanical Engineering, Chungnam National University, Daejeon 34134, Republic of Korea
* Correspondence: wklee@cnu.ac.kr

Abstract: Recently, the fourth industrial revolution has accelerated the application of multiple degrees-of-freedom (DOF) robot arms in various applications. However, it is difficult to utilize robot arms for precision motion control because of their low stiffness. External loads applied to robot arms induce deflections in the joints and links, which deteriorates the positioning accuracy. To solve this problem, control methods using a disturbance observer (DOB) with an external sensory system have been developed. However, external sensors are expensive and have low reliability because of noise and reliance on the surrounding environment. A disturbance-observer-based dual-position feedback (DOB-DPF) controller is proposed herein to improve the positioning accuracy by compensating for the deflections in real time using only an internal sensor. The DOB was designed to derive the unpredictable disturbance torque applied to each joint using the command voltage generated by the position controller. The angular deflection of each joint was calculated based on the disturbance torque and joint stiffness, which were identified experimentally. The DPF controller was designed to control the joint motor while simultaneously compensating for angular deflection. A five-DOF robot arm testbed with a position controller was constructed to verify the proposed controller. The contouring performance of the DOB-DPF controller was compared with that of a conventional position controller with an external load applied to the end effector. The increases in the root mean square values of the contour errors were 1.71 and 0.12 mm with a conventional position controller and the proposed DOB-DPF controller, respectively, after a 2.2 kg weight was applied to the end effector. The results show that the contour error caused by the external load is effectively compensated for by the DOB-DPF controller without an external sensor.

Keywords: robot machining system; contour error compensation; five-DOF robot arm

Citation: Kim, N.; Oh, D.; Oh, J.-Y.; Lee, W. Disturbance-Observer-Based Dual-Position Feedback Controller for Precision Control of an Industrial Robot Arm. *Actuators* **2022**, *11*, 375. https://doi.org/10.3390/act11120375

Academic Editor: Ioan Ursu

Received: 21 November 2022
Accepted: 13 December 2022
Published: 14 December 2022

Publisher's Note: MDPI stays neutral with regard to jurisdictional claims in published maps and institutional affiliations.

Copyright: © 2022 by the authors. Licensee MDPI, Basel, Switzerland. This article is an open access article distributed under the terms and conditions of the Creative Commons Attribution (CC BY) license (https://creativecommons.org/licenses/by/4.0/).

1. Introduction

Industrial robot arms are used in various industrial applications for transfer and assembly tasks. Recently, multiple-degree-of-freedom (DOF) robot arms have been employed for precision machining, offering various advantages compared with conventional machine tools comprising linear feed drives. Robot arms can machine multisized workpieces because they can cover a large workspace relative to their size. Moreover, a serial robot arm has a high DOF, which enables the machining of complex shapes. In addition, robot arms can perform various tasks, such as machining processes, inspection, and manipulation, owing to their high flexibility. In addition, robot arms cost 30% less than conventional machine tools with similar performance [1]; however, they cannot replace all such tools, owing to their low stiffness [2]. Generally, the stiffness of a robot arm is less than 1 N/μm, and that of a conventional machine tool is 50 N/μm or more [3]. Various predictable disturbances, such as self-weight, inertia, and friction, can cause angular deflections at the joints. Such disturbances can be estimated based on the stiffness of each joint and compensated for by the position controller [4]. Deflections caused by disturbances applied to the end effector, such as external weight and cutting force, are unpredictable and difficult to compensate for using a feedback controller because they are not recognized by feedback sensors [2]. These angular deflections overlap and cause a large end-effector position error, owing to the series connection. This position error deteriorates the machining accuracy and machining quality [5].

Recently, various studies have been conducted to improve the positioning accuracy of robots arm by compensating for the position error. Position error compensation techniques can be classified as either offline or online. In offline compensation methods, the position error is estimated by the physical model of the robot arm and predictable disturbances; subsequently, it is compensated for by applying an additional position command during control. Belchior et al. proposed an offline compensation method to correct tool path deviations induced by the compliance of industrial robots [6]. An elastic model of a robot arm was derived by finite element simulations and utilized to estimate the pose errors of the tool center position induced by elastic deformations. Munasinghe et al. proposed an offline trajectory compensation method to improve the contouring performance of industrial robot arms [7]. According to the proposed method, a realizable trajectory was generated from the objective trajectory, and its delay dynamics were compensated for using a forward compensator. Olabi et al. proposed an offline trajectory correction method to improve the positioning accuracy of an industrial robot [8]. Position errors of the end effector caused by the flexibility of the robot joints and kinematic errors in the transmission systems were predicted and compensated for by modifying the trajectory.

Offline compensation methods improve the positional accuracy of the robot arm without hardware changes. However, position errors caused by unpredictable external disturbances, such as the cutting force generated during the machining process, are difficult to compensate for. In online compensation methods, external disturbances applied to the end effector are measured with force or torque sensors in real time. Otherwise, the position error of the end effector is measured directly through external position sensors, such as a laser trackers or an image-based motion-capturing device, and applied to the control algorithm [9]. Xu et al. proposed a study on the dynamic modeling and compensation of a robot arm based on six-axis force/torque sensors [10]. Dynamic compensating devices were designed using a functional link artificial neural network, and a digital-signal-processor-based real-time dynamic compensation system was developed and evaluated. Park. et al. suggested a dual observer that estimates disturbance and states of the motors of industrial robots simultaneously [11]. Moeller et al. proposed an online position-error compensation method to improve the accuracy of a robot arm using a laser tracker [12]. The position error of the end effector was measured in real time and compensated for by modifying a programmed trajectory. Furuta et al. proposed a method for controlling the trajectory tracking of an articulated robot arm using sensory feedback [13]. Park et al. suggested a tuning method for PID according to several criteria, such as stability and tunability. This method was used to develop a robust, high-quality, linear PID tracking motion controller [14]. The dynamics of the robot arm were described in the task coordinate system, and a robust feedback controller was designed for feedback control based on a sensory feedback system. Other studies have been conducted on the optimization of the controllers of several actuators. Zhang et al. proposed a robust adaptive neural control algorithm for robust control a vehicle according to structural and gain-related uncertainties. They also developed a novel robust fuzzy control algorithm to deal with the path-following control problem of an unmanned sailboat robot [15,16]. Li et al. presented a novel cooperative design strategy for the path following of a mixed-order underactuated surface vehicle and unmanned aerial vehicle systems under the influence of external disturbances [17].

The aforementioned online compensation methods measure position errors directly and compensate for them in real time. However, external position sensors, which are generally expensive, are essential intended to configure real-time compensation. Moreover, it is difficult to guarantee the reliability of the compensation methods because obstacles in the working environment can block the external sensory system and render it unstable. Applying a state observer is an effective method to avoid the control performance deterioration caused by unstable sensor feedback signals. Liu et al. suggested sensorless force estimation by a disturbance observer and neural learning of friction approximation. The observer was modified to develop a disturbance Kalman-filter-based approach, and the uncertainty and measurement noise were analyzed by a neural network [18]. Tong et al. proposed observer-based adaptive control methods for the tracking control of uncertain nonlinear systems [19]. Cheng et al. suggested active disturbance rejection control based on dynamic feedforward to improve the control robustness and promote strong antidisturbance ability [20]. Yin et al. proposed an enhancing trajectory tracking accuracy method by formulating an adaptive control and robust control for robust adaptive control under the influence of both parametric uncertainties and external disturbances [21]. Mohammadi et al. proposed a general systematic approach to solve the design problem of a disturbance observer without restrictions on the number of degrees of freedom, the types of joints, or the manipulator configuration [22]. Hence, a disturbance-observer-based dual-position feedback (DOB-DPF) controller is proposed herein to improve the position accuracy of a five-DOF robot arm without external position sensors. The torques applied to the five joints were derived in real time based on the command voltage generated from the motion controller and the disturbance observer (DOB). The angular deflections of the five joints were calculated from the applied torque based on the physical and dynamic models of the robot arm. A DPF algorithm was applied to compensate for the position error of the end effector caused by the angular deflections. A five-DOF robot arm testbed with a position control system was constructed to evaluate the DOB-DPF controller. The contour errors of the conventional control algorithm and the DOB-DPF controller were compared in a circular interpolation to verify the performance of the proposed method. The root mean square (RMS) value of the contour errors increased by 1.71 and 0.12 mm for the conventional position controller and the proposed DOB-DPF controller, respectively, after a 2.2 kg weight was applied to the end effector.

Section 2 describes the design process of the DOB-DPF controller. Section 3 introduces the experimental setup of a five-DOF robot arm with a position controller, and he detailed design process of the robot arm hardware and the position controller, which comprises a numeric control kernel and motion control unit, are presented. Section 4 describes the tests performed to verify the performance of the DOB-DPF controller, as well as the verification test procedures and results. Finally, Section 5 concludes the paper.

2. Design of the DOB-DPF Controller

2.1. DOB Design

The driving torque of a robot arm joint comprises four components: inertial torque, internal disturbance, gravity, and external disturbance. The internal disturbance includes centrifugal and Coriolis force generation during operation. The external disturbance includes the load torque caused by the weight of the parts attached to the end effector and the force applied to the end effector during operation. The inertial torque and internal disturbance can be calculated based on dynamic and kinematic analyses of the robot. Therefore, the external disturbance (T_d) can be predicted by subtracting the inertial torque, internal disturbance, and gravity from the torque command as follows:

$$T_d = T_{com} - J(q)\ddot{q} - C(q,\dot{q})\dot{q} - G(q), \qquad (1)$$

where q is the angular position of the joints, which is measured by the encoder signal of each joint motor; matrices $J(q)$, $C(q,\dot{q})$, and $G(q)$ are the properties of inertia, inertial disturbance, and gravity, respectively, which are derived from the robot dynamics [23]; and T_{com} denotes the driving torque of the joint, which is calculated from the command voltage of the controller.

2.2. DPF Controller

The distribution profiles of the applied torque at each joint can be derived in real time using the DOB. The angular deflection of the joint can be calculated by dividing the applied torque by the stiffness of the joint. The actual position of the end effector is calculated based on the angular deflection of each joint and the kinematic analysis of the robot arm without an external position sensor. The position error can be compensated for online by controlling the actual angular position to follow the target angular position of each joint.

Figure 1a–c show block diagrams of a conventional a semi-closed loop, fully closed-loop, and the DPF control algorithm, respectively. A feedback controller comprises a proportional position loop and a proportional integral velocity loop, which is generally used for precision position control of the machine tool feed drives. The position loop generates the velocity command from the gap between the reference and actual positions measured by the position sensor. The velocity loop generates the current command from the gap between the velocity command and the actual velocity measured by the velocity sensor. A semi-closed loop is a typically used feedback control algorithm that refers to the position measured by an internal sensor and the velocity calculated from the measured position. A semi-closed loop cannot recognize and compensate for the position error caused by low stiffness. A fully closed loop is used to improve the positioning accuracy of a mechanical system containing both internal and external sensors. The aforementioned online compensation methods utilize also use a fully closed loop [10–12].

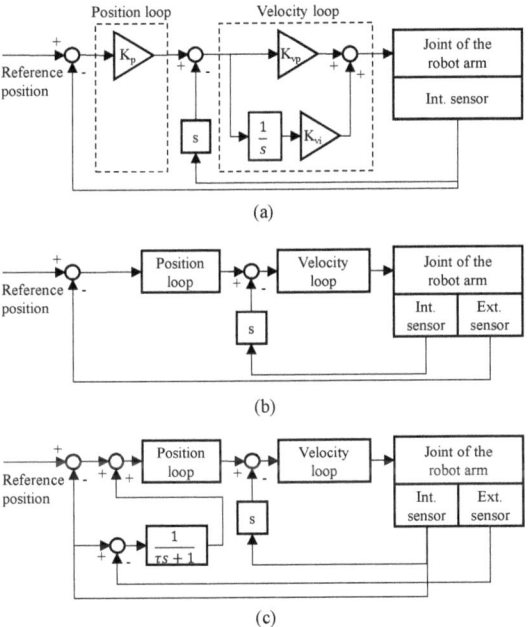

Figure 1. Block diagrams of (a) a conventional semi-closed loop, (b) fully closed loop, and (c) the DPF control algorithm.

In the DPF controller, the input value of the position loop (x_{in}) is calculated as follows:

$$x_{in} = x_{ref} - x_{int} + \frac{1}{\tau s + 1}(x_{int} - x_{ext}), \quad (2)$$

where x_{ref}, x_{int}, and x_{ext} represent the reference position, the position measured by the internal sensor, and the position measured by the external sensor, respectively. A first-order transfer function with a time constant (τ) is multiplied by the gap between the position measured by the internal and external sensors and added to the following error calculated by the position measured by the internal sensor. The transfer function reduces the noise and time skew caused by the external sensor and improves the stability. The DPF controller acts as a semi-closed loop when the time constant of the transfer function is set to a large value. Meanwhile, the DPF controller acts as a fully closed loop with a small time constant.

2.3. DOB-DPF Controller

The position error of the robot arm is compensated for by replacing the feedback position with an actual position measured by an external sensor. In this case, the control system becomes unstable when the external sensor includes noise. Although the feedback controller is configured based on an external sensor, an internal sensor is also required for velocity control. Therefore, time skew causes instability in the control performance when the sampling rates of the internal and external sensors differ [24]. In this regard, a DPF controller used for ultraprecision position control of the machine tool feed drive is utilized for online compensation of the position error.

Generally, position errors with various frequencies are generated during operation. We aimed to design a position controller to compensate for the low-frequency position error caused by the weight or low-frequency component of the cutting force. High-frequency vibrations caused by the high-frequency components of the cutting force, such as the force variation between cutters in the milling process, are not considered in this study. Although the transfer function reduces the bandwidth of the DPF controller compared to a fully closed loop, the DPF controller can stably compensate for the low-frequency position error. In this study, a new DPF system was suggested. Conventional DPF systems have to be constructed with an external sensory system and an internal sensory system. However, the suggested control methods that use DOB do require the use of external sensors. Therefore, the reliability does not decrease as a result of the noise of sensors, with an effective decrease in construction costs. Figure 2 shows a block diagram of the DOB-DPF controller. The DOB-DPF controller comprises a feedback controller, feedforward controller, and the DOB-DPF algorithm. The feedback controller controls each joint to follow the target angle based on a proportional position loop and a proportional integral velocity loop. The feedforward controller compensates for the additional torque caused by the self-weight, as well as the Coriolis and centrifugal forces. The DOB-DPF algorithm integrates the DOB to calculate the actual position and the DPF controller to compensate for the angular deflection.

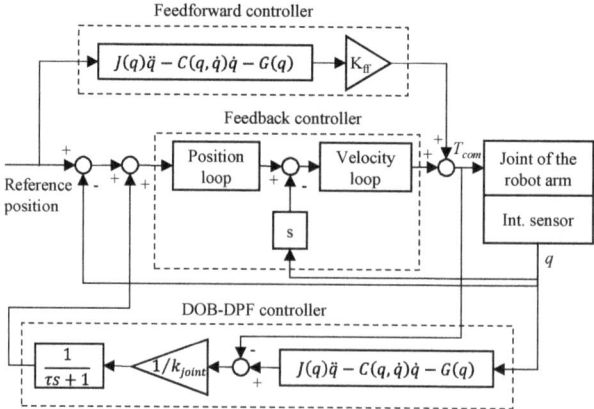

Figure 2. Block diagram of the DOB-DPF controller.

3. Design of a Five-DOF Robot Arm

3.1. Hardware Design

Figure 3a shows the experimental setup of the five-DOF robot arm. The payload of the robot arm was set to 50 N. The rated torque of the joint motors with reducers was designed based on the load torque applied to each joint. Joints 1 and 2 comprised a motor with a rated torque of 2.39 Nm (SGMAV-08A, Yaskawa) and a reducer with a gear ratio of 1/100 (PGX90-H100, ATG). Joint 3 comprised a motor with a rated torque of 1.27 Nm (SGMAV-04A, Yaskawa) and a reducer with a gear ratio of 1/100 (PGX62-H100, ATG). Joints 4 and 5, with relatively low loads, both had a rated torque of 0.159 Nm (SGMAV-04A, Yaskawa) and reduction gears (PGX44-H100, ATG) with a gear ratio of 1/100. Links 2 and 3 were each constructed with aluminum profiles measuring 40 mm × 80 mm and 40 mm × 40 mm, respectively. Figure 3b shows the Denavit–Hartenberg (DH) parameters, which represent the joint dimensions and relative angle of the robot processing system. Joints 1, 2, and 3 determine the position of the robot, whereas joints 4 and 5 determine the orientation of the robot. The designed five-DOF robot arm was installed on the surface of a plate table.

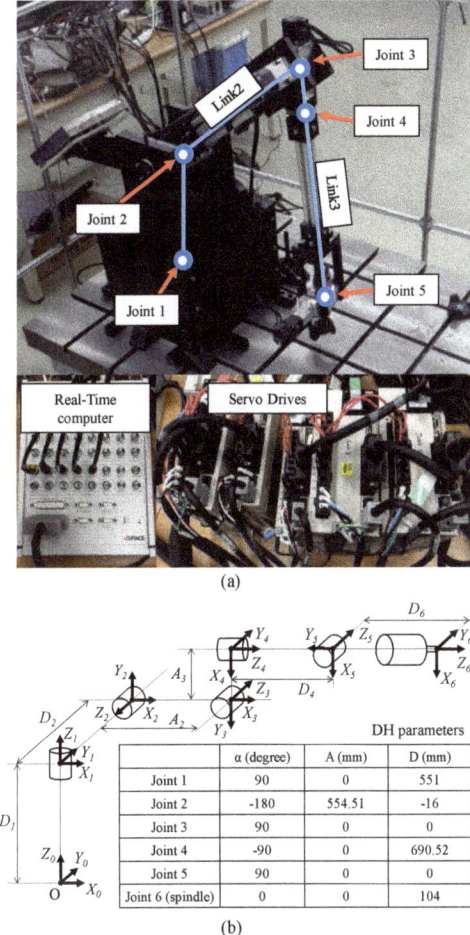

Figure 3. Experimental setup of the five-DOF robot arm: (a) photo and (b) Denavit–Hartenberg (DH) parameters, which represent the joint dimensions and relative angle.

3.2. Controller Design

A numerical control kernel and a motion control unit were designed for the position control of the five-DOF robot arm. The numeric control kernel comprises an interpolator and a velocity profiler that generate the target profiles of the angular position of each joint from the user input, which contains the target position and orientation of the end effector.

The interpolator calculates the target angular positions of the five joints to achieve the user input as follows.

Figure 4 shows the postures of links 1 to 3 corresponding to the angles of joints 1 to 3 of the robot arm. $(x_{J5}, y_{J5}, z_{J5})^{J1}$ indicates the position of joint 5 in the $J1$ coordinate system, $[X_{J1}, Y_{J1}, Z_{J1}]$, which is rotated by θ_1 in accordance with the global coordinate system $[X_G, Y_G, Z_G]$. The angular position of joint 1, (θ_1) can be calculated from the target position of the end effector in the global coordinate, $(x_{TP}, y_{TP}, z_{TP})^G$, as follows:

$$\theta_1 = tan^{-1}\left(\frac{y_{TP}}{x_{TP}}\right) - sin^{-1}\left(\frac{D_2}{\sqrt{x_{TP}^2 + y_{TP}^2}}\right), \tag{3}$$

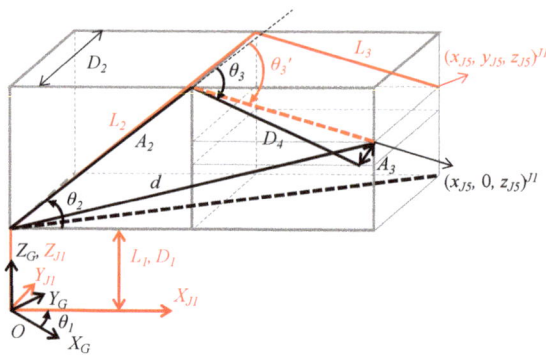

Figure 4. Postures of links 1 to 3 according to the angles of joints 1 to 3 of the robot arm.

$(x_{J5}, y_{J5}, z_{J5})^{J1}$ is derived from θ_1 and the unit vector of the target orientation in the global coordinate $(V_{TO} = (x_{TO}, y_{TO}, z_{TO})^G)$ using a rotational transformation matrix as follows:

$$\begin{bmatrix} x_{J5} \\ y_{J5} \\ z_{J5} \end{bmatrix} = \begin{bmatrix} cos\theta_1 & sin\theta_1 & 0 \\ -sin\theta_1 & cos\theta_1 & 0 \\ 0 & 0 & 1 \end{bmatrix} \begin{bmatrix} x_{TP} - D_6 \times x_{TO} \\ y_{TP} - D_6 \times y_{TO} \\ z_{TP} - D_6 \times z_{TO} \end{bmatrix}. \tag{4}$$

The angular position of joint 2 (θ_2) can be calculated as the sum of the angle between d and A_2 and the angle between d and x_{J1} as follows:

$$\theta_2 = cos^{-1}\left(\frac{A_2^2 + d^2 - L_3^2}{2 \cdot d \cdot L_3}\right) + tan^{-1}\left(\frac{z_{J5} - D_1}{x_{J5}}\right), \tag{5}$$

where d and L_3 are derived by $(x_{J5}, 0, z_{J5})^{J1}$ and the DH parameters, respectively. The angular position of joint 3 (θ_3) is the sum of the angle between D_4 and L_3, and $\theta_{3'}$, which denotes the angle between A_2 and L_3.

$$\theta_3 = cos^{-1}\left(\frac{d^2 - A_2^2 - L_3^2}{2 \cdot A_2 \cdot L_3}\right) + tan^{-1}\left(\frac{A_3}{D_4}\right), \tag{6}$$

The angular position of joint 4 (θ_4) is the angle between the y-axis unit vector of the coordinate system of joint 1 (Y_1) and the z-axis unit vector of the coordinate system of joint 5 (Z_5), which can be calculated as follows:

$$\theta_4 = cos^{-1}\left((-sin\theta_1, cos\theta_1, 0) \cdot \frac{X_3 \times V_{TO}}{||X_3 \times V_{TO}||}\right), \tag{7}$$

where X_3 is the x-axis unit vector of the coordinate system of joint 3, which is derived from θ_1 to θ_3 as follows:

$$X_3 = (\cos(\theta_2 - \theta_3)\cos\theta_1,\ \cos(\theta_2 - \theta_3)\sin\theta_1,\ \sin(\theta_2 - \theta_3))^G. \tag{8}$$

The angular position of joint 5 (θ_5) is the angle between V_{TO} and X_3, which is calculated as follows:

$$\theta_5 = \cos^{-1}(V_{TO} \cdot X_3). \tag{9}$$

The target profiles of the angular position can be derived by connecting the angular joints in the time domain. However, the acceleration and deceleration of the target profiles should be considered because large accelerations/decelerations increase the tracking error and instability of the robot arm. In this regard, a velocity profiler was designed to generate the target profiles of each joint, including the acceleration/deceleration section, as follows:

$$\omega_O[k] = \omega_O[k-1] + \frac{1}{m}\{\omega_i[k] - \omega_i[k-m]\}. \tag{10}$$

where $\omega_i[k]$ and $\omega_O[k]$ are the target angular velocities at the kth sampling before and after velocity profiling, respectively, and m is the number of samples corresponding to the linear acceleration/deceleration section. Figure 5a shows the target angles of joints 1 to 5 generated in the numerical control kernel with respect to the initial position of (300 mm, 0 mm, 100 mm) to the target position of (500 mm, 200 mm, 300 mm), maintaining the target orientation as (0, 0, −1). Figure 5b shows the posture of the robot arm at every second calculated by forward kinematics based on the DH parameters and the target profiles of joints 1 to 5. The motion control unit is the DOB-DPF controller mentioned in the previous section, which controls the joint corresponding to the target angular profiles generated by the numeric control kernel.

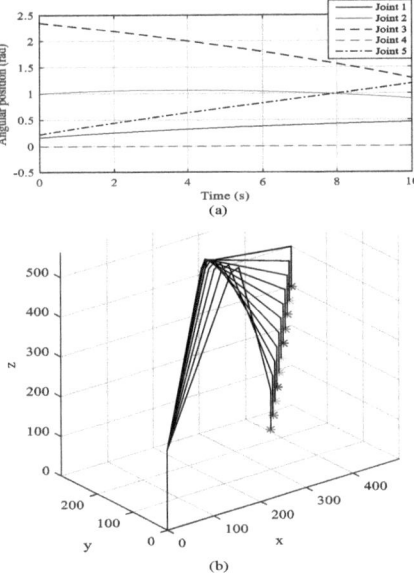

Figure 5. Simulation result with respect to the initial position of (300 mm, 0 mm, 100 mm) to the target position of (500 mm, 200 mm, 300 mm), maintaining the target orientation as (0, 0, −1): (**a**) target angles of joints 1 to 5 generated in the numerical control kernel and (**b**) posture of the robot arm.

3.3. Measurement of Stiffness

The angular deflection of each joint can be calculated by dividing the disturbance torque by the stiffness. The stiffness of the links was disregarded in this study because the stiffness of the joint is much lower than that of the links. The joint was controlled to keep the link parallel to the ground, and a capacitance sensor (CPL190, Lion precision) was installed above the end of the link. Subsequently, the increment in the gap between the capacitance sensor and the link was measured when a constant load was applied to the link. The increment of the stall torque of the joint in steady state was acquired by measuring the torque command of the joint motor. Finally, the stiffness of the joint was calculated by dividing the increment of the stall torque by that of the gap. The experiment was performed five times for each joint individually by increasing the applied load from 1 to 5 kg at intervals of 1 kg.

4. Evaluation of DOB-DPF Controller

4.1. Implementation of DOB-DPF Controller

The DOB-DPF controller was programmed using MATLAB and implemented on a robot arm using a real-time computer (Micro Lab Box, dSPACE). The sampling time was set to 0.001 s. The controller generated torque commands in the five joint motors as analog voltages in the range of -10 to 10 V. Each drive of the joint motor transferred the analog voltage to the target torque in a linear range of the rated torque and generated three phase-driving currents corresponding to the target torque. The encoder signal of each joint motor was transmitted to the digital input–output port of a real-time computer and decoded to the angular position. The angular position of the joint was derived by multiplying the gear ratio by the angular position of the joint motor and transmitted to the DOB-DPF controller.

The performance of the DPF controller is determined by the time constant of the first-order transfer function. In this study, the optimal value of the time constant was derived based on simulations. The simulation model of the five-DOF robot arm was constructed based on the position control algorithm and kinematic model of the robot arm. Using the simulation model, periodic disturbances with an amplitude 20 N were applied to the end effector while the robot arm was controlled to maintain the current position. Figure 6b shows the position of the end effector recognized by internal and external position sensors when the sinusoidal disturbance shown in Figure 6a was applied to the end effector. The black line indicates the compensation motion of the robot arm, and the red line is the position error of the end effector. Figure 6c shows the peak values of the position errors with respect to the time constant of the DPF controller. The result shows that a lower time constant leads to better control performance because the position error increases proportionally to the time constant. Figure 7b shows the position of the end effector when the square wave disturbance shown in Figure 7a is applied. Figure 7c shows the peak values of the acceleration of the end effector with respect to the time constants. The result shows that a small time constant causes large acceleration, which reduces the position accuracy and stability. The acceleration reduced rapidly at low time constants and saturated at a time constant of 0.05 s. Consequently, the time constant of the DPF controller was set to 0.05 s to improve position accuracy and robustness to external disturbance.

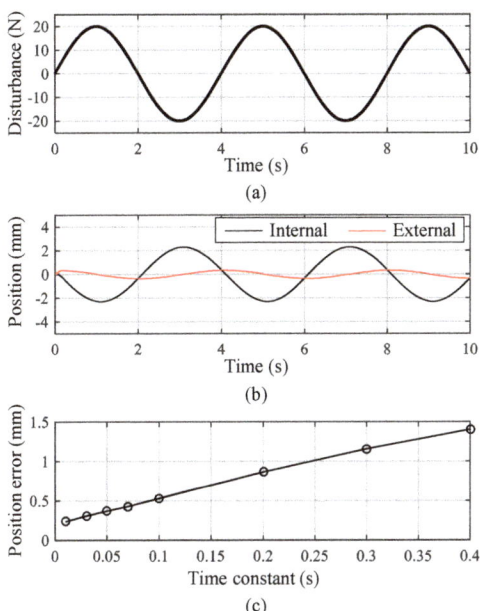

Figure 6. Simulation result of the dual-position feedback controller with sinusoidal wave disturbance: (**a**) disturbance; (**b**) position of the end effector measured by internal and external position sensors; (**c**) peak position errors of the end effector with respect to the time constants of the dual-position feedback controller.

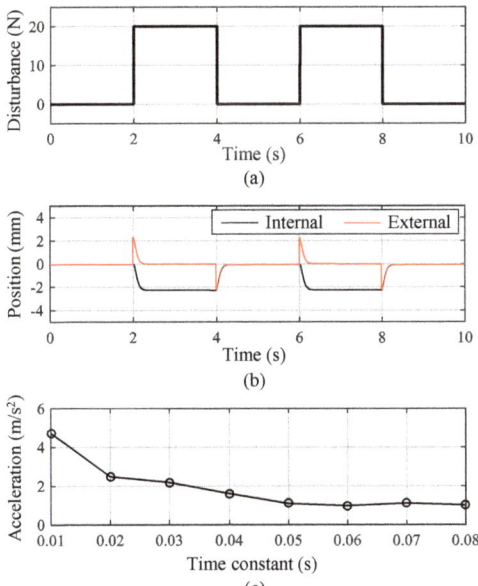

Figure 7. Simulation result of the dual-position feedback controller with square wave disturbance: (**a**) disturbance; (**b**) position of the end effector measured by internal and external position sensors; (**c**) peak acceleration of the end effector with respect to the time constants of the dual-position feedback controller.

4.2. External Position Sensing

An external position sensor (Vive, HTC) was installed to measure the actual contour error of the end effector. Figure 8 shows the three Cartesian coordinates (C_b, C_w, and C_G) used to calculate the actual position and contour error of the end effector. C_b is the coordinate of the Vive base station. The Vive acquires the three-dimensional position of the trackers with respect to the coordinates of the base station. The accuracy of the position measurement was 0.1 mm in our experimental setup. C_w and C_G denote the coordinates of the worktable and robot arm, respectively. The actual position of the robot arm was measured by attaching a tracker (T1) to the end effector; subsequently, it was converted to the worktable coordinate using a homogeneous transformation matrix (HTM). The HTMs of the worktable and base station coordinates were derived from the unit direction vectors of the worktable coordinates measured by three trackers (T2, T3, and T4) installed on the worktable. The target position of the robot arm was generated in the worktable coordinate and converted to the robot arm coordinate for position control. The contour error was calculated based on the target and actual positions of the end effector in the worktable coordinate. The HTMs of the robot arm and worktable coordinates were derived from the unit direction vectors of the robot arm coordinates calculated by measuring the position of tracker T1 when the robot was linearly moving along the x, y, and z axes.

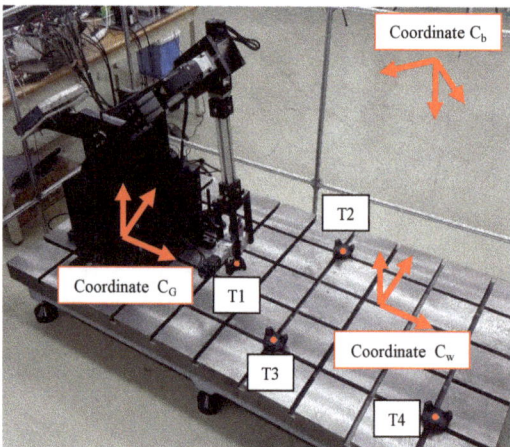

Figure 8. Three Cartesian coordinates (C_b, C_w, and C_G) and four trackers used to calculate the actual position and contour error of the end effector.

4.3. Evaluation Result

To evaluate the performance of the DOB-DPF controller, its contour errors were compared with those of a conventional controller comprising a feedback and feedforward module during circular interpolation. The trajectory of the robot arm was set to a circle with a radius of 100 mm in the xy plane of the worktable coordinate. Figure 9 compares the contouring performances of the two controllers before and after a constant weight of 2.2 kg was applied to the end effector. Figure 9a,b show that the position drop of the end effector caused by a significant weight reduction when the DOB-DPF controller is applied. The peak, root mean square (RMS), and standard deviation (STD) of the contour errors are listed in Table 1. The RMS value of the contour error of both the conventional and DOB-DPF controller was 0.59 mm when the external disturbance was zero. When a weight of 2.2 kg was applied to the end effector, the contour error of the conventional controller increased to 2.30 mm, whereas the contour error of the DOB-DPF controller increased to 0.71 mm. This result indicates that the contour error caused by the disturbance was compensated for by the DOB-DPF algorithm.

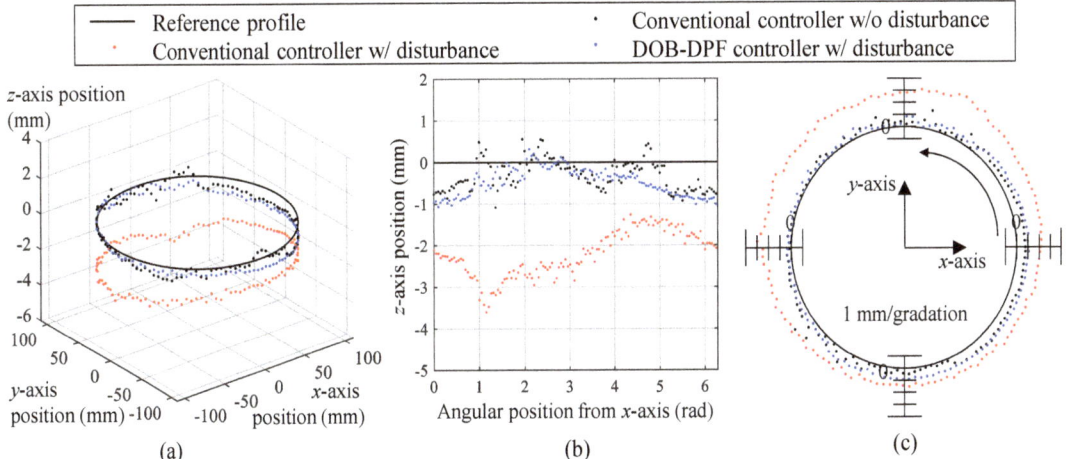

Figure 9. Contouring performances of the conventional controller and the DOB-DPF controller before and after a constant weight of 2.2 kg was applied to the end effector: position of the end effector in (a) three-dimensional and (b) two-dimensional (XZ plane) graph and (c) contour errors.

Table 1. Peak, RMS, and STD of the contour errors.

Control Method	Contour Error (mm)		
	Peak	RMS	STD
Conventional controller w/o disturbance	1.80	0.59	0.31
Conventional controller w/ disturbance	3.60	2.30	0.55
DOB-DPF controller w/ disturbance	1.08	0.71	0.32

5. Conclusions

A DOB-DPF controller was proposed in this paper to compensate for the position error of a five-DOF robot caused by low stiffness. Angular deflections caused by external disturbances were calculated by the DOB without using external position sensors and compensated by the DPF control algorithm. A five-DOF robot arm and its position controller were constructed to verify the proposed DOF-DPF controller. Contour errors of the conventional position and proposed DOB-DPF controllers were compared during circular interpolation using an external position sensor. In the conventional position controller, the RMS value of the contour error increased from 0.59 to 2.30 mm after a 2.2 kg weight was applied to the end effector, whereas it increased from 0.59 to 0.71 mm in the proposed DOB-DPF controller.

Author Contributions: Conceptualization, W.L. and N.K.; methodology, W.L. and N.K.; software, N.K. and D.O.; validation, N.K. and J.-Y.O.; formal analysis, investigation, resources, data curation, writing—original draft preparation, and visualization, W.L. and N.K.; supervision, project administration, and funding acquisition, W.L. All authors have read and agreed to the published version of the manuscript.

Funding: This research was supported in part by the Technology Development Program for Smart Controller in Manufacturing Equipment (20012834, Development of Smart CNC Control System Technology for Manufacturing Equipment) funded by the Ministry of Trade, Industry & Energy (MOTIE, Korea) and in part by the Korea Institute of Machinery and Materials for the project "Development of Technology for Mobile Platform-based Machining System" (No. NK210B).

Conflicts of Interest: The authors declare no conflict of interest.

References

1. Caro, S.; Dumas, C.; Garnier, S.; Furet, B. Workpiece placement optimization for machining operations with a KUKA KR270-2 robot. In Proceedings of the 2013 IEEE International Conference on Robotics and Automation, Karlsruhe, Germany, 6–10 May 2013; pp. 2921–2926.
2. Wang, J.; Zhang, H.; Fuhlbrigge, T. Improving machining accuracy with robot deformation compensation. In Proceedings of the 2009 IEEE/RSJ International Conference on Intelligent Robots and Systems, St. Louis, MO, USA, 10–15 October 2009; pp. 3826–3831.
3. Zhang, H.; Wang, J.; Zhang, G.; Gan, Z.; Pan, Z.; Cui, H.; Zhu, Z. Machining with flexible manipulator: Toward improving robotic machining performance. In Proceedings of the 2005 IEEE/ASME Interna-tional Conference on Advanced Intelligent Mechatronics, Monterey, CA, USA, 24–28 July 2005; pp. 1127–1132.
4. Lee, W.; Lee, C.-Y.; Jeong, Y.H.; Min, B.-K. Distributed component friction model for precision control of a feed drive system. IEEE/ASME Trans. Mechatron. 2015, 20, 1966–1974. [CrossRef]
5. Chen, Y.; Dong, F. Robot machining: Recent development and future research issues. Int. J. Adv. Manuf. Technol. 2012, 66, 1489–1497. [CrossRef]
6. Belchior, J.; Guillo, M.; Courteille, E.; Maurine, P.; Leotoing, L.; Guines, D. Off-line compensation of the tool path deviations on robotic machining: Application to incremental sheet forming. Robot. Comput.-Integr. Manuf. 2013, 29, 58–69. [CrossRef]
7. Munasinghe, S.R.; Nakamura, M.; Goto, S.; Kyura, N. Optimum contouring of industrial robot arms under assigned velocity and torque constraints. IEEE Trans. Syst. Man Cybern. 2001, 31, 159–167. [CrossRef]
8. Olabi, A.; Damak, M.; Bearee, R.; Gibaru, O.; Leleu, S. Improving the accuracy of industrial robots by offline compensation of joints errors. In Proceedings of the 2012 IEEE International Conference on Industrial Technology, Athens, Greece, 19–21 March 2012; pp. 492–497.
9. Schneider, U.; Drust, M.; Ansaloni, M.; Lehmann, C.; Pellic-ciari, M.; Leali, F.; Gunnink, J.W.; Verl, A. Improving robotic machining accuracy through experimental error investigation and modular compensation. Int. J. Adv. Manuf. Technol. 2016, 85, 3–15. [CrossRef]
10. Xu, K.-J.; Li, C.; Zhu, Z.-N. Dynamic modeling and compensation of robot six-axis wrist force/torque sensor. IEEE Trans. Instrum. Meas. 2007, 56, 2094–2100. [CrossRef]
11. Park, S.-K.; Lee, S.-H. Disturbance observer based robust control for industrial robots with flexible joints. In Proceedings of the 2007 International Conference on Control, Automation and Systems, Seoul, Republic of Korea, 17–20 October 2007.
12. Moeller, C.; Schmidt, H.C.; Koch, P.; Boehlmann, C.; Kothe, S.; Wollnack, J.; Hintze, W. Real time pose control of an industrial robotic system for machining of large scale components in aerospace industry using laser tracker system. SAE Int. J. Aerosp. 2017, 2, 100–108. [CrossRef]
13. Furuta, K.; Kosuge, K.; Mukai, N. Control of articulated robot arm with sensory feedback: Laser beam tracking system. IEEE Trans. Ind. Electron. 1988, 35, 31–39. [CrossRef]
14. Park, J.; Chung, W. Design of a robust H∞ PID control for industrial manipulators. J. Dyn. Sys. Meas. Control 2000, 122, 803–812. [CrossRef]
15. Zhang, G.; Li, J.; Jin, X.; Liu, C. Robust adaptive neural control for wing-sail-assisted vehicle via the multiport event-triggered approach. IEEE Trans. Cybern. 2021, 52, 12916–12928. [CrossRef] [PubMed]
16. Zhang, G.; Li, J.; Liu, C.; Zhang, W. A robust fuzzy speed regulator for unmanned sailboat robot via the composite ILOS guidance. Nonlinear Dyn. 2022, 110, 2465–2480. [CrossRef]
17. Li, J.; Zhang, G.; Shan, Q.; Zhang, W. A Novel Cooperative Design for USV-UAV Systems: 3D Mapping Guidance and Adaptive Fuzzy Control. IEEE Trans. Control. Netw. Syst. 2022. [CrossRef]
18. Liu, S.; Wang, L.; Wang, X. Sensorless force estimation for industrial robots using disturbance observer and neural learning of friction approximation. Robot. Comput.-Integr. Manuf. 2021, 71, 102168. [CrossRef]
19. Tong, S.; Min, X.; Li, Y. Observer-based adaptive fuzzy tracking control for strict-feedback nonlinear systems with unknown control gain functions. IEEE Trans. Cybern. 2020, 50, 3903–3913. [CrossRef] [PubMed]
20. Cheng, X.; Tu, X.; Zhou, Y.; Zhou, R. Active disturbance rejection control of multi-joint industrial robots based on dynamic feedforward. Electronics 2019, 8, 591. [CrossRef]
21. Yin, X.; Li, P. Enhancing trajectory tracking accuracy for industrial robot with robust adaptive control. Robot. Comput.-Integr. Manuf. 2018, 51, 97–102. [CrossRef]
22. Mohammadi, A.; Tavakoli, M.; Marquez, H.J.; Hashemzadeh, F. Nonlinear disturbance observer design for robotic manipulators. Control. Eng. Pract. 2013, 21, 253–267. [CrossRef]
23. Spong, M.W.; Hutchinson, S.; Vidyasagar, M. Robot Dynamics and Control, 2nd ed.; Wiley: Hoboken, NJ, USA, 2004; pp. 205–207.
24. Kim, N.; Kim, H.; Lee, W. Hardware-in-the-loop simulation for estimation of position control performance of machine tool feed drive. Precis. Eng. 2019, 60, 587–593. [CrossRef]

Article

Adaptive Fault Tolerant Non-Singular Sliding Mode Control for Robotic Manipulators Based on Fixed-Time Control Law

Saim Ahmed [1,2], Ahmad Taher Azar [1,2,3,*] and Mohamed Tounsi [1,2]

1. College of Computer and Information Sciences, Prince Sultan University, Riyadh 11586, Saudi Arabia
2. Automated Systems and Soft Computing Lab (ASSCL), Prince Sultan University, Riyadh 11586, Saudi Arabia
3. Faculty of Computers and Artificial Intelligence, Benha University, Benha 13518, Egypt
* Correspondence: aazar@psu.edu.sa or ahmad.azar@fci.bu.edu.eg or ahmad_t_azar@ieee.org

Abstract: This paper presents a fault tolerant scheme employing adaptive non-singular fixed-time terminal sliding mode control (AFxNTSM) for the application of robotic manipulators under uncertainties, external disturbances, and actuator faults. To begin, non-singular fixed-time terminal sliding mode control (FxNTSM) is put forth. This control method uses non-singular terminal sliding mode control to quickly reach fixed-time convergence, accomplish satisfactory performance in tracking, and produce non-singular and non-chatter control inputs. Then, without knowing the upper bounds beforehand, AFxNTSM is used as a reliable fault tolerant control (FTC) to estimate actuator faults and unknown dynamics. The fixed-time stability of the closed-loop system is established by the theory of Lyapunov analysis. The computer simulation results of the position tracking, control inputs, and adaptive parameters are presented to verify and illustrate the performance of the proposed strategy.

Keywords: robotic manipulators; fixed-time sliding mode control; fault tolerant control; actuator faults

1. Introduction

Recent developments in the field of control systems are having a profound impact on the fields of mechatronics and robotic systems. The problem of the robotic manipulator is one that is explored in the area of control theory. It is a highly unstable mechanical system that is nonlinear to a high degree. As a consequence of this, such a system must have a robust control law and must be capable of maintaining strong stability and trajectory tracking capabilities in the face of external disturbance and uncertainty [1]. In spite of the fact that a range of robust solutions have been offered for uncertain robotic systems, an additional problem arises when joint actuators fail to function properly. In this scenario, FTC is utilized to compensate for controller failures in order to ensure that the system continues to function correctly. Under real-world conditions, it is impossible to prevent the control failure from occurring. Therefore, an accurately functioning controlled system is impossible if the controller cannot tolerate faults in the system being regulated. As a consequence of this, there is a growing interest in the development of FTC methodologies, which have been subjected to extensive research and are being utilized in a variety of industries. The fundamental theory of FTC is that the designed controller needs to be robust in order to guarantee the achievement of the optimal level of stability and robustness in the event that the actuators fail to do their jobs [2].

The family of nonlinear controllers includes the sliding mode control (SMC). It is able to manage nonlinear systems with uncertainties, bounded disturbances, and low sensitivity to parameter variations in an effective manner. Terminal sliding mode control (TSM), which provides robust tracking and better precision, was created in [3] with the purpose of achieving finite-time stability. However, it suffers from slow convergence and singularity concerns. Then, SMC techniques were proposed as solutions to these challenges in order to meet the aims of attaining rapid convergence through the use of fast terminal SMC (FTSM), and getting rid of singularities through the use of fast non-singular terminal

Citation: Ahmed, S.; Azar, A.T.; Tounsi, M. Adaptive Fault Tolerant Non-Singular Sliding Mode Control for Robotic Manipulators Based on Fixed-Time Control Law. *Actuators* **2022**, *11*, 353. https://doi.org/10.3390/act11120353

Academic Editor: Guanghong Yang

Received: 22 October 2022
Accepted: 24 November 2022
Published: 29 November 2022

Publisher's Note: MDPI stays neutral with regard to jurisdictional claims in published maps and institutional affiliations.

Copyright: © 2022 by the authors. Licensee MDPI, Basel, Switzerland. This article is an open access article distributed under the terms and conditions of the Creative Commons Attribution (CC BY) license (https://creativecommons.org/licenses/by/4.0/).

SMC (FNTSM) [4,5]. In addition, the amount of time required for the finite-time system to converge is highly dependent on the initial values of the nonlinear system, and this amount of time would unquestionably increase as the initial values of the nonlinear system were raised. Therefore, fixed-time stability is an alternative, which may be utilized to precisely calculate the time of convergence regardless of the initial conditions [6,7]. Concerning finite-time convergence, several FTC algorithms have been proposed for robotic applications using adaptive control scheme to estimate the actuator faults [8].

Adaptive control is a well-known nonlinear control method that is gaining popularity in control engineering applications. It exhibits extraordinary adaptability to system uncertainty, external disturbances, and actuator failures, and improve the closed-loop system's tracking performance [9]. Various adaptive finite time SMC schemes have been proposed for the robotic manipulator with uncertainties and actuator failures. In [10], FTC using adaptive finite-time FTSM was designed for the robotic system under faults, in which faults were estimated using adaptive gains. A finite-time SMC based active FTC was proposed to estimate the unknown dynamics of the nonlinear robot with joint faults [11]. Another FTC scheme based on a class of third-order SMC was developed for the second-order nonlinear system in the presence of actuator faults [12]. Furthermore, a robust adaptive control approach with a quasi-continuous high-order SMC and neural network has been proposed for the unknown dynamics of the nonlinear system under joint actuator faults [13].

Interestingly, all of the aforementioned publications focused primarily on the adaptive scheme for the estimation of the upper bounds of uncertain dynamics and actuator faults utilizing finite-time FNTSM control [11–13]. According to our understanding, few works offer adaptive FxNTSM control [14,15], but none of them examined the FTC based on adaptive FxNTSM method under actuator failures. It is recognized that the primary advantage of FxNTSM control is singularity avoidance, strong robustness under system uncertainty and external disturbances; and convergence time does not depend on the initial values. In this study, we examine the fixed-time convergence and FTC for the nonlinear system in the presence of unknown dynamics. Therefore, we are proposing the adaptive fixed-time non-singular terminal SMC (AFxNTSM) for the application of uncertain and disturb robotic manipulators under actuator failures. The following is a summary of the key contributions of this work: (1) A sliding surface derived from the characteristics of non-singular fixed-time terminal SMC is devised. This sliding surface is designed to provide exceptional tracking performance, fixed-time convergence, and reduced chatter in the control torque. (2) Adaptive FTC approach is proposed with FxNTSM; bounded unknown dynamics and actuator failure are estimated to obtain the robust and sustainable performance for the robotic system. (3) The fixed-time stability analysis of the system is studied using the Lyapunov synthesis.

The other sections of this work are structured as follows: Section 2 presents the related works. Section 3 provides the system modelling and problem formulations. In Sections 4 and 5, respectively, the control design and stability analysis based on the Lyapunov theorem are described in detail. Section 6 then provides the numerical simulations to validate and demonstrate the performance of proposed scheme, and Section 7 addressed the discussion on the simulation results. The conclusions of the paper are presented in Section 8.

2. Related Work

In recent years, a significant number of researchers have focused their attention on the issue of the SMC schemes for nonlinear systems, which are distinguished by a fixed-time convergence. In [16], the authors proposed a singularity-free fixed-time SMC scheme for an uncertain robotic system with disturbances. The research that was published in [17] involved the creation of a new fixed-time sliding surface using constant and variable exponent coefficients for the second-order system. For the autonomous underwater vehicle, an event-triggered scheme using an integral fixed-time SMC technique has been presented in [18], and the formation control was constructed with the help of a fixed-time SMC, and disturbance was dealt with the assistance of a disturbance observer in [19]. Moreover, the author in [20] presented fast exponential fixed-time super-twisting SMC for the robotic manipulator and the finite-time high-order sliding mode observer to estimate the angular velocity and lumped disturbances. A fixed-time super-twisting sliding mode method subject to control input limitations was developed for a symmetric chaotic supply chain system [21]. A third-order fixed-time super-twisting-like SMC scheme was designed for the piezoelectric nanopositioning stage [22]. Another fixed-time control strategy based on robust observer was presented for n-DOF robot manipulators with uncertainty [23].

Faulty actuators can be compensated for by employing a variety of different adaptive techniques, which were presented in order to build FTC for a wide range of nonlinear systems. An adaptive non-singular TSM (AFTSMC) has been used in [10] to achieve fast response and lessen chattering and singularity problems, and adaptive control based FTC has been used to estimate uncertainties and actuator faults. Actuator failure compensation for an underactuated nonlinear system utilising an adaptive fuzzy SMC approach to adjust the uncertainties caused by actuator faults has been addressed in [24]. In [25], another adaptive technique has been developed for wind turbine under constant and variable actuator faults. In [26], FNTSM was designed and paired with adaptive control for attitude tracking of spacecraft in the presence of actuator faults, actuator saturations, external disturbances, and inertia uncertainty. Robust fault tolerant tracking control using fixed-time SMC and observer has been presented for an uncertain robotic manipulator [27].

3. Robot Dynamics and Problem Statement

The robotic manipulator's dynamic equation can be described as follows [28]:

$$M_0(q)\ddot{q} + \tilde{M}(q)\ddot{q} + C_0(q,\dot{q})\dot{q} + \tilde{C}(q,\dot{q})\dot{q} + G_0(q) + \tilde{G}(q) = u(t) + T_d + f(t-t_f)\mathcal{F}(q,\dot{q},\tau) \quad (1)$$

$$\implies M_0(q)\ddot{q} + C_0(q,\dot{q})\dot{q} + G_0(q) = u(t) + \Xi(q,\dot{q},\ddot{q},T_d,\mathcal{F}) \quad (2)$$

where $\Xi(q,\dot{q},\ddot{q},T_d,\mathcal{F}) = T_d + f(t-t_f)\mathcal{F}(q,\dot{q},\tau) - \tilde{M}(q)\ddot{q} - \tilde{C}(q,\dot{q})\dot{q} - \tilde{G}(q)$. The (2) can be rewritten as

$$\ddot{q} = M_0^{-1}(q)[u(t) - C_0(q,\dot{q})\dot{q} - G_0(q) + \Xi(q,\dot{q},\ddot{q},T_d,\mathcal{F})] \quad (3)$$

where $q \in \mathbb{R}^n$ is joints position, $\dot{q} \in \mathbb{R}^n$ is joint velocity and $\ddot{q} \in \mathbb{R}^n$ is joint acceleration. $M(q) \in \mathbb{R}^{n \times n}$ represents the inertia matrix and satisfies that $0 < \lambda_1(M(q)) \leq \|M(q)\| \leq \lambda_2(M(q))$ with λ_1 and λ_2 illustrate the min and the max eigenvalues of matrix $M(q)$. $C(q,\dot{q}) \in \mathbb{R}^{n \times n}$ denotes the coriolis, centripetal, and friction forces matrix; $G(q) \in \mathbb{R}^n$ is the gravitational vector. $M_0(q), C_0(q,\dot{q}), G_0(q)$ are nominal and $\tilde{M}(q), \tilde{C}(q,\dot{q}), \tilde{G}(q)$ are uncertain parameters. $T_d \in \mathbb{R}^n$ is a representation of the external disturbance, $u(t) \in \mathbb{R}^n$ is the input torque at the joints, the fault vector for a constant and/or time-varying actuator is defined by $\mathcal{F}(q,\dot{q},\tau) \in \mathbb{R}^n$, and the fault time profile is indicated by $f(t-Tf)$, where tf is the time at which the fault first occurs. The following notations throughout the paper will be used.

In addition, the following is the time profile of the faults that were discussed earlier, $f(\cdot)$, is defined:

$$f(t-t_f) = diag\{f_1(t-t_f), f_2(t-t_f), \cdots, f_n(t-t_f)\} \quad (4)$$

The time profile fault model is as follows, where f_i is the i_{th} state equation affected by the fault:

$$f_i(t-t_f) = \begin{cases} 0 & if\ t < t_f \\ 1 - e^{-\varsigma_i(t-t_f)} & if\ t \geq t_f \end{cases} \quad (5)$$

where $\varsigma_i > 0$ is the time constant that characterizes the unknown actuator fault's development. When ς_i is minor, the fault is referred to as an incipient fault. When $\varsigma_i \to \infty$, the f_i function begins to grow as a step, and the fault that was in the process of developing becomes an abrupt fault.

Using (3), we can express the trajectory tracking error as

$$\ddot{e} = M_0^{-1}(q)[u(t) - C_0(q,\dot{q})\dot{q} - G_0(q) + \Xi(q,\dot{q},\ddot{q},T_d,\mathcal{F})] - \ddot{q}_d \tag{6}$$

$$\Rightarrow \ddot{e} = M_0^{-1}(q)u(t) + \Omega(q,\dot{q}) + \tilde{\Xi}(q,\dot{q},\ddot{q},T_d,\mathcal{F}) \tag{7}$$

where $\Omega(q,\dot{q}) = -M_0^{-1}(q)[C_0(q,\dot{q})\dot{q} + G_0(q)] - \ddot{q}_d$ denotes the known nominal system dynamics and $\tilde{\Xi}(q,\dot{q},\ddot{q},T_d,\mathcal{F}) = M_0^{-1}(q)\Xi(q,\dot{q},\ddot{q},T_d,\mathcal{F})$. The tracking error $e = q - q_d$, where q is the actual and q_d is the desired position vector.

4. Control Design

This section begins with a discussion of the features of nonsingular fixed-time sliding surface and control design named FxNTSM. Moreover, the important Lemma and Assumption are given in this section.

4.1. Fixed-Time Non-Singular Terminal Sliding Manifold

In literature, sliding surfaces have been constructed to obtain the benefits of TSM while avoiding the singularity problem. Motivated by the aforementioned methodologies discussed in Section 1, the proposed FxNTSM surface can be designed as providing robust and precise trajectory tracking of the n-DOF robotic manipulators in fixed-time:

$$s(t) = \dot{e}(t) + \theta_1 sig^{\eta_1}(e(t)) + \theta_2 sig^{\eta_2}(e(t)) \tag{8}$$

where $s(t) \in \mathbb{R}^n$ is the sliding surface, $sig^y(\cdot) = |\cdot|^y sign(\cdot)$, $\theta_1 \in \mathbb{R}^+$ and $\theta_2 \in \mathbb{R}^+$ are positive constants, and the η_1 and η_2 are constants satisfying the relation $0 < \eta_1 < 1$ and $1 < \eta_2$.

The development of the sliding manifold is completed; now, the robustness against uncertainty and actuator faults will be achieved through the FxNTSM design for n-DOF robotic manipulators.

Assumption 1. *Conditional bounds on the uncertainty, external disturbance and fault vector are expressed by (9) that are shown below:*

$$\|\tilde{\Xi}(q,\dot{q},\ddot{q},T_d,\mathcal{F})\| \leq \Xi_1 + \Xi_2\|q\| + \Xi_3\|\dot{q}\|^2 \tag{9}$$

where Ξ_1, Ξ_2 and Ξ_3 are unknown constants of uncertainties, disturbances and actuator faults' upper bounds.

Lemma 1 ([29,30]). *Consider the following nonlinear system:*

$$\dot{x}(t) = f(t,x), \quad x(0) = x_0 \tag{10}$$

where $f(t,x)$ is a continuous nonlinear function. For fixed-time stability with fast time convergence, Lyapunov function $V(x)$ that satisfies
a. $V(x) = 0 \Leftrightarrow x = 0$
b. $\dot{V}(x) \leq -\beta_1 V^{\alpha_1}(x) - \beta_2 V(x)^{\alpha_2}$
where $\beta_1, \beta_2 > 0, 0 < \alpha_1 < 1$ and $\alpha_2 > 1$. Then, the system is fixed-time stable and the convergence time can be computed as

$$T \leq \frac{1}{\beta_1(1-\alpha_1)} + \frac{1}{\beta_2(\alpha_2-1)} \tag{11}$$

During the sliding motion, we have $s(t) = 0$. Thus, the following dynamics can be obtained according to (8) as

$$\dot{e}(t) = -\theta_1 sig^{\eta_1}(e(t)) - \theta_2 sig^{\eta_2}(e(t)) \tag{12}$$

The Lyapunov function is considered as follows:

$$V_e(t) = \frac{1}{2}e(t)^T e(t) \tag{13}$$

The derivative of $V_e(t)$ can be obtained with (12) as

$$\dot{V}_e(t) = e(t)^T \dot{e}(t) = e(t)^T[-\theta_1 sig^{\eta_1}(e(t)) - \theta_2 sig^{\eta_2}(e(t))] \tag{14}$$

$$\begin{aligned}\dot{V}_e(t) &\leq -\theta_1\|e(t)\|^{\eta_1+1} - \theta_2\|e(t)\|^{\eta_2+1}\\ &\leq -2^{\frac{\eta_1+1}{2}}\theta_1 V_e^{\frac{\eta_1+1}{2}} - 2^{\frac{\eta_2+1}{2}}\theta_2 V_e^{\frac{\eta_2+1}{2}}\end{aligned} \tag{15}$$

According to Lemma 1, the sliding surface (8) will reach zero in a fixed-time, and the time it takes to converge is bounded by

$$\begin{aligned}T_1 &= \frac{1}{2^{\frac{\eta_1+1}{2}}\theta_1\left(1-\frac{\eta_1+1}{2}\right)} + \frac{1}{2^{\frac{\eta_2+1}{2}}\theta_2\left(\frac{\eta_2+1}{2}-1\right)}\\ &= \frac{\sqrt{2}}{2^{\eta_1/2}\theta_1(1-\eta_1)} + \frac{\sqrt{2}}{2^{\eta_2/2}\theta_2(\eta_2-1)}\end{aligned} \tag{16}$$

4.2. FxNTSM Control Design

To control a robotic manipulator in the presence of known bounded uncertainties, external disturbances, and actuator failures, the FxNTSM control law can be defined as follows:

$$u(t) = u_1(t) + u_2(t) \tag{17}$$

where $u_1(t)$ is the control input that is utilized in the control of the nominal dynamics, and $u_2(t)$ is used to mitigate the uncertainties and actuator fault:

$$u_1(t) = -M_0(q)\left(\Omega(q,\dot{q}) + \theta_1\Pi(q)\dot{e}(t) + \theta_2\eta_2|e(t)|^{\eta_2-1}\dot{e}(t)\right) \tag{18}$$

where $\Pi(e(t)) = \begin{cases} \eta_1|e(t)|^{\eta_1-1} & \text{if } e(t) \neq 0 \\ 0 & \text{if } e(t) = 0 \end{cases}$ satisfies the non-singularity in the control input:

$$u_2(t) = -M_0(q)\left((\Xi_1 + \Xi_2\|q\| + \Xi_3\|\dot{q}\|^2)sign(s) + \gamma_1 sig^{\gamma_{10}}(s(t)) + \gamma_2 sig^{\gamma_{20}}(s(t))\right) \tag{19}$$

where $\gamma_1 \in \mathbb{R}^+$ and $\gamma_2 \in \mathbb{R}^+$ are positive constants, and γ_{10} and γ_{20} are constants satisfying the relation $0 < \gamma_{10} < 1$ and $1 < \gamma_{20}$, respectively.

5. Stability Analysis

In this section, the stability of the overall system using FxNTSM scheme is established through the application of the Lyapunov theorem. Afterward, the fault tolerant control structure with adaptive laws is subsequently designed to provide AFxNTSM for uncertain robotic manipulators under varying actuator faults at joint(s). Then, stability analysis using AFxNTSM method is investigated by the Lyapunov theorem.

Theorem 1. *Taking into account the defined robotic manipulator (3), the proposed sliding manifold (8) and the proposed FxNTSM controller (17) allow for the desired augular position of the uncertain robotic manipulator to converge in a fixed-time along with (9).*

Proof. The following is the Lyapunov function selected as

$$V_s(t) = \frac{1}{2}s(t)^T s(t) \tag{20}$$

The calculation for the derivative of $V_s(t)$ can be written as

$$\dot{V}_s(t) = s(t)^T \dot{s}(t) \tag{21}$$

The derivative of (8) when substituted into Equation (21) yields

$$\dot{V}_s(t) = s(t)^T \left[\ddot{e}(t) + \theta_1 \Pi(q) \dot{e}(t) + \theta_2 \eta_2 |e(t)|^{\eta_2-1} \dot{e}(t) \right] \tag{22}$$

By substituting error Equation (7) in (22), one has

$$\dot{V}(t) = s(t)^T \left\{ \begin{array}{l} M_0^{-1}(q)u + \Omega(q,\dot{q}) + \tilde{\Xi}(q,\dot{q},\ddot{q},T_d,\mathcal{F}) \\ + \theta_1 \Pi(q) \dot{e}(t) + \theta_2 \eta_2 |e(t)|^{\eta_2-1} \dot{e}(t) \end{array} \right\} \tag{23}$$

By substituting control input (17) in (23), one obtains

$$\dot{V}_s(t) = s(t)^T \left\{ \begin{array}{l} (-\Xi_1 - \Xi_2 \|q\| - \Xi_3 \|\dot{q}\|^2) sign(s(t)) - \Omega(q,\dot{q}) \\ -\gamma_1 sig^{\gamma_{10}}(s(t)) - \gamma_2 sig^{\gamma_{20}}(s(t)) \\ -\theta_1 \Pi(q) \dot{e}(t) - \theta_2 \eta_2 |e(t)|^{\eta_2-1} \dot{e}(t) + \Omega(q,\dot{q}) \\ +\tilde{\Xi}(q,\dot{q},\ddot{q},T_d,\mathcal{F}) + \theta_1 \Pi(q)\dot{e}(t) + \theta_2 \eta_2 |e(t)|^{\eta_2-1} \dot{e}(t) \end{array} \right\} \tag{24}$$

$$\dot{V}_s(t) = s(t)^T \left\{ \begin{array}{l} (-\Xi_1 - \Xi_2 \|q\| - \Xi_3 \|\dot{q}\|^2) sign(s(t)) + \tilde{\Xi}(q,\dot{q},\ddot{q},T_d,\mathcal{F}) \\ -\gamma_1 sig^{\gamma_{10}}(s(t)) - \gamma_2 sig^{\gamma_{20}}(s(t)) \end{array} \right\}$$

$$\leq (-\Xi_1 - \Xi_2 \|q\| - \Xi_3 \|\dot{q}\|^2) \|s(t)\| + \|\tilde{\Xi}(q,\dot{q},\ddot{q},T_d,\mathcal{F})\| \|s(t)\| \tag{25}$$

$$-\gamma_1 \|s(t)\|^{\gamma_{10}+1} - \gamma_2 \|s(t)\|^{\gamma_{20}+1}$$

According to Assumption 1, one can obtain

$$\dot{V}_s(t) \leq -\gamma_1 \|s(t)\|^{\gamma_{10}+1} - \gamma_2 \|s(t)\|^{\gamma_{20}+1} \tag{26}$$

$$\dot{V}_s(t) \leq -2^{\frac{\gamma_{10}+1}{2}} \gamma_1 \{V_s(t)\}^{\frac{\gamma_{10}+1}{2}} - 2^{\frac{\gamma_{20}+1}{2}} \gamma_2 \{V_s(t)\}^{\frac{\gamma_{20}+1}{2}} \tag{27}$$

Thus, the system trajectory approaches to $s(t)$ in a fixed-time. According to Lemma 1, the convergence time can be formulated as

$$T_2 = \frac{1}{2^{\frac{\gamma_{10}+1}{2}} \gamma_1 \left(1 - \frac{\gamma_{10}+1}{2}\right)} + \frac{1}{2^{\frac{\gamma_{20}+1}{2}} \gamma_2 \left(\frac{\gamma_{20}+1}{2} - 1\right)} \tag{28}$$

By the combination of T_1 and T_2, the total fixed settling time can be calculated as

$$T_{10} = T_1 + T_2 = \frac{\sqrt{2}}{2^{\gamma_{10}/2} \gamma_1 (1-\gamma_{10})} + \frac{\sqrt{2}}{2^{\gamma_{20}/2} \gamma_2 (\gamma_{20}-1)} + \frac{\sqrt{2}}{2^{\eta_1/2} \theta_1 (1-\eta_1)} + \frac{\sqrt{2}}{2^{\eta_2/2} \theta_2 (\eta_2-1)} \tag{29}$$

Hence, this shows that the proposed scheme is fixed-time SMC. □

AFxNTSM Based FTC Control Design

For the unknown dynamics and actuator faults, the control input using adaptive scheme is designed as follows:

$$u(t) = u_3(t) \tag{30}$$

where

$$u_3(t) = -M_0(q) \left(\begin{array}{l} (\hat{\Xi}_1 + \hat{\Xi}_2 \|q\| + \hat{\Xi}_3 \|\dot{q}\|^2) sign(s(t)) + \Omega(q,\dot{q}) \\ +\gamma_1 sig^{\gamma_{10}}(s(t)) + \gamma_2 sig^{\gamma_{20}}(s(t)) \\ +\theta_1 \Pi(q) \dot{e}(t) + \theta_2 \eta_2 |e(t)|^{\eta_2-1} \dot{e}(t) \end{array} \right) \tag{31}$$

where $\hat{\Xi}_1$, $\hat{\Xi}_2$ and $\hat{\Xi}_3$ represent the estimates of Ξ_1, Ξ_2 and Ξ_3, respectively.

For the compensation of uncertainties, external disturbances and actuator faults, adaptive laws are designed as follows:

$$\begin{cases} \dot{\hat{\Xi}}_1 = \frac{1}{\lambda_1}\|s\| \\ \dot{\hat{\Xi}}_2 = \frac{1}{\lambda_2}\|q\|\|s\| \\ \dot{\hat{\Xi}}_3 = \frac{1}{\lambda_3}\|\dot{q}\|^2\|s\| \end{cases} \quad (32)$$

where λ_1, λ_2 and λ_3 are positive constants, and the proposed model is given in Figure 1.

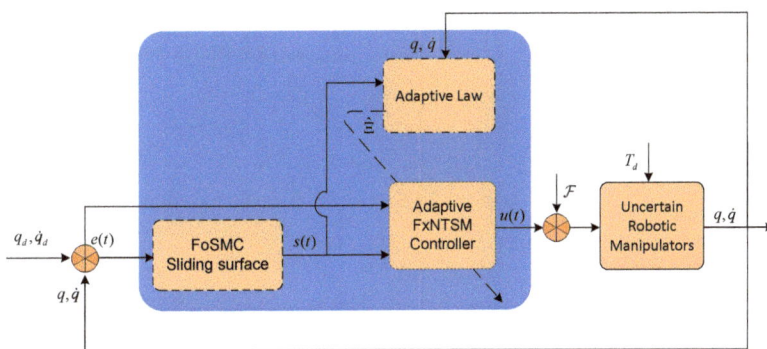

Figure 1. Structure of the proposed scheme.

The upper bounds of the uncertainties, external disturbances and actuator faults can be compensated using (32). Hence, the AFxNTSM scheme formulates the tracking performance of the uncertain robotic manipulators under actuator faults.

Theorem 2. *Taking into account the defined robotic manipulator (3), which is subject to a number of problems such as uncertainties, external disturbances and joint actuator failures. Therefore, the proposed sliding surface (8), AFxNTSM control input (30) and adaptive laws (32) make it possible for the desired angular position of the robotic manipulator to converge in a fixed-time with the condition of Assumption 1.*

Proof. The Lyapunov functional candidate is chosen as follows:

$$V_a(t) = \frac{1}{2}s(t)^T s(t) + \frac{1}{2}\lambda_1 \Delta \Xi_1^2 + \frac{1}{2}\lambda_2 \Delta \Xi_2^2 + \frac{1}{2}\lambda_3 \Delta \Xi_3^2 \quad (33)$$

where $\Delta \Xi_1 = \hat{\Xi}_1 - \Xi_1$, $\Delta \Xi_2 = \hat{\Xi}_2 - \Xi_2$, $\Delta \Xi_3 = \hat{\Xi}_3 - \Xi_3$ are adaptation errors.

The derivative of $V_a(t)$ can be obtained as

$$\dot{V}_a(t) = s(t)^T \dot{s}(t) + \lambda_1 \Delta \Xi_1 \dot{\hat{\Xi}}_1 + \lambda_2 \Delta \Xi_2 \dot{\hat{\Xi}}_2 + \lambda_2 \Delta \Xi_3 \dot{\hat{\Xi}}_3 \quad (34)$$

The substitution of derivative of (8) into (34), one obtains

$$\dot{V}_a(t) = s(t)^T \left\{ \begin{array}{l} M_0^{-1}(q)u(t) + \Omega(q,\dot{q}) + \tilde{\Xi}(q,\dot{q},\ddot{q},T_d,\mathcal{F}) \\ +\theta_1 \Pi(q)\dot{e}(t) + \theta_2 \eta_2 |e(t)|^{\eta_2 - 1}\dot{e}(t) \end{array} \right\} \quad (35)$$
$$+\lambda_1 \Delta \Xi_1 \dot{\hat{\Xi}}_1 + \lambda_2 \Delta \Xi_2 \dot{\hat{\Xi}}_2 + \lambda_3 \Delta \Xi_3 \dot{\hat{\Xi}}_3$$

The substitution of control input (30) into (35), one obtains

$$\dot{V}_a(t) = s(t)^T \begin{Bmatrix} (-\hat{\Xi}_1 - \hat{\Xi}_2\|q\| - \hat{\Xi}_3\|\dot{q}\|^2)sign(s(t)) - \Omega(q,\dot{q}) \\ -\gamma_1 sig^{\gamma_{10}}(s(t)) - \gamma_2 sig^{\gamma_{20}}(s(t)) \\ -\theta_1\Pi(q)\dot{e}(t) - \theta_2\eta_2|e(t)|^{\eta_2-1}\dot{e}(t) + \Omega(q,\dot{q}) \\ +\tilde{\Xi}(q,\dot{q},\ddot{q},T_d,\mathcal{F}) + \theta_1\Pi(q)\dot{e}(t) + \theta_2\eta_2|e(t)|^{\eta_2-1}\dot{e}(t) \end{Bmatrix} \\ + \lambda_1 \Delta\Xi_1 \hat{\Xi}_1 + \lambda_2 \Delta\Xi_2 \hat{\Xi}_2 + \lambda_3 \Delta\Xi_3 \hat{\Xi}_3 \quad (36)$$

$$\dot{V}_a(t) = s(t)^T \begin{Bmatrix} (-\hat{\Xi}_1 - \hat{\Xi}_2\|q\| - \hat{\Xi}_3\|\dot{q}\|^2)sign(s(t)) \\ -\gamma_1 sig^{\gamma_{10}}(s(t)) - \gamma_2 sig^{\gamma_{20}}(s(t)) + \tilde{\Xi}(q,\dot{q},\ddot{q},T_d,\mathcal{F}) \end{Bmatrix} \\ + \lambda_1 \Delta\Xi_1 \hat{\Xi}_1 + \lambda_2 \Delta\Xi_2 \hat{\Xi}_2 + \lambda_3 \Delta\Xi_3 \hat{\Xi}_3 \quad (37)$$

$$\dot{V}_a(t) \leq -\gamma_1\|s(t)\|^{\gamma_{10}+1} - \gamma_2\|s(t)\|^{\gamma_{20}+1} \\ -\hat{\Xi}_1\|(s(t))\| - \hat{\Xi}_2\|q\|\|(s(t))\| - \hat{\Xi}_3\|\dot{q}\|^2\|(s(t))\| \\ +\|\tilde{\Xi}(q,\dot{q},\ddot{q},T_d,\mathcal{F})\|\|s(t)\| + \lambda_1\Delta\Xi_1\hat{\Xi}_1 + \lambda_2\Delta\Xi_2\hat{\Xi}_2 + \lambda_3\Delta\Xi_3\hat{\Xi}_3 \quad (38)$$

Using (32), (38) can be simplified as follows:

$$\dot{V}_a(t) \leq -\gamma_1\|s(t)\|^{\gamma_{10}+1} - \gamma_2\|s(t)\|^{\gamma_{20}+1} \quad (39)$$

Hence, the robotic manipulator that is used for the precise trajectory tracking is fixed-time stable if and only if certain conditions are met. As a result, the proof of stability is thoroughly examined. □

Now, we will determine the fixed settling time, and the preceding equation can be represented as [26]

$$\dot{V}_a(t) \leq -\gamma_1\{2(V_a(t) - \Phi)\}^{\frac{\gamma_{10}+1}{2}} - \gamma_2\{2(V_a(t) - \Phi)\}^{\frac{\gamma_{20}+1}{2}} \quad (40)$$

where $\Phi = \frac{1}{2}\lambda_1\Delta\Xi_1^2 + \frac{1}{2}\lambda_2\Delta\Xi_2^2 + \frac{1}{2}\lambda_3\Delta\Xi_3^2$.

$$\dot{V}_a(t) \leq -2^{\frac{\gamma_{10}+1}{2}}\gamma_1\left\{1-\frac{\Phi}{V_a(t)}\right\}^{\frac{\gamma_{10}+1}{2}}V_a(t)^{\frac{\gamma_{10}+1}{2}} - 2^{\frac{\gamma_{20}+1}{2}}\gamma_2\left\{1-\frac{\Phi}{V_a(t)}\right\}^{\frac{\gamma_{20}+1}{2}}V_a(t)^{\frac{\gamma_{20}+1}{2}} \quad (41)$$

Using Lemma 1, the fixed-time can be computed as

$$T_3 = \frac{1}{\sigma_1\left(1-\frac{\gamma_{10}+1}{2}\right)} + \frac{1}{\sigma_2\left(\frac{\gamma_{20}+1}{2}-1\right)} = \frac{2}{\sigma_1(1-\gamma_{10})} + \frac{2}{\sigma_2(\gamma_{20}-1)} \quad (42)$$

where $\sigma_1 = 2^{\frac{\gamma_{10}+1}{2}}\gamma_1\left\{1-\frac{\Phi}{V_a(t)}\right\}^{\frac{\gamma_{10}+1}{2}}$, $\sigma_2 = 2^{\frac{\gamma_{20}+1}{2}}\gamma_2\left\{1-\frac{\Phi}{V_a(t)}\right\}^{\frac{\gamma_{20}+1}{2}}$.

By the combination of of T_1 and T_3, the fixed time convergence can be computed as

$$T_{20} = \frac{2}{\sigma_1(1-\gamma_{10})} + \frac{2}{\sigma_2(\gamma_{20}-1)} + \frac{\sqrt{2}}{2^{\eta_1/2}\theta_1(1-\eta_1)} + \frac{\sqrt{2}}{2^{\eta_2/2}\theta_2(\eta_2-1)} \quad (43)$$

As a result, the state trajectory will approach to zero in fixed-time.

Remark 1. *Applying the proposed method to the uncertain dynamics of robotic system (1), which includes the sliding surface (8), the proposed control input (30) and the adaptive laws (32), implies the tracking error tends to zero. In the following part, the numerical simulation will be provided.*

6. Simulation Results and Comparative Analyses

In order to validate the proposed FxNTSM and AFxNTSM methods, a 2DOF manipulator is used to show the simulation performance. A 2DOF robotic manipulator under actuator faults with external disturbances and uncertainty will be used. Therefore, there are two cases that are presented with and without actuator faults to demonstrate the high performance of FxNTSM and AFxNTSM, and simulations using MATLAB/Simulink are illustrated. Their model parameters, intended trajectories and uncertainties are given, and the dynamic of 2DOF robotic manipulators is described as:

$$M(q) = \begin{bmatrix} M_{11} & M_{12} \\ M_{21} & M_{22} \end{bmatrix}, C(q,\dot{q}) = \begin{bmatrix} C_1 \\ C_2 \end{bmatrix}, G(q) = \begin{bmatrix} G_1 \\ G_2 \end{bmatrix},$$

$$u(t) = \begin{bmatrix} u_1 \\ u_2 \end{bmatrix}, q_d = \begin{bmatrix} 1.45 - 1.4e^{-t} + 0.6e^{-4t} \\ 1.25 + e^{-t} - 0.5e^{-4t} \end{bmatrix}, T_d = \begin{bmatrix} 1 - e^{-t} \\ 1 - e^{-t} \end{bmatrix}.$$

where $M_{11} = m_1 r_1^2 + m_1(r_1^2 + l_1^2) + 2\cos(q_2)m_2 l_1 r_2 + J_2 + J_1$, $M_{12} = m_2 r_2^2 + \cos(q_2)m_2 r_2 l_1 + J_2$, $M_{21} = M_{12}$, $M_{22} = m_2 r_2^2 + J_2$, $C_1 = -\sin(q_2)m_2 r_2 l_1 \dot{q}_1 \dot{q}_2 - \sin(q_2)m_2 r_2 l_1 (\dot{q}_1 + \dot{q}_2)\dot{q}_2$, $C_2 = \sin(q_2)m_2 r_2 l_1 \dot{q}_1 \dot{q}_1$, $G_1 = \cos(q_1)(m_1 r_1 + m_2 l_1)g + \cos(q_1 + q_2)m_2 r_2 g$, $G_2 = \cos(q_1 + q_2)m_2 r_2 g$.

The length of the links $l_1 = 1$ m, $l_2 = 1$ m, centroid length of joints $r_1 = 0.5$ m, $r_2 = 0.85$ m, mass of the links $\bar{m}_1 = 0.5$ kg, $\bar{m}_2 = 1.5$ kg, nominal mass of links $m_{10} = 0.4$ kg, $m_{20} = 1.2$ kg, moment of inertia $J_1 = J_2 = 5$ kg·m^2 and gravitational constant $g = 9.8$ m/s^2. In addition, the physical model of 2-DOF robotic manipulator is given in Figure 2.

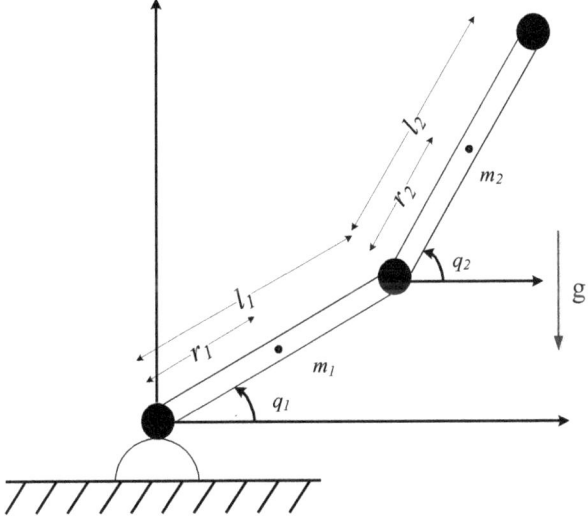

Figure 2. 2-DOF robotic manipulator.

6.1. Case-1: Proposed Scheme without Actuator Faults

In this subsection, the proposed FxNTSM method is applied on the 2-DOF robotic manipulator with known uncertainties and external disturbances and the joint actuator faults are not considered. The parameters of FxNTSM are selected as follows: for (8), parameters are chosen as $\theta_1 = 6$, $\theta_2 = 1$, $\eta_1 = 0.8$, $\eta_2 = 1.5$. The parameters of (17) are selected as $\gamma_1 = 50$, $\gamma_2 = 50$, $\gamma_{10} = 0.65$, $\gamma_{20} = 1.5$. The initial conditions of joint positions are chosen as $q_1(0) = 1$ and $q_2(0) = 1.5$.

Figures 3–10 exhibit, accordingly, the position tracking performance, tracking errors, control inputs, and sliding mode surfaces, which correspond to the simulation findings of the proposed method on 2-DOF robotic manipulators.

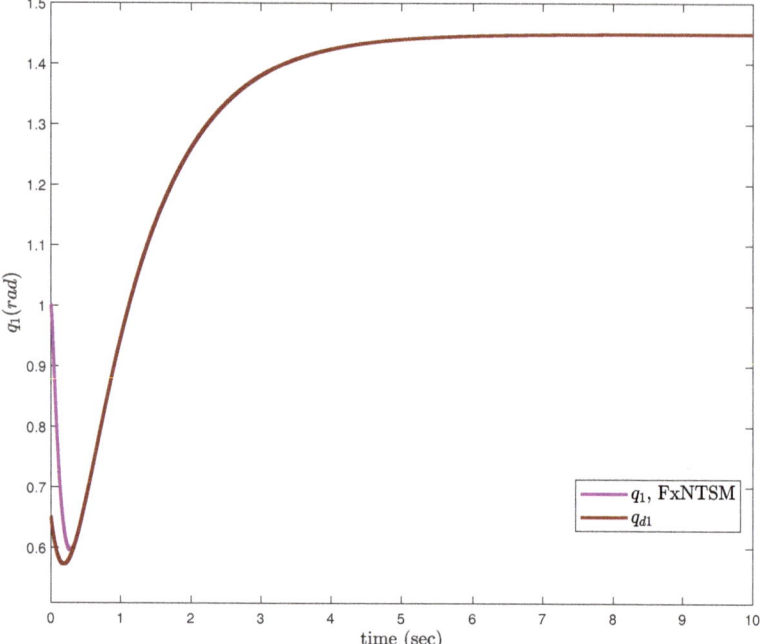

Figure 3. Position tracking—Joint 1.

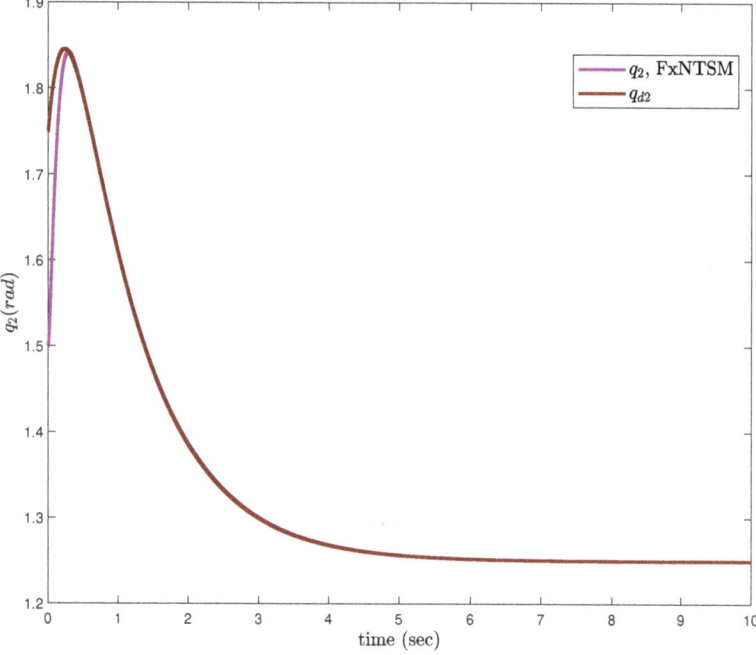

Figure 4. Position tracking—Joint 2.

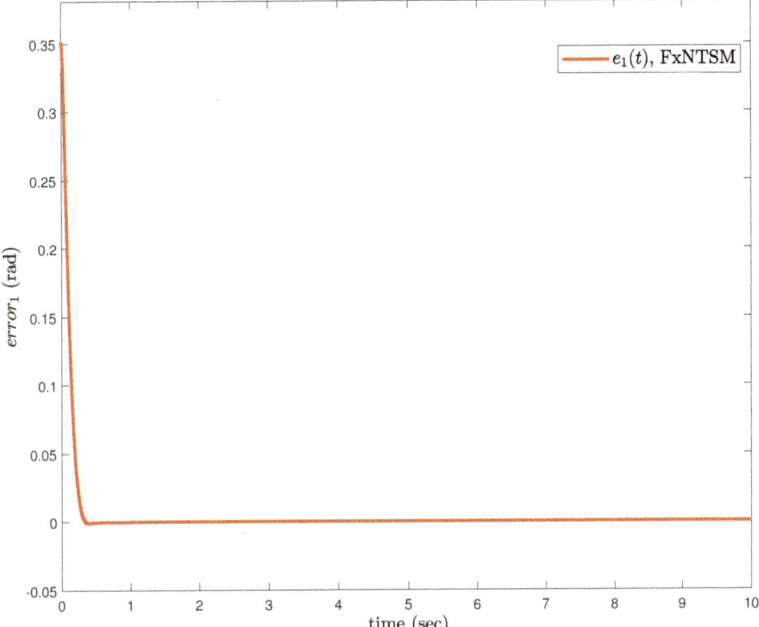

Figure 5. Tracking error—Joint 1.

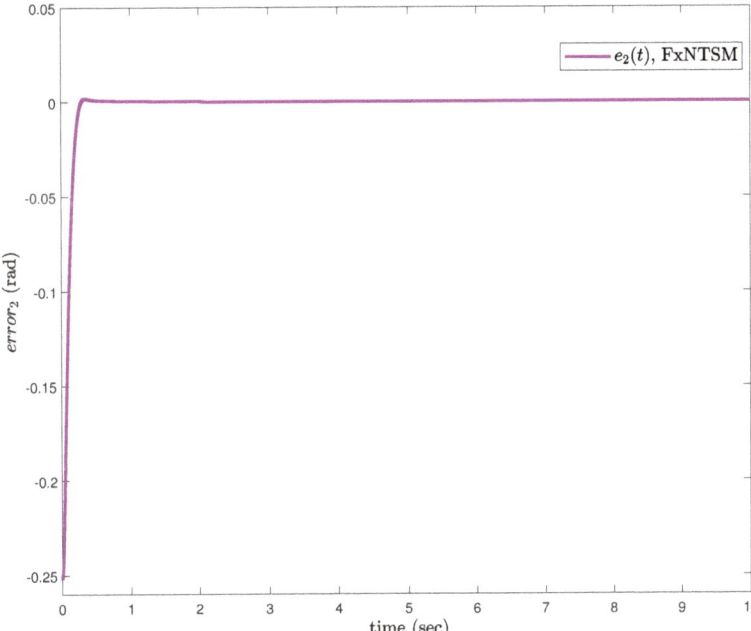

Figure 6. Tracking error—Joint 2.

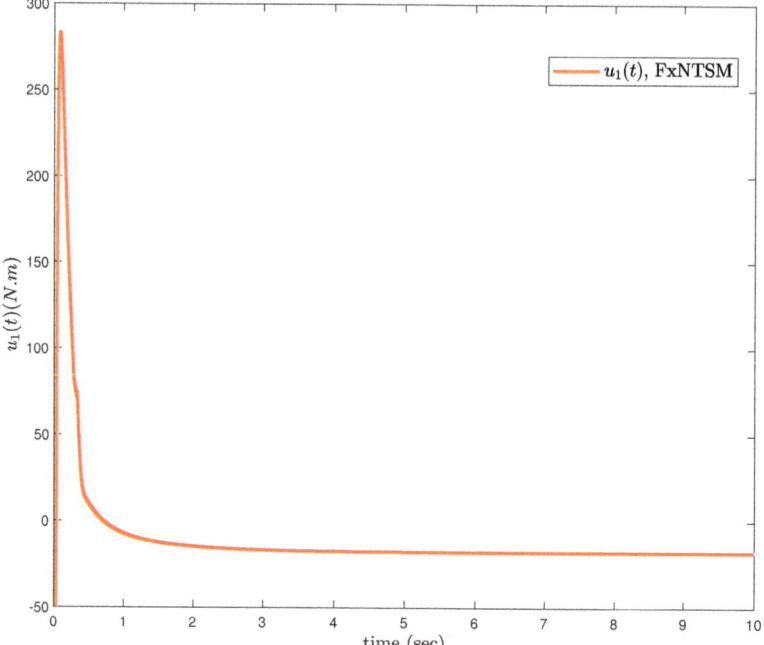

Figure 7. Control input—Joint 1.

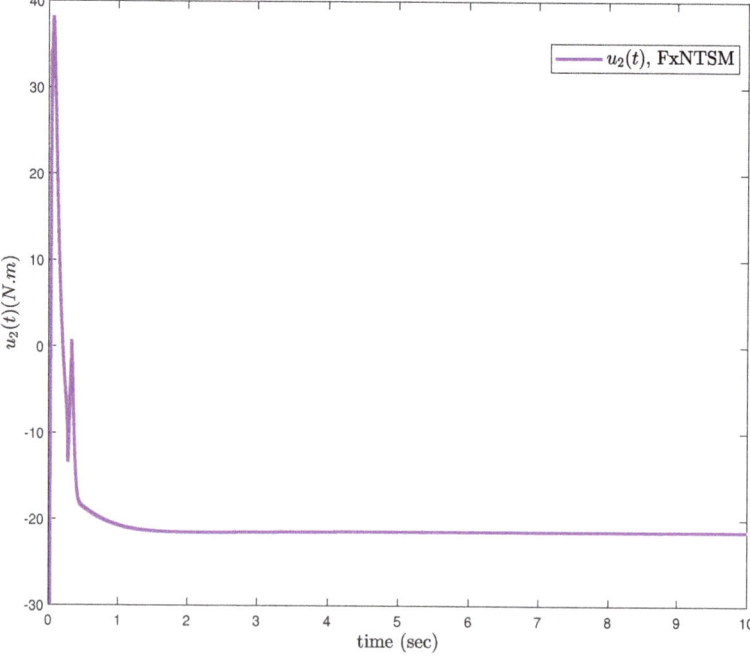

Figure 8. Control input—Joint 2.

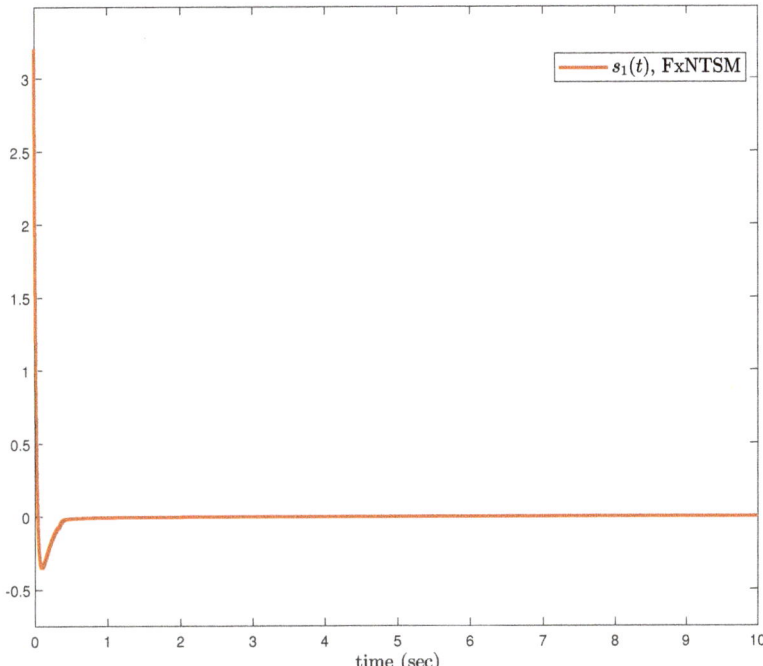

Figure 9. Sliding surface—Joint 1.

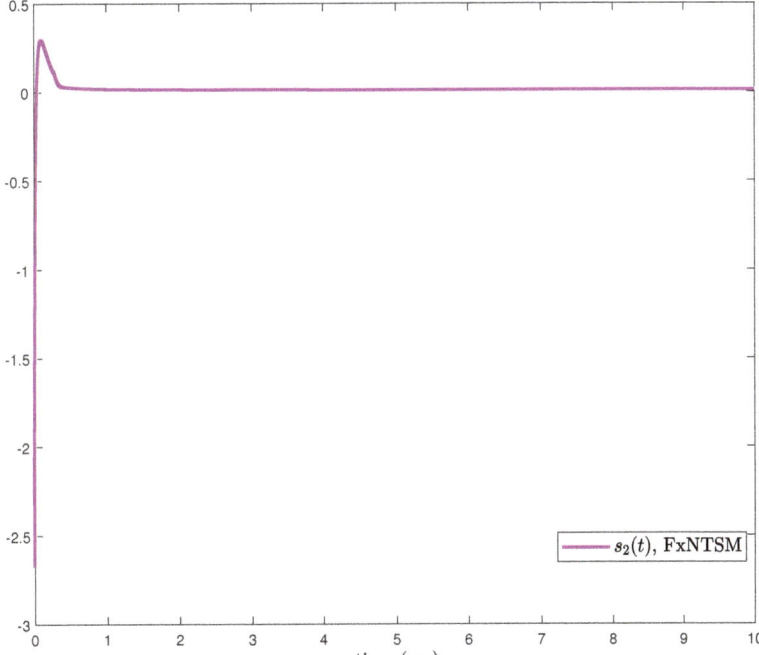

Figure 10. Sliding surface—Joint 2.

Taking into consideration the high tracking and robustness against the known bounded system's uncertainties, the proposed FxNTSM has superior performance and obtains angular position fast tracking performance in Figures 3 and 4, smaller tracking errors in Figures 5 and 6, and chatter-free control inputs in Figures 7 and 8.

6.2. Case-2: Comparative Analysis under Unknown Dynamics and Actuator Faults

In this subsection, the proposed adaptive approach with FxNTSM method is employed to compensate the unknown dynamics of the uncertain 2-DOF robotic manipulator in the existence of unknown bounded external disturbances and actuator faults. Moreover, it is compared with adaptive fractional-order non-singular terminal sliding mode control (AFONTSM) [10] to show the effectiveness of the proposed method. The fault occurs at 2 s for joint-2 such as $\mathcal{F} = [0,\ 0.7u_2(2s)]^T$, the parameters of (30) are selected the same as (17), and the parameters of (32) are selected as $\lambda_1 = 20$, $\lambda_2 = 20$ and $\lambda_3 = 20$. The performances under unknown dynamics and actuator faults, the compared benchmark simulations of trajectories, control inputs and sliding surfaces of the proposed AFxNTSM scheme with AFONTSM are given in Figures 11–16. In addition, the adaptive parameter estimations of unknown dynamics are illustrated in Figure 17.

The compared obtained results show that the AFxNTSM has enhanced tracking performance, chatter-free control inputs and precise adaptive values in the presence of uncertainties, external disturbances and actuator failures. In Figures 11–14, it is clearly seen that the proposed method under external disturbances and at the occurrence of actuator faults provides the better convergence and trajectory tracking performance while the AFONTSM method shows the large angular position error and the less robust to unknown dynamics. Moreover, the root mean square (RMS) error of the proposed AFxNTSM method and AFONTSM technique are computed as $e_{1RMS} = 0.0294$, $e_{2RMS} = 0.0208$ and $e_{1RMS} = 0.0320$, $e_{2RMS} = 0.0237$, respectively.

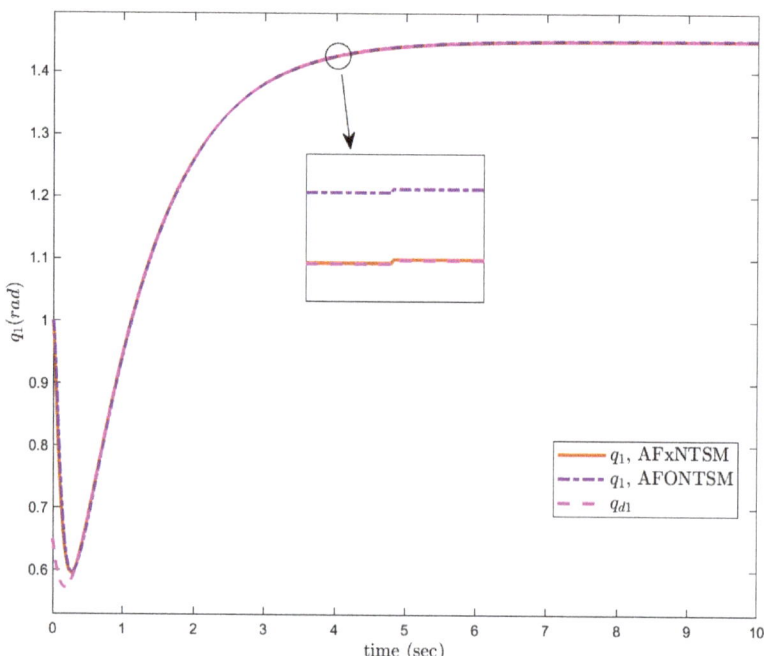

Figure 11. Position tracking method under fault and disturbances—Joint 1.

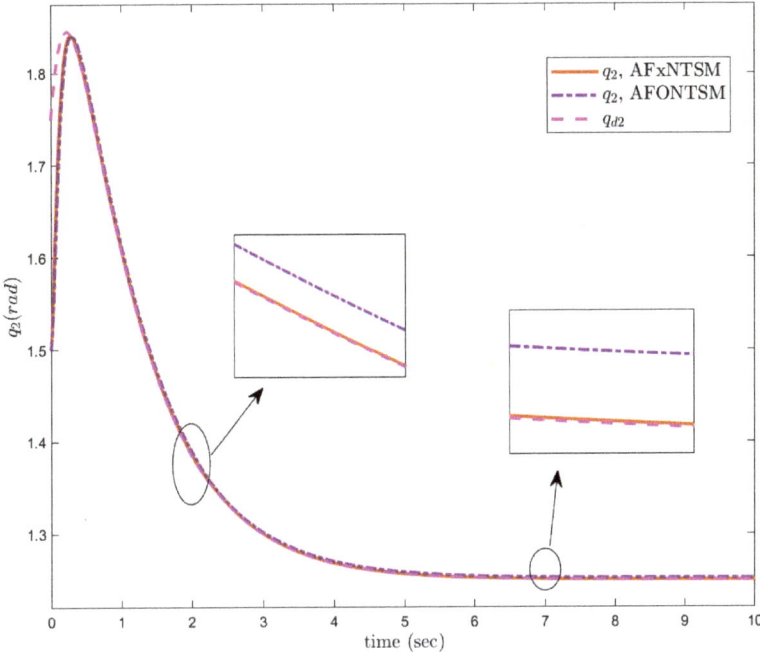

Figure 12. Position tracking method under fault and disturbances—Joint 2.

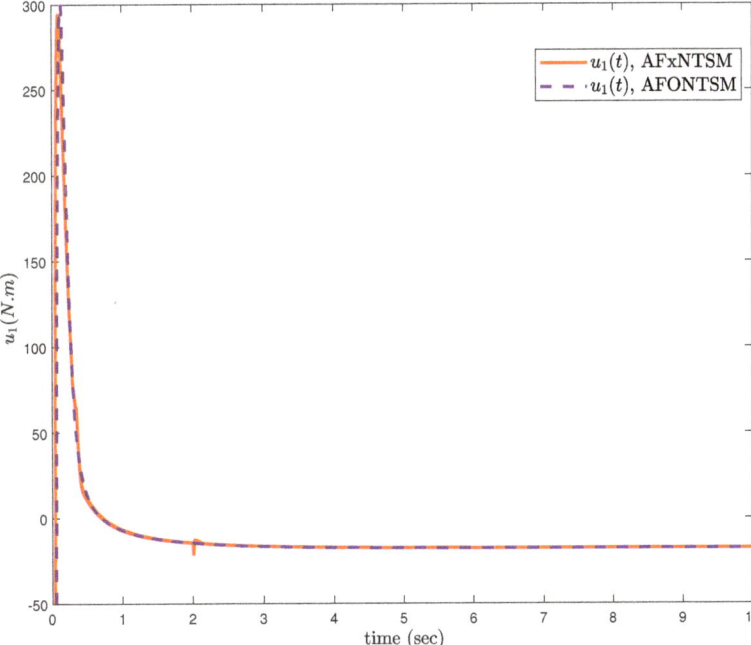

Figure 13. Control input under fault and disturbances—Joint 1.

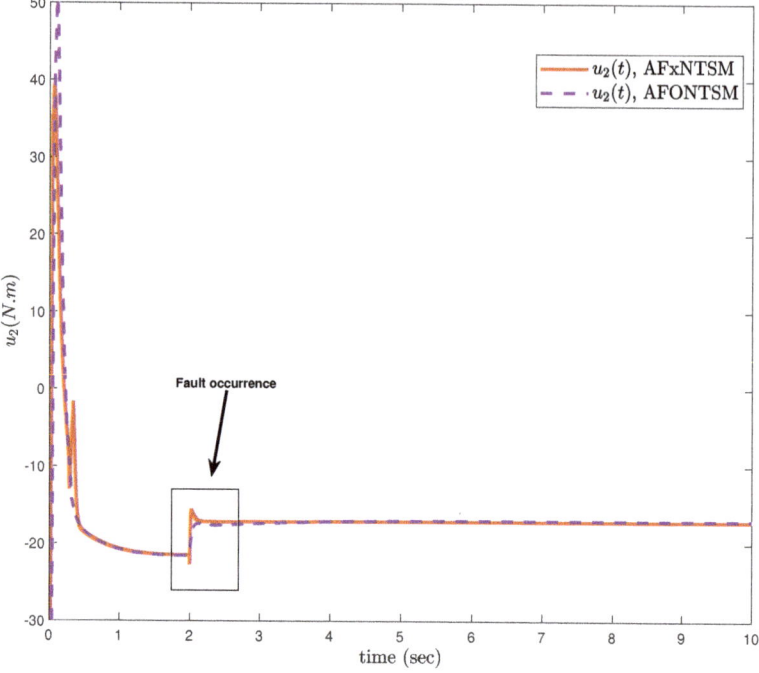

Figure 14. Control input under fault and disturbances—Joint 2.

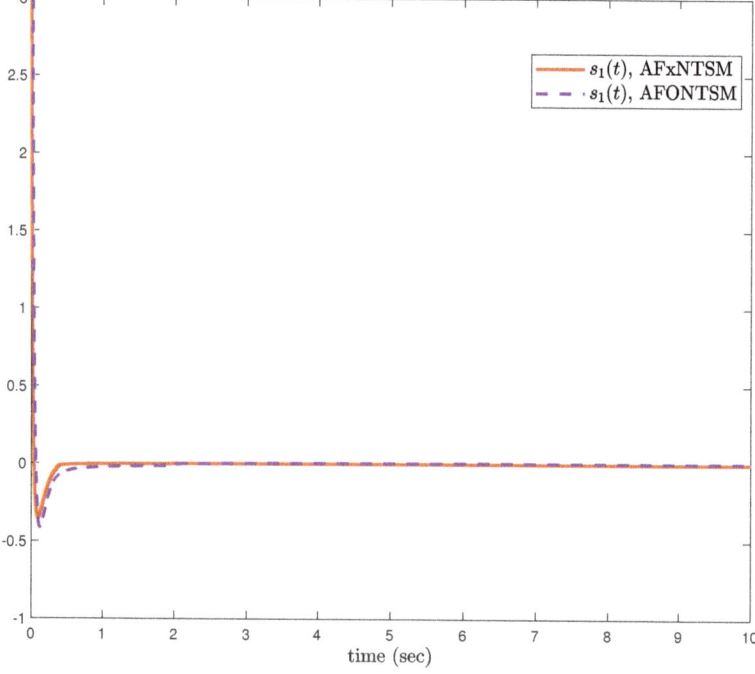

Figure 15. Sliding surface under fault and disturbances—Joint 1.

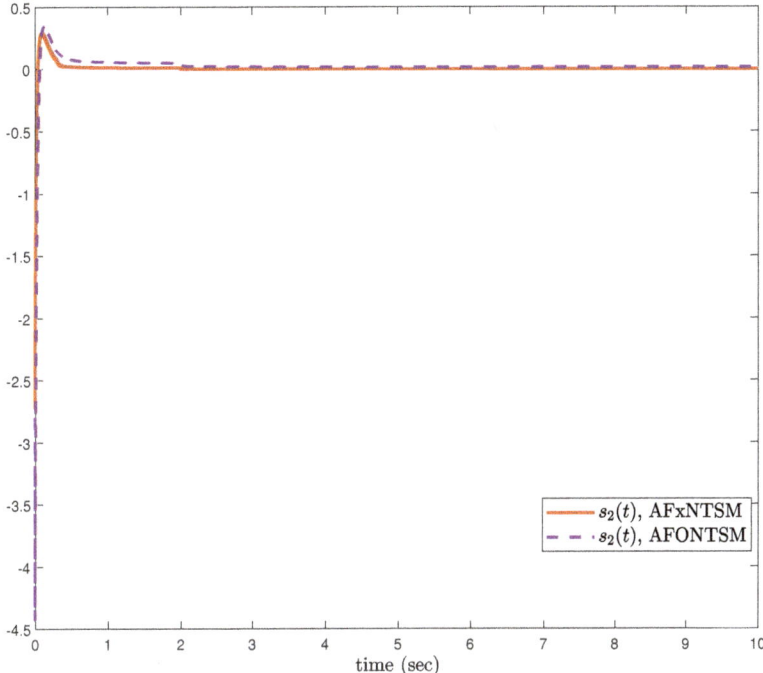

Figure 16. Sliding surface under fault and disturbances—Joint 2.

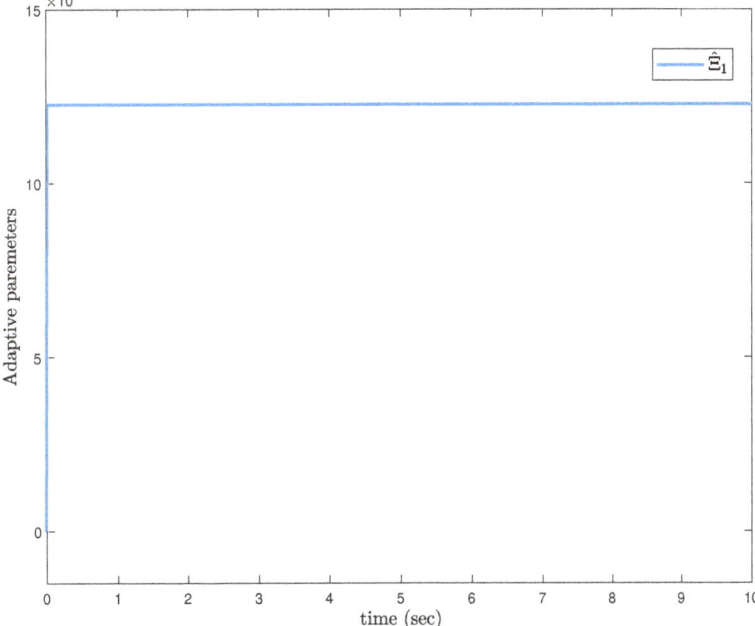

Figure 17. *Cont.*

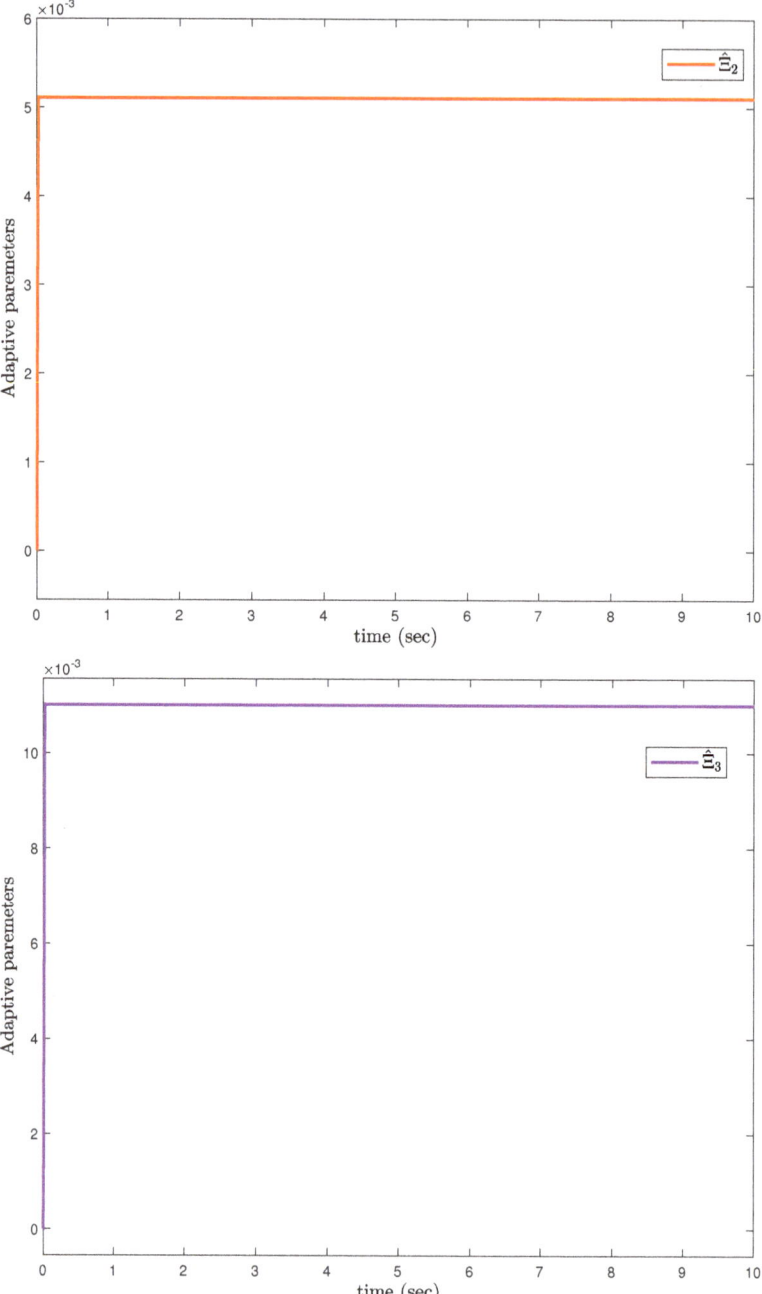

Figure 17. Adaptive parameters.

7. Discussion

In this section, the discussion related to the simulated results of the proposed FxNTSM and AFxNTSM are presented. In addition, the limitations of the suggested controller are briefly discussed in terms parameters and stability analyses. Moreover, the future aspects of the proposed method with the nonlinear system are also discussed.

A comparison is made between the suggested control approach and the AFONTSM and the parameters of both schemes are fairly selected. Thus, it is evident from Figures 11 and 12 that the suggested controller has the minimum tracking error and the shortest time to converge. In addition, the control inputs of the two joints can be seen in Figures 13 and 14, and it can be observed that the suggested solution provides the smoothest and efficient control input. Moreover, the adaptive estimation is given in Figure 17, which estimates the unknown parameters and compensates the effects of uncertainties, external disturbance and actuator faults, and shows that there is no drifting problem in adaptive control laws.

The parameters of the suggested control strategy are selected according to the range that was stated, such as $\theta_1 > 0, \theta_2 > 0, 0 < \eta_1 < 1, \eta_2 > 1, \gamma_1 > 0, \gamma_2 > 0, 0 < \gamma_{10} < 1$ and $\gamma_{20} > 1$. If these are not taken care of, the closed-loop system will not remain fixed-time stable. It is easy to see, based on the results of (29) and (43) that T_{10} and T_{20} are inversely proportional to θ_i and γ_i, whereas θ_i and γ_i are directly proportional to $u(t)$ in (17) and (30). Therefore, the appropriate values of θ_i and γ_i need to be chosen in order to obtain fixed-time convergence as well as closed-loop system stability at the same time. Furthermore, the ranges of the other parameters are known, which enables one to choose the suitable value in a manner that is appropriate. In addition, this work can further be extended to consider the non-smooth nonlinearities for the nonlinear robotic systems such as a robotic manipulator, inverted pendulum, mobile robots etc.

8. Conclusions

For robotic manipulator trajectory tracking with uncertainties, external disturbances and actuator faults, an AFxNTSM based FTC is developed. In order to estimate the unknown bounds of actuator faults, uncertainties and disturbances, fixed-time sliding surface is developed and then the FxNTSM control is designed utilising an adaptive approach, allowing for fixed-time convergence and tracking performance. FxNTSM and AFxNTSM are applied on the 2-DOF manipulator with and without actuator faults to show and justify the efficacy of the proposed approach. Simulation results show that the proposed FxNTSM and AFxNTSM outperform in terms of response time, trajectory tracking error, faults control, and better uncertainties and disturbances rejection capability.

Author Contributions: Conceptualization, S.A., A.T.A.; Formal analysis, S.A., A.T.A., M.T.; Funding acquisition, M.T.; Investigation, A.T.A., M.T.; Methodology, S.A., A.T.A., M.T.; Project administration, M.T.; Resources, S.A., M.T.; Software, S.A.; Supervision, A.T.A., M.T.; Validation, A.T.A., M.T.; Visualization, S.A., A.T.A.; Writing—original draft, S.A.; Writing—review & editing, S.A., A.T.A., M.T. All authors have read and agreed to the published version of the manuscript.

Funding: This research was funded by Prince Sultan University, Riyadh, Saudi Arabia.

Institutional Review Board Statement: Not applicable.

Informed Consent Statement: Not applicable.

Data Availability Statement: Not applicable.

Acknowledgments: The authors would like to acknowledge the support of Prince Sultan University, for paying the Article Processing Charges (APC) of this publication. Special acknowledgement to Automated Systems & Soft Computing Lab (ASSCL), Prince Sultan University, Riyadh, Saudi Arabia. In addition, the authors wish to acknowledge the editorial office and anonymous reviewers for their insightful comments, which have improved the quality of this publication.

Conflicts of Interest: The authors declare no conflict of interest.

References

1. Ahmed, S.; Wang, H.; Tian, Y. Modification to model reference adaptive control of 5-link exoskeleton with gravity compensation. In Proceedings of the 2016 35th Chinese Control Conference (CCC), Chengdu, China, 27–29 July 2016; pp. 6115–6120.
2. Hagh, Y.S.; Asl, R.M.; Cocquempot, V. A hybrid robust fault tolerant control based on adaptive joint unscented Kalman filter. *ISA Trans.* **2017**, *66*, 262–274. [CrossRef] [PubMed]
3. Zhao, D.; Li, S.; Gao, F. A new terminal sliding mode control for robotic manipulators. *Int. J. Control.* **2009**, *82*, 1804–1813. [CrossRef]
4. Feng, Y.; Yu, X.; Man, Z. Non-singular terminal sliding mode control of rigid manipulators. *Automatica* **2002**, *38*, 2159–2167. [CrossRef]
5. Yang, L.; Yang, J. Nonsingular fast terminal sliding-mode control for nonlinear dynamical systems. *Int. J. Robust Nonlinear Control* **2011**, *21*, 1865–1879. [CrossRef]
6. Moulay, E.; Lechappe, V.; Bernuau, E.; Defoort, M.; Plestan, F. Fixed-time sliding mode control with mismatched disturbances. *Automatica* **2022**, *136*, 110009. [CrossRef]
7. Ton, C.; Petersen, C. Continuous fixed-time sliding mode control for spacecraft with flexible appendages. *IFAC-PapersOnLine* **2018**, *51*, 1–5. [CrossRef]
8. Mekki, H.; Boukhetala, D.; Azar, A.T. Sliding modes for fault tolerant control. In *Advances and Applications in Sliding Mode Control Systems*; Springer: Cham, Switzerland, 2015; pp. 407–433.
9. Tao, G. Multivariable adaptive control: A survey. *Automatica* **2014**, *50*, 2737–2764.
10. Ahmed, S.; Wang, H.; Tian, Y. Fault tolerant control using fractional-order terminal sliding mode control for robotic manipulators. *Stud. Inform. Control* **2018**, *27*, 55–64. [CrossRef]
11. Truong, T.N.; Vo, A.T.; Kang, H.J.; Van, M. A Novel Active Fault-Tolerant Tracking Control for Robot Manipulators with Finite-Time Stability. *Sensors* **2021**, *21*, 8101. [CrossRef]
12. Van, M.; Ge, S.S.; Ren, H. Robust fault-tolerant control for a class of second-order nonlinear systems using an adaptive third-order sliding mode control. *IEEE Trans. Syst. Man Cybern. Syst.* **2016**, *47*, 221–228. [CrossRef]
13. Van, M.; Kang, H.J. Robust fault-tolerant control for uncertain robot manipulators based on adaptive quasi-continuous high-order sliding mode and neural network. *Proc. Inst. Mech. Eng. Part C J. Mech. Eng. Sci.* **2015**, *229*, 1425–1446. [CrossRef]
14. Abadi, A.S.S.; Hosseinabadi, P.A.; Mekhilef, S. Fuzzy adaptive fixed-time sliding mode control with state observer for a class of high-order mismatched uncertain systems. *Int. J. Control Autom. Syst.* **2020**, *18*, 2492–2508. [CrossRef]
15. Hu, Y.; Yan, H.; Zhang, H.; Wang, M.; Zeng, L. Robust Adaptive Fixed-Time Sliding-Mode Control for Uncertain Robotic Systems with Input Saturation. *IEEE Trans. Cybern.* **2022**, 1–11. [CrossRef]
16. Zhang, L.; Wang, Y.; Hou, Y.; Li, H. Fixed-time sliding mode control for uncertain robot manipulators. *IEEE Access* **2019**, *7*, 149750–149763. [CrossRef]
17. Moulay, E.; Lechappe, V.; Bernuau, E.; Plestan, F. Robust Fixed-Time Stability: Application to Sliding-Mode Control. *IEEE Trans. Autom. Control* **2021**, *67*, 1061–1066. [CrossRef]
18. Su, B.; Wang, H.; Li, N. Event-triggered integral sliding mode fixed time control for trajectory tracking of autonomous underwater vehicle. *Trans. Inst. Meas. Control* **2021**, *43*, 3483–3496. [CrossRef]
19. Gao, Z.; Guo, G. Fixed-time sliding mode formation control of AUVs based on a disturbance observer. *IEEE/CAA J. Autom. Sin.* **2020**, *7*, 539–545. [CrossRef]
20. Zhai, J.; Li, Z. Fast-exponential sliding mode control of robotic manipulator with super-twisting method. *IEEE Trans. Circuits Syst. II Express Briefs* **2021**, *69*, 489–493. [CrossRef]
21. Wang, B.; Jahanshahi, H.; Volos, C.; Bekiros, S.; Yusuf, A.; Agarwal, P.; Aly, A.A. Control of a symmetric chaotic supply chain system using a new fixed-time super-twisting sliding mode technique subject to control input limitations. *Symmetry* **2021**, *12*, 1257. [CrossRef]
22. Wang, G.; Wang, B.; Zhang, C. Fixed-time third-order super-twisting-like sliding mode motion control for piezoelectric nanopositioning stage. *Mathematics* **2021**, *9*, 1770. [CrossRef]
23. Vo, A.T.; Truong, T.N.; Kang, H.J.; Van, M. A Robust Observer-Based Control Strategy for n-DOF Uncertain Robot Manipulators with Fixed-Time Stability. *Sensors* **2021**, *21*, 7084. [CrossRef] [PubMed]
24. Abro, G.E.M.; Zulkifli, S.A.B.; Asirvadam, V.S.; Ali, Z.A. Model-free-based single-dimension fuzzy SMC design for underactuated quadrotor UAV. *Actuators* **2021**, *10*, 191. [CrossRef]
25. Fekih, A.; Mobayen, S.; Chen, C.C. Adaptive robust fault-tolerant control design for wind turbines subject to pitch actuator faults. *Energies* **2021**, *14*, 1791. [CrossRef]
26. Han, Z.; Zhang, K.; Yang, T.; Zhang, M. Spacecraft fault-tolerant control using adaptive non-singular fast terminal sliding mode. *IET Control Theory Appl.* **2010**, *10*, 1991–1999. [CrossRef]
27. Liu, L.; Zhang, L.; Wang, Y.; Hou, Y. A novel robust fixed-time fault-tolerant tracking control of uncertain robot manipulators. *IET Control Theory Appl.* **2021**, *15*, 195–208. [CrossRef]
28. Ahmed, S. Robust model reference adaptive control for five-link robotic exoskeleton. *Int. J. Model. Identif. Control* **2021**, *39*, 324–331. [CrossRef]

29. Zimenko, K.; Polyakov, A.; Efimov, D.; Perruquetti, W. On simple scheme of finite/fixed-time control design. *Int. J. Control* **2020**, *93*, 1353–1361. [CrossRef]
30. Huang, S.; Wang, J. Fixed-time fractional-order sliding mode control for nonlinear power systems. *J. Vib. Control* **2020**, *26*, 1425–1434. [CrossRef]

Article

Robust Stabilization of Underactuated Two-Wheeled Balancing Vehicles on Uncertain Terrains with Nonlinear-Model-Based Disturbance Compensation

Yongkuk Kim and SangJoo Kwon *

School of Aerospace and Mechanical Engineering, Korea Aerospace University, Goyang 10540, Republic of Korea; cooperkim@kau.kr
* Correspondence: sjkwon@kau.ac.kr

Abstract: Two-wheeled inverted pendulum (TWIP) vehicles are prone to lose their mobility and postural stability owing to their inherently unstable and underactuated dynamic characteristics, specifically when they encounter abruptly changed slopes or ground friction. Overcoming such environmental disturbances is essential to realize an agile TWIP-based mobile platform. In this paper, we suggest a disturbance compensation method that is compatible with unmanned TWIP systems in terms of the nonlinear-model-based disturbance observer, where the underactuated dynamic model is transformed to a fully actuated form by regarding the gravitational moment of the inverted pendulum as a supplementary pseudo-actuator to counteract the pitch-directional disturbances. Consequently, it enables us to intuitively determine the disturbance compensation input of the two wheels and the pitch reference input accommodating to uncertain terrains in real time. Through simulation and experimental results, the effectiveness of the proposed method is validated.

Keywords: two-wheeled inverted pendulum; underactuated system; disturbance rejection control; nonlinear disturbance observer (NDOB)

1. Introduction

Due to its maneuverability and high payload-to-weight ratio, the two-wheeled inverted pendulum (TWIP), typically with two parallel wheels, is still receiving much attention as a mobile platform for personal transporters [1], autonomous vehicles [2,3], robotic wheelchairs [4], wheeled humanoids [5,6], and wheeled bipedal robots [7]. It belongs to inherently unstable and underactuated systems with fewer actuators than the degrees of freedom needed for their control, which can be justified only when the instability of the pendulum is actively utilized to accomplish agile motions committed to diverse manipulation tasks. Inevitably, it is highly sensitive to external disturbances caused by uncertain environments, and the risk of turnover becomes higher while autonomously driving on unknown surfaces with varying slope and ground friction.

As a matter of fact, the posture control performance of unmanned TWIPs can be greatly improved by modifying the structural design. For example, a movable center of gravity enables more swift movements at the start and stop of the run [8]. The reaction wheel is also effective in compensating for the internal disturbances caused by embedded manipulators [9]. However, the TWIP employing the additional actuators is not an underactuated system anymore and requires paying the price of a much heavier weight and complicated mechanism.

Error-based linear feedback controls such as PID controls and LQRs [10] are certainly limited in covering the wide range of pitch motions that the TWIP robot can experience as the terrain slope and wheel friction are unexpectedly changed. In other words, a set of control gains well-adjusted for a plain does not guarantee postural stability and driving performance on a different slope because the strong nonlinear effect is closely concerned with the pitch motion. The nonlinear control schemes including the adaptive control [11], the Lyapunov-based control [12], the SDRE optimal control [13], etc., can be applied to extend the range of possible pitch angles until the turnover happens. Nonetheless, to make the inverted pendulum motion quickly converge to the equilibrium point, it is desired to adopt an anticipative compensation input to directly cope with the lumped uncertainty, including modeling errors and the external disturbances not considered in the error-based nominal feedback control design.

The preceding results on the robust compensator design of TWIP can be classified into the extended state observer [14], the nonlinear disturbance observer [15], sliding mode control methods [16,17], as well as the combined synthesis of a disturbance observer and a sliding control [18]. These works prove that it is a challenging problem to determine the disturbance compensation input for underactuated systems because they do not have a one-to-one correspondence between the actuators and the degrees of freedom. Despite the rigorous outcomes mostly in terms of Lyapunov-based designs, they are taking rather highly complicated forms of many tuning parameters and switching functions to ensure the asymptotic stability for lumped disturbances. Thus, aside from the mathematical completeness, this could inevitably raise an implementation issue for real systems because the driving performance highly depends on a sophisticated gain-tuning process.

Focusing more on the slope-climbing problem for unmanned TWIP systems, the dynamic equations on an inclined surface were described with respect to the 2D longitudinal motion [19] and the 3D motion [20]. The slope angle of the terrain was estimated by using a disturbance observer in [21]. The effects of the terrain inclination on the stability of TWIP were accounted for in [22]. The reaction torque observer against the ramp disturbances was suggested to determine the equilibrium pitch angle in [23]. A so-called second sliding controller was designed to improve the velocity tracking performance on inclined surfaces in [16]. These examples demonstrate that the terrain uncertainty with an unknown slope is a dominant factor that determines the tracking performance and postural stability of TWIPs.

In this paper, we propose a new solution to tackle the stabilization problem of unmanned TWIP-balancing vehicles in uncertain terrains in terms of the nonlinear-model-based disturbance observer (NDOB). The highlight of this study lies in regarding the gravitational moment acting on the inverted pendulum as a pseudo-actuator and transforming the dynamic model of the underactuated TWIP into a fully actuated one by modulating the input matrix. As relevant performances were carried out through the whole-body coordination control in [5–7], how to aggressively utilize the gravity of the pendulum is essential to accomplish the balanced agile motions of a TWIP system. In the previous robust control frameworks [14–18] for underactuated TWIPs, it cannot be clearly described how the disturbance estimates along the forward, pitch, and yaw motions are resolved into the compensation input channels. In contrast, the proposed scheme clarifies that the forward and yaw directional disturbances can be compensated through two input channels, and the body disturbances hindering the pitch motion can be indirectly attenuated in terms of a real-time pitch reference input dealing with the pitch directional disturbance estimates. Thus, the proposed method has the merit of explicitly reflecting the dynamic correlations of the underactuated TWIP by using a compensation input design and making the feedback gain tuning easier.

The rest of this paper is organized as follows: In Section 2, a description is provided in terms of how the unmanned TWIP robot behaves on a ramp while it performs both velocity and posture control at the same time. In Section 3, the related issues in applying the NDOB to the TWIP as an underactuated system are discussed, and finally, an effective compensation strategy for suppressing lumped disturbances is proposed with real-time pitch reference generation. Section 4 is devoted to the driving simulations and experiments on slopes to verify the effectiveness of the proposed method. Finally, conclusions are drawn in Section 5.

2. Dynamic Characteristics of TWIP on Inclined Surfaces

2.1. Dynamic Model

The schematic of the TWIP robot is represented in Figure 1, and the parameters and variables are defined in Table 1, where it has two inputs (T_L, T_R) corresponding to the left and right wheel torques and three outputs (x, θ, ψ) to describe the three degrees of freedom. As has been described in [24], seven holonomic and three nonholonomic constraints for the wheeled mobile robot can be considered in formulating the dynamic model of the TWIP. However, it finally leaves the following set of differential equations with respect to the three controlled states of forward velocity, pitch, and yaw rate as

$$M(q)\ddot{q} + C(q,\dot{q})\dot{q} + G(q) = B\tau$$
$$M(q) = \begin{bmatrix} m_{11} & m_{12} & 0 \\ m_{21} & m_{22} & 0 \\ 0 & 0 & m_{33} \end{bmatrix}, \; C(q,\dot{q}) = \begin{bmatrix} 0 & c_{12} & c_{13} \\ 0 & 0 & c_{23} \\ c_{31} & c_{32} & 0 \end{bmatrix} \quad (1)$$
$$G(q) = \begin{bmatrix} g_1 \\ g_2 \\ g_3 \end{bmatrix}, \; B = \begin{bmatrix} 1/r & 1/r \\ -1 & -1 \\ d/2r & -d/2r \end{bmatrix}, \; \tau = \begin{bmatrix} T_R \\ T_L \end{bmatrix}$$

where $q = [x, \theta, \psi]^T$ is the generalized coordinates, $M(q)$ is the inertia matrix, $C(q,\dot{q})$ is the Coriolis and centrifugal matrix, $G(q)$ is the gravity vector, B is the input matrix, and τ is the input vector. The elements of the matrices and vectors are specified in Appendix A.

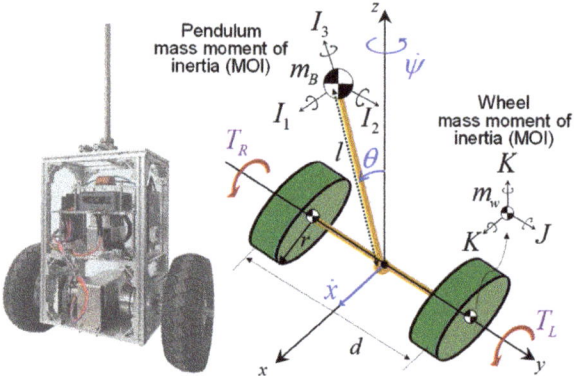

Figure 1. Prototype and schematic of TWIP with two parallel wheels.

Table 1. Variables and parameters of TWIP robot.

x	Displacement along the forward direction
θ	Pitch angle of inverted pendulum
$\dot{\psi}$	Yaw rate of the entire TWIP robot
T_L, T_R	Torque of left and right wheels
d	Distance between the parallel wheels
l	Distance from the wheel axis to the center of gravity (length of inverted pendulum)
m_B, m_w	Mass of inverted pendulum and each wheel
I_1, I_2, I_3	MOI of inverted pendulum body
K, J	MOI of each wheel body
r	Radius of wheel

Considering the dynamic characteristics of TWIP systems, pitch and forward motions are strongly coupled, as the off-diagonal elements in the first and second row of the inertia matrix indicate, whereas the yaw motion is rarely affected by the other motions, although the Coriolis and centrifugal terms define the correlation among them. Hence, the performances of the pitch and velocity control are highly interdependent since the two states $(\dot{x}, \theta)$ must be simultaneously controlled by sharing the single input of $\tau = T_R + T_L$ from the two wheels in the longitudinal direction, whereas the yaw rate for steering can be independently controlled through the difference between the two wheel torques. If a linear system analysis is conducted for the TWIP around an equilibrium point, the closed-loop transfer function regarding the pitch and velocity control will have the same characteristic equation.

The TWIP robot belongs to the acrobot [25] where the two wheels and the inverted pendulum share the wheel axis as the common rotational hinge, and the wheel actuators are mounted on the chassis as a part of the pendulum body, which results in input couplings between the wheel and the pendulum body due to the reaction torque. When a driving torque is exerted to rotate the wheels, the same amount of reverse torque is delivered to the inverted pendulum, and it brings about a pitch motion. The opposite direction of the first and second row in the input matrix B in Equation (1) indicates the input coupling between the forward and pitch motions. The TWIP mechanism distinctly differs from the pendubot [25] systems, such as a cart–pendulum system, where the wheel torques do not directly work on the pendulum. However, a few studies adopted the cart–pendulum system as the nominal model of the TWIP [26].

2.2. Finding Static Equilibrium Point on Inclined Surfaces

For a quick understanding of the effect of uncertain terrains with an arbitrary slope angle and surface friction, the longitudinal motion of the TWIP is represented in Figure 2. If the TWIP robot keeps its static equilibrium state on a slope at a constant speed or standstill, the sum of the gravitational moments with respect to the contact point by the weights of the wheels and the inverted pendulum body is equal to zero. That is,

$$\begin{aligned}\sum M_A &= M_w - M_B \\ &= 2m_w g r \sin\alpha - m_B g (l \sin\theta - r \sin\alpha) \\ &= (m_B + 2m_w) g r \sin\alpha - m_B g l \sin\theta = 0\end{aligned} \quad (2)$$

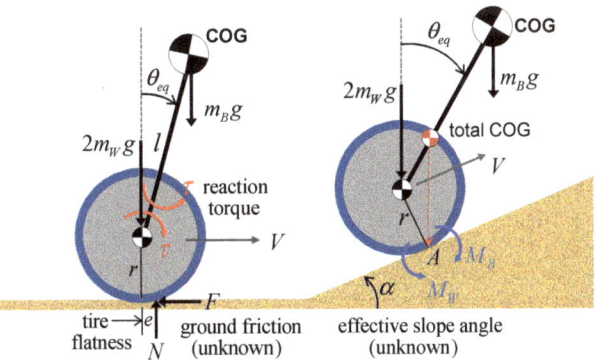

Figure 2. Static equilibrium state of TWIP.

Then, we have the equilibrium pitch angle against the slope as

$$\theta_{eq} = \sin^{-1}\left[\frac{(m_B + 2m_w)r}{m_B l}\sin\alpha\right] \quad (3)$$

The above relationship holds by assuming a point contact between the wheels and the ground surface. As denoted in the left of Figure 2, even when the TWIP is moving with a constant speed on a plane, it has a nonzero equilibrium pitch angle because of the tire flatness and ground friction. Hence, the time-varying slope angle on the right of Figure 2 can be regarded as an effective ramp disturbance including the frictional effect in the longitudinal direction.

When the TWIP mobile robot meets an unexpected slope, it slows down in uphill climbing and accelerates downhill. To surmount the ramp disturbances, the pitch angle of the inverted pendulum must be swiftly transferred near the equilibrium point. In the case of human-riding TWIP transporters, a skillful rider can readily travel on a ramp by leaning the pitch angle of the body to find the equilibrium point. In other words, the human rider is involved in the control loop as an additional actuator to supplement the underactuated inverted pendulum. However, the safety, and the driving performance of the unmanned TWIP mobile robot on uncertain terrains, highly depend on how quickly the equilibrium pitch angle can be found by the control system against the ramp disturbances.

2.3. Limit of Error-Based Feedback Control

As a typical error-based feedback controller, the PID control law has the robustness property for a certain range of biased disturbances and are widely applied in practical systems. However, a TWIP robot on a slope is a good example where the error-based controls with a fixed gain setting, including linear and nonlinear schemes, show performance limitations. Since the pitch and forward motions of the TWIP are dynamically coupled, and their control performances are in a trade-off relationship, it is time-consuming to attain the final gains satisfying both performances even in numerical simulations. Moreover, the optimal values of the gain setting are varied depending on the inclination of the terrain, because the equilibrium point of the pitch angle is accordingly moved.

The simulation result in Figure 3 compares the uphill driving performance of the prototype in Figure 1 when the velocity reference is 1 m/s, and the PID control is applied with the same gain setting adjusted for the flat surface, where the TWIP robot meets the slopes with different angles at 4 s. When the integral control action is activated, the pitch angle finally converges to the equilibrium point according to the relationship in Equation (3), and although the zero-pitch reference is assigned for the unknown terrain, the velocity tracking performance is greatly degraded as the slope angle increases. This means that the PID controller is vulnerable to ramp disturbances, mainly because it takes some time to reach the pitch equilibrium point, and usually puts more weight on the conservative pitch control gains for the safety of the TWIP from turnovers.

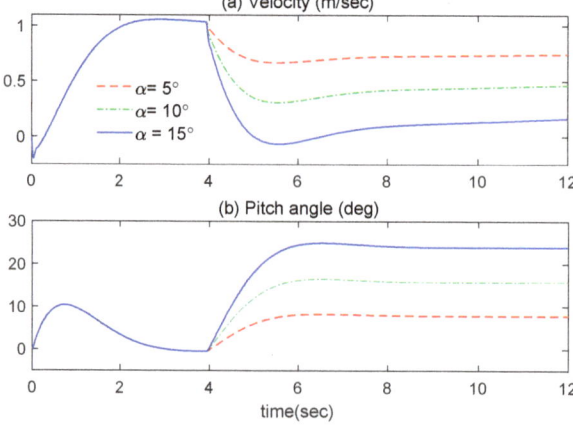

Figure 3. Uphill driving simulation on an inclined surface.

As another example, Figure 4 shows the experimental results for the prototype, where the two cases concerned with the gain tuning issue are compared, while the robot is accelerated and decelerated on a flat surface. Case 1 employs the control gains that give more weight to the pitch control than the velocity tracking performance, whereas Case 2 is the opposite. Naturally, Case 2 with a velocity-weighted controller shows a better tracking performance, but it accompanies a large pitch motion to make the robot rapidly accelerate and decelerate by utilizing the gravity of the inverted pendulum. The pitch-weighted control of Case 1 is advantageous in keeping the upright posture of the robot, but it sacrifices swift velocity tracking. In summary, when an error-based feedback controller is applied, the velocity tracking performance and the posture stabilization of the inverted pendulum are irreconcilable on uncertain terrains unless the pitch equilibrium point is given in real time.

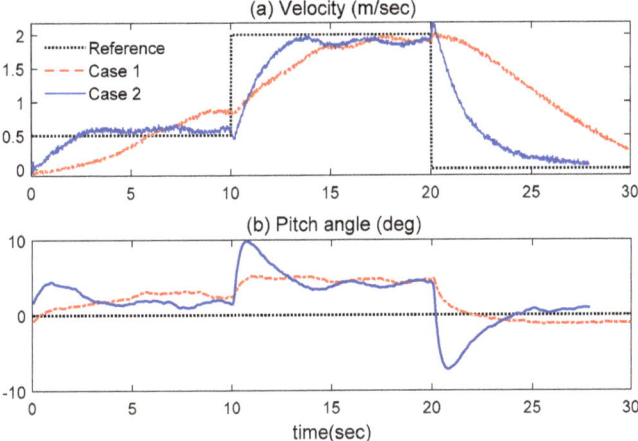

Figure 4. Velocity tracking control experiment on a flat surface.

3. NDOB-Based Disturbance Compensation

3.1. NDOB Application to Underactuated TWIPs

A great merit of applying the disturbance observer technique is that it can deal with the lumped disturbance, including the model's parametric uncertainties and external disturbances, and it allows for the freedom to maintain the current nominal feedback controller, whether it is a linear scheme or a nonlinear one [27]. Considering the strong nonlinear dynamic characteristics of the inverted pendulum, which could happen due to the wide pitch variations against the ramp disturbances, it is reasonable to adopt a nonlinear disturbance observer (NDOB) directly based on differential equations rather than a transfer-function-based linear observer.

Although there exist a few different versions in the NDOB formulations depending on the incorporated state equations and filtering structure [27–29], the fundamental notion is that the lumped disturbance at the current time can be equivalently estimated using the nominal model as

$$\hat{D}(t) = Q \cdot [M\ddot{q}(t) + C\dot{q}(t) + G(t) - B\tau(t-\lambda)] \qquad (4)$$

under the assumption that the input variation between the control intervals λ is very small, i.e., $\tau(t) \approx \tau(t-\lambda)$, and all the states are available. The linear operator Q represents a low-pass filter to suppress the high-frequency noises in sensor signals and data. One of the main issues in implementing Equation (4) is how to construct the acceleration terms since the acceleration data are not available in most robotic systems. To eliminate the requirement of any acceleration measurement, an auxiliary variable vector was used in the modified

NDOB [29], and the setup of the relevant parameters of the TWIP was developed in [15]. In reality, the acceleration data can be obtained by applying filtered derivatives to the joint measurements, and it works well, as the mobile robot is traveling near a constant speed without high maneuvers.

Prior to establishing a disturbance rejection scheme based on the NDOB, we need to ascertain the drawback of the conventional NDOB in applying it to the underactuated TWIP systems. The dynamic model for the underactuated TWIP in Equation (1) can be rewritten by considering the lumped disturbance reflecting all the internal and environmental uncertainties other than the nominal parameters as

$$M^{n \times n}(q)\ddot{q} + C^{n \times n}(q,\dot{q})\dot{q} + G^{n \times 1}(q) = B^{n \times r}\tau^{r \times 1} + D^{n \times 1}$$
$$D^{n \times 1} = d_m^{n \times 1} + d_u^{n \times 1} = B^{n \times r}\tau_d^{r \times 1} + d_u^{n \times 1} \tag{5}$$

where $r = 2$ is the number of inputs, $n = 3$ is the number of outputs, and $D = [d_1 \ d_2 \ d_3]^T$ is the lumped disturbance with three elements, which can be defined as the wheel disturbance for the forward motion of the two wheels, the body disturbance for the pitch motion of the inverted pendulum, and the yaw disturbance for the steering motion, respectively. Again, the lumped disturbance vector can be divided into the matched disturbance d_m, satisfying the matching condition, and the unmatched disturbance d_u, which does not exist in the column space of the input matrix in Equation (1). In Equation (5), τ_d can be thought of as the transformation of the matched disturbance into the input channels.

To determine the compensation torques for the disturbance estimates through the input channels, the compensation input τ_c must satisfy the relationship of $B\tau_c = -\hat{D} = [-\hat{d}_1 \ -\hat{d}_2 \ -\hat{d}_3]^T$. However, the nonsquare input matrix has only the left inverse $B^+ = (B^T B)^{-1} B^T$ since the number of rows is larger than the columns. Then, if the conventional NDOB compensation input $\tau_c = -B^+ \hat{D}$ is applied, the compensation error is equivalent to

$$\begin{aligned}\tilde{D} &\triangleq D - \hat{D} = D + B\tau_c = D - BB^+\hat{D} \\ &= (B\tau_d + d_u) - BB^+(B\hat{\tau}_d + \hat{d}_u) \\ &= \underbrace{(B\tau_d - B(B^+B)\hat{\tau}_d)}_{\approx 0} + (d_u - BB^+\hat{d}_u)\end{aligned} \tag{6}$$

where the first part corresponding to the matched disturbance can be almost rejected since $B^+B = I$, but the residual compensation error caused by the unmatched disturbance still perturbs the system response since $BB^+ \neq I$.

On the other hand, by taking the left pseudo-inverse of the input matrix in Equation (1), we have

$$\tilde{D} = D - BB^+\hat{D} = \begin{bmatrix} d_1 - \frac{1}{(1+r^2)}\hat{d}_1 + \frac{r}{(1+r^2)}\hat{d}_2 \\ d_2 - \frac{r^2}{(1+r^2)}\hat{d}_2 + \frac{r}{(1+r^2)}\hat{d}_1 \\ d_3 - \hat{d}_3 \end{bmatrix} \tag{7}$$

As the first and second elements represent, the wheel disturbance and the body disturbance cannot be clearly attenuated, because when both estimates are transferred to the underactuated input channels, they are directly correlated by the input coupling of the acrobot. The last yaw disturbance compensation error is not affected by the other two compensation elements since the yaw motion is free of the input coupling. However, if the lumped disturbance of the TWIP satisfies the matching condition, the relationship of $\hat{d}_2 = -r\hat{d}_1$ holds, as depicted in Figure 5. A simple example of the matched disturbance is the viscous and Coulomb friction exerted on the wheel axis. In this case, the compensation error Equation (7) is reduced to

$$\tilde{D} = \begin{bmatrix} d_1 - \hat{d}_1 & d_2 - \hat{d}_2 & d_3 - \hat{d}_3 \end{bmatrix}^T \tag{8}$$

which indicates that the matched disturbances are completely rejected through the input channels if all the states in Equation (4) can be exactly reconstructed in real time.

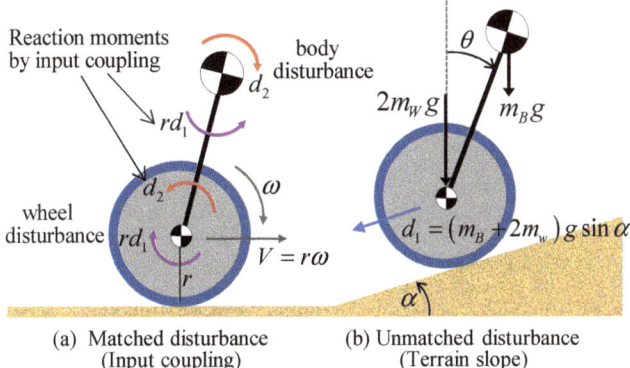

(a) Matched disturbance
(Input coupling)

(b) Unmatched disturbance
(Terrain slope)

Figure 5. Examples of matched and unmatched disturbances.

A great part of the lumped disturbance acting on the TWIP robot can be classified as unmatched disturbances, e.g., model parametric errors, rolling resistance due to the tire flatness, wheel–slip phenomena, the eccentric center of the gravity of the pendulum from the wheel axis, and most importantly, the environmental disturbance by the inclined terrains. If the effective slope angle in Figure 2 is considered in the nominal model Equation (1), the pitch angle θ in the elements of matrices of M and C is changed to $\theta + \alpha$, as shown in Appendix A, and the first element of the gravity vector has $g_1 = (m_B + 2m_W)g \sin \alpha$ [16,20]. As the static equilibrium condition in Equation (2) implies, this additional gravity term arising from the unknown terrain, as denoted in Figure 5, dominantly affects the velocity tracking performance and the upright posture stabilization of the TWIP as a wheel disturbance. Assuming only a ramp disturbance due to terrain uncertainty, the lumped disturbance of the TWIP at a steady state can be represented by

$$D_{ramp} = \begin{bmatrix} -(m_B + 2m_W)g \sin \alpha \\ 0 \\ 0 \end{bmatrix} \qquad (9)$$

The above disturbance certainly does not satisfy the matching condition because it does not exist in the column space of the input matrix. In other words, it cannot be expressed as a linear combination of the column vectors of B in Equation (1).

3.2. Disturbance Rejection by Input Matrix Modulation

As we have seen, the conventional NDOB techniques generating equivalent compensation torques to the lumped disturbances through the input channels are fundamentally limited in attenuating the unmatched disturbances of underactuated systems. Related to this issue, the NDOB-combined sliding mode controls employed the so-called dynamic surface in [15], and a novel sliding surface in [18], to achieve an asymptotically stable sliding mode for unmatched disturbances. Additionally, the second sliding controller in [16], the integral-type sliding surface suggested in [17] for TWIP systems, and the second-order sliding control suggested for underactuated systems in [30] belong to this class. However, the chattering problem due to the switching control action is unavoidable when the behavior of the TWIP deviates far from the nominal sliding dynamics, and the complicated parameters and gain structures, which were inevitable to guarantee the Lyapunov stability, would be a great barrier to find an appropriate gain setting for the stable convergence of the inverted pendulum to the equilibrium point.

Compared with nominal error-based feedback controls, the above-mentioned robust control schemes can significantly contribute to the stabilization of underactuated TWIPs as the system's uncertainty increases. However, it will reach a certain limit of velocity tracking performance if the zero-pitch reference is kept for unknown ramp disturbances because it intrinsically violates the static equilibrium condition in Figure 2. Although the center of gravity (COG) movement of the inverted pendulum, along with the pitch motion, bothers the upright posture of the TWIP, it must be actively utilized to implement high-maneuver manipulations in terms of the balanced mobile platform and keep the static equilibrium state on inclined surfaces.

The inverted pendulum body of TWIP systems can be regarded as a gravitational actuator if the pitch motion is fairly stabilized all the time. The whole-body controls in [5–7] are good examples utilizing the gravity of the inverted pendulum. However, they can be enabled only when appropriate pitch references are given for the center of gravity through an extra planning process. In this regard, a dynamic-model-based trajectory in [31] has been proposed for swift velocity transition on flat surfaces. In this paper, we suggest how the real-time pitch reference of the TWIP accommodating to uncertain terrains can be generated in terms of the NDOB. First, the gravity term of the nominal model in Equation (1) is merged into the input vector by regarding it as a pseudo-actuator. Then, we have

$$M(q)\ddot{q} + C(q,\dot{q})\dot{q} = \tilde{B}u + D$$
$$\tilde{B} = \begin{bmatrix} 1/r & 1/r & 0 \\ -1 & -1 & 1 \\ d/2r & -d/2r & 0 \end{bmatrix}, u = \begin{bmatrix} \tau_R \\ \tau_L \\ m_B g l \sin\theta \end{bmatrix}, D = \begin{bmatrix} d_1 \\ d_2 \\ d_3 \end{bmatrix} \quad (10)$$

where the modulation of the input matrix into a full-rank and square one temporarily makes the TWIP system a fully actuated system. Then, the compensation input satisfying the relationship of $\tilde{B}\tau_c = -\hat{D}$ for the disturbance estimates in terms of a specific NDOB formulation can be determined by

$$\tau_c = \begin{bmatrix} \tau_R \\ \tau_L \\ m_B g l \sin\theta_{ref} \end{bmatrix} = -\tilde{B}^{-1}\hat{D} = \begin{bmatrix} -\left(\frac{r}{2}\hat{d}_1 + \frac{r}{d}\hat{d}_3\right) \\ -\left(\frac{r}{2}\hat{d}_1 - \frac{r}{d}\hat{d}_3\right) \\ -\left(r\hat{d}_1 + \hat{d}_2\right) \end{bmatrix} \quad (11)$$

Hence, the compensation input consists of two direct torque inputs (τ_R, τ_L) for the right and left wheels and an indirect gravitational moment, which can be generated in real time by assigning the pitch reference input as follows:

$$\theta_{ref} = -\sin^{-1}\left(\frac{r\hat{d}_1 + \hat{d}_2}{m_B g l}\right) \quad (12)$$

which satisfies a dynamic equilibrium between the disturbance input and the gravitational moment. Then, as far as the pitch control loop successfully follows the pitch reference, we have the disturbance compensation error, $\tilde{D} = D - \tilde{B}\tilde{B}^{-1}\hat{D} = D - \hat{D}$ in the same form as Equation (8) instead of Equation (7). As shown, the wheel disturbance as well as the body disturbance, as defined in Equation (5), are involved in the equilibrium condition according to the input coupling effect. If only the uncertain slope is considered as a dominant disturbance denoted in Equation (9), and the TWIP is moving at a constant speed, the pitch reference is supposed to be coincident with the equilibrium pitch angle in Equation (3). On the other hand, it goes to zero when it meets $\hat{d}_2 = -r\hat{d}_1$ for the matched disturbances depicted in Figure 5. However, this happens only if the wheels make a point of contact when traveling on flat surfaces, which cannot occur in reality.

Some researchers investigated how to generate a pitch reference for the smooth climbing of the TWIP on inclined surfaces. For example, state estimators including the slope angle [21] and a pitch angle disturbance observer [23] were synthesized based on the linear models around the equilibrium point. However, they are inadequate to cover a wide range of pitch motions, which can arise via abrupt slope changes and other heavy disturbances. Above all, the current formulation has the merit of consistently generating the torque compensation input and the real-time pitch reference input simultaneously, without an extra trajectory planner and irrespective of the disturbance estimation algorithm.

The overall schematic of the proposed dynamic compensation scheme is represented in Figure 6, where the disturbances associated with the forward and yaw motions are attenuated by the torque compensation inputs of the two wheels according to Equations (4) and (11), and the body disturbance is suppressed as the pitch control loop is activated with the pitch reference assignment according to Equation (12). Separately from the disturbance compensation input, the nominal feedback control loop for the three-degree-of-freedom motion is fundamentally based on the error-based PID control logic. The velocity and steering commands $(\dot{x}_{ref}, \dot{\psi}_{ref})$ can be given arbitrarily, but the pitch reference command θ_{ref} is highly dependent upon the terrain's condition. When the controllers for the velocity, pitch, and yaw motion are generated as (u_x, u_θ, u_ψ), respectively, the nominal control inputs of the right and left wheels can be determined by

$$u_R = \frac{u_x + u_\theta + u_\psi}{2}, \quad u_L = \frac{u_x + u_\theta - u_\psi}{2} \tag{13}$$

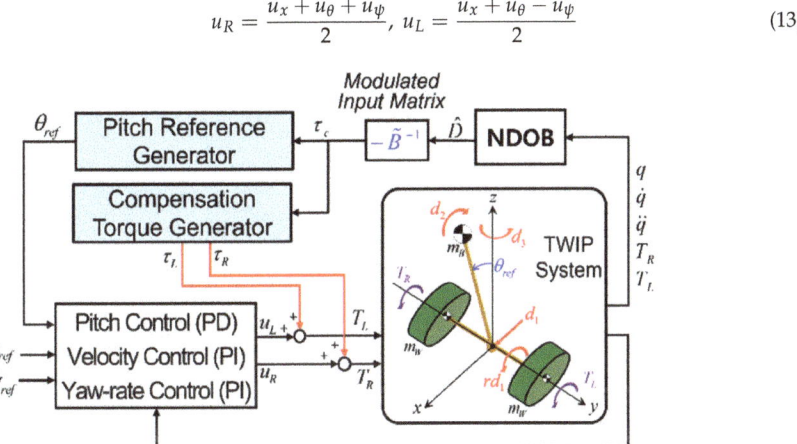

Figure 6. NDOB-based dynamic compensator with real-time pitch reference generation.

As indicated, if the pseudo-fully actuated system model in Equation (10) is incorporated in the NDOB-based compensator design, it does not discriminate the matched and unmatched disturbances, and the relationship between the disturbance estimates and compensation inputs becomes clarified. Applying it to TWIP systems, the complicated design issues in [15–18] concerning multiple sliding surfaces and switching control gains to ensure the robust stability of underactuated systems can be much reduced.

4. Numerical Simulations

To demonstrate the robustness of the proposed technique with respect to uncertain terrains with arbitrary slopes, comparative simulations were carried out using the Simscape Multibody Toolbox [32]. This software provides a dynamic simulation environment for multibody systems and useful tools for modeling the spatial contact force between the wheels and driving surfaces based on the stick–slip friction model. The parameters of the prototype TWIP mobile robot are given in Table 2. The PID controller was applied as a nominal controller for the forward velocity, the pitch angle, and the yaw rate for steering. The gain setting of the nominal controller was adjusted for smooth traveling on plains with more weighting on keeping the upright posture, as previously mentioned in

Section 2.3. The video clips related to the simulation results in Figures 7–10 can be found at https://youtu.be/YqzDefO85s8 (accessed on 25 May 2022).

Table 2. Dimensions of TWIP robot.

m_B, m_w	17.6, 2.2 (kg)
l, d, r	0.15, 0.47, 0.127 (m)
I_1, I_2, I_3	0.4032, 0.3297, 0.1907 (kg m^2)
K, J	0.010, 0.018 (kg m^2)

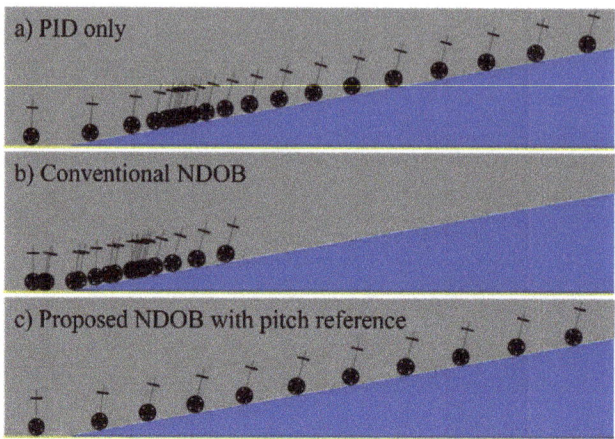

Figure 7. Climbing a ramp with an unknown slope of 10 degrees.

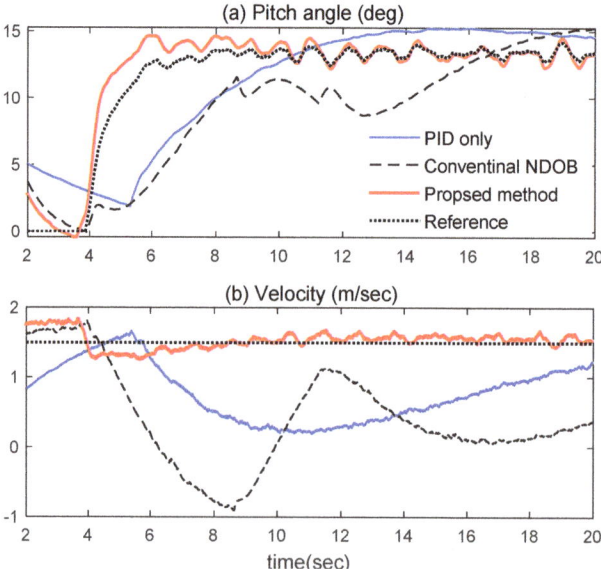

Figure 8. Climbing a ramp with an unknown slope of 10 degrees. The pitch references for PID and conventional NDOB were zero.

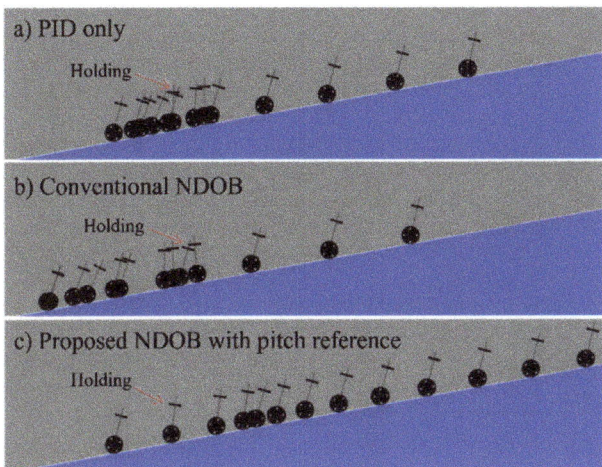

Figure 9. Holding a standstill position on a ramp with an unknown slope of 10 degrees.

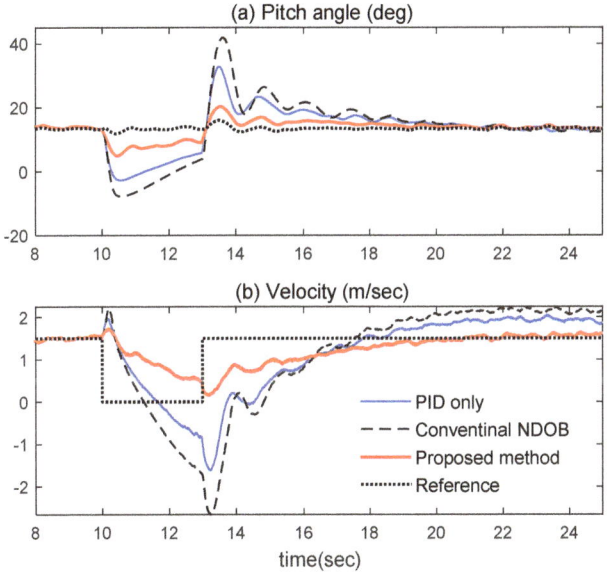

Figure 10. Holding a standstill position on a ramp with an unknown slope of 10 degrees. The pitch references for PID and conventional NDOB were zero.

Firstly, as shown in Figures 7 and 8, the TWIP had a reference velocity of 1.5 m/s, and it entered the ramp with an unknown slope at around 4 s. (1) In the case of only the PID controller with no pitch reference, the velocity tracking performance deteriorated as soon as the robot encountered the ramp disturbance. For smoothly climbing an inclined surface, the pitch angle of the inverted pendulum had to be transferred to a new equilibrium point as the feedback control was activated. Although the robot managed to climb the ramp again owing to the integral control action, it took quite a long time until the final velocity reached the reference value; (2) when a conventional NDOB compensation input was added to the nominal controller, the tracking performance was more degraded. This is mainly because the reaction torque delivered to the pendulum body in response to the compensation input occurred at the pitch-up moment, and it hindered the pitch motion from reaching the equilibrium point; (3) finally, when the proposed compensation method was applied, it generated the pitch references for the inverted pendulum in real time to keep the equilibrium state compatible to the inclined surface, and it caused the robot to steadily ascend the uncertain slope following the reference velocity.

Secondly, as shown in Figures 9 and 10, as the TWIP robot steadily climbed the ramp, the velocity reference changed from 1.5 m/s to 0 m/s at 10 s to hold a stationary state for 3 s. (1) When applying only the PID controller with a zero-pitch reference, it had great difficulty in making the robot stand still on a ramp. As indicated in Figure 10a, when the zero-velocity command was assigned, it tended to recover the upright posture, which resulted in a severe retreat of the TWIP owing to the gravitational moment acting on the wheels; (2) the compensation input by the conventional NDOB was not helpful at all to keep the standstill position, because the residual disturbance in Equation (7) due to the input couplings continually perturbed the forward and pitch motion at the same time; (3) the proposed NDOB with the real-time pitch reference generation enabled us to have a smooth stop and restart during the uphill movement.

As indicated in Section 2.3, even if a PID controller is applied, a steady traveling of the TWIP on a specific slope can be realized by sophisticated gain tuning for the uphill or downhill driving with more emphasis on the tracking performance rather than keeping the upright posture. However, it does not guarantee an identical transient performance on a different slope and accompanies poor postural stability for unexpected body disturbances, because the static equilibrium point of the inverted pendulum moves according to the varying slope.

For uphill traveling with ramp disturbances, another practical issue that must be considered about the PID controller, as a representative error-based nominal controller, is the actuator saturation problem induced by a long-time accumulation of tracking errors. Although the integral control function is indispensable for overcoming the gravitational effect, it could invoke a large overshoot and rapid increase in velocity as soon as the ramp disturbance vanishes. An anti-windup scheme, such as the clamping technique in [33], can be applied to solve this problem. In contrast, the NDOB-based robust compensation method proposed in this paper greatly relaxes the burden of the nominal feedback gains to achieve a consistent tracking performance regardless of the terrain condition. Additionally, it makes the nominal PID controller free of the anti-windup issue since the additional disturbance compensation input fundamentally has an integral control property to counteract gravitational disturbances. Thus, it enables us to apply moderate velocity gains, and even the integral function can be excluded from the nominal controller.

5. Experimental Results

The prototype in Figure 11 had the same nominal parameters as those listed in Table 2. The experiments were classified into three cases: (1) standing still on a flat surface for an arbitrary longitudinal eccentricity as a dominant body disturbance; (2) straight traveling on a flat surface for a lateral eccentricity as a dominant yaw disturbance; (3) velocity tracking on a ramp as a dominant wheel disturbance. The video clips related to the experimental results in Figures 12–17 can be found at https://youtu.be/fvrYeNSiiH4 (accessed on 25 May 2022).

As shown in Figure 12, while the robot was holding its upright posture on the plane, a dummy weight was placed on the body to make a longitudinal eccentricity of the COG with respect to the wheel axis. When the PID control was the only function to stabilize the pitch motion, the robot drifted away quite a long distance from the initial position until the feedback system made the pitch angle converge to the new equilibrium point. However, when the proposed NDOB compensation scheme was activated, the moving distance was minimal owing to the prompt generation of the pitch references shown in Figure 12a. The symmetrical shape of the disturbance estimates in Figure 12c for the longitudinal motion of the wheel and body indicated the input coupling of the acrobot.

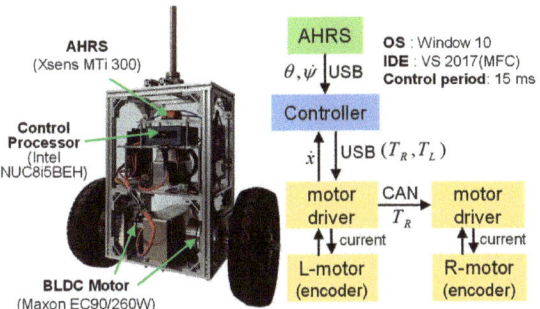

Figure 11. System architecture of the TWIP prototype.

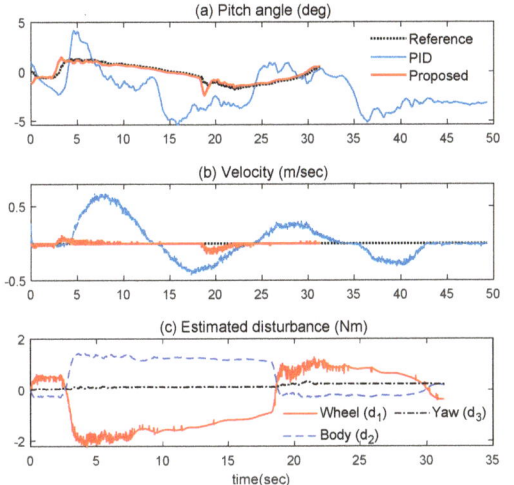

Figure 12. Effect of the longitudinal eccentricity.

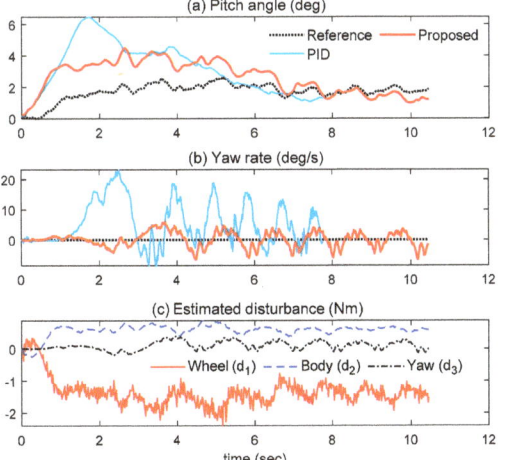

Figure 13. Effect of the lateral eccentricity.

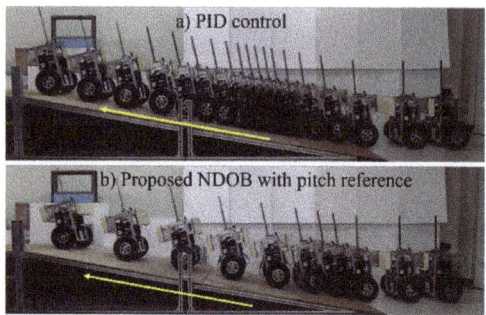

Figure 14. Effect of the terrain uncertainty during uphill driving.

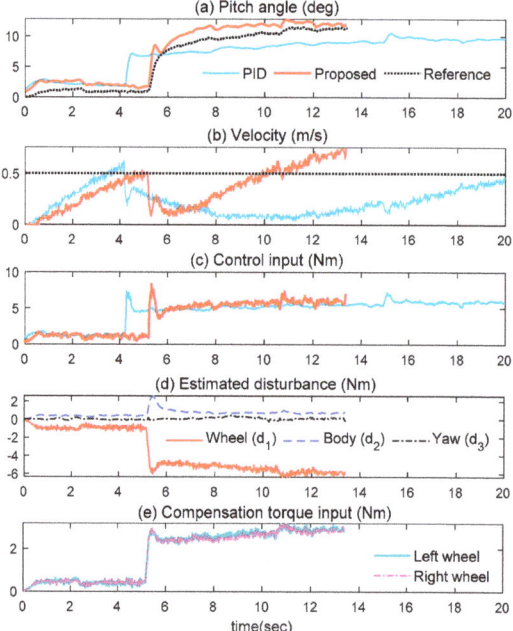

Figure 15. Effect of the terrain uncertainty during uphill driving.

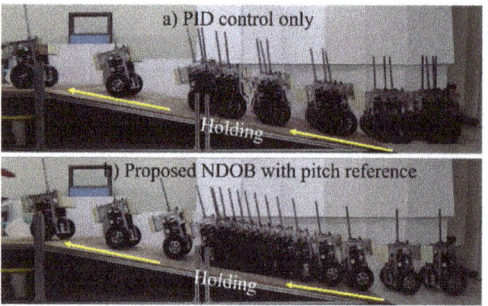

Figure 16. Holding a standstill position on the slope.

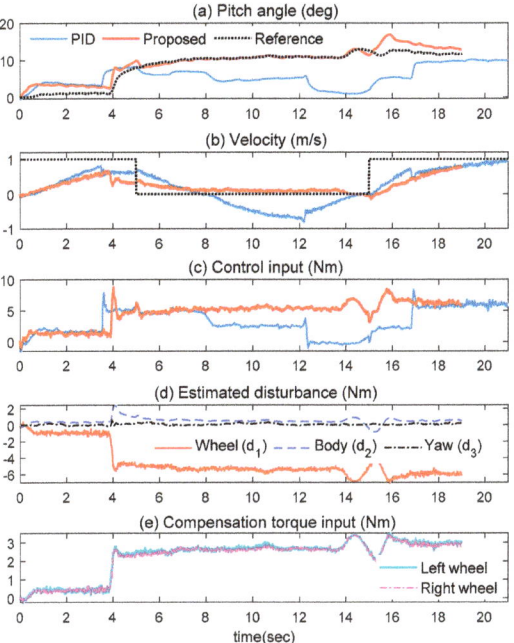

Figure 17. Holding a standstill position on the slope.

As shown in Figure 13, the COG of the pendulum was intentionally biased in the lateral direction. As a result, it predominantly worked as a yaw disturbance. Without the yaw attitude control, the lateral eccentric effect made the robot deviate far from the straight line in a short period of time when it was only under the PID yaw-rate control. In contrast, the proposed dynamic compensator prevented the robot from drifting by producing the appropriate torque compensation input for the yaw disturbance. On the other hand, the estimates in Figure 13c corresponding to the wheel and the body disturbances were mainly derived from the parametric errors due to the extra dummy weight.

An uphill driving experiment was then conducted to validate the robustness of the proposed scheme for uncertain terrains. As shown in Figures 14 and 15, the TWIP robot met the inclined surface while driving on a flat plain with a reference velocity of 0.5 m/s and climbed the ramp with an unknown slope of 10 degrees. The results were almost the same as anticipated in the simulation studies. With only the nominal PID controller, the TWIP robot could hardly travel on a ramp since it took quite some time to reach the static equilibrium corresponding to the slope. Although a little slowdown of the speed occurred at the uphill entry, the proposed method enabled the TWIP to steadily climb the ramp by combining the quick generation of the pitch equilibrium angle and the torque compensation input in Equation (11). In the downhill phase, the situation was reversed. Under only the PID control, the robot greatly accelerated, due to the gravitational effect, until the pitch angle converged to the equilibrium point, but the real-time pitch reference in terms of the NDOB prevented a rapid increase in speed and achieved steady downhill movement.

Finally, as shown in Figures 16 and 17, a zero-velocity command was given to the robot for 10 s in the middle of climbing. As shown, using the PID controller without an appropriate pitch reference generation, holding a standstill position on an unknown slope was almost impossible for the underactuated TWIP robot. However, in the NDOB-based robust control approach, the ramp disturbance could be promptly detected, and the posture control performance could be greatly improved by assigning the time-varying pitch reference according to the real-time disturbance estimates.

6. Conclusions

Compared with the previous results on the robust control of the TWIP as an underactuated system, a great merit of the proposed method lies in its physical intuitiveness in drawing the compensation input to tackle uncertain terrains. A sound understanding of the static equilibrium on the slope, the input coupling of the acrobot, and the performance limit of conventional NDOBs for unmatched disturbances led to the establishment of a clear relationship between the disturbance estimates and the compensation input. In addition to unmanned, two-wheeled balancing vehicles, the dynamic compensation scheme developed in this paper can be effectively applied to enhance the control capabilities of wheeled humanoids and mobile manipulators, which are fundamentally based on the TWIP technology, specifically when they are performing on uncertain terrains.

Author Contributions: Conceptualization, Y.K.; formal analysis, Y.K.; funding acquisition, S.K.; investigation, Y.K. and S.K.; methodology, Y.K.; project administration, S.K.; software, Y.K.; supervision, S.K.; writing—original draft preparation, Y.K.; writing—review and editing, S.K. All authors have read and agreed to the published version of the manuscript.

Funding: This work was supported by the National Research Foundation of Korea, grant number NRF-2022R1F1A1073383.

Conflicts of Interest: The authors declare no conflict of interest.

Appendix A

Elements of the Matrices and Vectors in Equation (A1)

$$\begin{aligned}
m_{11} &= m_B + 2m_w + 2J/r^2 \\
m_{12} &= m_{21} = m_B l \cos\theta \\
m_{22} &= m_B l^2 + I_2 \\
m_{33} &= I_3 + 2K + (d^2/2)(m_w + J/r) - (I_3 - I_1 - m_B l^2)\sin^2\theta \\
c_{12} &= -(m_B l \sin\theta)\dot\theta^2, \quad c_{13} = -(m_B l \sin\theta)\dot\psi^2 \\
c_{23} &= (I_3 - I_1 - m_B l^2)(\sin\theta \cos\theta)\dot\psi^2 \\
c_{31} &= (m_B l \sin\theta)\dot\psi\dot x \\
c_{32} &= -2(I_3 - I_1 - m_B l^2)\dot\theta\dot\psi \\
g_1 &= g_3 = 0 \\
g_2 &= -m_B g l \sin\theta
\end{aligned} \qquad (A1)$$

References

1. Segway, A. Two-Wheeled Self-Balancing Personal Transporter. Available online: https://en.wikipedia.org/wiki/Segway (accessed on 25 May 2022).
2. Personal Urban Mobility and Accessibility (PUMA). Available online: https://en.wikipedia.org/wiki/Personal_Urban_Mobility_and_Accessibility (accessed on 17 November 2022).
3. Vermeiren, L.; Dequidt, A.; Guerra, T.M.; Rago-Tirmant, H.; Parent, M. Modeling, control and experimental verification on a two-wheeled vehicle with free inclination: An urban transportation system. *Control Eng. Pract.* **2011**, *19*, 744–756. [CrossRef]
4. Takahashi, Y.; Kohda, M. Human riding experiments on soft front wheel raising of robotic wheelchair with inverse pendulum control. In Proceedings of the 2005 IEEE International Conference on Industrial Technology, Hong Kong, China, 14–17 December 2005; pp. 266–271.
5. Boston Dynamics. Available online: https://www.bostondynamics.com/legacy (accessed on 25 May 2022).
6. Zafar, M.; Hutchinson, S.; Theodorou, E.A. Hierarchical optimization for whole-body control of wheeled inverted pendulum humanoids. In Proceedings of the 2019 International Conference on Robotics and Automation (ICRA), Montreal, QC, Canada, 20–24 May 2019; pp. 7535–7542.
7. Klemm, V.; Morra, A.; Gulich, L.; Mannhart, D.; Rohr, D.; Kamel, M.; de Viragh, Y.; Siegwart, R. LQR-Assisted Whole-Body Control of a Wheeled Bipedal Robot With Kinematic Loops. *IEEE Robot. Autom. Lett.* **2020**, *5*, 3745–3752. [CrossRef]
8. Huang, J.; Ding, F.; Fukuda, T.; Matsuno, T. Modeling and velocity control for a novel narrow vehicle based on mobile wheeled inverted pendulum. *IEEE Trans. Control Syst. Technol.* **2013**, *22*, 1607–1617. [CrossRef]
9. Larimi, S.R.; Zarafshan, P.; Moosavian, S.A.A. A New Stabilization Algorithm for a Two-Wheeled Mobile Robot Aided by Reaction Wheel. *J. Dyn. Syst. Meas. Control* **2014**, *137*, 011009. [CrossRef]

10. Chan, R.P.M.; Stol, K.A.; Halkyard, C.R. Review of modelling and control of two-wheeled robots. *Annu. Rev. Control* **2013**, *37*, 89–103. [CrossRef]
11. Li, Z.; Yang, C. Neural-Adaptive Output Feedback Control of a Class of Transportation Vehicles Based on Wheeled Inverted Pendulum Models. *IEEE Trans. Control Syst. Technol.* **2011**, *20*, 1583–1591. [CrossRef]
12. Ravichandran, M.T.; Mahindrakar, A. Robust Stabilization of a Class of Underactuated Mechanical Systems Using Time Scaling and Lyapunov Redesign. *IEEE Trans. Ind. Electron.* **2010**, *58*, 4299–4313. [CrossRef]
13. Kim, S.; Kwon, S. Nonlinear Optimal Control Design for Underactuated Two-Wheeled Inverted Pendulum Mobile Platform. *IEEE/ASME Trans. Mechatron.* **2017**, *22*, 2803–2808. [CrossRef]
14. Canete, L.; Takahashi, T. Disturbance compensation in pushing, pulling, and lifting for load transporting control of a wheeled inverted pendulum type assistant robot using the extended state observer. In Proceedings of the 2012 IEEE/RSJ International Conference on Intelligent Robots and Systems, Vilamoura-Algarve, Portugal, 7–12 October 2012; pp. 5373–5380.
15. Huang, J.; Ri, S.; Liu, L.; Wang, Y.; Kim, J.; Pak, G. Nonlinear Disturbance Observer-Based Dynamic Surface Control of Mobile Wheeled Inverted Pendulum. *IEEE Trans. Control Syst. Technol.* **2015**, *23*, 2400–2407. [CrossRef]
16. Huang, J.; Guan, Z.-H.; Matsuno, T.; Fukuda, T.; Sekiyama, K. Sliding-Mode Velocity Control of Mobile-Wheeled Inverted-Pendulum Systems. *IEEE Trans. Robot.* **2010**, *26*, 750–758. [CrossRef]
17. Xu, J.-X.; Guo, Z.-Q.; Lee, T.H. Design and Implementation of Integral Sliding-Mode Control on an Underactuated Two-Wheeled Mobile Robot. *IEEE Trans. Ind. Electron.* **2013**, *61*, 3671–3681. [CrossRef]
18. Huang, J.; Zhang, M.; Ri, S.; Xiong, C.; Li, Z.; Kang, Y. High-order disturbance-observer-based sliding model control for mobile wheeled inverted pendulum systems. *IEEE Trans. Ind. Electron.* **2020**, *67*, 2030–2041. [CrossRef]
19. Dai, F.; Gao, X.; Jiang, S.; Liu, Y.; Li, J. A multi-DOF two wheeled inverted pendulum robot climbing on a slope. In Proceedings of the 2014 IEEE International Conference on Robotics and Biomimetics (ROBIO 2014), Bali, Indonesia, 5–10 December 2014; pp. 1958–1963.
20. Peng, K.; Ruan, X.; Zuo, G. Dynamic model and balancing control for two-wheeled self-balancing mobile robot on the slopes. In Proceedings of the 10th World Congress on Intelligent Control and Automation, Beijing, China, 6–8 July 2012; pp. 3681–3685.
21. Takei, T.; Matsumoto, O.; Komoriya, K. Simultaneous estimation of slope angle and handling force when getting on and off a human-riding wheeled inverted pendulum vehicle. In Proceedings of the 2009 IEEE/RSJ International Conference on Intelligent Robots and Systems, St. Louis, MO, USA, 10–15 October 2009; pp. 4553–4558.
22. Kausar, Z.; Stol, K.; Patel, N. The Effect of Terrain Inclination on Performance and the Stability Region of Two-Wheeled Mobile Robots. *Int. J. Adv. Robot. Syst.* **2012**, *9*, 218. [CrossRef]
23. Hirata, K.; Kamatani, M.; Murakami, T. Advanced motion control of two-wheel wheelchair for slope environment. In Proceedings of the IECON 2013-39th Annual Conference of the IEEE Industrial Electronics Society, Vienna, Austria, 10–13 November 2013; pp. 6436–6441.
24. Kim, S.; Kwon, S. Dynamic modeling of a two-wheeled inverted pendulum balancing mobile robot. *Int. J. Control Autom. Syst.* **2015**, *13*, 926–933. [CrossRef]
25. Liu, Y.; Yu, H. A survey of underactuated mechanical systems. *IET Control Theory Appl.* **2013**, *7*, 921–935. [CrossRef]
26. Dinale, A.; Hirata, K.; Zoppi, M.; Murakami, T. Parameter Design of Disturbance Observer for a Robust Control of Two-Wheeled Wheelchair System. *J. Intell. Robot. Syst.* **2014**, *77*, 135–148. [CrossRef]
27. Chen, W.-H.; Yang, J.; Guo, L.; Li, S. Disturbance-Observer-Based Control and Related Methods—An Overview. *IEEE Trans. Ind. Electron.* **2015**, *63*, 1083–1095. [CrossRef]
28. Chen, W.-H. Disturbance Observer Based Control for Nonlinear Systems. *IEEE/ASME Trans. Mechatron.* **2004**, *9*, 706–710. [CrossRef]
29. Chen, W.-H.; Ballance, D.J.; Gawthrop, P.J.; Gribble, J.J.; Reilly, J.O. A nonlinear disturbance observer for two link robotic manipulators. *IEEE Trans. Ind. Electron.* **2000**, *47*, 932–938. [CrossRef]
30. Riachy, S.; Orlov, Y.; Floquet, T.; Santiesteban, R.; Richard, J. Second order sliding mode control of underactuated me-chanical systems I: Local stabilization with application to an inverted pendulum. *Int. J. Robust Nonlinear Control* **2008**, *18*, 529–543. [CrossRef]
31. Kim, S.; Kwon, S.J. Robust transition control of underactuated two-wheeled self-balancing vehicle with semi-online dy-namic trajectory planning. *Mechatronics* **2020**, *68*, 102366. [CrossRef]
32. Simscape. Available online: https://mathworks.com/products/simscape-multibody.html (accessed on 25 May 2022).
33. Tariq, M.; Bhattacharya, T.K.; Varshney, N.; Rajapan, D. Fast response Anti windup PI speed controller of Brushless DC motor drive: Modeling, simulation and implementation on DSP. *J. Electr. Syst. Inf. Technol.* **2016**, *3*, 1–13. [CrossRef]

Article

Time-Optimal Trajectory Planning of 6-DOF Manipulator Based on Fuzzy Control

Feifan He [1] and Qingjiu Huang [2,*]

[1] School of Information and Electronic Engineering, Zhejiang Gongshang University, Hangzhou 310018, China
[2] Control System Laboratory, Graduate School of Engineering, Kogakuin University, Tokyo 163-8677, Japan
* Correspondence: huang@cc.kogakuin.ac.jp

Abstract: Currently, the teaching programming or offline programming used by an industrial manipulator can manually set the running speed of the manipulator. In this paper, to consider the running speed and stability of the manipulator, the time-optimal trajectory planning (TOTP) of the manipulator is transformed into a nonlinear optimal value search problem under multiple constraints, and a time-search algorithm based on fuzzy control is proposed, so that the end of the manipulator can run along the given path in Cartesian space for the shortest time, and the angular velocity and angular acceleration of each joint is within a limited range. In addition, a simulation model of a 6-DOF manipulator is established in MATLAB, taking a straight-line trajectory of the end of the manipulator in Cartesian space as an example, and the effectiveness and efficiency of the algorithm proposed in this paper are proved by comparing the execution time with the bisection algorithm and the traditional gradient descent method.

Keywords: manipulator; trajectory planning; fuzzy control; time optimization; minimum–maximum rule

1. Introduction

In current industrial production, both the teaching and offline programming can set the running speed of industrial manipulators, but the running speed of the manipulator is still relatively slow in many industrial applications. This is because reducing the running speed of the manipulator can reduce the angular velocity and angular acceleration of the joints of the manipulator, thereby reducing the vibration and jitter during the operation of the manipulator, improving its operation stability, and prolonging its service life [1]. However, reducing the running speed of the manipulator also reduces its production benefits [2,3].

Research into manipulators is divided into several aspects, such as manipulator control algorithms, trajectory planning and servo drive. Trajectory planning is an important part of the design process of manipulator control systems. At present, the mainstream research direction of trajectory planning is to optimize the trajectory of manipulators, including time optimization, jerk optimization [4], energy optimization [5], and multi-objective optimization considering time, jerk and energy [6]. In addition, manipulator obstacle avoidance [7] has become an increasing focus of trajectory planning.

The main goal of this paper is to perform TOTP in Cartesian space, making the planned trajectory time-optimal and smooth. Below, the research background and research methods of the TOTP of the manipulator will be elaborated from joint space and Cartesian space.

For TOTP in joint space, so far, there are some study methods, including limiting the joint torque rate [8], expressing joint torque and joint velocity constraints as functions of path coordinates to generate velocity limit curves [9], and the CPG method based on kinematic constraints [10]. Moreover, some algorithms are used to solve for TOTP, such as the bisection algorithm [11], input-shaping algorithm [12], hybrid-improved whale optimization and particle-swarm optimization (IWOA-PSO) algorithm [13], adaptive cuckoo search (ACS) algorithm [14], genetic algorithm (GA) [3,15], firefly algorithm [16], and simulated annealing (SA) algorithm [17]. Deep learning is also used to plan the trajectory of the grasping movement of the manipulator [18], which greatly shortens the calculation time of trajectory planning.

The above methods can plan a time-optimal and smooth trajectory; however, the TOTP in joint space only allows the manipulator to perform point-to-point (PTP) tasks, such as handling, pick-and-place, and palletizing. If the end of the manipulator moves along straight lines, arcs, or free curves, it is necessary to plan a Cartesian space trajectory.

For the TOTP of Cartesian space, there are two study methods. The first considers the distance and velocity of the end effector along a specified path as the state vector and converts the nonlinear dynamic constraints of the manipulator into state-related constraints of acceleration along the path [2]. The second transforms the time-optimal path tracking problem into a convex optimal control problem of a single state [19]. On the basis of these two study methods, there is a method based on the reachability analysis theory to transform the TOTP problem and achieve efficient solutions through multiple linear programming [20], and the other method that transforms the TOTP problem into a finite-dimensional second-order cone programming problem [21]. The sequential quadratic programming method (SQP) [22] is also used to solve the TOTP of the end of the manipulator along the spline curve, taking into account the continuity of joint acceleration and jerk. However, none of the references [2,19–21] consider acceleration continuity at the end of the manipulator, therefore, during the moving process, the joint torque of the manipulator will change abruptly, resulting in vibration and shaking, which affect the stability and accuracy of the manipulator.

In view of the above research background, to solve the problem of joint space trajectory planning that can only perform PTP tasks, and to solve the problem of manipulator instability caused by the sudden change in joint torque in the TOTP in Cartesian space, this paper proposes a new offline algorithm for TOTP of manipulators based on fuzzy control, which makes the end of the manipulator run with the shortest time along a given path in Cartesian space and avoids sudden changes in the angular velocity and angular acceleration of each joint, thus compensating for the shortcomings of the above research. First, the kinematic and dynamic model of a universal 6-joint industrial robot is established. Subsequently, the TOTP problem of the manipulator is transformed into a nonlinear optimal value search problem under multiple constraints, and an adaptive time search algorithm based on fuzzy control (ATSA-FC) is proposed to calculate the shortest time of Cartesian space trajectory under the constraints of the angular velocity and angular acceleration of each joint of the manipulator. Furthermore, a simulation model of the above-mentioned manipulator is established in MATLAB. Taking a straight-line trajectory of the end of the manipulator in Cartesian space as an example, the method proposed in this paper is used to calculate the shortest time of this trajectory. At the same time, two common nonlinear search algorithms are also selected: the bisection algorithm (BA) [11,23] and the gradient descent method with constant proportional coefficient (GDM-CPC) [24]. The trajectory times and execution times of these two algorithms are compared with ATSA-FC proposed in this paper to verify the efficiency of ATSA-FC.

The remainder of this paper is organized as follows. Section 2 introduces kinematic and dynamic models of the manipulator. Section 3 introduces the trajectory planning method for the end of the manipulator. Section 4 introduces the transformation of TOTP to a nonlinear optimal value search problem and three TOTP algorithms used in this paper, which are BA, GDM-CPC, and ATSA-FC. Section 5 introduces the simulation of TOTP of the manipulator based on MATLAB. Section 6 presents the conclusions of this paper.

2. Manipulator Kinematics and Dynamics Model

The manipulator used in this paper is a 6-DOF wrist-separated manipulator which satisfies the Piper criterion and has a closed solution [25]. The position-level kinematic model of this type of manipulator is established using the standard D-H method, and the D-H parameters table of the manipulator is shown in Table 1.

Table 1. D-H Parameter of the 6-DOF Manipulator.

Link i	θ_i (°)	d_i (m)	a_i (m)	α_i (°)
1	0	1	0	90
2	90	0	2	0
3	0	0	0	90
4	0	2	0	90
5	90	0	0	−90
6	0	1	0	0

Using the above D-H parameters, the schematic diagram of the manipulator in this paper is shown in Figure 1.

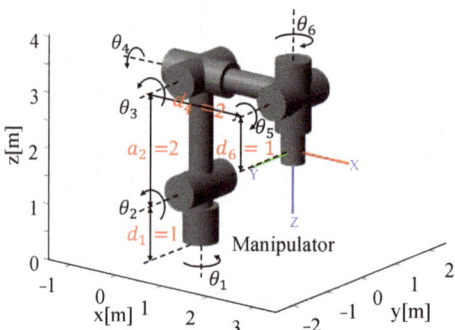

Figure 1. Schematic of the manipulator.

Forward position-level kinematic of the manipulator solves the position and attitude of the end of the manipulator relative to the base by the given joint angles. Let $^{i-1}_{i}T$ be the homogeneous transformation matrix of the connecting rod coordinate system Σ_{i-1} to Σ_i. According to the D-H rule, $^{i-1}_{i}T$ is shown in Equation (1).

$$^{i-1}_{i}T = \begin{bmatrix} c\theta_i & -s\theta_i c\alpha_i & s\theta_i s\alpha_i & a_i c\theta_i \\ s\theta_i & c\theta_i c\alpha_i & -c\theta_i s\alpha_i & a_i s\theta_i \\ 0 & s\alpha_i & c\alpha_i & d_i \\ 0 & 0 & 0 & 1 \end{bmatrix} \quad (1)$$

where $c\theta_i = \cos\theta_i$, $c\alpha_i = \cos\alpha_i$, $s\theta_i = \sin\theta_i$, $s\alpha_i = \sin\alpha_i$.

Therefore, the homogeneous matrix of the manipulator end coordinate system Σ_n relative to the base coordinate system Σ_0 is shown in Equation (2).

$$^{0}_{n}T = {}^{0}_{1}T(\theta_1){}^{1}_{2}T(\theta_2)\cdots{}^{n-1}_{n}T(\theta_n) = fkine(\theta) \quad (2)$$

This paper uses the axis/angle notation to represent the attitude at the end of the manipulator. For any rotation matrix R, it can be considered as a single rotation around an appropriate axis in space through an appropriate angle, and the axis/angle representation is shown in Equation (3).

$$R = R_{(k,\phi)} \quad (3)$$

where k is the unit vector defining the axis of rotation, ϕ is the angle rotated around axis k, and the pair (k,ϕ) is called the axis/angle representation of R [26].

Given any rotation matrix R, whose element is a_{ij}, the corresponding rotation angle ϕ and axis k are shown in Equations (4) and (5), respectively.

$$\phi = acos(\frac{tr(R)-1}{2}) \tag{4}$$

$$k = \frac{1}{2\sin\phi}[a_{32}-a_{23} \quad a_{13}-a_{31} \quad a_{21}-a_{12}]^T = [k_x \quad k_y \quad k_z]^T \tag{5}$$

The axis/angle notation for the rotation matrix R is not unique because the rotation angle ϕ about axis k and the rotation angle $-\phi$ about axis $-k$ are equivalent, as shown in Equation (6).

$$R_{(k,\phi)} = R_{(-k,-\phi)} \tag{6}$$

If $\phi = 0$, then R is the identity matrix and axis k is not defined at this time. Because k is a unit vector, the equivalent axis/angle representation can be represented by a single vector r, and the vector r is shown in Equation (7).

$$r = \phi k = [\alpha \quad \beta \quad \gamma]^T \tag{7}$$

where $\alpha = \phi k_x$, $\beta = \phi k_y$, $\gamma = \phi k_z$. The length of vector r is the angle ϕ, and the direction of vector r is the equivalent axis of rotation k.

Therefore, in addition to using a homogeneous transformation matrix to represent the position and attitude of the end of the manipulator, it can also be represented by a 6-dimensional vector X_e, where X_e is shown in Equation (8).

$$X_e = [x_e \quad y_e \quad z_e \quad \alpha_e \quad \beta_e \quad \gamma_e]^T \tag{8}$$

where y_e, z_e represent the positions of the end of the manipulator, and α_e, β_e, γ_e represent the attitudes of the end of the manipulator.

The linear velocity v_e and linear acceleration a_e at the end of the manipulator are shown in Equations (9) and (10), respectively.

$$v_e = [\dot{x}_e \quad \dot{y}_e \quad \dot{z}_e]^T \tag{9}$$

$$a_e = [\ddot{x}_e \quad \ddot{y}_e \quad \ddot{z}_e]^T \tag{10}$$

The attitude angular velocity w_e and the attitude angular acceleration $\dot{w}_e$ are shown in Equations (11) and (12), respectively.

$$w_e = [\dot{\alpha}_e \quad \dot{\beta}_e \quad \dot{\gamma}_e]^T \tag{11}$$

$$\dot{w}_e = [\ddot{\alpha}_e \quad \ddot{\beta}_e \quad \ddot{\gamma}_e]^T \tag{12}$$

According to Equations (9)–(12), the velocity at the end of manipulator $\dot{X}_e$ and the acceleration at the end of manipulator $\ddot{X}_e$ are shown in Equations (13) and (14).

$$\dot{X}_e = [\dot{x}_e \quad \dot{y}_e \quad \dot{z}_e \quad \dot{\alpha}_e \quad \dot{\beta}_e \quad \dot{\gamma}_e]^T \tag{13}$$

$$\ddot{X}_e = [\ddot{x}_e \quad \ddot{y}_e \quad \ddot{z}_e \quad \ddot{\alpha}_e \quad \ddot{\beta}_e \quad \ddot{\gamma}_e]^T \tag{14}$$

The transfer matrix between the joint angular velocity and the end velocity of the manipulator is called the Jacobian matrix J. The Jacobian matrix is a function of joint angle θ, as shown in Equation (15).

$$J = J(\theta) \tag{15}$$

The forward velocity-level kinematic equation of the manipulator is shown in Equation (16).

$$\dot{X}_e = J\dot{\theta} \qquad (16)$$

where $\dot{\theta}$ represents the joint velocity.

When J is a reversible square matrix, the inverse velocity-level kinematic equation of the manipulator can be obtained from Equation (16), as shown in Equation (17).

$$\dot{\theta} = J^{-1}\dot{X}_e \qquad (17)$$

Taking the derivation of both sides of Equation (16), the forward acceleration-level kinematic equation of the manipulator can be obtained, as shown in Equation (18).

$$\ddot{X}_e = J\ddot{\theta} + \dot{J}\dot{\theta} \qquad (18)$$

When J is a reversible square matrix, the inverse acceleration-level kinematic equation of the manipulator can be obtained from Equation (18), as shown in Equation (19).

$$\ddot{\theta} = J^{-1}(\ddot{X}_e - \dot{J}\dot{\theta}) \qquad (19)$$

$\dot{J}$ is the derivative of the Jacobian matrix with respect to time, as shown in Equation (20).

$$\dot{J} = \lim_{t \to 0} \frac{J(\theta + \dot{\theta}) - J(\theta)}{t} \qquad (20)$$

The dynamic equation of the manipulator [8] is shown in Equation (21).

$$\tau = M(\theta)\ddot{\theta} + C(\theta,\dot{\theta})\dot{\theta} + G(\theta) \qquad (21)$$

where $M(\theta)$ is the inertia force matrix, $C(\theta,\dot{\theta})$ is the cordial force and centrifugal force matrix, $G(\theta)$ is the gravity term matrix, and τ is the joint torque vector.

3. Trajectory Planning

There are two main types of trajectory planning for manipulators; one is trajectory planning in joint space and the other is trajectory planning in Cartesian space [27]. Given that trajectory planning in joint space is not capable of high-precision work, this paper performs trajectory planning of Cartesian space for the manipulator, and then uses the kinematic model in Section 2 to obtain the corresponding joint-space trajectory.

The traditional trapezoidal velocity curve at the end of the manipulator is shown in Figure 2, and the acceleration curve of the trapezoidal velocity is shown in Figure 3. As shown in Figure 3, the acceleration curve of the trapezoidal velocity changes abruptly. It can be seen from Equation (19) that when the acceleration of the end of the manipulator changes abruptly, the angular acceleration of the joint also changes abruptly.

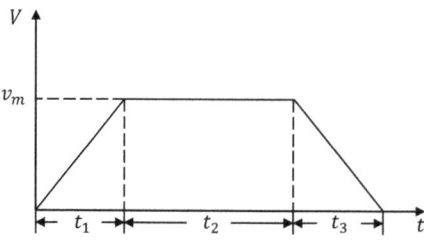

Figure 2. Trapezoidal velocity curve.

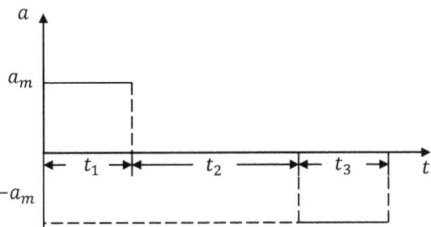

Figure 3. Acceleration curve of trapezoidal velocity.

According to Equation (21), it can be shown that an abrupt change in the angular acceleration of the joint indicates an abrupt change in the torque of the joint motor, which causes mechanical vibration, impacting and affecting the accuracy and service life of the manipulator [28]. Conversely, a continuous change in joint angular velocity and angular acceleration causes a continuous change in joint torque. Therefore, in this paper, the S-shaped velocity curve [13] is used to replace the trapezoidal velocity curve shown in Figure 2. The S-shaped velocity curve is shown in Figure 4, and the acceleration curve of the S-shaped velocity is shown in Figure 5. The acceleration and deceleration segments of the S-shaped velocity curve are 5th order polynomials. It can be seen from Figures 4 and 5 that the S-shaped velocity curve and acceleration curve of the S-shaped velocity change continuously. Equations (17) and (19) show that the joint angular velocity and angular acceleration of the manipulator change continuously, so the torque of the manipulator also changes continuously.

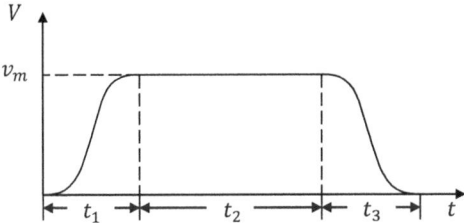

Figure 4. S-shaped velocity curve.

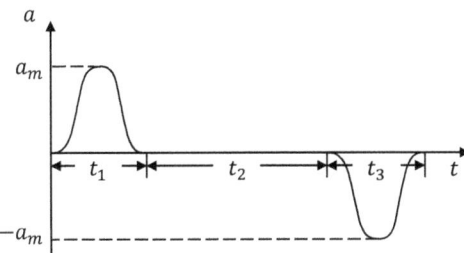

Figure 5. Acceleration curve of the S-shaped velocity.

In this paper, trajectory planner P was designed to plan a trajectory with continuously changing acceleration in Cartesian space. P is represented by Equation (22).

$$X_e, \dot{X}_e, \ddot{X}_e = P(t, kt, p, r, n) \qquad (22)$$

where t is the trajectory running time, kt is the trajectory type, p is the constraint points set of the trajectory, which is represented by homogeneous matrices, r is the ratio of acceleration and deceleration time, and n is the number of trajectory points.

To plan a straight-line trajectory in Cartesian space, two constraint points are required and the distance between the two constraint points is used as the planning distance. To plan an arc trajectory, three constraint points are required, and the central angle of the arc where these three points are located is used as the planning distance.

Assuming that a straight-line trajectory is planned, the known spatial distance of the two constraint points is l, total running time is t, and ratio of acceleration to deceleration time is r.

The velocity $v(x)$ of this trajectory is shown in Equation (23).

$$v(x) = \begin{cases} v_a(x), & x \in [0, rt) \\ v_b(x), & x \in [rt, (1-r)t) \\ v_c(x), & x \in [(1-r)t, t] \end{cases} \quad (23)$$

where $v_a(x)$ denotes the 5th order polynomial velocity curve of the acceleration segment, $v_b(x)$ denotes the velocity of the uniform velocity segment, and $v_c(x)$ denotes the 5th order polynomial velocity curve of the deceleration segment.

$$l = \int_0^t v(x)dx \quad (24)$$

$$l_a = \int_0^{rt} v_a(x)dx \quad (25)$$

$$l_c = \int_{(1-r)t}^t v_c(x)dx \quad (26)$$

Let $v_b(x) = v_m$, then v_m can be written as Equation (27).

$$v_m = \frac{l - l_a - l_c}{(1 - 2r)t} \quad (27)$$

Because the first and second derivatives of $v_a(x)$ and $v_c(x)$ at 0, rt, $(1-r)t$ and t are both 0, l_a and l_c can be written as Equation (28).

$$l_a = l_c = \frac{v_m rt}{2} \quad (28)$$

Thus, v_m can be written as Equation (29).

$$v_m = \frac{l}{(1 - r)t} \quad (29)$$

When a uniform velocity v_m is obtained, the 5th order polynomial velocity planning can be performed.

Suppose the time period starting from t_s to t_e, the velocity of the end of the manipulator is $v(t)$, and $v(t)$ is shown in Equation (30).

$$v(t) = at^5 + bt^4 + ct^3 + dt^2 + et + f \quad (30)$$

There are the following six boundary conditions,

$$v(t_s) = v_s, v'(t_s) = a_s, v''(t_s) = j_s$$
$$v(t_e) = v_e, v'(t_e) = a_e, v''(t_e) = j_e$$

The first-order derivative $v'(t)$ and the second-order derivative $v''(t)$ of $v(t)$ are shown in Equations (31) and (32), respectively.

$$v'(t) = 5at^4 + 4bt^3 + 3ct^2 + 2dt + e \quad (31)$$

$$v''(t) = 20at^3 + 12bt^2 + 6ct + 2d \tag{32}$$

Substituting the above six boundary conditions into Equations (30)–(32), the following six equations can be obtained, as shown in Equations (33)–(38).

$$at_s^5 + bt_s^4 + ct_s^3 + dt_s^2 + et_s + f = v_s \tag{33}$$

$$at_e^5 + bt_e^4 + ct_e^3 + dt_e^2 + et_e + f = v_e \tag{34}$$

$$5at_s^4 + 4bt_s^3 + 3ct_s^2 + 2dt_s + e = a_s \tag{35}$$

$$5at_e^4 + 4bt_e^3 + 3ct_e^2 + 2dt_e + e = a_e \tag{36}$$

$$20at_s^3 + 12bt_s^2 + 6ct_s + 2d = j_s \tag{37}$$

$$20at_e^3 + 12bt_e^2 + 6ct_e + 2d = j_e \tag{38}$$

Equations (33)–(38) can be written in the form of matrix multiplication, as shown in Equation (39).

$$Ax = y \tag{39}$$

where

$$A = \begin{bmatrix} t_s^5 & t_s^4 & t_s^3 & t_s^2 & t_s & 1 \\ t_e^5 & t_e^4 & t_e^3 & t_e^2 & t_e & 1 \\ 5t_s^4 & 4t_s^3 & 3t_s^2 & 2t_s & 1 & 0 \\ 5t_e^4 & 4t_e^3 & 3t_e^2 & 2t_e & 1 & 0 \\ 20t_s^3 & 12t_s^2 & 6t_s & 2 & 0 & 0 \\ 20t_e^3 & 12t_e^2 & 6t_e & 2 & 0 & 0 \end{bmatrix}$$

$$x = \begin{bmatrix} a & b & c & d & e & f \end{bmatrix}^T$$

$$y = \begin{bmatrix} v_s & v_e & a_s & a_e & j_s & j_e \end{bmatrix}^T$$

Because A is invertible, Equation (39) can be rewritten as Equation (40).

$$x = A^{-1}y \tag{40}$$

By substituting the boundary conditions of the acceleration, uniform velocity, and deceleration into Equation (40), the velocity change curve can be obtained, and the acceleration and displacement change curves can be obtained through differentiation and integration, respectively.

Similarly, the angular velocity and angular acceleration of the attitude at the end of the manipulator only need to be planned by changing the spatial distance l to the attitude angle ϕ.

Through the trajectory constraint points of the trajectory planner P, the attitude matrices R_s and R_e at the initial and final moments of the end of the manipulator can be determined, and R_e is shown in Equation (41).

$$R_e = R_t R_s \tag{41}$$

where R_t is the rotation matrix that changes from R_s to R_e, and R_t is shown in Equation (42).

$$R_t = R_e R_s^{-1} \tag{42}$$

Substituting R_t into Equations (4) and (5), attitude rotation angle ϕ and rotation axis k can be obtained. The rotation matrix R_i corresponding to the attitude of each trajectory point, is shown in Equation (43).

$$R_i = c_{\phi_i} E_3 + (1 - c_{\phi_i}) kk^T + s_{\phi_i} k^\times \tag{43}$$

where ϕ_i represents the rotation angle corresponding to the i-th trajectory point, E_3 is the unit matrix of 3×3, $k^\times$ is the antisymmetric matrix of vector k, and $k^\times$ is shown in Equation (44).

$$k^\times = \begin{bmatrix} 0 & -k_z & k_y \\ k_z & 0 & -k_x \\ -k_y & k_x & 0 \end{bmatrix} \quad (44)$$

4. Time-Optimal Trajectory Planning Algorithm

In this paper, the trajectory running time t is used as the control variable, the joint angular velocity and joint angular acceleration of the manipulator are used as the state variables, and the TOTP problem of the manipulator in Cartesian space is regarded as an optimal-value search problem under multiple constraints. In this paper, the minimum–maximum rule is used to solve the problem of multiple constraints, and avoids the situation of local optimal solution when using time-search algorithms to find the trajectory shortest time.

4.1. Problem Description of Time-Optimal Trajectory Planning

In the process of trajectory planning, if only the constraint condition of the angular acceleration of joint i is considered, then a time t can be found such that when the manipulator is running along the trajectory, the maximum angular acceleration of joint i reaches the angular acceleration constraint condition of joint i; t at this time is the shortest time that only considers the constraint condition of the angular acceleration of joint i. A block diagram of TOTP is shown in Figure 6. The joint parameters $(\theta, \dot{\theta}, \ddot{\theta})$ after each trajectory planning and inverse kinematic were compared with the joint constraints, and a time search was performed.

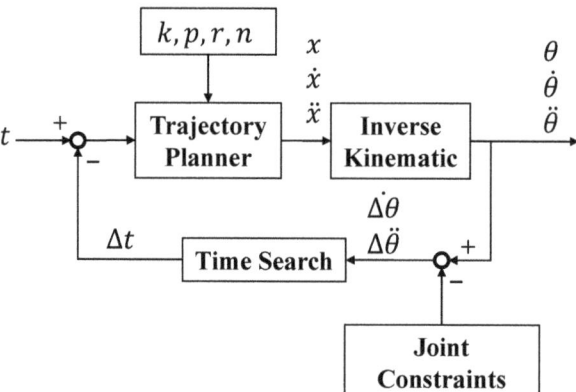

Figure 6. The block diagram of time-optimal trajectory planning.

The joint constraints of the manipulator are listed in Table 2; $\dot{\theta}_{ilim}$ represents the joint angular velocity constraint, $\ddot{\theta}_{ilim}$ represents the joint angular acceleration constraint. There were 12 constraints corresponding to the 12 shortest times. Using the minimum–maximum rule, the maximum value of the 12 shortest times is the shortest time of the trajectory.

Table 2. Joint Constraints of The Manipulator.

Joint i	Angular Velocity $\dot{\theta}_{ilim}$ (°/s)	Angular Acceleration $\ddot{\theta}_{ilim}$ (°/s²)
1	$\dot{\theta}_{1lim}$	$\ddot{\theta}_{1lim}$
2	$\dot{\theta}_{2lim}$	$\ddot{\theta}_{2lim}$
3	$\dot{\theta}_{3lim}$	$\ddot{\theta}_{3lim}$
4	$\dot{\theta}_{4lim}$	$\ddot{\theta}_{4lim}$
5	$\dot{\theta}_{5lim}$	$\ddot{\theta}_{5lim}$
6	$\dot{\theta}_{6lim}$	$\ddot{\theta}_{6lim}$

If $\dot{\theta}_{imax}$ or $\ddot{\theta}_{imax}$ satisfies Equations (45) and (46), joint i is considered to have reached the angular velocity or angular acceleration constraint.

$$\dot{\theta}_{imax} \in \dot{\Theta}_{ilim} \tag{45}$$

$$\ddot{\theta}_{imax} \in \ddot{\Theta}_{ilim} \tag{46}$$

Among them,

$$\dot{\Theta}_{ilim} = \dot{\theta}_{ilim} \times 99.8\% \pm 0.2\% = [0.996 \times \dot{\theta}_{ilim}, \dot{\theta}_{ilim}]$$

$$\ddot{\Theta}_{ilim} = \ddot{\theta}_{ilim} \times 99.8\% \pm 0.2\% = [0.996 \times \ddot{\theta}_{ilim}, \ddot{\theta}_{ilim}]$$

$i = 1, 2, \ldots, 6$, $\dot{\theta}_{imax}$ and $\ddot{\theta}_{imax}$ are the maximum angular velocity and maximum angular acceleration generated by the i-th joint during operation, respectively.

Let $\min t_{1i}$ be the shortest time that only considers the angular velocity constraint of joint i, $\min t_{2i}$ is the shortest time that only considers the angular acceleration constraint of joint i, and $\min T$ is the shortest time that the manipulator runs along the Cartesian space trajectory. The problem of TOTP can be described by Equations (47)–(49).

$$\min T = \max\{t_{1i}, t_{2i}\} \tag{47}$$

$$\begin{cases} \min t_{1i} \\ \text{s.t.} \\ t_{1i} > 0 \\ X_e, \dot{X}_e, \ddot{X}_e = P(t_{1i}, k, p, r, n) \\ \theta = ikine(X_e) \\ \dot{\theta} = J^{-1}(\theta)\dot{X}_e \\ \dot{\theta}_{imax} \in \dot{\Theta}_{ilim} \end{cases} \tag{48}$$

$$\begin{cases} \min t_{2i} \\ \text{s.t.} \\ t_{2i} > 0 \\ X_e, \dot{X}_e, \ddot{X}_e = P(t_{2i}, k, p, r, n) \\ \theta = ikine(X_e) \\ \dot{\theta} = J^{-1}(\theta)\dot{X}_e \\ \ddot{\theta} = J^{-1}(\theta)(\ddot{X}_e - \dot{J}(\theta)\dot{\theta}) \\ \ddot{\theta}_{imax} \in \ddot{\Theta}_{ilim} \end{cases} \tag{49}$$

where $i = 1, 2, \ldots, 6$. $X_e, \dot{X}_e, \ddot{X}_e$ are the position, velocity, and acceleration of the trajectory planner to plan the trajectory of the end of the manipulator in Cartesian space, respectively, and *ikine* represents the inverse position-level kinematic.

It can be seen from Equations (47)–(49) that, to solve the shortest time, Equation (48) or Equation (49) needs to be calculated at least once. To solve min T, Equations (48) and (49) must be calculated at least 12 times. Therefore, to reduce the amount of calculation, let $minT_1$ be the shortest time of the trajectory satisfying the angular velocity constraints of the six joints of the manipulator, and let $minT_2$ be the shortest time of the trajectory satisfying the angular acceleration constraints of the six joints of the manipulator. The shortest time min T of the Cartesian space trajectory can be expressed as Equations (50)–(52).

$$minT = \max(T_1, T_2) \tag{50}$$

$$\begin{cases} minT_1 \\ s.t. \\ T_1 > 0 \\ X_e, \dot{X}_e, \ddot{X}_e = P(T_1, k, p, r, n) \\ \theta = ikine(X_e) \\ \dot{\theta} = J^{-1}(\theta)\dot{X}_e \\ \forall \dot{\theta}_i \leq \dot{\theta}_{ilim} \\ \exists \dot{\theta}_{imax} \in \Theta_{ilim} \end{cases} \tag{51}$$

$$\begin{cases} minT_2 \\ s.t. \\ T_2 > 0 \\ X_e, \dot{X}_e, \ddot{X}_e = P(T_2, k, p, r, n) \\ \theta = ikine(X_e) \\ \dot{\theta} = J^{-1}(\theta)\dot{X}_e \\ \ddot{\theta} = J^{-1}(\theta)(\ddot{X}_e - \dot{J}(\theta)\dot{\theta}) \\ \forall \ddot{\theta}_i \leq \ddot{\theta}_{ilim} \\ \exists \ddot{\theta}_{imax} \in \Theta_{ilim} \end{cases} \tag{52}$$

Solving min T requires calculating Equations (51) and (52) at least once, which reduces the amount of computation to 1/6 compared with using Equations (48) and (49). Considering the 12 constraints of the manipulator joints, the shortest time min T of the Cartesian space trajectory can be further expressed by Equation (53).

$$\begin{cases} minT \\ s.t. \\ T > 0 \\ X_e, \dot{X}_e, \ddot{X}_e = P(T, k, p, r, n) \\ \theta = ikine(X_e) \\ \dot{\theta} = J^{-1}(\theta)\dot{X}_e \\ \ddot{\theta} = J^{-1}(\theta)(\ddot{X}_e - (\theta)\dot{\theta}) \\ \forall \dot{\theta}_i \leq \dot{\theta}_{ilim} \cap \forall \ddot{\theta}_i \leq \ddot{\theta}_{ilim} \\ \exists \dot{\theta}_{imax} \in \Theta_{ilim} \cup \exists \ddot{\theta}_{imax} \in \Theta_{ilim} \end{cases} \tag{53}$$

The min T can be obtained by computing Equation (53) at least once. The condition for determining whether the trajectory is time-optimal is shown in Equation (54).

$$\begin{array}{c} \forall \dot{\theta}_i \leq \dot{\theta}_{ilim} \cap \forall \ddot{\theta}_i \leq \ddot{\theta}_{ilim} \\ \exists \dot{\theta}_{imax} \in \Theta_{ilim} \cup \exists \ddot{\theta}_{imax} \in \Theta_{ilim} \end{array} \tag{54}$$

Equation (53) describes the TOTP problem for the Cartesian spatial. Next, it is necessary to use a nonlinear search algorithm to determine the shortest time t of the trajectory, such that the trajectory of the joint space of the manipulator satisfies Equation (54).

4.2. Time-Search Algorithm

This section introduces three kinds of time-search algorithms, which are BA, GDM-CPC, and ATSA-FC. By judging whether the joint trajectory corresponding to the shortest time satisfies Equation (54), the validity of the trajectory is verified. By comparing the execution times of the three algorithms, the efficiency of the ATSA-FC algorithm is verified.

The BA is a widely used search method. Its computational complexity is $O(log(n))$. Therefore, despite the large amount of data, this search method ensures high computational efficiency [23]. The premise of using BA is that the data must be an ordered sequence, and the time series is exactly an ordered sequence, which makes it suitable for using BA. In this paper, the BA method was used to search for the shortest time of the trajectory in the time interval $[t_l, t_r]$. The input time for the initial trajectory planner is t_r. The flowchart of BA is shown in Figure 7.

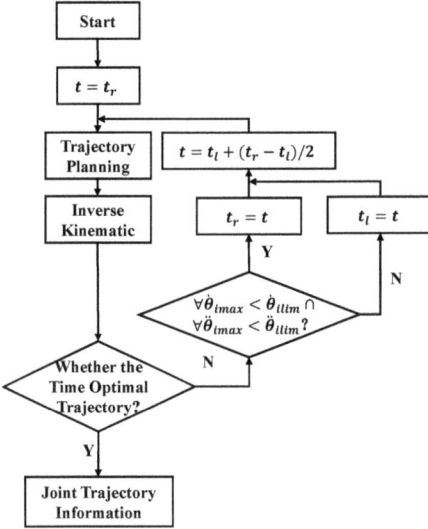

Figure 7. The flow chart of BA.

The algorithm first uses t_r as the running time to plan the trajectory. If the planning result does not satisfy the conditions of the time-optimal trajectory, it is necessary to determine whether the maximum angular velocity and maximum angular acceleration of all joints are within the constraints of the angular velocity and angular acceleration of the joints. The judgment condition is shown in Equation (55).

$$\forall \dot{\theta}_{imax} < \dot{\theta}_{ilim} \cap \forall \ddot{\theta}_{imax} < \ddot{\theta}_{ilim} \tag{55}$$

If the joint trajectory satisfies Equation (55), then let $t_r = t$, otherwise, let $t_l = t$. Then, let $t = t_l + (t_r - t_l)/2$, input it into the trajectory planner as the running time of the trajectory, iterate continuously, and finally determine the shortest time t.

However, these algorithms have limitations. When the shortest time of the trajectory is not in the given time interval, the algorithm will fail and enter an infinite loop, and the time of each planning will be infinitely close to the boundary of the given time interval.

Therefore, this paper uses GDM-CPC to solve this problem. GDM-CPC is a first-order optimization algorithm that can search for a local minimum of the function. Because this paper uses Equation (54) as the judgment condition of time-optimal trajectory, there is only one joint to reach its maximum constraint, and the angular velocity and angular acceleration of the other joints are less than their maximum constraint. Therefore, the use of GDM-CPC here will not fall into the local optimal situation, and must be able to obtain a shortest time of trajectory that satisfies all joint constraints. GDM-CPC first provides an initial trajectory running time t_{init}, and then determines whether the joint trajectory satisfies Equation (54) after obtaining the joint trajectory of the manipulator through trajectory planning and inverse kinematics. If Equation (54) is not satisfied, then searching for a new trajectory running time, and the shortest running time of the trajectory, will finally be obtained. The advantage of this algorithm is that it only needs to provide a time value greater than 0 to converge to the shortest time of the trajectory, thereby avoiding the limitations of BA.

The flowchart of GDM-CPC is shown in Figure 8.

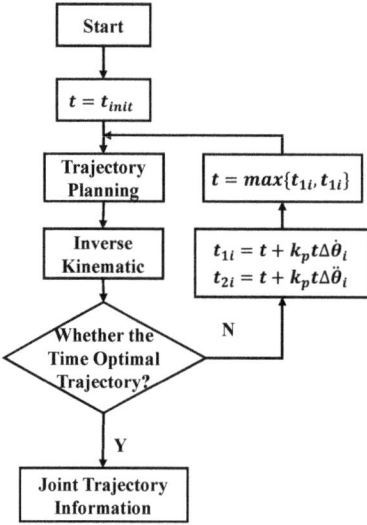

Figure 8. The flow chart of GDM-CPC.

Among them, $\Delta \dot{\theta}_i$ is shown in Equation (56) and $\Delta \ddot{\theta}_i$ is shown in Equation (57).

$$\Delta \dot{\theta}_i = \frac{\dot{\theta}_{imax} - \dot{\theta}_{ilim} \times 0.998}{\dot{\theta}_{ilim} \times 0.998} \tag{56}$$

$$\Delta \ddot{\theta}_i = \frac{\ddot{\theta}_{imax} - \ddot{\theta}_{ilim} \times 0.998}{\ddot{\theta}_{ilim} \times 0.998} \tag{57}$$

where t_{1i} is the time at which joint i is optimized with $k_p t \Delta \dot{\theta}_i$ each time and t_{2i} is the time at which joint i is optimized with $k_p t \Delta \ddot{\theta}_i$ each time.

If $\Delta \dot{\theta}_i > 0$, the current input time is small, and the maximum angular velocity of joint i exceeds its angular velocity constraint during the trajectory planning process. The time change is $k_p t \Delta \dot{\theta}_i > 0$, which increases the input time to reduce the maximum angular velocity of joint i. If $\Delta \dot{\theta}_i < 0$, the current input time is large, and the maximum angular velocity of joint i is less than its angular velocity constraint during the trajectory planning process. The time change is $k_p t \Delta \dot{\theta}_i < 0$, reducing the input time to increase the maximum angular velocity of joint i. The joint angular acceleration has the same adjustment process. Take the maximum value of t_{1i} and t_{2i} and assign it to t as the input of the trajectory planner. In the continuous iterative process, the shortest time t of the trajectory will be obtained.

Because k_p must be adjusted many times, the algorithm will have fewer convergence steps. Therefore, this paper proposes an ATSA-FC. This method adaptively adjusts k_p according to $\Delta \dot{\theta}_i$ and $\Delta \ddot{\theta}_i$ by using fuzzy control.

Fuzzy control is a control method that combines an expert system, fuzzy set theory, and control theory, and is very different from traditional control theory based on the mathematical model of the controlled process [29]. The behavior and experience of human experts can be added to fuzzy control. Fuzzy control is practical when establishing a mathematical model for a controlled process is difficult.

This paper considers a design for a first-order fuzzy controller to adjust the value of k_p. First, the input linguistic variable is fuzzified. Let the input linguistic variable be $\Delta\vartheta$, where $\Delta\vartheta$ is the smallest absolute value between $\Delta\dot{\theta}_i$ and $\Delta\ddot{\theta}_i$. Let the domain of $\Delta\vartheta$ be U_1, $U_1 \in [-a, a]$, and divide it into five fuzzy sets, which are NB, N, ZE, P, and PB, respectively. NB stands for negative big, N for negative, ZE for zero, P for positive, PB for positive big. The membership function corresponding to each fuzzy set is a Gaussian distribution function, as shown in Figure 9.

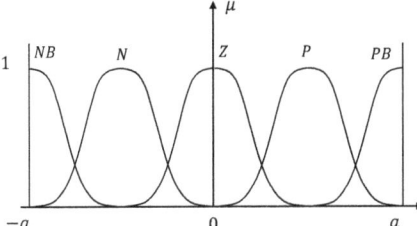

Figure 9. The membership function corresponding to the input fuzzy set.

The expression of the membership function for each fuzzy set is shown in Equation (58).

$$\begin{cases} NB(x) = e^{-\frac{(x+a)^2}{2\sigma^2}} \\ N(x) = e^{-\frac{(x+\frac{a}{2})^2}{2\sigma^2}} \\ ZE(x) = e^{-\frac{x^2}{2\sigma^2}} \\ P(x) = e^{-\frac{(x-\frac{a}{2})^2}{2\sigma^2}} \\ PB(x) = e^{-\frac{(x-a)^2}{2\sigma^2}} \end{cases} \quad (58)$$

where $-a < x < a$.

Second, the output linguistic variable is fuzzified. Let the output linguistic variable be k_p, and let the domain of k_p be U_2, $U_2 \in [b, c]$, and divided into three fuzzy sets, which are S, M, L. S represents small k_p values, M represents medium k_p values, and L represents large k_p values. The membership function corresponding to each fuzzy set is a Gaussian distribution curve, as shown in Figure 10.

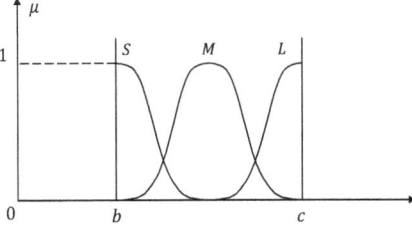

Figure 10. The membership function corresponding to the output fuzzy set.

The expression of the function corresponding to each fuzzy set is shown in Equation (59).

$$\begin{cases} S(y) = e^{-\frac{(y-b)^2}{2\sigma^2}} \\ M(y) = e^{-\frac{(y-\frac{b+c}{2})^2}{2\sigma^2}} \\ L(y) = e^{-\frac{(y-c)^2}{2\sigma^2}} \end{cases} \tag{59}$$

where $b < y < c$.

Fuzzy control rules are then established and fuzzy reasoning is performed. After determining the fuzzy sets of the input and output linguistic variables, fuzzy conditional statements in the form of an IF–THEN are used to establish fuzzy control rules. The fuzzy rules are as follows:

IF $\Delta\vartheta$ is NB THEN k_p is L
IF $\Delta\vartheta$ is B THEN k_p is M
IF $\Delta\vartheta$ is ZE THEN k_p is S
IF $\Delta\vartheta$ is P THEN k_p is M
IF $\Delta\vartheta$ is PB THEN k_p is L

When $\Delta\vartheta$ is NB or PB, it indicates that the difference between the maximum joint angular velocity or maximum angular acceleration and the constraints is large. At this time, a larger k_p value should be output and the convergence step should be increased. When $\Delta\vartheta$ is N or P, it indicates that the difference is medium, and a medium k_p value should be output at this time. When $\Delta\vartheta$ is Z, it indicates that the difference is small. A small k_p value should be output to reduce the convergence step and avoid repeated oscillations.

The flowchart of ATSA-FC is shown in Figure 11.

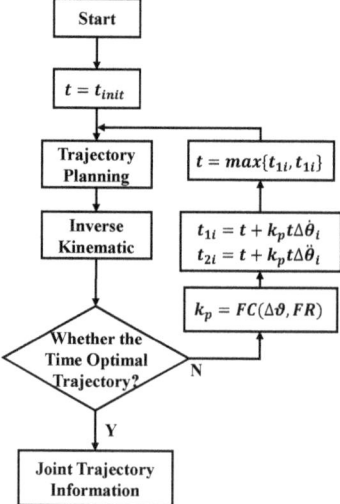

Figure 11. The flow chart of ATSA-FC.

The FC is the fuzzy control function, and the FR is the fuzzy control rule, and $\Delta\vartheta$ is shown in Equation (60).

$$\Delta\vartheta = \min\{\min\{|\Delta\dot{\theta}_i|\}, \min\{|\Delta\ddot{\theta}_i|\}\} \tag{60}$$

Take the maximum value of t_{1i} and t_{2i} and assign it to t as the input of the trajectory planner. In the continuous iterative process, the shortest time t of the trajectory will be obtained.

5. Simulation

The simulation section first sets the parameters of the simulation, and then analyses the simulation results.

5.1. Parameter Setting of the Simulation

This paper simulates TOTP based on the MATLAB environment. The Robotics Toolbox is used to establish the manipulator.

The constraints of each joint angular velocity $\dot{\theta}_{ilim}$ and angular acceleration $\ddot{\theta}_{ilim}$ set in the simulation environment are listed in Table 3.

Table 3. Joint Constraints of the Simulation Environment.

Joint i	Angular Velocity $\dot{\theta}_{ilim}$ (°/s)	Angular Acceleration $\ddot{\theta}_{ilim}$ (°/s²)
1	150	300
2	160	320
3	170	340
4	320	640
5	400	800
6	460	920

The position and attitude of the end of the manipulator is set at the initial and end moments of the straight-line path, which are represented by homogeneous matrices T_{st} and T_{end}, respectively. T_{st} is shown in Equation (61) and T_{end} is shown in Equation (62).

$$T_{st} = \begin{bmatrix} 1 & 0 & 0 & 3 \\ 0 & 0.5000 & -0.8660 & -2 \\ 0 & 0.8660 & 0.5000 & 2 \\ 0 & 0 & 0 & 1 \end{bmatrix} \quad (61)$$

$$T_{end} = \begin{bmatrix} 0.6124 & -0.3536 & 0.7071 & 2 \\ -0.5000 & -0.8660 & 0 & 2 \\ 0.6124 & -0.3536 & -0.7071 & 0.5000 \\ 0 & 0 & 0 & 1 \end{bmatrix} \quad (62)$$

Set the initial time of the trajectory planner P to $t = 10$ s, $n = 1000$, the ratio of acceleration and deceleration time to $r = 0.3$, the trajectory type to be a straight-line, and the constraint points to be T_{st} and T_{end}.

The linear trajectory of the end of the manipulator in Cartesian space is shown in Figure 12. The red triangle represents the starting point and the red circle represents the end point.

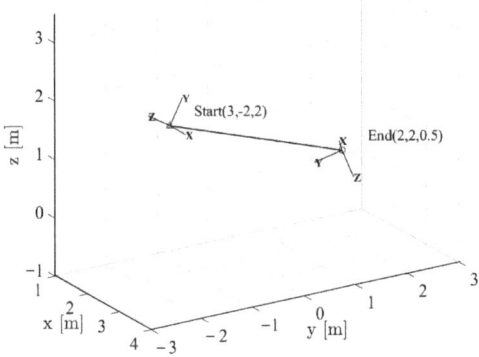

Figure 12. Straight-line trajectory in Cartesian space.

Using Equation (42), the rotation transformation matrix R_t of the attitude at the initial and end moments is calculated, and R_t is shown in Equation (63).

$$R_t = \begin{bmatrix} 0.6124 & -0.7891 & 0.0474 \\ -0.5000 & -0.4330 & -0.7500 \\ 0.6124 & 0.4356 & -0.6597 \end{bmatrix} \quad (63)$$

From Equations (4) and (5), the rotation axis/angle representation of R_t can be obtained, and the rotation angle ϕ is shown in Equation (64), the axis of rotation k is shown in Equation (65).

$$\phi = 137.7448° \quad (64)$$

$$k = \begin{bmatrix} 0.8816 & -0.4201 & 0.2150 \end{bmatrix}^T \quad (65)$$

For fuzzy control, the Fuzzy Logic Toolbox in MATLAB is used in this paper to build a fuzzy inference system.

The membership function of each fuzzy set of input linguistic variables is shown in Equation (58), where $x \in [-1, 1]$, $\sigma = 0.2142$. The membership function of each fuzzy set of output linguistic variables is shown in Equation (59), where $y \in [0.35, 1]$, $\sigma = 0.1$. The membership function corresponding to the input linguistic variables and output linguistic variables are shown in Figure 13. For input linguistic variable, $x \in [-1, 1]$, which is due to the normalization of Equations (56) and (57). In order to ensure the completeness of the membership function [30], the membership degree at the intersection of the two membership functions is 0.5, combined with the experience summarized in the simulation debugging process of this study, the σ can be set to be 0.2142. For output language variable, it has three fuzzy sets. In order to make the membership of S and L at 0.675 tend to 0, so that the output has better clarity, the σ can be set to be 0.1.

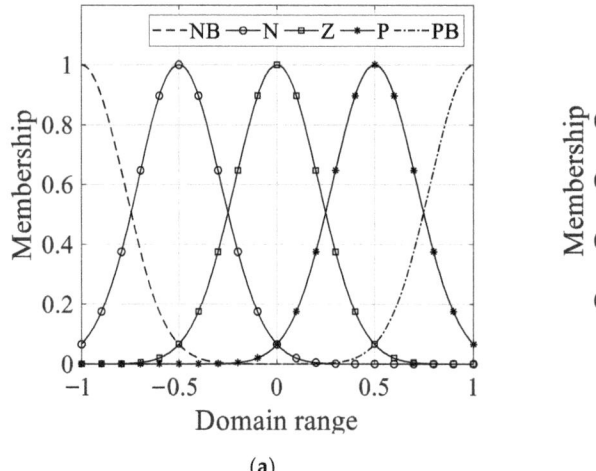
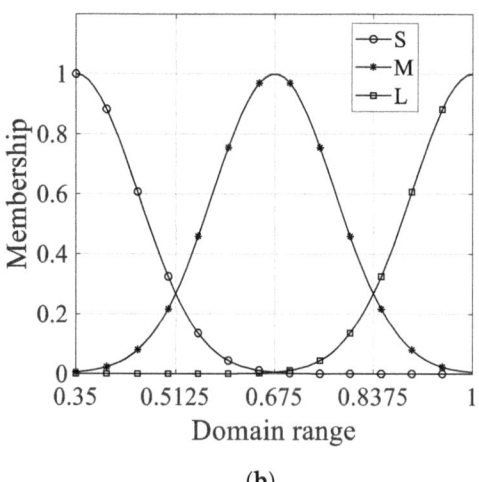

(a) (b)

Figure 13. The membership function corresponding linguistic variable: (a) input linguistic variable; (b) output linguistic variable.

Using the fuzzy rules established in Section 4, the mapping curve of the input and output of the fuzzy control is obtained, as shown in Figure 14.

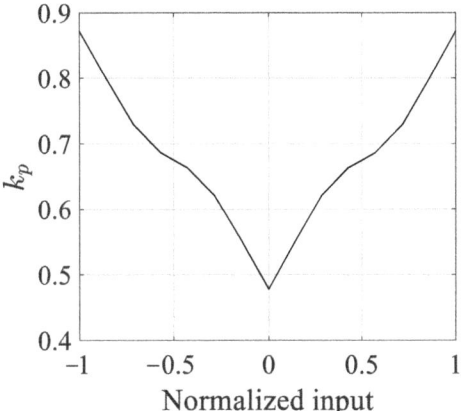

Figure 14. The input and output mapping curve.

5.2. Results of the Simulation

The convergence curves of the controlled time of the three algorithms using BA, GDM-CPC with $k_p = 0.5$, and ATSA-FC are shown in Figure 15.

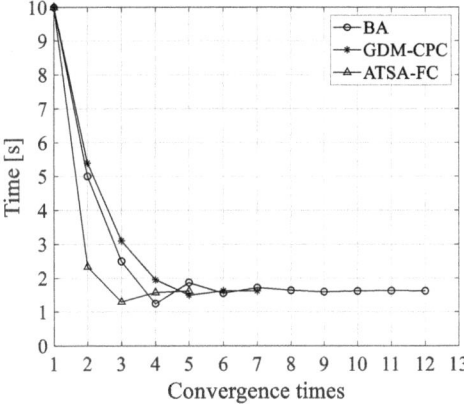

Figure 15. Convergence curve of controlled time of three algorithms.

As shown in Figure 16, under the same initial conditions, to get the trajectory shortest time, BA required 12 times, GDM-CPC required seven times, and ATSA-FC required five times. It can also be seen that the convergence curves of the controlled time of these three algorithms have oscillation phenomena, in which the convergence step of BA at each iteration is taken as half of the updated time interval at each iteration, since BA simply adjusts the time and does not take into account the difference with the constraint. It has the largest number of convergence steps. GDM-CPC has the smallest convergence step size at the first convergence and produces the smallest oscillation amplitude. The ATSA-FC has the largest convergence step size at the first convergence, but there is only one oscillation phenomenon, and the shortest time to the trajectory is obtained by using the least number of convergence steps, which reflects the superiority of ATSA-FC.

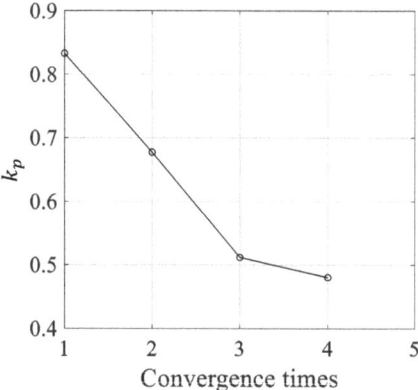

Figure 16. k_p changes with input at each iteration.

The variation in k_p with the number of convergences is shown in Figure 16. The k_p value obtained from the current iteration is used to update the input time for the next trajectory planning. Because the input time of the 5th trajectory planning meets the shortest time requirement of the trajectory, k_p has only four iterations.

The trajectory shortest times obtained by three algorithms are listed in Table 4.

Table 4. The trajectory shortest time solved by the three algorithms.

Algorithm	The Trajectory Shortest Time (s)
BA	1.6260
GDM-CPC	1.6248
ATSA-FC	1.6237

It can be seen from Table 4 that the trajectory shortest time planned by BA is the largest, which is 1.6260 s. The trajectory shortest time planned by GDM-CPC is 1.6248 s, which is 1.2 ms less than that of BA. The trajectory shortest time planned by ATSA-FC is 1.6237 s, which is 2.3 ms less than that of BA. Since the judgment condition for reaching the maximum joint parameter specified in Equations (45) and (46) is 99.6–100% of the joint constraints, the trajectory shortest time difference obtained by these three algorithms is very small.

The execution times of the three algorithms are measured using the timing function in MATLAB, as listed in Table 5.

Table 5. Execution time of three algorithms.

Algorithm	The Algorithm Execution Time (s)
BA	8.38
GDM-CPC	5.26
ATSA-FC	4.24

As shown in Table 5, the execution time of BA is 8.38 s, and the execution time of GDM-CPC is 5.26 s, which is 37.23% less than that of BA. The execution time of ATSA-FC is 4.24 s, which is 19.39% less than that of GDM-CPC and 49.40% less than that of BA, which proves the efficiency of the ATSA-FC proposed in this paper.

Using the trajectory shortest time obtained by the ATSA-FC, S-shaped velocity planning of the end of the manipulator along the trajectory in Figure 12 is performed. The change curves of the joint angle, angular velocity, and angular acceleration are shown in Figure 17.

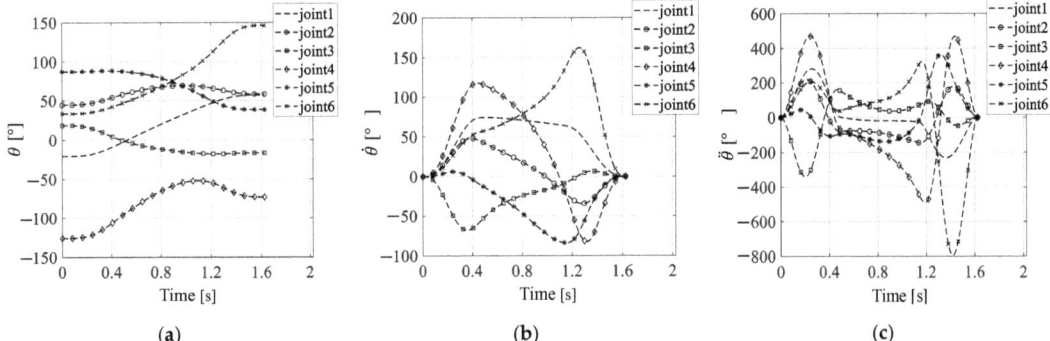

Figure 17. The change curves of each joint: (**a**) angle; (**b**) angular velocity; (**c**) angular acceleration.

As shown in Figure 17, the angular velocity and angular acceleration of each joint obtained by using the S-shaped velocity curve change continuously, and it can be inferred that the operation of the manipulator is stable. It can be seen from Figure 17b,c that in the process of TOTP in Cartesian space, the maximum angular acceleration of joint 3 plays a major limiting role, satisfying the maximum angular acceleration judgment condition of the joint. The angular velocity and angular acceleration of other joints do not reach their constraints. This also shows that it is feasible to use the minimum–maximum rule to solve the multi-constraint problem in TOTP.

Because the shortest times of the trajectories obtained by these three algorithms are very close, the difference between the overall angular velocity and angular acceleration cannot be seen in the comparison chart, so only the local enlarged pictures at the maximum angular velocity and maximum angular acceleration of the joint are given here, as shown in Figure 18.

It can be seen from Figure 18a,b that the angular velocity and angular acceleration of the joint are negatively correlated with the trajectory time of the manipulator. Since the ATSA-FC calculates the minimum trajectory shortest time, the corresponding joint trajectory also has the largest peak.

To determine the trajectory planning effect of these three algorithms, beyond comparing the shortest time of the trajectory, it can also be measured by using the degree of TOTP. The degree of TOTP can be described by the ratio of the maximum joint parameters that plays the major limitation role in the joint constraints, and in this simulation, joint 3's acceleration plays the major role, so the degree of TOTP can be calculated by Equation (66).

$$\rho = \frac{\ddot{\theta}_{3max}}{\ddot{\theta}_{3lim}} \tag{66}$$

When using BA, GDM-CPC and ATSA-FC, the $\dot{\theta}_{imax}$, $\Delta\dot{\theta}_i$, $\ddot{\theta}_{imax}$ and $\Delta\ddot{\theta}_i$ of each joint at trajectory shortest time are shown in Tables 6–8, respectively.

Table 6. The joint information table of BA.

Joint	$\dot{\theta}_{imax}$ (°/s)	Δ	$\ddot{\theta}_{imax}$ (°/s²)	$\Delta\ddot{\theta}_i$
1	74.2030	−0.5053	280.2118	−0.0660
2	47.9242	−0.7005	218.7880	−0.3163
3	67.7642	−0.6014	338.8432	−0.0034
4	117.3646	−0.6332	491.0460	−0.2327
5	83.9523	−0.7901	364.3361	−0.5446
6	162.0533	−0.6477	792.0519	−0.1391

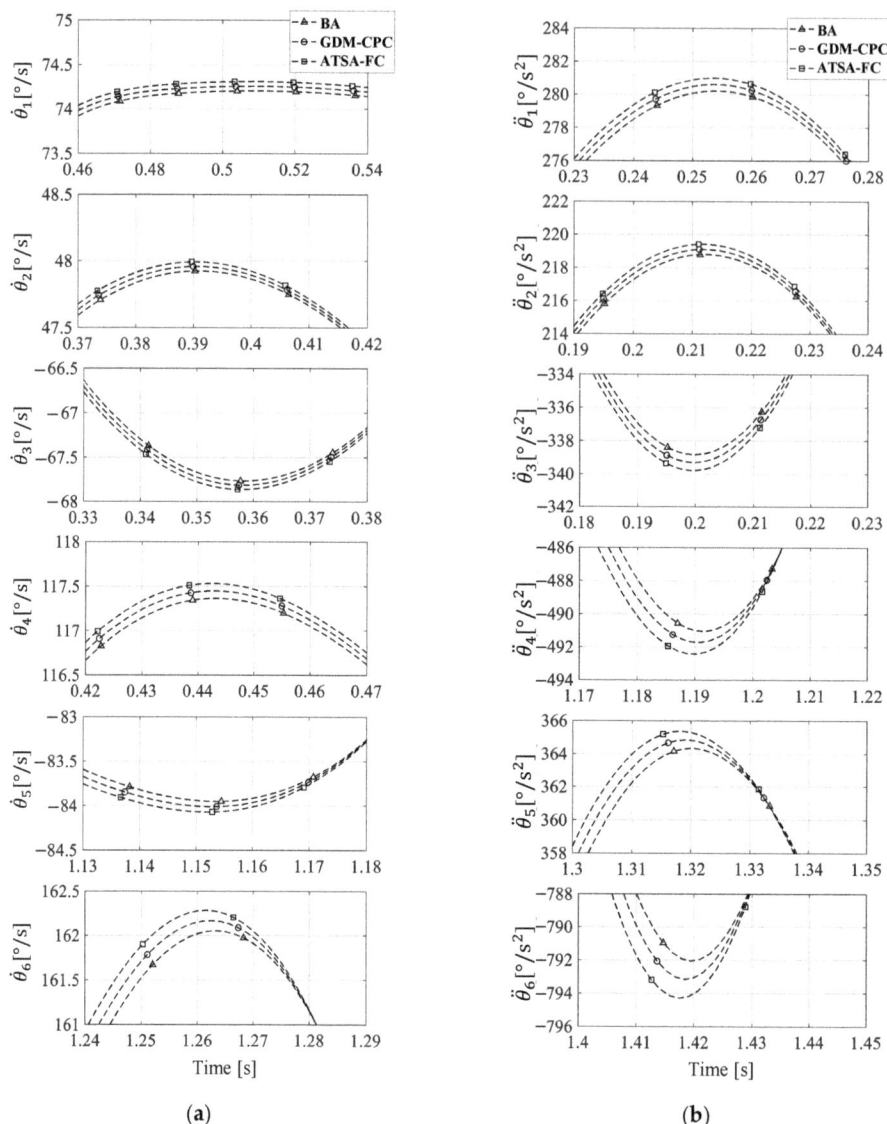

Figure 18. Comparison of joint maximum angular information planned by three algorithms: (**a**) angular velocity; (**b**) angular acceleration.

Table 7. Joint information table of GDM-CPC.

Joint	$\dot{\theta}_{imax}$ (°/s)	$\Delta \dot{\theta}_i$	$\ddot{\theta}_{imax}$ (°/s^2)	$\Delta \ddot{\theta}_i$
1	74.2548	−0.5050	280.6037	−0.0647
2	47.9577	−0.7003	219.0941	−0.3153
3	67.8166	−0.6011	339.3172	−0.0020
4	117.4466	−0.6330	491.7329	−0.2317
5	84.0110	−0.7900	364.8458	−0.5439
6	162.1666	−0.6475	792.1599	−0.1379

Table 8. Joint information table of ATSA-FC.

Joint	$\dot{\theta}_{imax}$ (°/s)	$\Delta \dot{\theta}_i$	$\ddot{\theta}_{imax}$ (°/s^2)	$\Delta \ddot{\theta}_i$
1	74.3078	−0.5046	281.0043	−0.0633
2	47.9919	−0.7001	219.4069	−0.3144
3	67.8600	−0.6008	339.8017	-5.8336×10^{-4}
4	117.5304	−0.6327	492.4349	−0.2306
5	84.0710	−0.7898	365.3667	−0.5433
6	162.2823	−0.6472	794.2922	−0.1366

As shown in Tables 6–8, the maximum angular velocity and angular acceleration of the six joints are within the joint constraints, and the maximum angular accelerations of joint 3 planned by these three algorithms are 338.8432°/s^2, 339.3172°/s^2, and 339.8017°/s^2, and their degrees of TOTP are 99.66%, 99.80%, and 99.94%, respectively. The maximum angular acceleration constraints of joint 3 are $\ddot{\Theta}_{3lim}$, $\ddot{\Theta}_{3lim} = [338.64, 340]$, and the maximum angular acceleration of joint 3 planned by these three algorithms are all within $\ddot{\Theta}_{3lim}$. Therefore, the joint trajectories planned by these three algorithms satisfy Equation (54), which proves that the shortest time of the trajectory obtained by the above three algorithms is effective, and ATSA-FC has the highest degree of TOTP.

In fact, the degree of TOTP is not only related to the algorithm itself, but also to the judgment condition's range set in Equations (45) and (46), which determines the upper and lower limits of the degree of TOTP. In the simulation, the judgment condition's range is 99.6%–100% of the maximum joint parameters, so according to Equation (54), no matter how the algorithm is run, the degree of TOTP will always be between 99.6% and 100%.

Adjust Equations (45) and (46) and simulate a different range of judgment conditions. The trajectory shortest times and algorithm execution times planned by each algorithm are listed in Table 9. Let $\dot{\Theta}_{ilim} = [Er \times \dot{\theta}_{ilim}, \dot{\theta}_{ilim}]$ and $\ddot{\Theta}_{ilim} = [Er \times \ddot{\theta}_{ilim}, \ddot{\theta}_{ilim}]$, where Er is the lower limit of degree of TOTP.

Table 9. The table of each algorithm's execution time and the trajectory shortest time.

Er	The Algorithm Execution Time (s)			The Trajectory Shortest Time (s)		
	BA	GDM-CPC	ATSA-FC	BA	GDM-CPC	ATSA-FC
96%	6.8173	4.8556	4.4596	1.6406	1.6447	1.6386
96.5%	6.1426	6.0968	4.3226	1.6406	1.6426	1.6364
97%	5.9353	4.6736	4.2043	1.6406	1.6405	1.6342
97.5%	5.9040	4.6402	4.2660	1.6406	1.6383	1.6321
98%	7.8637	4.6664	4.2799	1.6309	1.6362	1.6299
98.5%	7.8450	4.6422	4.2874	1.6309	1.6341	1.6279
99%	7.8179	5.3306	4.2909	1.6309	1.6273	1.6260
99.5%	8.4473	5.2891	4.2913	1.6260	1.6252	1.6241

As shown in Table 9, under all Er conditions, the ATSA-FC had the shortest execution time. In addition, among the three algorithms, the trajectory shortest time planned by ATSA-FC is also the smallest. Thus, the superiority and effectiveness of the ATSA-FC are verified.

6. Conclusions

In this paper, the problem of TOTP of the manipulator in Cartesian space is studied, and ATSA-FC is proposed, so that the end of the manipulator can run along the given trajectory of Cartesian space with the shortest running time, while avoiding the sudden change in torque of each joint.

In the simulation, taking a straight-line path of the manipulator in Cartesian space as an example, BA, GDM-CPC, and ATSA-FC are used to calculate the shortest time of this trajectory. By comparing the trajectory shortest time and the execution time of these three algorithms, the superiority and efficiency of the proposed algorithm is proved. The main contributions of this article are as follows:

1. An adaptive time-search algorithm based on fuzzy control is proposed, which can adaptively adjust the time-search step by using fuzzy control based on the results of the previous feedback. The algorithm execution time and the degree of TOTP is better than BA and GDM-CPC.
2. The TOTP problem is transformed into a nonlinear optimization problem under multi-constraints, and the minimum–maximum rule is used to consider the multi-constraints, as shown in Equations (53) and (54), to avoid falling into the situation of local optimal solution when using the time-search algorithm.
3. The range of maximum judgment conditions is 99.6–100% of the maximum joint parameters, as shown in Equations (45) and (46), which can reduce the number of iterations and have little impact on the maximum running speed of the trajectory. At the same time, this range also specifies the upper and lower limits of the optimal trajectory planning degree of time.

In conclusion, the TOTP algorithm based on fuzzy control proposed in this study is not only efficient, but also calculates the shortest trajectory time under the same trajectory constraints.

In the follow-up, based on the research in this paper, the dynamic constraints of the manipulator and the quality of the links and joints will be considered, and the TOTP will be carried out under the dynamic constraints.

Author Contributions: Conceptualization, Q.H.; methodology, Q.H.; software, F.H.; supervision, Q.H.; validation, F.H.; visualization, F.H.; writing—original draft, F.H.; writing—review and editing, F.H. and Q.H. All authors have read and agreed to the published version of the manuscript.

Funding: This research received no external funding.

Institutional Review Board Statement: Not applicable.

Informed Consent Statement: Not applicable.

Data Availability Statement: Not applicable.

Conflicts of Interest: The authors declare no conflict of interest.

References

1. Huang, J.; Hu, P.; Wu, K.; Zeng, M. Optimal time-jerk trajectory planning for industrial robots. *Mech. Mach. Theory* **2018**, *121*, 530–544. [CrossRef]
2. Bobrow, J.E.; Dubowsky, S.; Gibson, J.S. Time-optimal control of robotic manipulators along specified paths. *Int. J. Robot. Res.* **1985**, *4*, 3–17. [CrossRef]
3. Yu, X.; Dong, M.; Yin, W. Time-optimal trajectory planning of manipulator with simultaneously searching the optimal path. *Comput. Commun.* **2022**, *181*, 446–453. [CrossRef]
4. Wang, F.; Wu, Z.; Bao, T. Time-Jerk optimal Trajectory Planning of Industrial Robots Based on a Hybrid WOA-GA Algorithm. *Processes* **2022**, *10*, 1014. [CrossRef]
5. Zhang, X.; Shi, G. Multi-objective optimal trajectory planning for manipulators in the presence of obstacles. *Robotica* **2022**, *40*, 888–906. [CrossRef]
6. Garriz, C.; Domingo, R. Trajectory Optimization in Terms of Energy and Performance of an Industrial Robot in the Manufacturing Industry. *Sensors* **2022**, *22*, 7538. [CrossRef]
7. Yu, Y.; Zhang, Y. Collision avoidance and path planning for industrial manipulator using slice-based heuristic fast marching tree. *Robot. Comput. Integr. Manuf.* **2022**, *75*, 102289. [CrossRef]
8. Constantinescu, D.; Croft, E.A. Smooth and Time-Optimal Trajectory Planning for Industrial Manipulators along Specified Paths. *J. Robot. Syst.* **2000**, *17*, 233–249. [CrossRef]
9. Ding, Y.; Wang, Y.; Chen, B. Smooth and Proximate Time-Optimal Trajectory Planning of Robotic Manipulators. *Trans. Can. Soc. Mech. Eng.* **2022**, *46*, 466–476. [CrossRef]
10. Fang, Y.; Hu, J.; Liu, W.; Chen, B.; Qi, J.; Ye, X. A CPG-Based Online Trajectory Planning Method for Industrial Manipulators. In Proceedings of the 2016 Asia-Pacific Conference on Intelligent Robot Systems (ACIRS), Tokyo, Japan, 20–24 July 2016. [CrossRef]

11. Barnett, E.; Gosselin, C. A Bisection Algorithm for Time-Optimal Trajectory Planning Along Fully Specified Paths. *IEEE Trans. Robot.* **2021**, *37*, 131–145. [CrossRef]
12. Zhang, T.; Zhang, M.; Zou, Y. Time-optimal and Smooth Trajectory Planning for Robot Manipulators. *Int. J. Control Autom. Syst.* **2021**, *19*, 521–531. [CrossRef]
13. Zhao, J.; Zhu, X.; Song, T. Serial Manipulator Time-Jerk Optimal Trajectory Planning Based on Hybrid IWOA-PSO Algorithm. *IEEE Access* **2022**, *10*, 6592–6604. [CrossRef]
14. Zhang, L.; Wang, Y.; Zhao, X.; Zhao, P.; He, L. Time-optimal Trajectory Planning of Serial Manipulator based on Adaptive Cuckoo Search Algorithm. *J. Mech. Sci. Technol.* **2021**, *35*, 3171–3181. [CrossRef]
15. Liu, Y.; Guo, C.; Weng, Y. Online Time-optimal Trajectory Planning for Robotic Manipulators Using Adaptive Elite Genetic Algorithm with Singularity Avoidance. *IEEE Access* **2019**, *7*, 146301–146308. [CrossRef]
16. Guo, X.; Bo, R.; Jia, J.; Li, R. Time-optimal Trajectory Planning of Manipulator Based on Improved Firefly Algorithm. *Mach. Des. Res.* **2021**, *37*, 55–59. [CrossRef]
17. Zhu, Y.; Jiao, J. Automatic Control System Design for Industrial Robots Based on Simulated Annealing and PID Algorithms. *Adv. Multimed.* **2020**, *2022*, 9226576. [CrossRef]
18. Ichnowski, J.; Avigal, Y.; Satish, V.; Goldberg, K. Deep learning can accelerate grasp-optimized motion planning. *Sci. Robot.* **2022**, *5*, eabd7710. [CrossRef]
19. Verscheure, D.; Demeulenaere, B.; Swevers, J.; De Schutter, J.; Diehl, M. Time-Optimal Path Tracking for Robots: A Convex Optimization Approach. *IEEE Trans. Automat. Contr.* **2009**, *54*, 2318–2327. [CrossRef]
20. Pham, H.; Pham, Q.C. A New Approach to Time-Optimal Path Parameterization Based on Reachability Analysis. *IEEE Trans. Robot.* **2018**, *34*, 645–659. [CrossRef]
21. Shen, J.; Kong, M.; Zhu, Y. Trajectory Optimization Algorithm Based on Robot Dynamics and Convex Optimization. In Proceedings of the 2019 IEEE 3rd Advanced Information Management, Communicates, Electronic and Automation Control Conference (IMCEC), Chongqing, China, 11–13 October 2019. [CrossRef]
22. Liu, H.; Lai, X.; Wu, W. Time-optimal and jerk-continuous trajectory planning for robot manipulators with kinematic constraints. *Robot. Comput. -Integr. Manuf.* **2013**, *29*, 309–317. [CrossRef]
23. Zhu, K.G.; Shi, G.Y.; Liu, J. Improved flattening algorithm for NURBS curve based on bisection feedback search algorithm and interval reformation method. *Ocean Eng.* **2022**, *247*, 110635. [CrossRef]
24. Xue, Y.; Wang, Y.; Liang, J. A self-adaptive gradient descent search algorithm for fully-connected neural networks. *Neurocomputing* **2022**, *478*, 70–80. [CrossRef]
25. Liang, B.; Xu, W. *Space Robotics: Modeling, Planning and Control*; Tsinghua University Press: Beijing, China, 2017; pp. 93–94. ISBN 978-7-302-47258-2.
26. Spong, M.W.; Hutchinson, S. *Robot Modeling and Control*; John Wiley & Sons Inc.: New York, NY, USA, 2005; pp. 57–60. ISBN 978-0-471-64990-8.
27. Gasparetto, A.; Zanotto, V. A technique for time-jerk optimal planning of robot trajectories. *Robot. Comput. Integr. Manuf.* **2008**, *24*, 415–426. [CrossRef]
28. Wan, J.; Wu, H.; Ma, R.; Zhang, L. A study on avoiding joint limits for inverse kinematics of redundant manipulators using improved clamping weighted least-norm method. *J. Mech. Sci. Technol.* **2018**, *32*, 1367–1378. [CrossRef]
29. Driankov, D.; Hellendoorn, H.; Reinfrank, M. *An Introduction to Fuzzy Control*; Springer Science & Business Media: Berlin/Heidelberg, Germany, 2013; pp. 1–3. ISBN 978-3-662-11131-4.
30. Su, J.; Ren, J.; Pan, H. An improved self-structuring neuro-fuzzy algorithm. In Proceedings of the 2008 International Conference on Information and Automation, Changsha, China, 20–23 June 2008. [CrossRef]

MDPI
St. Alban-Anlage 66
4052 Basel
Switzerland
www.mdpi.com

Actuators Editorial Office
E-mail: actuators@mdpi.com
www.mdpi.com/journal/actuators

Disclaimer/Publisher's Note: The statements, opinions and data contained in all publications are solely those of the individual author(s) and contributor(s) and not of MDPI and/or the editor(s). MDPI and/or the editor(s) disclaim responsibility for any injury to people or property resulting from any ideas, methods, instructions or products referred to in the content.

www.ingramcontent.com/pod-product-compliance
Lightning Source LLC
LaVergne TN
LVHW070408100526
838202LV00014B/1411